TECH INTERVIEWS

AN INSIDER GUIDE TO ACE SYSTEM DESIGN, BEHAVIOURAL, & DATA STRUCTURES AND ALGORITHMS INTERVIEWS

Accelerate your readiness for
any software engineering role

SHALINI GOYAL & ALOK SHARAN

ISBN

Hardcase 979-8-89632-872-8
Paperback 979-8-89632-691-5

Dedicated to

Our Mom and Dad

Praise for the Book

This invaluable guide excels in breaking down the complex topics into easy to understand concepts, making it useful for both experienced professionals and beginners.

– Payal Agrawal,
VP, Engineering, JP Morgan

Awesome Tech Interviews' is a comprehensive guide that truly covers every topic you'll ever need to prepare for your next interview. The content feels remarkably current, reflecting the most recent trends and patterns in modern hiring processes. What stood out to me was how straightforward and accessible the explanations are—complex concepts are broken down into simple, easy-to-grasp sections. It's also clear that Shalini Goyal and Alok Sharan bring a wealth of hands-on industry experience to the table, as each chapter is packed with practical insights and real-world examples. Highly recommend it for anyone preparing for any tech interview.

– Rohit Jain,
Senior Software Engineer, Amazon
Highest Rated Udemy Instructor

As a former tech recruiter who has been involved in thousands of tech interviews I was intrigued by Awesome Tech Interviews. The book is a meticulously crafted guide that addresses every facet of the modern technical interview process. Authors have masterfully condensed their years of experience into a comprehensive yet accessible resource. Whether you're an aspiring developer, a seasoned engineer, or an executive honing your hiring strategies, this book equips you with actionable insights and structured preparation techniques. Its clarity in explaining complex concepts like system design, alongside practical tips for behavioral and coding interviews, sets it apart from other guides in this space. By bridging technical acumen with a strategic approach to interviews, the authors empower readers to land their dream role in tech. This is a must-read for anyone navigating the fiercely competitive tech landscape.

– Rich Wilson,
CEO and Co-Founder, Gigged.AI

Preface

Early 2024, I received a call from a friend in the UK. After spending nine years at the same company, he had suddenly been made redundant. Despite having all these years of experience in the industry, he sounded lost. His question was simple but loaded with anxiety: "What should I study to prepare for an interview when the opportunity comes?"

I asked him what kinds of roles he was targeting. His response, though unsurprising, was telling: "Basically anything." His list included hands on technical to mid-to-senior level role in software industry. He wasn't just certain about his next step - he was grappling with the overwhelming possibilities of a shifting job market.

We spoke for over an hour, outlining a strategy, identifying skills to focus on, and clarifying how he should approach his job search.

In the same year, there was another similar incident. This time, it was a former colleague from Gurgaon, India. He had been working as an engineering manager at a medium size firm for two years but was uncertain about continuing in his role, since the role was not producing enough challenges. He now wanted to take a leap towards big tech companies but wasn't sure where/how to start. During the call, his request was simple: "Can you please guide me around the topics I should start learning?"

As the idea of this book was just taking shape, it got firmed up as I spoke with someone within friends and family (in India) who is pursuing bachelor degree in computing science. His goal after completing his studies is to join a big tech company, such as Google, Amazon, or Facebook. He is a bright student, but the institute he attends is not one where these companies recruit from campus. He wanted a pathway to follow his dreams. We worked together to create a plan for him to crack into FAANG.

And the patterns kept repeating!

These conversations were the inspiration for this book. They confirmed my belief that if so many people were feeling this uncertainty, there is a real need for a comprehensive all-in-one guide. This book in your hands is a roadmap to success that empowers individuals to navigate today's increasingly complex and competitive job market. It aims to equip them with the tools and strategies not only to survive but to excel in this constantly evolving landscape.

Starting this book was a challenge, but once I began, it was hard to stop. Each subject, from 'system design' to 'behavioral interviews' to 'data structures & algorithms (DSA)', is vast. The goal here isn't just to teach the concepts but to provide readers with actionable insights and resources those are freely available to dive deeper into when needed. The book has been structured into four parts –

- The system design section covers core concepts and provides links to resources for those who want a more in-depth understanding.
- The behavioral section explores every aspect of preparation, focusing on real-world scenarios and how to present experience confidently.
- As for DSA, it's more of a roadmap—learning DSA is about practice, more than theory. So I've focused on strategies, resources, and techniques to help people gain the necessary expertise through hands-on experience.
- Resources Library: This section contains a wealth of free-to-use references including links to websites, books and video tutorials as needed.

This book is a culmination of those conversations, experiences, and the need to fill a gap. It's designed to guide people through their preparation, no matter where they start from. I hope it gives them the clarity, confidence, and structure they need as they navigate their next career move.

Good luck!

About the Authors

Shalini Goyal is a technology leader with over two decades of experience in the software industry. Having worked with top-tier global organizations such as Amazon, J.P. Morgan, and Tata Consultancy Services, she brings a unique insider's perspective of the big tech world.

Shalini holds a master's degree and is a passionate advocate for equality in education. She is dedicated to empowering individuals by helping them navigate their career path.

As an established mentor, keynote speaker, and thought leader, she frequently speaks at conferences, YouTube channels, and participates in podcasts, inspiring others to grow in the tech space.

In 2024, she was honored as a finalist for the prestigious TechWomen100 award in the UK, recognizing her exceptional contributions to technology and mentorship.

Alok Sharan an experienced technology expert helping enterprises achieve their business objectives through innovative designs, development, and architecture.

Throughout his career, Alok has worked with a broad range of technologies. He specializes in digital transformation, guiding organizations through on-premise to AWS cloud migrations, and delivering robust Identity and Access Management solutions.

He is known for his ability to create purpose-built solutions, underpinned by strong problem-solving skills. His expertise is further demonstrated by a number of industry-recognized certifications, including TOGAF, AWS Solutions Architect, and AWS Machine Learning Specialty.

Table of Contents

PART 2: BEHAVIORAL INTERVIEWS

PART 3: CODING INTERVIEWS

PART 4: RESOURCES LIBRARY

Introduction

Whether you're a seasoned professional or just starting your career, this guide is designed to help you confidently navigate both technical and behavioral interviews. The tech industry is fiercely competitive, and excelling in interviews requires more than just the technical expertise. You need to prepare across multiple areas to truly stand out. This book is designed to help you accomplish that.

To set you up for success, this book starts by equipping you with the essential information to effectively plan your interview journey. You'll find strategies designed to help you structure and optimize your preparation, ensuring you're aware and well-prepared for every stage of the interview process.

After the foundation planning, the book is structured into 4 essential parts:

Part 1: System Design Interviews

System design interviews are critical, particularly for mid-level to senior roles, as they assess your ability to design scalable, efficient, and reliable systems. In this section, you will:

- Understand the fundamentals of system design, including key concepts like scalability, load balancing, and fault tolerance.
- Explore how to design common systems like social networks, e-commerce platforms, and messaging systems.
- Learn various architectural patterns, such as microservices, distributed systems, and event-driven architecture.
- Discover best practices for approaching system design interviews, from clarifying requirements to creating high-level designs and discussing trade-offs.

By the end of this section, you will have the knowledge and tools to excel in system design interviews, showcasing your ability to architect complex systems.

Part 2: Behavioral Interviews

Behavioral interviews are often overlooked but are crucial for assessing how well you fit into a company's culture and handle real-world situations. In this section, you will:

- Learn how to structure your responses using the STAR (Situation, Task, Action, Result) method for clear, impactful answers.
- Discover common behavioral questions, along with sample answers, to help you prepare.
- Master advanced strategies for handling curveball questions, managing stress, and tailoring your responses to different interviewers.
- Explore post-interview strategies, such as following up, reflecting on your performance, and using feedback to improve.

This part of the guide will help you effectively articulate your experiences, making a lasting impression on your interviewers.

Part 3: Coding Interviews (Data Structures and Algorithms)

Coding interviews are often the most challenging part of the tech interview process, testing your ability to solve problems using data structures and algorithms (DSA). In this section, you will:

- Get 6 months DSA Roadmap to follow and help you learn about the core data structures such as arrays, linked lists, trees, graphs, heaps, and more.
- Master algorithmic techniques, including sorting, searching, dynamic programming, backtracking, and greedy algorithms.
- Discover problem-solving strategies to approach coding challenges effectively, break down complex problems, and optimize your solutions.
- Practice with collection of problems along with step-by-step explanation to refine your skills.

This section will help you build a strong foundation in DSA, enabling you to confidently tackle any coding challenge.

Part 4: Resources

Mastering interviews goes beyond a single guide; it requires continuous learning and practice. This section emphasizes the importance of external resources to deepen your understanding and enhance your skills. Here's what this part covers:

- Explore books, articles, and tutorials that dive deeper into data structures, algorithms, and system design. Consistent coding practice and learning new patterns will sharpen your problem-solving abilities.
- Use practical frameworks to structure your answers, like storytelling techniques for real-life examples. Engaging with case studies and reflective exercises can help you develop concise, impactful responses.

This part encourages you to explore beyond the basics and adopt a growth mindset. The more you engage with various resources, the better prepared you'll be for interviews and career success.

How to Use This Guide

This guide has been structured to take you through each interview part step-by-step. Whether you're focusing on system design, behavioral interviews or coding, it is recommended that you start by reviewing the relevant section and then dive into practice. Each part is designed to build your confidence and competence, giving you a comprehensive preparation for your interviews.

Take your time with each section, practice diligently, and revisit the material as needed. The more familiar you are with the concepts and techniques, the better equipped you'll be to tackle any challenge that comes your way.

Contacting the Authors

We would welcome any comments and feedback you may have on this book. To share your feedback or ask any questions, you can reach out to us at: nobleapproachbooks@gmail.com

Pre-interview Planning

When preparing for a software engineering interview at any level, it's essential to create a plan that can help you get ready for the success. From researching the company and understanding the job description to refine your approach, this chapter covers everything you need. At the end of it, you should have a plan for yourself to start your preparation.

Five Key Strategies

There are 5 key pillars for any interview preparation in the software engineering role which you must consider to create a roadmap.

Goal Alignment

- You must tailor your plan to match the specific requirements of the job you're pursuing. By aligning your efforts with the skills and competencies the role demands, you maximize your chances of success during interviews and on the job.
- **How to Do It**: Start by thoroughly analyzing the job description to identify key skills and qualifications. Then, focus your preparation on strengthening those areas through targeted practice and study, ensuring you meet the role's specific expectations.

Coding Proficiency

- Start by mastering the basics of your chosen programming language. Anchor on writing clean, bug-free code by practicing simple problems on platforms like LeetCode. Every day, dedicate at least 30 minutes to solving basic problems (e.g., reverse a string, find the maximum in an array) to build your coding muscle.
- **How to Do It**: Use LeetCode's 'Easy' problems section. Aim to solve 5 problems per day. After that, review your solution against the most optimized one in the discussion forum to learn better approaches.

Problem-Solving Skills

- Develop a systematic approach to problem-solving. When faced with a problem, break it down into smaller parts:

1. Understand the problem statement: Restate it in your own words.
2. Identify the inputs and outputs: Clearly define what the problem is asking for.
3. Brainstorm possible solutions: Think of multiple ways to solve it.
4. Choose the most efficient way out: Consider both time in hand and solution complexity.

- **How to Do It**: Practice this approach with every problem you solve. Initially, you can also write down these steps on paper until they become your second nature.

System Design Abilities (for mid-level to senior roles)

- Start learning basic system design concepts like load balancing, caching, and database sharding. Don't just read about these concepts; implement simple versions of them in small projects.
- **How to Do It**: Begin with a small project, like designing a URL shortener. Implement basic functionalities like creating a short link, redirecting, and counting hits. Use tools like Lucidchart to create design diagrams and think how you will explain your choices.

Cultural Fit and Communication Skills

- Develop the habit of explaining your thought process clearly and succinctly. Go through the different values companies publish on their website. Practice by discussing them with someone else, or even to yourself in front of a mirror.
- **How to Do It**: After solving a problem, explain your solution as if you were teaching it to a beginner. Record yourself or use a voice memo app to listen back and improve your clarity.

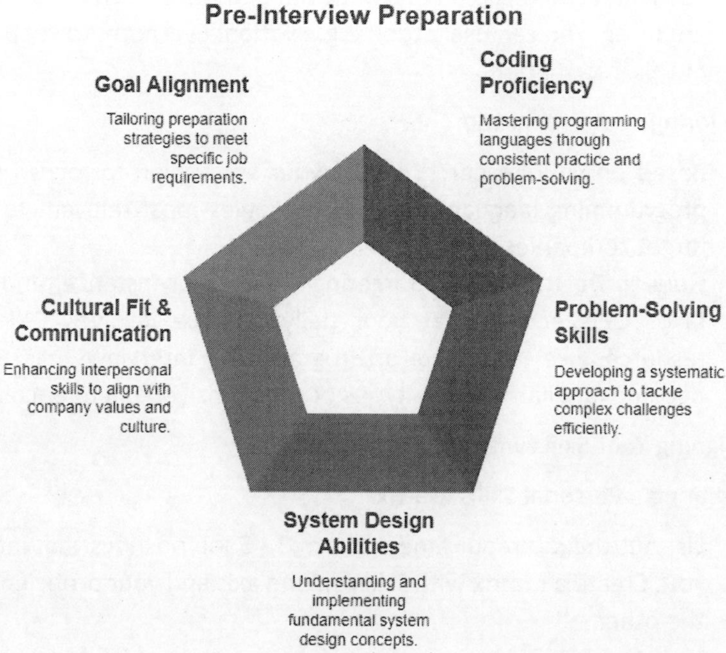

Figure – 1

Create a Detailed Plan

Once you have grasped the above strategies required for your preparation, you need to learn how you can effectively apply each one of them. You might already be an expert in one or more of them but will still need to focus on the rest for a complete plan. Let us break them down further and explore the key points to help you create the detailed plan.

1. Defining Clear Objectives

► Identifying Your Target Companies

- Researching Companies
    - Create a list of 10 companies you are interested in. For each, research their commonly used tech stack, preferred languages, and interview process.
    - **How to Do It**: Use LinkedIn to follow these companies, join relevant groups, and connect with current employees. Spend 10 minutes

each day reading up on recent developments or technologies they are using. You can use a tool (e.g., Notion, Evernote) to keep track of this information.

- Tailoring Your Preparation
    - Based on your research, adjust your study plan to focus on the programming languages and technologies most relevant to your target companies.
    - **How to Do It**: If you're targeting Google, for instance, and they favor C++, ensure that your daily practice involves C++. Use resources like "Elements of Programming Interviews in C++" to become familiar with the types of problems you might encounter.

► Aligning Your Skills with Job Requirements

- Creating a Personal Skills Matrix
    - List out the job requirements from 3 - 5 job postings that interest you. Create a matrix with skills on one axis and your proficiency on the other.
    - **How to Do It**: Rate yourself honestly on a scale of 1-5 for each skill. Focus your study plan on the skills where you rate yourself 3 or below. Reassess every month to track improvement.
- Strategies for Upskilling
    - Identify one growth area and dedicate a full week to improving it. For instance, if you're weak in dynamic programming (DP), spend that week solving only DP problems.
    - **How to Do It**: Use the 'Topics' section on LeetCode to find DP problems. Start your week with easy problems, progress to medium by mid-week, and tackle hard ones towards the end of the week. At last, review all the problems you solved and understand the patterns.

2. Creating a Study Plan for Problem Solving

► Structured Approach

- Daily Routine
    - Create a daily routine that includes reading, coding, and review sessions.

- **How to Do It**: Allocate time slots for different activities:
  - 1 hour of coding practice (e.g., solving 2-3 LeetCode problems).
  - 30 minutes of reading theory (e.g., algorithms from "Introduction to Algorithms" by Cormen).
  - 15 minutes of reviewing previous solutions and notes.
  - You can use tools like Google Calendar to block out these times and stick to them.

- Weekly Checkpoints
  - Every weekend, review what you've learned during the week and take a timed practice test.
  - **How to Do It**: Use LeetCode's weekly contest problems to simulate real interview pressure. After the contest, spend time reviewing each problem, understanding where you went wrong, and revising your approach.

- Monthly Milestones
  - Set a major goal for each month, such as mastering all sorting algorithms or completing 50 problems on a specific topic.
  - **How to Do It**: Break down the milestone into weekly and daily tasks. For example, if your monthly goal is to master sorting algorithms, week one could focus on bubble sort and selection sort, week two on merge sort and quick sort, and so on.

▶ Using the DSA Roadmap

- Month-by-Month Breakdown
  - This book provides 6-month roadmap which you should follow, adjusting the pace based on your comfort level. The roadmap is discussed in part 3 of the book.
  - **How to Do It**:

    <u>Month 1:</u> Basic Data Structures (Arrays & Strings)

    Why: Fundamental for most coding problems, builds a strong foundation.

    Goal: Solve 10 problems per week to reinforce key concepts and patterns. If you can only do 5 problems: Focus on understanding each problem deeply, like an Agile sprint, gradually increasing velocity.

Month 2: Recursion, Backtracking, Basic Algorithms

Why: Core algorithms prepare you for more advanced topics and complex problems.
Goal: Gradually increase difficulty, mastering recursion and backtracking.

Month 3-4: Trees, Graphs, Dynamic Programming

Why: Essential for tackling complex data structures and algorithms.
Goal: Solve mixed problems that combine multiple concepts.

Month 5-6: Mock Interviews & Timed Problem Solving

Why: Prepares you for real-world interview scenarios, highlights weak areas.
Goal: Focus on applying knowledge under time constraints, reviewing major topics.

- Integrating Mock Interviews

  Schedule at least two mock interviews per month starting from month 3.
  How to Do It: Use platforms like igotanoffer.com or interview with a study partner. Record these sessions if possible, and critically review your performance, focusing on areas for improvement.

3. Mastering the Programming Language

► Language Choice and Commitment

- Once you choose a language, commit to solving at least 100 problems in that language before considering switching.
  - **Why**: This helps build fluency in the language's syntax and strengths, reducing hesitation when solving problems. Switching too early can hinder your progress.
  - **How to Do It**: Track your progress using tools like Trello or an Excel sheet. For each solved problem, note any new language features or techniques you discovered, such as unique syntax or built-in functions.

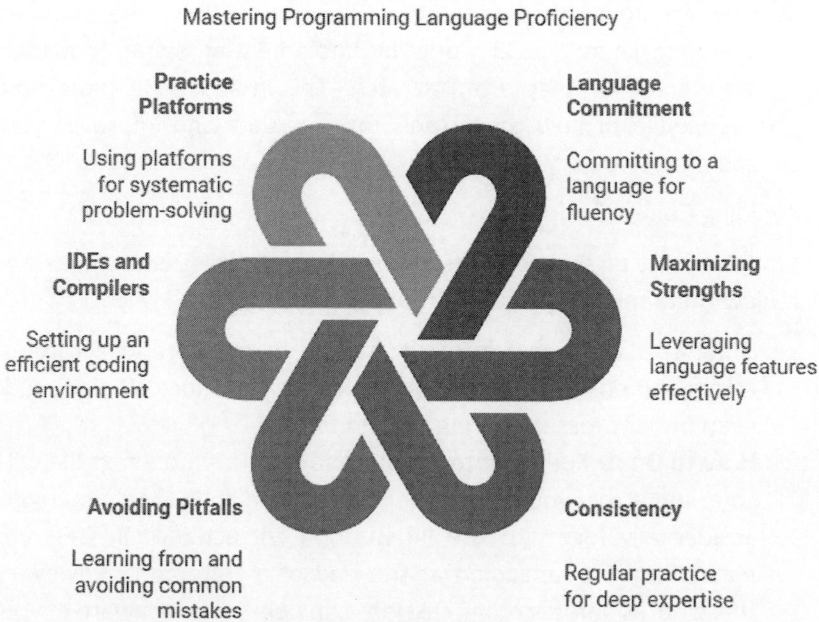

Figure – 2

► Maximizing Language Strengths

- Learn and leverage the most efficient data structures and libraries your chosen language provides.
    - **Why**: This can significantly optimize your solutions and reduce the coding time for you. You will be able to solve problems effectively and efficiently during interviews.
    - **How to Do It:** For example, if you're using Python, master collections like defaultdict and Counter, which simplify complex problems such as frequency counts or grouping data. In C++, make use of STL (Standard Template Library) containers like vector, set, or map to handle data efficiently.

► Importance of Consistency

- Focus on identifying and understanding the internals of your language's most-used features for building deep expertise.
    - **Why**: Gaining deeper insights into how core libraries and structures work helps you solve problems faster and more accurately in interviews, where writing code from scratch may be required.

- **How to Do It:** If you're using C++, explore how the Standard Template Library (STL) works by implementing some containers like vector or map from scratch. This exercise deepens your knowledge of how these tools manage data and improves your coding proficiency.

► Avoiding Common Pitfalls

- Compile a list of syntax errors or mistakes you frequently make and review them regularly to avoid repeating them.
  - **Why:** This will help you build muscle memory, reduce careless errors and ensure that you write cleaner and more efficient code even under pressure during the interviews.
  - **How to Do It:** Keep a note in your phone or a simple text file with common errors you encounter. For example, in Python, you might accidentally forget to use indentation correctly, or in C++, you might forget a semicolon at the end of a statement. Reviewing these notes before coding sessions can help you stay aware of your common pitfalls.

► IDEs, Compilers, and Practice Platforms

- You should set up your coding environment. *Choose an IDE* and configure it with the necessary extensions or plugins that enhance coding efficiency.
  - **Why:** A well configured environment will allow you smoother coding, faster debugging, and improved focus on problem solving.
  - **How to Do It:** For example, if you choose VSCode, install extensions like Python, C++ Intellisense, or Prettier for code formatting. Create a custom workspace with shortcuts for running code, debugging, and accessing documentation quickly.

► Leveraging Practice Platforms

- Use platforms like *LeetCode, HackerRank, or Codeforces* systematically. Focus on one problem category at a time and track your performance.
  - **Why:** This approach helps you build expertise in specific areas, identify your strengths and weaknesses and gradually improve your problem-solving skills.
  - **How to Do It:** For each problem you solve, document the problem statement, your initial approach, any issues faced, and the

final optimized solution. Use a tool *of your choice* (e.g., Notion, Evernote) to organize this information by topic and difficulty level.

4. Learning System Design

Mastering the Concepts and Practice

- Learn key system design topics
  - Start by learning the basic concepts like load balancing, caching, database sharding, replication, and estimations. Understand trade-offs involved in choices like SQL vs. No-SQL.
  - **How to Do It:** List down the topics you are unaware of and start exploring each of them. System Design section of this book covers all the basics you would require.
- Sample System Design Problems
  - Familiarize yourself with common system design interview questions and various case studies.
  - **How to Do It:** Refer the resources section provided in this book to learn about different blogs and videos you can go through to see how the solutions work. Additionally, once you consider yourself ready for the interview, set up some mock-up interviews to practice with someone.

5. Building the Right Mindset

Once you have created a roadmap for your preparation using the above strategies, it is important to get into a mindset that fosters progress. With so much to learn and accomplish for interview preparation, it is easy to feel overwhelmed. That's why developing a growth mindset is essential to stay motivated and focused on improvements.

Growth Mindset for Continuous Improvement

- Developing Resilience
  - Embrace challenges as opportunities to learn rather than obstacles.
  - **How to Do It**: Each time you encounter a problem you can't solve, instead of feeling discouraged, document the problem, research the solution, and revisit the problem later. Reflect on your progress regularly to see how far you've come.

- Daily Reflection
    - At the end of each day, spend 10 minutes reflecting on what you learned, what challenges you faced, and how you overcame them.
    - **How to Do It**: Use a journal or a digital note-taking app. This reflection process helps solidify your learning and maintain a positive attitude towards continuous improvement.

Strategies to Overcome Imposter Syndrome

- Building Confidence
    - Celebrate small wins regularly. Each time you solve a problem or master a concept, acknowledge it.
    - **How to Do It**: Keep a "Victory Log" where you note down every accomplishment, no matter how small. Review this log whenever you feel self-doubt creeping in.
- Positive Reinforcement
    - Surround yourself with positive influences—join study groups, engage in forums where people encourage and help each other.
    - **How to Do It**: Join online communities like Reddit's '*r/cscareerquestions*' or specific Discord servers focused on interview prep. Actively participate in discussions, ask questions, and share your own insights.

Final Thoughts

By now you should have a written plan for yourself and identified areas where you need to focus more. You can pick up any part of the book below and start from there. All the parts are independent from each other and do not need any prior knowledge to begin with.

PART 1

SYSTEM DESIGN INTERVIEWS

Chapter 01

Foundations of System Design Interviews

Imagine designing a system that can be used by millions of users worldwide in real time—think of platforms like Facebook or Instagram. How do you ensure it serves the desired business function, scalability, reliability, and performance of such large-scale distributed systems under immense pressure and limited time window? That's what system design interviews try to evaluate - a candidate's ability to understand stated business problems and come up with a solution approach that serves core business problems (both functional and stated/agreed non-functional) as well as prepared for future changes i.e. flexibility.

System design interview is a decisive component of overall hiring process, especially for senior engineering roles. Unlike coding interviews that focus on algorithms and problem-solving, system design interviews evaluate a candidate's ability to drive the conversation, demonstrate creativity, and teamwork to prepare a near real blueprint of a reliable system.

In real-world scenarios, engineers often deal with systems that must accommodate a growing user base, comply with specific performance standards, ensure data consistency, and security. A system design interview tests how well a candidate can balance these aspects while considering into account both functional and non-functional constraints.

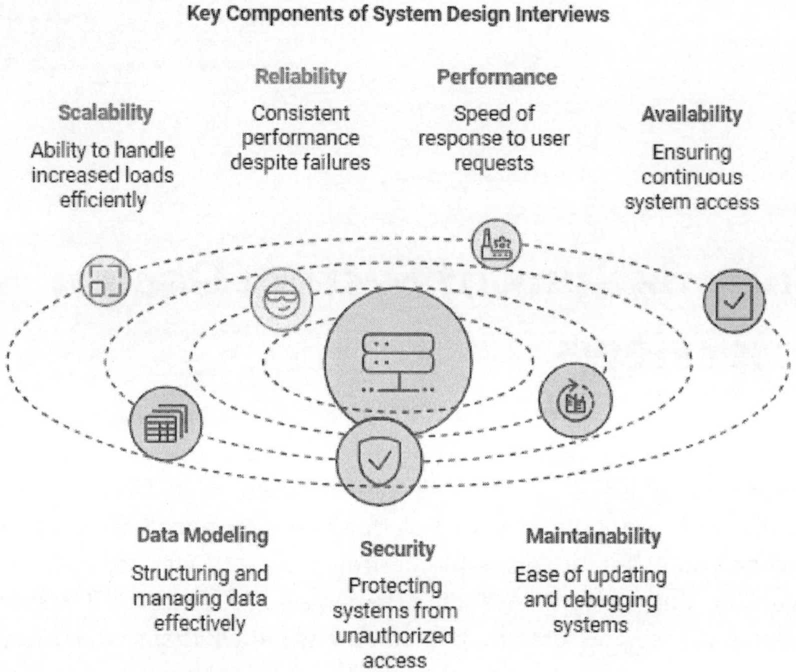

Figure – 1.1

Core Concepts in System Design Interviews

Let's look at some of the core concepts that candidates are expected to be familiar with:

Scalability: Scalability means ability and readiness of a system to deal with change in access patterns, usually considered in terms of spikes/increase in system load. It means a system can handle increased demands by either adding more machines (horizontal scaling) or enhancing existing ones (vertical scaling). Think of it as adding more cash registers in a busy supermarket or making the existing ones process items faster. One of the primary goals of system design is to design a system that scales efficiently.

Example: A social media platform must be able to handle a growing number of users without significant degradation in performance. The system can scale horizontally to handle this increased load by employing techniques like load balancing and database sharding.

Reliability: A reliable system is one that can perform its intended function consistently and accurately for a specified time under a given set of operating conditions. There are multiple components that contributes towards a system's reliability. It includes redundancy, replication, failover and disaster recovery plans, testing & quality control, systems monitoring & alerting, improving security posture and many more.

Example: In a banking application, reliability is critical because even a small data inconsistency could result in financial losses or user mistrust. Techniques like distributed database replication, reconciliation, audit, disaster recovery plans, and failover mechanisms help to ensure reliability of the system.

Performance: System performance is often measured by how fast it can respond to user requests. Low-latency systems are crucial for applications like real-time gaming or stock trading platforms where every millisecond counts.

Example: For an e-commerce website, users expect product pages to load within milliseconds. Implementing caching strategies (like storing frequently accessed data in a cache rather than fetching it from the database each time) improves performance.

Availability: Availability measures how often a system is accessible and functional. A highly available system ensures continuous access, even during peak usage or hardware failures, by leveraging redundancy and automatic failover mechanisms.

Example**:** For a platform like Netflix, availability is essential. If one server or data center fails, a backup system kicks in without the user noticing any disruption, ensuring smooth streaming at all times.

Data Modeling: Data modeling defines how information is structured and managed within a system. It includes choosing the right database type, creating schema designs, and planning data partitioning for scalability and performance.

Example**:** An online store might use a relational database like MySQL to store structured data, such as customer orders, and a NoSQL database like MongoDB to manage product reviews. This combination offers both consistency and flexibility.

Security: Security ensures that data and systems are protected from unauthorized access and cyber threats. This includes authentication, authorization, encryption, and secure communication protocols to safeguard user information.

Example: A payment platform must protect sensitive data like card information through encryption. Multi-factor authentication and secure communication channels like TLS ensure that data remains safe during transactions.

Maintainability: A maintainable system is easy to update and debug. This involves creating clean, modular architectures where individual components can be updated without affecting the entire system.

Example: A microservices architecture breaks down the system into independent components, allowing each service to be updated or scaled independently. This increases the maintainability of the system.

Following chapters cover these core concepts in detail along with appropriate examples to help you understand as well as implement them when needed.

1.1 Types of Systems Typically Designed in Interviews

Candidates are often asked to design systems that are similar to widely used services or platforms but simplified for the purpose of the interview. Common examples include:

▶ **Design a URL Shortener (e.g., bit.ly)**

A URL shortener transforms long URLs into compact, easy-to-share links. This service must handle high traffic, generate unique short URLs, support custom aliases, and provide analytics tracking for users to monitor link performance. It also needs to manage edge cases, like detecting and preventing malicious links.

Key Components:

- Database: Stores the mapping between long and short URLs, expiration time, and analytics data.
- Hashing/Encoding Logic: Converts long URLs into unique short codes. A base62 encoding is often used for compact representation.
- Custom Alias Support: Allows users to create personalized short URLs instead of auto-generated codes.
- Analytics Tracking: Tracks metrics such as click count, referrer, and geographic location.

- Scalability: Uses caching to manage frequent requests and ensure quick redirects.

Example:

If a user shortens the URL https://example.com/long-url, the system generates a code like bit.ly/abc123. Upon clicking the short link, the system retrieves and redirects to the original URL.

► Design a Social Media Platform (e.g., Twitter or Instagram)

A social media platform allows users to post updates, follow others, and view timelines. It must handle real-time interactions, offer personalized content, and manage a vast amount of data efficiently.

Key Components:

- User Service: Manages user profiles, relationships (followers and following), and authentication.
- Post Management: Stores text, images, videos, and hashtags.
- News Feed Generation: Retrieves posts from users the current user follows and ranks them using algorithms.
- Scalability: Uses distributed databases and caching mechanisms to handle millions of active users.
- Storage: Media files are stored using a CDN to ensure fast access and availability.

Example:

When a user posts an update, followers see the new post appear in their timelines. Real-time notifications alert them about new activity, like comments or likes.

► Design a Chat System (e.g., WhatsApp or Slack)

A chat system allows real-time communication between individuals or groups. It needs to ensure reliable message delivery even under network failures and handle concurrent users effectively.

Key Components:

- Message Service: Manages the sending, receiving, and storage of messages. Messages are often stored temporarily until they are delivered.
- Group Management: Handles group creation, member management, and permissions.

- Delivery Acknowledgment: Supports features like “read receipts” and “message seen” indicators.
- Offline Messaging: Ensures messages sent while a user is offline are delivered when they come online.
- Scalability: Uses a combination of load balancers and message queues to manage high traffic.

Example:

When a user sends a message to a friend, the system guarantees delivery with proper acknowledgment. In case of network issues, the message will be retried until successfully delivered.

► Design a Video Streaming Service (e.g., Netflix or YouTube)

Video streaming platforms enable users to watch content on demand. The system needs to handle large-scale video uploads, streaming, and personalized recommendations while maintaining smooth playback even during network fluctuations.

Key Components:

- Content Delivery Network (CDN): Distributes videos closer to users for faster access and minimal latency.
- Video Encoding: Converts videos into multiple resolutions and formats to support various devices.
- Streaming Protocols: Uses adaptive streaming (e.g., HLS or DASH) to adjust video quality based on the user’s internet speed.
- Recommendation Engine: Suggests videos based on user preferences and behavior.
- Analytics Tracking: Monitors engagement metrics like watch time and drop-off points.

Example:

When a user clicks on a video, the system selects the nearest CDN server to stream the content and adjusts the resolution automatically to avoid buffering.

► Design a Recommendation Engine

A recommendation engine suggests relevant items (e.g., products, videos, or articles) to users based on their behavior or preferences. It can use collaborative filtering, content-based filtering, or hybrid approaches to generate recommendations.

Key Components:

- User Profiles: Stores user interactions, such as search history, purchases, and likes.
- Item Database: Maintains metadata about the items (e.g., genre, type, category).
- Filtering Algorithms: Uses collaborative filtering to recommend items based on other users' activity and content-based filtering to match items with user preferences.
- Real-Time Updates: Continuously adjusts recommendations based on new user activity.
- Scalability: Uses distributed storage and batch processing for large datasets.

Example:

A music app might suggest new songs based on a user's past listening habits, as well as popular tracks among users with similar tastes.

▶ Design a News Feed System

A news feed system presents a stream of posts, articles, or updates to users, typically ranked by relevance or engagement. It needs to fetch, sort, and display content in real time, ensuring that users see the most relevant updates.

Key Components:

- Content Aggregation: Collects posts from sources such as followed accounts or subscribed channels.
- Ranking Algorithm: Sorts content based on factors like engagement, relevance, and recency.
- Personalization: Adapts the feed based on user preferences and activity.
- Caching: Stores frequently accessed data to reduce load times.
- Notifications: Alerts users about new posts, mentions, or activity.

Example:

When a user opens their feed, the system displays the latest updates from their connections, prioritized by relevance, such as recent posts with high engagement or posts tagged with their interests.

1.2 What Do Interviewers Look For?

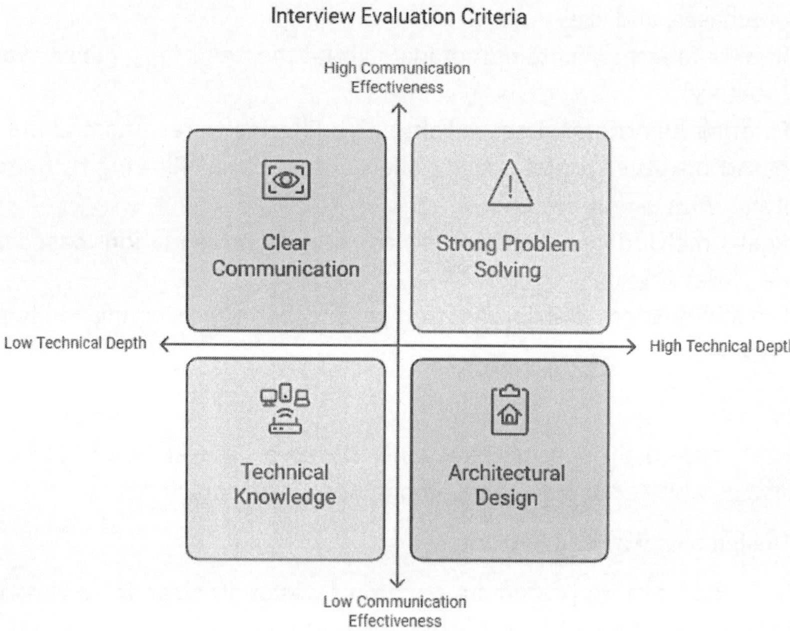

Figure – 1.2

System design interviews are not just about coming up with the "right" solution; rather, they are about demonstrating your thought process, problem-solving skills, and ability to address different constraints. Interviewers typically evaluate the following:

Problem Solving Approach

Interviewers want to see if you understand the problem clearly and can break it down well or not. Are you asking relevant clarifying questions? Do you understand the users of the system, the expected traffic, and the main features the system must support? Are you considering edge cases and special scenarios that could affect the design?

Example Questions:

- Who will be the users of this system, and what activities they will perform? What user volume is expected.
- Does the system require to remain functional all the time or some downtime is acceptable?

- Are there any special security concerns or compliance issues to consider?
- Is there a requirement to maintain the stored data for 'n' years?

Architectural Design and Breakdown of Components

The interviewer is interested in seeing how you divide the system into smaller, manageable components. This includes identifying the key building blocks of the system, such as web servers, databases, caches, load balancers, and message queues.

Example: In designing a social media feed, you might break down the system into the following components:

- **Client Layer**: Where the user interacts with the system (e.g., web or mobile application).
- **Authentication Layer**: To authenticate users and the clients they will be using e.g. web, mobile.
- **API Gateway**: Acts as an intermediary between the client and backend services.
- **Backend Services**: Microservices that handle user data, posts, and timelines.
- **Database**: Stores user profiles, posts, and relationships (followers/following).
- **Cache**: Frequently accessed data, like user timelines, is cached to reduce database load.

Technical Knowledge

Interviewers evaluate your understanding of distributed systems and how well you can apply the right technologies to solve problems. They also assess your ability to make informed decisions, explaining trade-offs between different approaches. Knowing when to use certain tools or architectures—like relational databases versus NoSQL, or monolith versus microservices—is crucial. Your design should address scalability, reliability, and performance while showing an awareness of constraints such as cost and complexity.

Example: If asked to design a URL shortener, you might explain the trade-offs between using a relational database for strict consistency versus a NoSQL database for scalability. You could also discuss how caching mechanisms and load balancers reduce latency under heavy usage. The key is demonstrating that you can weigh the pros and cons for each component.

Communication Skills

Effective communication is a must in system design interviews. Interviewers want to see if you can clearly express your thought process, collaborate on design ideas, and take feedback constructively. They look for structured thinking—how you break down a complex problem into smaller pieces and explain your approach step-by-step. It's also important to ask clarifying questions and confirm requirements to ensure your solution aligns with the interviewer's expectations.

Example: While designing a chat system, you might start by clarifying whether the system requires real-time messaging or if occasional delays are acceptable. You would then walk through your plan for handling message storage, delivery confirmation, and offline messaging, asking the interviewer for feedback along the way. Clear communication shows that you can not only build systems but also work effectively in collaborative environments.

Chapter 02

Effective Time Management

A common comment from every candidate who comes out of System Design interview is – *'I wish I had more time to complete the design or add more components to highlight my knowledge'*. Candidates are often expected to cover multiple aspects of a system, from requirement gathering to bottleneck resolution, all within a relatively short period (usually 45-60 minutes). Given the complexity of designing large-scale systems, you must allocate time wisely across different sections to ensure the coverage of all necessary areas.

In this chapter, we will break down each phase of the system design interview, providing a timeline and detailed explanation of how to handle each part efficiently. The goal is to help you optimize your approach and ensure that no aspect of the design is overlooked.

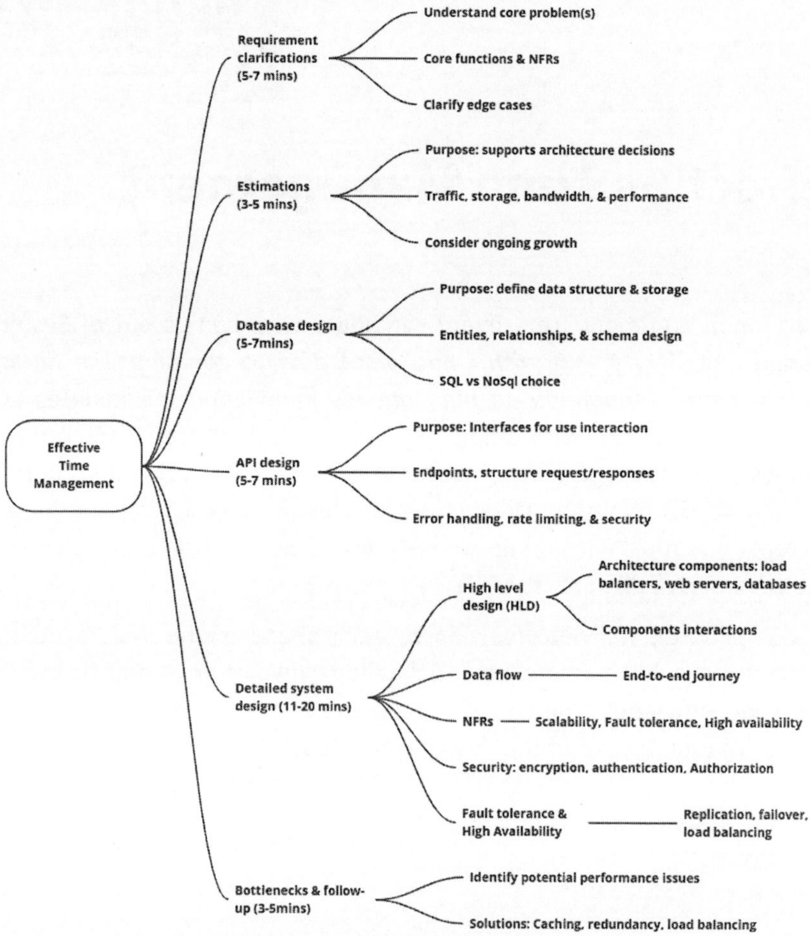

Figure – 2.1

2.1 Suggested Timeline Breakdown

Here's a general guideline for how to divide your time during a system design interview:

- Requirement Clarifications (5-7 minutes)
- Estimations (3-5 minutes)
- Database Design (5-7 minutes)
- API Design (5-7 minutes)
- System's Detailed Design (15-20 minutes)
- Resolving Bottlenecks and Follow-up Questions (3-5 minutes)

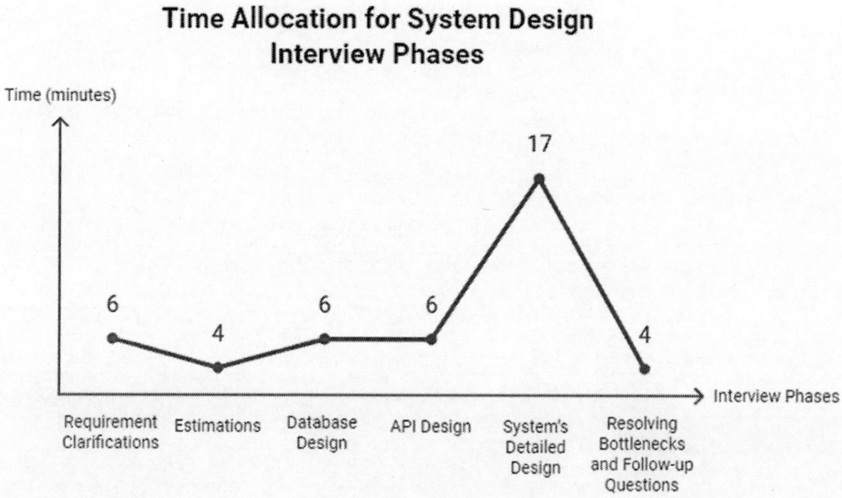

Figure – 2.2

Each section should be approached methodically, ensuring that you address the most critical elements of the design while staying within the time limits. Let's see each of these at a high level to understand how the time distribution should work.

2.2 Requirement Clarifications (5-7 minutes)

The first phase of the interview focuses on understanding the problem and clarifying the requirements. This is the most important step, as it lays the foundation for your entire design process. Misunderstanding the requirements, including making assumptions without clarifying or overlooking key details, could lead to a flawed design. This is also the start of the engagement process with interviewers where you start driving the conversation.

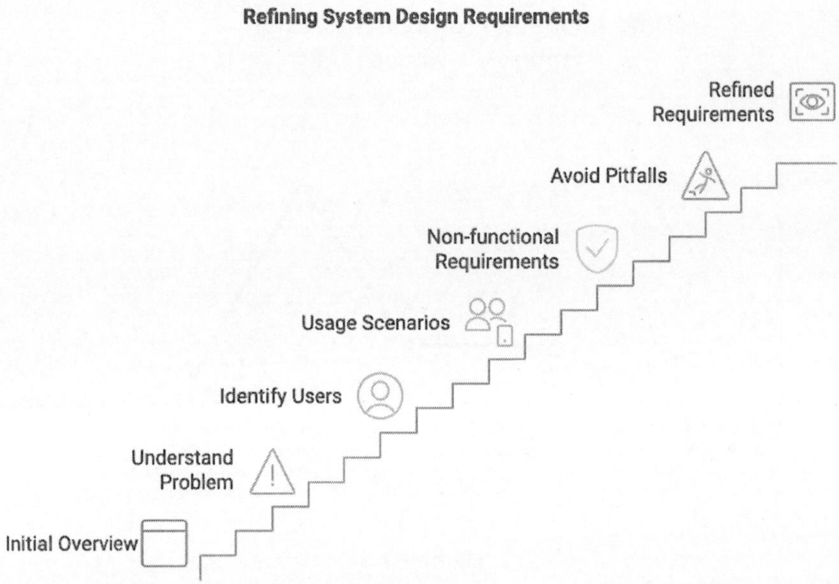

Figure – 2.3

Steps to Follow

i. Understand the Core Problem

Start by asking the interviewer for a brief overview of the system. Clarify the primary functionality, user interactions, non-functional expectations, and the overall goal of the system. Let's consider we are looking at a design for URL Shortening Service.

Example:

- "Should the service only shorten URLs, or should it also support features like click analytics to track the number of clicks on each shortened URL?"
- "Do we need to allow users to customize their short URLs, or will the service only generate auto-created short URLs?"

ii. Identify the Users

Understanding who will use the system is key to making informed design decisions. Different types of users (e.g., general users, business clients, administrators) may have varying needs. Clarify whether the system will serve a broad user base or specific segments.

Example:

- "Will the service cater to general external users only, or will businesses also use it for their marketing needs?"
- "Are there any administrative users who need access to advanced analytics or data controls?"

iii. Discuss Usage Scenarios

Define the core use cases for the system to ensure the design meets the most common user needs. Understanding user actions and system responses helps you structure an effective design.

Example:

- Creating a short URL.
- Tracking click analytics for each shortened URL.
- Enabling URL expiration and customization options for premium users.
- Redirecting users from the short URL to the original URL.

iv. Clarify Non-functional Requirements

Along with functional requirements, clarify non-functional requirements like performance, scalability, availability, and security. These requirements often shape the architecture, selected components, and trade-offs made in design.

Example:

- "How many users per day will use the system? Also, at a given time how many of them can be active?" – Based on this information users/second can also be estimated.
- "Do we need high availability or fault tolerance to ensure short URLs remain accessible?"
- "Do we want users to authenticate themselves before accessing the service?"

v. Pitfalls to Avoid

- **Rushing Through Requirements:** Don't rush through this phase. It's better to take a few extra minutes to fully understand the problem than to design a solution based on assumptions or insufficient understanding.
- **Not Clarifying Edge Cases:** Always ask about edge cases that could impact the system's performance or user experience. For instance, "What happens if a user tries to shorten a URL that has already been shortened?" or "How should expired URLs be handled?"

2.3 Estimations (3-5 minutes)

Once you understand the problem and requirements, the next step is to estimate the scale of the system. Estimating traffic, storage, and performance requirements helps you make informed decisions about the architecture, particularly when it comes to choosing databases, load balancing strategies, and caching mechanisms. Depending upon the system you have been asked to build, some or all of the following can be applicable.

1. Traffic Estimates

Begin by estimating how much traffic the system will handle. This includes both read (e.g., users accessing a web page or data) and write (e.g., users creating new content or sending messages) requests. These estimates help to answer a few core questions downstream e.g. can I use any database for my design or I need something more specific? Can my design meet the system performance implicitly because of the choices I have made for my components or should I consider to introduce something more specialized say, caching?

Example:

For a URL shortening service, if you expect 1 million users and each user shortens 10 URLs per month, this results in:

- 10 million URL shortenings per month.
- Roughly 350,000 URL shortenings per day.
- Peak traffic might be 4-5 requests per second.

Any database can meet the above request/second requirement and hence we can easily infer that this number is insignificant for us while deciding a database for the problem in hands.

2. Data Storage Estimates

Next, estimate how much data the system will need to store. This includes user data, logs, metadata, and any additional information (like analytics data or multimedia files). While estimating data storage, also consider future-proofing in terms of year-on-year data growth as well as retention policy as applicable.

Example:

If each shortened URL consumes 100 bytes, and the service handles 10 million URLs per month, you would need roughly 1 GB of storage per month (without accounting for replication, metadata, or analytics).

Now, consider additional storage for:

- User accounts (if needed).
- Analytics data (e.g., number of redirects, referrers, geolocation data).
- Keeping the data for 'n' months.

3. Bandwidth Estimates

Estimate how much data will be transmitted over the network to anticipate bandwidth needs and potential costs. For a URL shortening service, this includes both the traffic generated from URL shortening requests and the redirections.

Example:

- Each redirection request involves a small data transfer (about 100 bytes), so for 100 million redirects per month, the bandwidth required for redirection alone is around 10 GB per month.
- URL shortening requests (assuming similar size) would need about 1 GB per month, resulting in a total bandwidth estimate of approximately 11 GB per month.

Factoring in bandwidth helps to plan for network costs, and whether a CDN is required to reduce latency for users in different locations.

4. Performance Requirements

Determine the acceptable performance levels for the system, particularly in terms of response times and latency. Depending on the system and nature of the consumer, users may expect responses in milliseconds, or they may tolerate slower response times.

Example:

- URLs to be shortened and returned to the user within 100-200ms.
- Redirection from the shortened URL to the original URL should happen in less than 100ms.

5. Estimation Pitfalls

- **Overestimating Traffic**: While it's important to account for growth, overestimating traffic can lead to over-complicating your design.
- **Ignoring Data Growth**: Always consider how data grows over time, especially in systems that need to store historical data like analytics or logs.

2.4 Database Design (5-7 minutes)

Designing a database schema defines how data will be structured, stored, and retrieved efficiently. This is crucial for ensuring the system performs well, can scale as needed, and remains reliable.

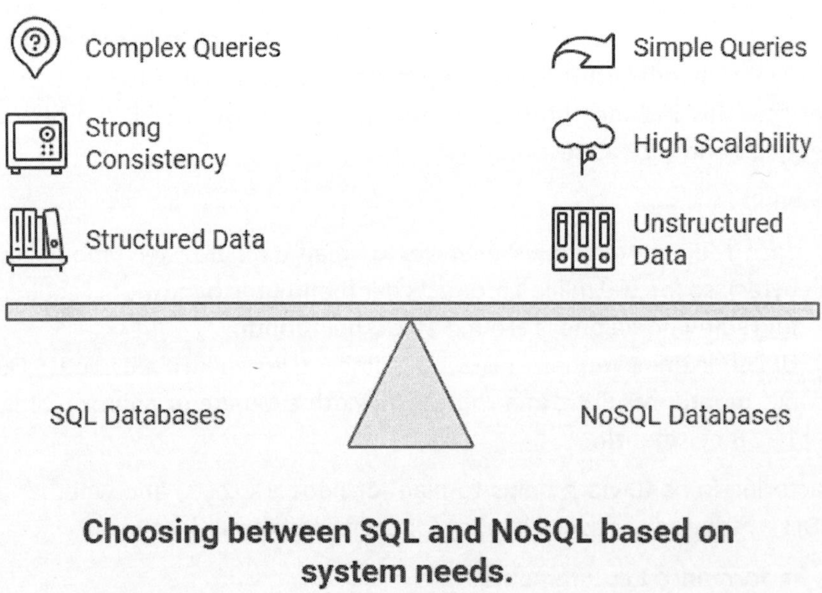

Figure – 2.4

Steps to Follow:

1. Identify Key Entities

Start by identifying the core entities that will be stored in your database. Each entity represents a key data object that your system will interact with. In SQL databases, each entity typically corresponds to a table, while in NoSQL databases, entities may map to collections.

Example:

- URLs: Represents both the original URL and the shortened URL.
- Users: Stores user details if the service includes user accounts.
- Analytics: Tracks usage data for shortened URLs, such as access count, referrers, and timestamps.

2. Define Relationships Between Entities

Next, define the relationships between these entities. In a relational (SQL) database, this often involves establishing relationships using foreign keys. In NoSQL databases, you may choose to embed related data within documents or link collections.

Example:

- URLs Table: Stores original and shortened URLs, user ID (if applicable), and timestamps for tracking.
- Analytics Table: Tracks each shortened URL's access count, referrer data, and the last access date.
- User to URLs Relationship: If a user can create multiple shortened URLs, there would be a one-to-many relationship between the Users and URLs tables.

3. Schema Design

Think carefully how the schema is going to look like.

Example:

URLs Table

- `id` (Primary Key)
- `original_url` (VARCHAR)
- `short_url` (VARCHAR, unique)
- `user_id` (Foreign Key, references Users table)

- `created_at` (TIMESTAMP)
- `expiration_date` (TIMESTAMP, optional)

Analytics Table

- `id` (Primary Key)
- `short_url_id` (Foreign Key, references URLs table)
- `access_count` (INTEGER)
- `last_accessed` (TIMESTAMP)
- `referrer` (VARCHAR)

Users Table (if applicable)

- `id` (Primary Key)
- `username` (VARCHAR, unique)
- `email` (VARCHAR, unique)
- `password_hash` (VARCHAR)
- `created_at` (TIMESTAMP)

4. NoSQL vs. SQL

Choose between a relational (SQL) or non-relational (NoSQL) database based on the system's needs. Consider factors such as scalability, consistency, and how the data will be accessed.

- SQL: Ideal for structured data with clear relationships, requiring strong consistency and support for complex queries.
- NoSQL: Suitable for unstructured or semi-structured data, systems needing high scalability, or scenarios prioritizing availability over strict consistency (e.g., social media timelines).

5. Common Pitfalls

- **Overcomplicating the Schema:** Keep the schema as simple as possible to meet the system's core requirements. Remember, this design is for the interview setting and does not need to be production-ready, so focus on simplicity.
- **Ignoring Future Growth:** Consider how the database will scale over time. Design the schema with potential growth in mind, ensuring it can support millions of rows and handle efficient querying as the dataset expands.

2.5 API Design (5-7 minutes)

After clarifying requirements and estimating the system's scale, the next step is defining the interfaces through which users or clients will interact with the system. API design is essential for making the system user-friendly, adaptable, and resilient in handling both normal and edge-case requests.

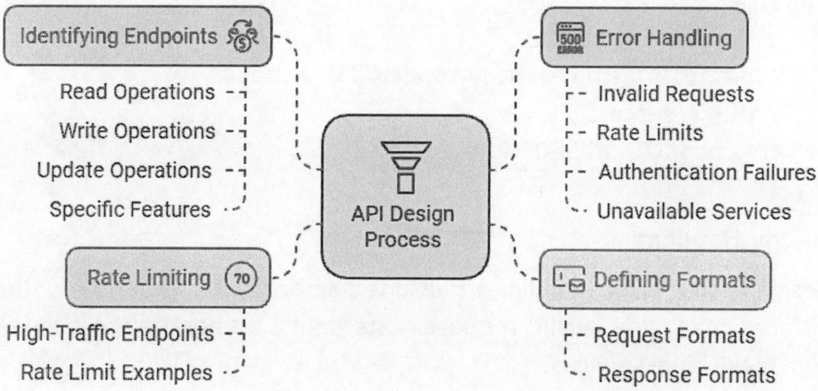

Figure – 2.5

Steps to Follow:

1. Identify Key Endpoints

Start by identifying the primary endpoints that will be exposed to clients. This includes endpoints for read, write, update operations, and any specific features like analytics.

Example:

- POST /shorten: Shortens a given URL.
- GET /{shortURL}: Redirects to the original URL.
- GET /stats/{shortURL}: Retrieves analytics for a specific shortened URL.
- DELETE /{shortURL} (Optional): Deletes a shortened URL, if allowed for users.

2. Define Request and Response Formats

Define the request and response structure for each endpoint, specifying the required fields and data types for requests and responses.

Example for POST /shorten Endpoint:

Request: Contains the original URL and an optional custom alias.

{
  "original_url": "http://example.com",
  "custom_alias": "myalias"
}

Response: Returns the shortened URL, creation date, and a status message.

{
  "short_url": "http://short.ly/myalias",
  "status": "success",
  "created_at": "2024-09-01T12:00:00Z"
}

3. Error Handling

Design robust error handling to ensure a smooth user experience. This includes managing invalid requests, rate limits, authentication failures, and unavailable services.

Example for Error Handling in POST /shorten Endpoint:

- 400 Bad Request: Returned if the original URL is invalid.
- 409 Conflict: Returned if the custom alias is already in use.
- 401 Unauthorized: Returned if the user attempts to shorten a URL without valid authentication.
- 403 Forbidden: Returned if the user lacks sufficient permissions to access certain endpoints (like deleting a URL or accessing analytics).

Authentication and Authorization Error Handling: Incorporate checks for user authentication and permissions:

- Authentication: For example, if using OAuth tokens, validate the token and return a 401 Unauthorized error if it's invalid or expired.
- Authorization: Return a 403 Forbidden error if the user lacks permission to access or modify specific data (e.g., deleting URLs created by other users).

4. Rate Limiting and Throttling

To manage server load and prevent abuse, implement rate limiting for high-traffic endpoints, such as URL shortening and redirection.

- Example: For the POST /shorten endpoint, apply rate limits (e.g., 100 requests per hour per user). Return 429 Too Many Requests if a user exceeds their rate limit, along with a message indicating when they can retry.

2.6 System's Design (15-20 minutes)

The design phase is where you architect the system and layout all its components to meet both functional and non-functional requirements like scalability, fault tolerance, and audit capabilities. This phase combines both top-down and bottom-up approaches, ensuring that each component supports the system's goals and contributes to a cohesive and high-performance solution. By integrating these elements methodically, we establish a reliable, scalable, and efficient infrastructure capable of handling future growth and complex interactions.

In this book, we adopt a top-down approach for system design. Starting with a high-level overview, we move into specific component details and then consider how these components fit into the broader system to achieve the desired results. This approach ensures that each part of the system aligns with overarching business goals and operational requirements.

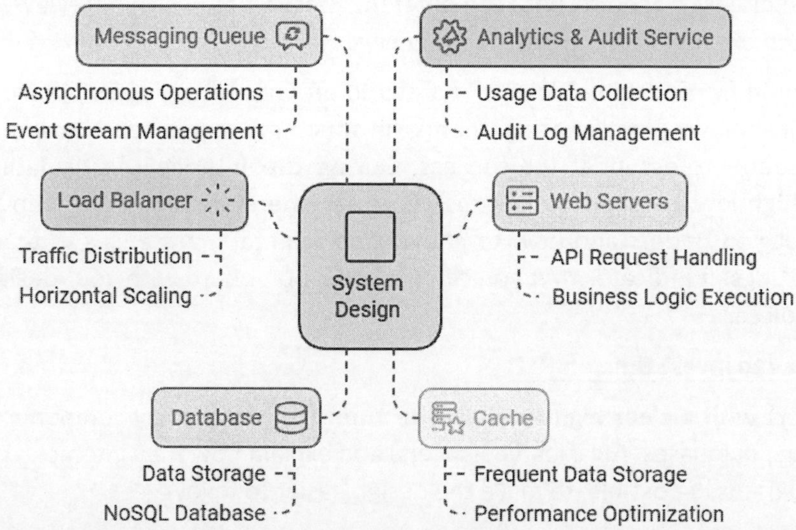

Figure – 2.6

High-Level Design (HLD)

It is the first visual output you should produce that will be expanded later-on to produce a detailed design, meeting the requirements in your hands. A high-level design should reflect -

Clarity of Vision: High-level design demonstrates that you understand the core architecture and structure of the system, including how the major components interact. Interviewers want to see that you can design a system that solves the problem efficiently, rather than getting lost in the details. Starting with a high-level design helps you lay out a clear roadmap before diving into specifics.

Effective Communication: A well-articulated high-level design shows that you can communicate complex systems in a way that's easy for others to understand. This is a critical skill in real-world scenarios where you need to align with other engineers, managers, and stakeholders. In the interview, it also helps ensure that both you and the interviewer are on the same page before you proceed to more detailed discussions.

Problem-Solving Approach: By focusing on high-level design, you show that you can break down a complex problem into manageable parts. This is crucial for designing scalable, reliable systems. It also helps you identify and discuss trade-offs between different approaches, which interviewers often expect in system design interviews.

Buy-In from Stakeholders: In real-world projects, securing buy-in from stakeholders—engineering teams, product managers, and business leaders—is essential for success. During the interview, articulating a high-level design that makes sense for the system's needs; shows that you understand how to gather and maintain consensus in team settings. It indicates that you can get others on board with your design choices.

How to invest time on HLD

Start with a clear high-level architecture: Lay out the key components (e.g., databases, APIs, load balancers) and explain how they interact. Use diagrams, if possible, to make the design easier to follow.

Communicate the "why" behind your choices: As you present your design, explain why you chose certain components or approaches (e.g., microservices vs. monolithic architecture). This shows that you've carefully considered trade-offs and thought through your decisions.

Invite feedback: While presenting, ask the interviewer if they'd like to dive into specific areas. This mirrors real-world stakeholder engagement, where buy-in is key to making sure everyone understands and agrees on the system's direction.

Iterate based on feedback: Be open to adjusting your design based on questions or feedback from the interviewer, just as you would in a real project. This shows that you can handle constructive input and align your vision with the team's goals.

Taking an example, in designing a system like a URL shortening service, key architectural components include:

Client Requests: Users initiate actions (e.g., shorten or access a URL) through the client interface, whether on a web or mobile platform i.e.user submits a URL for shortening

Load Balancer: Distributes traffic across multiple servers, enhancing availability and ensuring no single server is overwhelmed.

Web Servers: Process API requests, execute business logic, and interface with data layers.

Cache: Temporarily stores frequently accessed URLs to optimize performance by reducing database load. The web server first checks the cache for an existing shortened URL. If found, the server returns this URL immediately, saving time and resources.

Database: Persistently stores primary data (e.g., original and shortened URLs, analytics, user information). If the URL isn't found in the cache, the web server queries the database. If no existing entry is found, a new shortened URL is generated, saved to the database, as well as added to the cache.

Analytics & Audit Service: Collects and processes usage data, managing audit logs to meet compliance and tracking requirements. Each URL access is recorded for auditing and analytics processing.

The example above provides a scalable and resilient framework, balancing real-time performance needs with effective data management and user interaction handling.

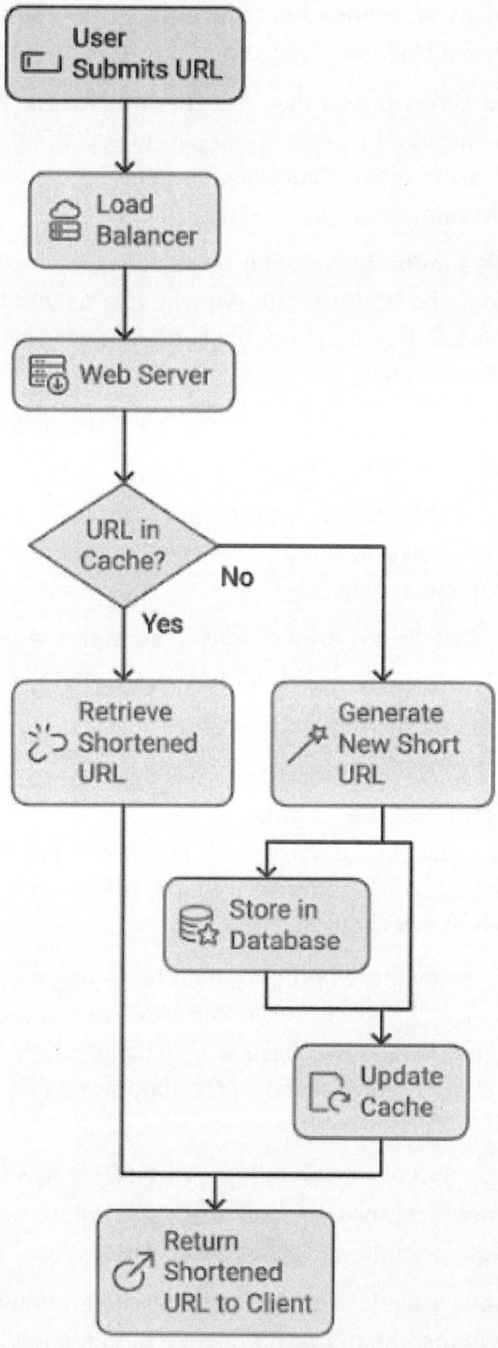
User
Submits URL
Load
Balancer
Web Server
URL in
Cache?
No
Yes
Retrieve
Shortened
URL
Generate
New Short
URL
Store in
Database
Update
Cache
Return
Shortened
URL to Client

Figure – 2.7

Non-Functional Requirements (NFRs)

NFRs guarantee a comprehensive, dependable, and scalable system design that considers both functionality and long-term success. They are essential for the following reasons –

Comprehensive System Design: NFRs like performance, security, scalability, and fault tolerance ensure your system performs effectively under live conditions. Addressing these shows you understand both functionality and operational efficiency.

Real-World Relevance: NFRs are essential for systems to work at scale. Discussing them in the interview demonstrates your ability to design solutions that can handle real-world challenges like high traffic, security threats, and scalability.

Audit and Compliance: Audit support is key for regulatory compliance in a few industries e.g. finance and healthcare. Mentioning logging, traceability, and security measures shows you're considering the compliance aspects of system design.

System Monitoring: Incorporating system monitoring improves overall reliability by facilitating transparency on performance tracking, error detection, and troubleshooting. Highlighting monitoring tools (e.g., dashboards, alerts) proves you're thinking about system health and proactive maintenance.

Risk Management: Addressing NFRs like security shows you're designing with risk management in mind.

► Scaling the System

Companies need systems that can handle increased load as their user base, data, and traffic grow. Demonstrating an understanding of scalability shows you can design solutions that not only work today but will remain functional and efficient as demand increases. We will discuss this in detail in chapter 9.

► Fault Tolerance and High Availability

Fault tolerance and high availability ensure the system remains operational and resilient, even in the face of hardware or software failures. It ensures business continuity even when some components fail. Interviewers want to see that you can design systems capable of handling failures gracefully, minimizing downtime, and maintaining availability, which are crucial for most real-world applications.

Many candidates cover scaling and performance but fail to adequately address how to ensure the system remains available during outages or failures. Showing your knowledge of fault tolerance will set you apart by highlighting your focus on designing resilient systems that meet high service level agreements (SLAs).

► **Security**

Security should be addressed with clarity and intention. It is a non-negotiable aspect of any system design. In today's digital landscape, vulnerabilities can lead to data breaches, financial losses, and damage to a company's reputation. Interviewers expect candidates to be proactive in addressing potential security risks as part of a robust design. Chapter 13 will provide more details on this topic.

How to Invest time on NFRs

Integrate NFRs into your design discussion, showing how your system will handle factors like performance, security, and scalability.

Mention system monitoring: Explain how monitoring tools will track system health, detect issues, and support long-term maintenance.

2.7 Resolving Bottlenecks and Follow-up Questions (3-5 minutes)

In the final phase of the interview, you'll need to identify potential bottlenecks in your system and suggest ways to resolve them. This is also the time to address any follow-up questions from the interviewer.

Steps to Follow

1. Identifying Bottlenecks

Look for areas in your system where performance or scalability could be compromised. Bottlenecks can occur at various points in the system, such as:

Single Points of Failure: For example, if the system relies on a single database instance, a failure of that instance could bring down the entire service.

Database Load: If the system queries the database too frequently, this could lead to performance degradation.

2. Resolving Bottlenecks

For each bottleneck, propose a solution. This could involve adding redundancy, caching, or load balancing to distribute the load. Such as:

Single Points of Failure: In case of a single database, you can propose a database replica or an active-active setup as per the use case.

Database Load: If the system queries the database too frequently, propose efficient cache implementation.

Example

Your high-traffic URL shortening service faces a sudden DDoS attack, overwhelming servers with fake requests. Adding more servers might help temporarily but doesn't address the root issue.

Approach

Rate Limiting & Throttling: Limit requests per IP within a timeframe. Throttling deprioritizes attackers' requests, reducing load from malicious traffic.

Web Application Firewall (WAF): Deploy a WAF to filter out suspicious requests before they hit your servers, based on IP origin, headers, or specific endpoints.

DDoS Protection Services: Services like Cloudflare or AWS Shield intercept and mitigate attacks at the network edge, ensuring legitimate traffic flows smoothly.

Strategic Caching: Cache frequently accessed resources to reduce load on backend servers. Legitimate repeated requests can be served from cache, limiting database strain. Also consider the use of CDN for a candidate use case.

Load Balancing with Health Checks: Use intelligent load balancing to reroute traffic to less-burdened servers, ensuring uninterrupted service for real users.

Final Thoughts

At the end of the interview, keep a few mins to briefly summarize your design, highlighting its strengths and connecting it back to the requirements captured at the beginning of the discussion. Even at this moment you should be prepared for any follow-up questions or challenges from the interviewer.

Chapter 03

Clarifying the Requirements

Requirement clarification is the first thing you do as the interview begins. Many candidates rush through this part, but not asking the questions would mean skipping a part where you can get score from interviewer. Secondly, before jumping into architecture, databases, or scalability, you must fully understand what the problem statement really requires.

In this chapter, we will break down the process of gathering and understanding requirements in a system design interview. We will cover different types of requirements and how to ask the right questions to clarify these.

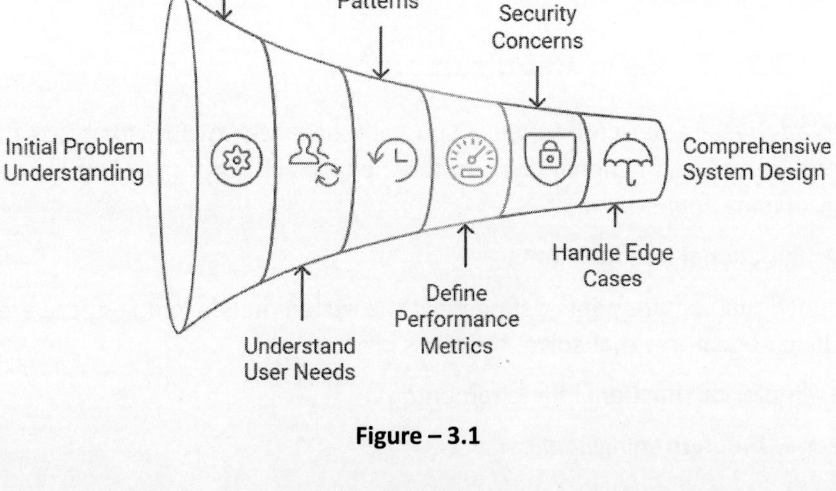

Figure – 3.1

3.1 Importance of Requirement Clarifications

The interviewer expects you to ask clarifying questions and call out any assumptions that lead you toward the right solution. By spending time in the beginning to clarify what is expected, you can ensure that your design focuses on the right goals and constraints. Skipping this step can lead to misunderstandings, incorrect designs, and missed requirements.

Why Candidates Fail to Clarify Requirements

Lack of Functional Domain Knowledge: If the question is related to shortening URL but candidate has never heard of this term i.e. does not understand the basic high-level behavior. In such a case, it becomes even harder to work towards a possible solution.

Lack of Focus on Edge Cases: Many candidates only focus on the core features but ignore edge cases. For example, in a URL shortening service, what happens when a user tries to shorten a duplicate URL or when the custom alias is already taken?

Failure to Address Non-functional Requirements: Focusing solely on functionality without considering scalability, availability, or latency is a common mistake. These factors can affect the entire architecture.

Jumping Straight to Design: Candidates often feel pressured to jump straight into coding or system design without fully understanding the problem. This leads to poor designs that don't meet the actual requirements.

3.2 Types of Requirements

In any system design interview, you will encounter two major types of requirements: functional and non-functional. Each plays an essential role in shaping your system.

► Functional Requirements

Functional requirements define what the system needs to do—these are the core features that solve the user's problem.

Examples of Functional Requirements

For a URL Shortening Service:

- Shorten a long URL and return the short version.

- Redirect users from the short URL to the original URL.
- Allow users to create custom short URLs (e.g., mycompany.com/myalias).

For a Social Media Platform:

- Allow users to post updates, like, share, and comment.
- Follow and unfollow users.
- View real-time updates on a timeline or newsfeed.

For a Messaging Service:

- Send and receive messages in real-time.
- Support one-to-one and group conversations.
- Attach media (e.g., images, videos, files).

How to Clarify Functional Requirements

Start by asking general questions to understand the core functionalities, but then move into specific scenarios. Here are the types of questions you can ask:

- "What are the main user actions this system needs to support?"
- "Are there any special user roles like admin or moderator that require different functionality?"
- "What should happen if a user tries to perform an invalid action?

▶ Non-functional Requirements

Non-functional requirements are equally critical in system design. They define how the system performs under various conditions and influence how you design your system architecture, database, and scalability solutions.

Examples of Non-functional Requirements

Scalability: How will the system handle increased traffic or data growth?

Performance: What is the acceptable latency or response time for API calls or page loads?

Reliability: How important is system uptime? What are the recovery mechanisms in case of failures?

Security: What security considerations should be in place? For example, should all data be encrypted both in transit and at rest?

Compliance: Are there any regulatory requirements (e.g., GDPR, PCI/DSS) that the system must adhere to?

How to Clarify Non-functional Requirements

To clarify non-functional requirements, ask questions that focus on system performance and how it should behave under various conditions. Some useful questions include:

"What are the expected traffic patterns? Are there peaks, such as during holidays or special events?"

"Is low latency critical for this system? What are acceptable response times?"

"How important is high availability? Can we afford downtime, or do we need 99.99% uptime?"

3.3 Key Questions to Ask

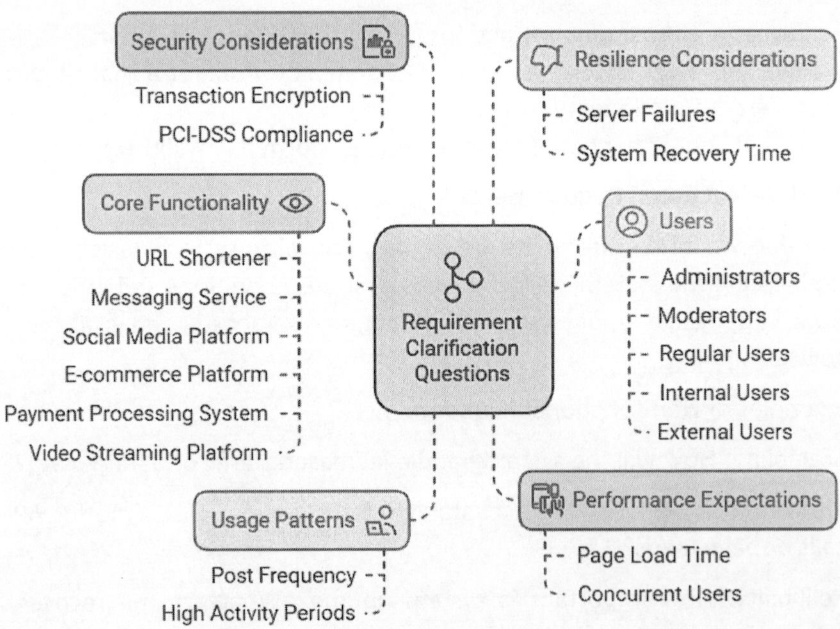

Figure – 3.2

Here are the types of questions you should ask during the requirement clarification phase:

▶ What is the Core Functionality?

This question is crucial because it ensures that you and the interviewer are aligned on the fundamental purpose of the system. If you're unclear on this point, your entire design might go off course.

Example for a URL Shortener: What is the primary purpose of this URL shortening service? Is it simply to shorten URLs, or are we also tracking analytics like click-through rates?

▶ Who Are the Users?

Understanding the users will help you design the system to meet their needs. Different users may encounter different system behavior guided by permissions and access levels.

Example for a Messaging Service: Will there be different types of users, such as administrators, moderators, regular, internal to the system or external users? What permissions does each type of user have?

▶ What Are the Expected Usage Patterns?

Knowing how users will interact with the system helps you design for peak loads and scalability.

Example for a Social Media Platform: How often will users post updates? Will there be periods of high activity (e.g., during major events)?

▶ What Are the Performance Expectations?

Performance metrics are critical for ensuring that your system remains responsive, especially under load.

Example for an E-commerce Platform: What is the acceptable page load time during peak traffic hours? How many concurrent users should the system support?

▶ What Are the Security Considerations?

Security is non-negotiable in most systems, especially those dealing with sensitive data like personal information or payment details.

Example for a Payment Processing System: Should all transactions be encrypted? How will we ensure compliance with payment industry standards like PCI-DSS? Note that If your system is holding payment card information in any fashion then PCI compliance is a basic requirement. If you know it then better reflect the same in your conversation with interviewers.

► **What Are the Resilience Considerations?**

Every system must be designed to handle failure scenarios, such as server crashes, network outages, or database downtime.

Example for a Video Streaming Platform: What should happen if a server fails while a user is streaming a video? How quickly should the system recover?

Handling Edge Cases and Special Scenarios

In real-world systems, edge cases often create the most challenges. Clarifying how your system should behave in these cases is crucial for designing a robust solution. Edge cases may not occur frequently, but they can lead to system failure or performance issues if not handled properly.

Common Edge Cases –

Number of Characters: What if the URL to shorten is huge? What if the URL to shorten is shorter than shortened outcome?

Deduplication: How should the system handle duplicate inputs? For example, what happens if a user tries to shorten the same URL multiple times?

Traffic Spikes: What happens if the system experiences a sudden surge in traffic? For example, would load balancing be enough or we need to think about throttling?

System Failure: What will be the behavior if the system is not responding because of any unforeseen reason e.g. Shortening service fails before completing a request processing.

3.4 Prioritizing Requirements During an Interview

In a real-world system, it's impossible to build everything at once. The same applies in a designing a system. Some features are more critical than others (The MoSCoW method), and understanding that helps you focus on what matters first.

During the interview, you might realize that some features are not core to the system. Discuss this openly with the interviewer and prioritize must-have features that will drive the core functionality. The nice-to-have one can be parked (unless they are not taking your additional efforts) to be discussed at a later stage.

For example, in a URL shortening service:

Must-have (absolutely needed) : Shortening URLs, redirecting users to the original URL.

Nice-to-have (Should): Allowing users to create custom short URLs, analytics tracking.

Requirement Clarification Examples

Let's go through a few examples to solidify your understanding of requirement clarifications.

URL Shortener

Scenario

You're asked to design a URL shortening service like bit.ly.

Questions to Ask

"Who will be my users?"
"What happens if a user inputs a URL that has already been shortened?"
"Do we need to support custom aliases for shortened URLs?"
"Should we track analytics for each shortened URL?"

Non-functional Clarifications

"What is the expected traffic during normal and peak times?"
"What is the acceptable latency for redirecting users from the shortened URL to the original URL?"

Messaging Service

Scenario

Design a messaging service similar to WhatsApp, considering text based messaging.

Questions to Ask

"Should the system support both one-on-one and group chats?"
"What happens if a message fails to be sent due to network issues?"

Non-functional Clarifications

"What kind of uptime is required? Should messages be stored in case of server failures?"
"What is the average user volume and during the peak? How should the system handle spikes in message traffic?"
"Is there a need for message encryption or end-to-end security?"

Chapter 04

Estimations in Action

Many a times, interviewers look for estimations that can serve as the foundation of your proposed solution. Estimations are vital in determining the architecture, technology stack, and scaling strategies for a system. The ability to make sound back-of-the-envelope calculations is a key consideration in interviews.

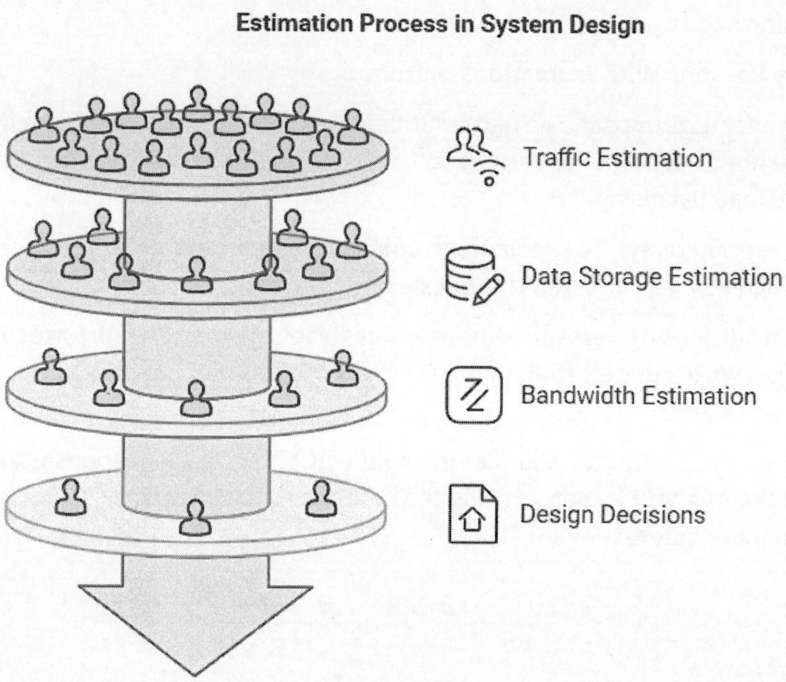

Figure – 4.1

Without proper estimates, you risk designing a system that is over-engineered (leading to resource wastage) or under-engineered (leading to failures under load). This chapter will dive deep into the process of estimating traffic, data storage, and bandwidth—essential elements of system design.

Why Estimations Are Critical in System Design

The importance of estimations cannot be overstated in system design. These numbers drive nearly all major design decisions, from selecting databases and servers to configuring load balancers and caching mechanisms. Miscalculations can lead to system failures, performance bottlenecks, or unnecessary costs. In a system design interview, making estimations demonstrates that you can think critically about scalability, performance, and resource allocation.

For example, without estimating the number of requests per second (RPS) or storage requirements, you might choose an inadequate database that fails under load, or an overly expensive setup that isn't justified by traffic needs.

Key Reasons Why Estimations Matter

Architectural Impact: The right estimations guide decisions about whether you need horizontal or vertical scaling, database sharding, caching layers, and load balancing.

System Stability: By predicting traffic spikes and data growth, you can design a system that doesn't buckle under unexpected loads.

Cost Efficiency: Overestimating resources leads to expensive infrastructure bills, while underestimating resources causes service outages and downtime.

Performance Tuning: Estimations help you optimize for response times and throughput by determining the best places to use caching, CDNs, and database indexes.

4.1 Estimation Primitives

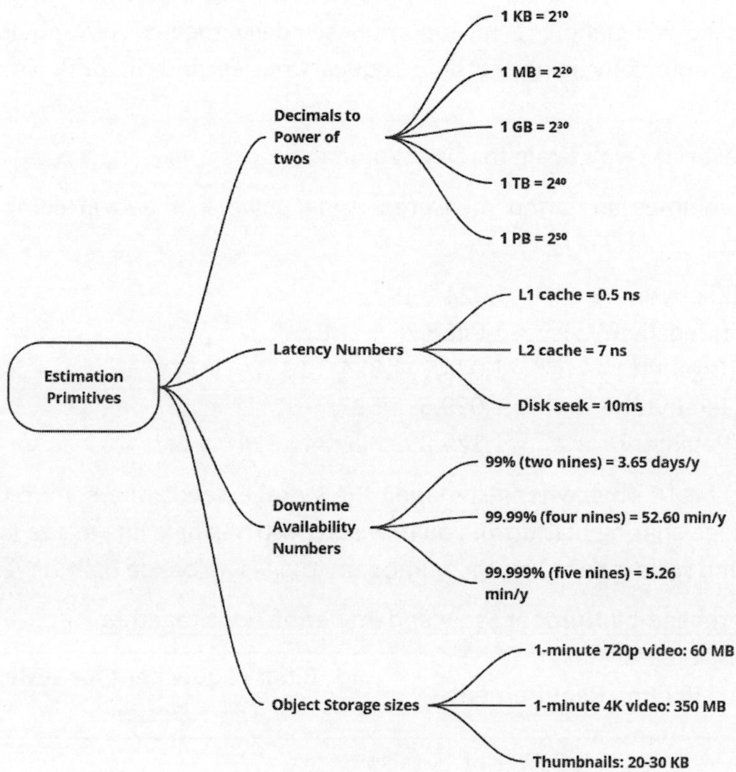

Figure – 4.2

You'll often be asked to estimate critical metrics such as Queries Per Second (QPS), storage, bandwidth, and other performance factors in your design. These "back-of-the-envelope" calculations showcase your ability to understand the scale of a problem and offer practical solutions.

Below are key estimates that every candidate must be familiar with:

► Number Scale

Understanding number scales (power of 10) is required for making estimations at scale:

1 thousand (1K) : 3 zeroes
1 million (1M) : 6 zeroes
1 billion (1B) : 9 zeroes
1 trillion (1T) : 12 zeroes
1 quadrillion(1P) : 15 zeroes

These number scales come into play when estimating user counts, requests per second, and data volumes. For example, estimating that a system will handle 1 million requests daily means you should be comfortable converting that into requests per second or traffic volume estimates.

► Power of Two's Scale for Data Volumes

Data volumes are often measured using powers of two in computer science:

1 KB (Kilobyte) : 2^{10} = 1,024 ~ 1K
1 MB (Megabyte) : 2^{20} = 1,048,576 ~ 1M
1 GB (Gigabyte) : 2^{30} = 1,073,741,824 ~ 1B
1 TB (Terabyte) : 2^{40} = 1,099,511,627,776 ~ 1T
1 PB (Petabyte). : 2^{50} = 1,125,899,906,842,624 ~ 1 Qd

In practical terms, when estimating the storage needs of a system (e.g., an image-sharing platform), you may start with a single image size (say 3 MB) and scale it based on the number of images uploaded daily or yearly.

Comprehending **Number Scale** and **Power of Twos** together

Volume Requirement		**Binary Equivalent for system Design**	
General Term	Power of 10 (also called number of zeros)	Binary term	Power of 2 representation
1 thousand (1K)	3	1KB (Kilobyte)	2^{10}
1 million (1M)	6	1MB (Megabyte)	2^{20}
1 billion (1B)	9	1GB (Gigabyte)	2^{30}
1 trillion (1T)	12	1TB (Terabyte)	2^{40}
1 quadrillion(1Q)	15	1PB (Petabyte)	2^{50}

Table – 4.1

How to Use This Table

If the requirement talks about 100 million users, you can use the table above to convert this number into binary form as; 100 millions (first column in the table) = 100 MB (as per third column in the table) = 100 x 2^{20} (as per fourth column) = 0.1 GB or 0.1 x 2^{30}

If furthermore the question says 100 million users with 10 requests per day, you can calculate the total number of requests as 100 million x 10 request = 1000 million request = 1000 x 2^{20} = 2^{10} x 2^{20} = 2^{30}

Note: 1000 = 1 thousand (i.e. 3 zeros) = 1KB = 2^{10}

▶ Latency Numbers

Latency refers to how long it takes for a system to respond to a request. Understanding typical latency numbers is important because it informs system performance and helps you make realistic decisions on infrastructure.

Here's a list of key latency numbers. In general, the mentioned numbers can be used to make your calculations. These numbers in actual may vary but as a general principle for interview, they can be used as below.:

L1 cache reference: 0.5 ns
Branch mispredict: 5 ns
L2 cache reference: 7 ns
Mutex lock/unlock: 100 ns
Main memory reference: 100 ns
Compress 1K bytes with Zippy: 10,000 ns (10 μs)
Send 2K bytes over 1 Gbps network: 20,000 ns (20 μs)
Read 1 MB sequentially from memory: 250,000 ns (250 μs)
Round trip within the same datacenter: 500,000 ns (500 μs)
Disk seek: 10,000,000 ns (10 ms)
Read 1 MB sequentially from network: 10,000,000 ns (10 ms)
Read 1 MB sequentially from disk: 30,000,000 ns (30 ms)
Send packet CA (California) → Netherlands → CA: 150,000,000 ns (150 ms)

Knowing these latency figures helps when designing systems that need quick response times, such as real-time messaging apps. For instance, to achieve sub-200ms latency for an API, you might use in-memory caching to avoid slower disk seeks.

▶ Availability Numbers

Availability refers to the operational time of a system. Achieving high availability is critical for services that must be online 24/7. Below is a breakdown of availability percentages and the corresponding downtime:

Availability Percentage	Downtime Per Year	Downtime Per Month	Downtime Per Day
90% (one nine)	36.53 days	73.05 hours	2.40 hours
99% (two nines)	3.65 days	7.31 hours	14.40 minutes
99.9% (three nines)	8.77 hours	43.83 minutes	1.44 minutes
99.99% (four nines)	52.60 minutes	4.38 minutes	8.64 seconds
99.999% (five nines)	5.26 minutes	26.30 seconds	864 milliseconds
99.9999% (six nines)	31.56 seconds	2.63 seconds	86.4 milliseconds

Table – 4.2

For systems that require 99.99% availability, the design should include features like replication, load balancing, and failover strategies to ensure minimal downtime. This also ties into your storage and traffic estimations, as you need to ensure that replication across multiple regions doesn't affect performance.

► Blob/Object Storage Sizes

In many systems, you'll need to estimate the size of objects such as images, videos, and documents to calculate storage needs. Below are common storage sizes you can consider for various data types during interview though they can vary depending upon system in use:

char: 1 byte
char (Unicode): 2 bytes
UUID: 16 bytes
Thumbnails: 20-30 KB
Website image: 200-300 KB
Mobile image: 2-3 MB
Documents (books, reports, etc.): 1-3 MB
Audio files (songs, recordings): 4-5 MB
1-minute 720p video: 60 MB
1-minute 1080p video: 130 MB
1-minute 4K video: 350 MB

If you're designing a cloud storage platform, these numbers are essential in calculating how much data storage is needed. For instance, if users upload 1 million 1080p videos a month (each 130 MB), your storage requirements would grow by 130 TB/month. Calculated as:

No of videos = 1 million = 2^{20} videos/month

Each video size = 130 MB = 130 x 2^{20} bytes

Total storage size = (No of videos) x (each video size) = 2^{20} x 130 x 2^{20} = 130 x 2^{40} = 130 TB/Month

4.2 Types of Estimations

In system design, there are a few key types of estimations you need to focus on:

Traffic Estimates: Understanding how many users interact with the system and the volume of requests it generates.

Data Storage Estimates: Knowing how much data needs to be stored over time.

Bandwidth Estimates: Determining how much data needs to be transmitted over the network.

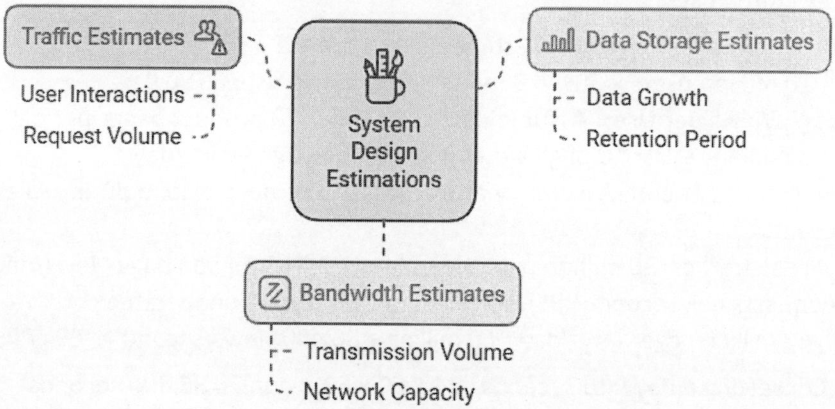

Figure – 4.3

Let's dive into each type and explore them in greater detail.

▶ **Traffic Estimates**

Traffic estimation determines everything from the architecture to the type of servers and databases you use. You should be able to accurately estimate how many users will use the system and how many requests each user will generate.

Breaking Down Traffic Estimation

Here's how to break down traffic estimation step by step:

Total Users: The total number of users the system needs to account for. Start by estimating the total registered users.

Daily Active Users (DAU): Not all users will use the system every day. Estimate the percentage of daily active users (usually 10-30% of the total user base, depending on the application).

Requests per User: Estimate how many actions (e.g., page views, API calls) each active user performs in a given day. This varies depending on the type of service—social media users may post 5 times a day, while e-commerce users may browse 10 products.

Peak Traffic: Systems experience peak loads (traffic spikes), and you must plan for these. Peak traffic might be 2x or even 10x the average traffic depending upon the use-case.

Example: Estimating Traffic for an E-Commerce Website

Let's estimate the traffic for an e-commerce website with 10 million registered users.

Daily Active Users (DAU): Assume 30% of users are active daily.
  10 million users × 30% = 3 million daily active users (DAU)
Page Views per User: Assume each user views 10 product pages per day.
  3 million DAU × 10 page views = 30 million page views/day
Peak Traffic Factor: Assume peak traffic is 2x the normal load during sales events.
  Peak traffic = 30 million page views/day × 2 = 60 million page views/day
Requests per Second (RPS): To calculate RPS during peak traffic:
  60 million page views/day = 60 million ÷ 86,400 views/second = ~694 RPS

(Converting a day into seconds : 24 x 60 x 60 seconds=86,400 seconds)

Therefore, your system needs to handle **694 requests per second** at peak traffic.

How Traffic Affects Design Choices

Once you've estimated the RPS, you can make several key decisions:

Horizontal Scaling: Add more servers to handle increasing RPS during peak traffic.

Load Balancers: You'll likely need a load balancer to distribute traffic across multiple servers.
Caching: Implement caching for frequently viewed pages to reduce the load on your database.

Handling Traffic Spikes

Always design for peak traffic. For instance, Black Friday might bring a 10x traffic surge for e-commerce platforms, and failure to account for this could result in outages.

Example: If your normal traffic is 700 RPS, but you experience a 10x surge during a sale, your system should handle 7,000 RPS at peak. Design your web servers, load balancers, and databases to handle such surges without crashing.

▶ Data Storage Estimates

Data storage estimation helps you understand how much storage your system will need to handle user data, logs, and metadata. This requires an understanding of the nature of the data, how it's structured, and how it grows over time.

Steps for Calculating Storage Requirements

Identify the Types of Data You Will Store

Each application will have different types of data, such as user profiles, content uploads (like videos or images), logs, metadata, etc.
For each type of data, you need to know the average size and the number of entries or records stored.

Determine the Size of Each Record

Break down each record or entry into its components (e.g., fields in a database row or keys and payload size for semi-structured/unstructured data) and estimate the size of each component.
Consider the structure of the data and whether it's text, binary, or JSON, as each format requires different amounts of storage.

Estimate Number of Records

You need to estimate how many records will be stored at any given time. For instance, if you are designing a system for 1 million users, you must estimate how many records each user will generate per day, week, or month.

Calculate Total Storage Needs

Multiply the average record size (as per step B) by the estimated number of records (as per step C). This will give you an approximate storage size.
Keep in mind that storage grows over time, so you should factor in long-term growth (e.g., over 1 year or 5 years).

Include Overhead

Always include extra storage for indexing, metadata, backups, and logs, which are not part of the raw data but are essential for system functionality.

Example: Estimating Data Storage for a Social Media Platform

Let's estimate storage needs for a social media platform where users can post text, images, and videos.

1. Text Posts: Assume each text post is 1 KB (2-3 paragraphs).

   1 million users post 2 updates per day = 2 million posts/day.
   2 million posts/day × 1 KB/post = 2 GB/day

2. Image Uploads: Assume each image is 2 MB.

   1 million users upload 1 image/day = 1 million images/day.
   1 million images/day × 2 MB/image = 2 TB/day

3. Video Uploads: Assume each video is 100 MB.

   100,000 users upload 1 video/day = 100,000 videos/day.
   100,000 videos/day × 100 MB/video = 10 TB/day

4. Total Storage Needs: Combining text, images, and videos:

   Text : 2 GB/day i.e. 0.002 TB.
   Images : 2 TB/day.
   Videos : 10 TB/day.

5. Thus, the system generates approx **12 TB** of new data per day.

6. Annual Storage Growth: Multiply by 365 days for yearly storage.

   12 TB/day × 365 = ~4.38 PB/year (without replication).
   Note: If the calculation is too complex, then using approximation is just fine. Do not spend time performing complex mathematical

calculations. E.g. For calculation in step 6 above, approximation to 4PB/y or 5PB/y will not make much difference overall during the interview.

7. Impact of Data Replication on Storage

   If you implement 3x replication for fault tolerance and redundancy: Total Storage with Replication = 4.38 PB/year × 3 = ~13.14 PB/year

8. Planning for Future Data Growth

   Data growth is often exponential in social media platforms. Assume the user base grows by 20% annually
   Year 1: 4.38 PB (without Replication).
   Year 2: 4.38 PB × 1.2 = 5.26 PB
   Year 3: 5.26 PB × 1.2 = 6.31 PB

After three years, your total data storage requirement (with replication) could exceed **16 PB**.

► Bandwidth Estimates

Bandwidth estimates are required when dealing with large amounts of data transfer, such as streaming services or file-sharing applications. It is used to determine how much data has to be sent over a network in a given amount of time. This ensures system scalability and efficiency by assisting in calculating the necessary network bandwidth to manage user requests, data streaming, and API interactions without experiencing performance bottlenecks.

Estimating Bandwidth for a Video Streaming Platform

Let's estimate bandwidth for a video streaming platform like Netflix.

Average Video Size: Assume a 1080 pixel video requires 5 Mbps of bandwidth.

Simultaneous Streams: If 100,000 users are streaming videos simultaneously:

Total Bandwidth = 100,000 users × 5 Mbps = 500,000 Mbps = 500 Gbps

Handling Bandwidth Spikes

During peak hours, such as evenings, the number of simultaneous streams might surge from 100,000 to 500,000 users:

Peak Bandwidth = 500,000 users × 5 Mbps = 2500 Gbps = **2.5 Tbps**

Thus, the network must handle **2.5 terabits per second** of data transfer during peak times.

4.3 Back-of-the-Envelope Estimations

Let's dive into an example where we apply these estimations in a system design scenario. WE will use a video streaming service as the case study.

▶ Example Scenario: Designing a Video Streaming Service

In this example, you're asked to design a video streaming service like YouTube or Netflix. In order to do that, we will use back-of-the-envelope techniques to calculate how much storage, traffic, and performance capacity the system will need.

Requirement

Functional Requirements

- Users can upload, stream, and download videos.
- There are 1 million users for the system with average 10 videos per month upload
- The system should support user authentication and personalized video recommendations.

Non-Functional Requirements

- High availability (99.99% uptime).
- Low latency to ensure smooth video streaming (sub-200ms response time).

Let's assume we have a few more details on the requirements so that we can move to the estimation part.

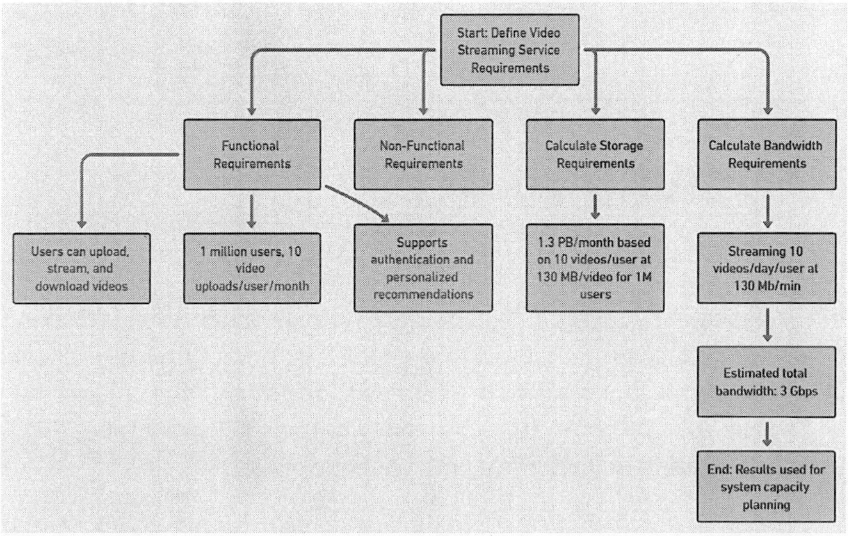

Figure – 4.4

Estimations

Storage Estimates

Let's estimate the storage requirements for users uploading videos

- Each user uploads 10 videos per month, and each video is say 130 MB (1-minute long, 1080p video).
- If there are 1 million users:

  10 videos/user × 130 MB/video × 1 million users = 1.3 PB/month

Thus, your system would need to store approximately **1.3 Petabytes of video data per month**.

Bandwidth Estimates

Next, calculate the bandwidth needed for streaming:

- Assume each user streams 10 videos per day, with each video (being 1 minute long) at 130 Mb/min for 1080p video.
- For 1 million users, the required bandwidth is 3 Gbps. Calculated as:

  [A]---> 10 videos/user day =10/(24x60x60) videos/user seconds

  [B]---> 130 Mb/min × 1M users = 130/60 Mb/s x [1 x 2^{20}] users= [(130 x 2^{20})/60 b/s] x.[2^{20}]

  Total bandwidth = [A] x [B] = [10/(24x60x60)] x [(130 x 2^{20})/60] x [2^{20}] = 0.003 x 2^{40} bps = 3 x 2^{30} bps = 3 Gbps

Chapter 05

Designing an API

API (Application Programming Interface) design allows different parts of a system to communicate. It also enables external systems or clients interaction with your system. In interviews, designing a robust, scalable, and secure APIs demonstrates your ability to think holistically about how users and systems will interface with your application.

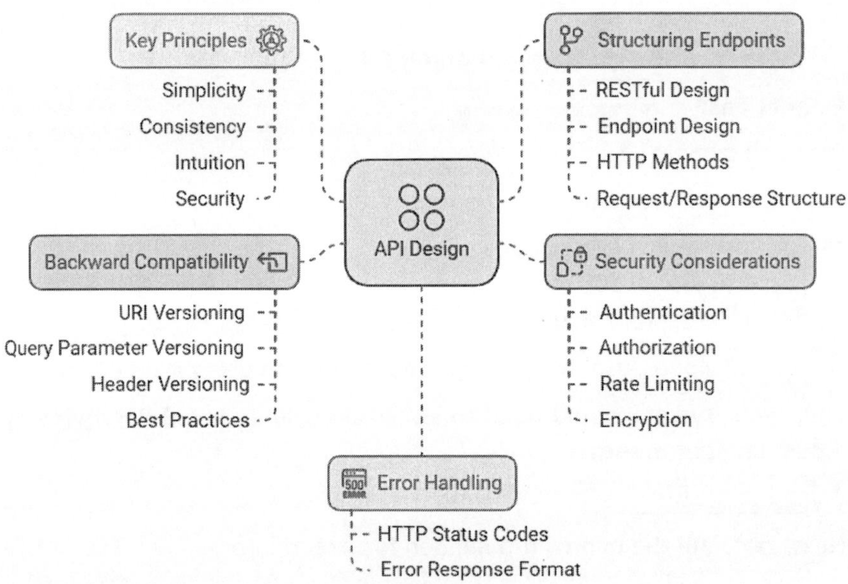

Figure – 5.1

A well-designed API is not just about how the endpoints are named or how data is structured. It also involves considering scalability, security, performance, ease of use, and maintainability. This chapter dives into the key concepts and best practices that will help you create a top-notch API in any system design interview. We will explore the following here:

5.1 Key Principles

An API should be simple, consistent, intuitive, and secure. This should be reflected during designing an endpoint including the name used for interfaces and resources, use of verbs with regards to intended action while creating a method.

Example of a complex endpoint can be –

```
POST/api/userAction?method=create&username=johndoe&role=admin
```

Whereas a corresponding simpler endpoint may look like –

```
POST /users
{
 "username": "johndoe",
 "role": "admin"
}
```

In the example above POST indicates the behavior (create a resource) while the name of the endpoint clearly talks about the resource in question. Similarly, other methods (for fetching, updating, and deleting *users*) on the resource will be –

```
GET /users/{id}
PUT /users/{id}
DELETE /users/{id}
```

Security is an integral part of any API design. APIs expose critical business functions and data, making them a target for attacks. You must incorporate appropriate security mechanism for your endpoints from the start. Following mechanism should be well thought -

Authentication ensures that users are who they claim to be.

Authorization ensures that users have the right permissions for the requested actions.

Rate limiting prevents abuse by limiting the number of requests a user can make in a specific time frame. This prevents our system from becoming overwhelmed.

Encryption ensures that sensitive data remains secure while in transit.

5.2 Endpoints

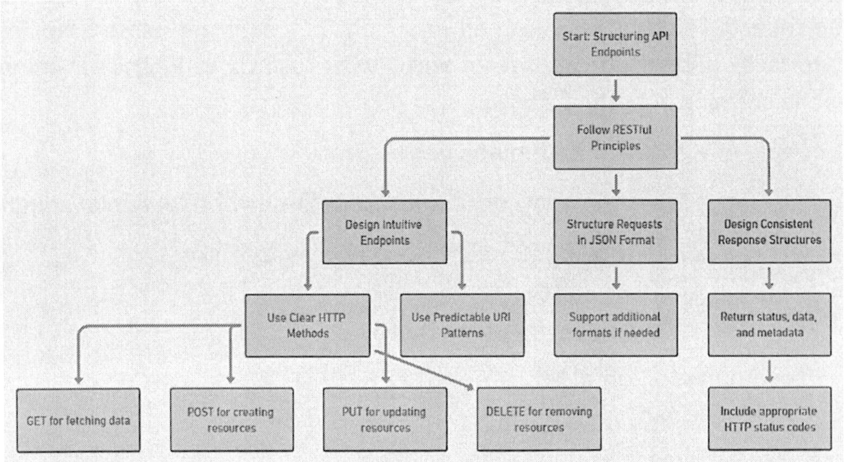

Figure – 5.2

APIs typically follow REST (Representational State Transfer) principles, but there are also other paradigms such as GraphQL. In this section, the focus is on RESTful design, which is widely used in system design interviews.

RESTful API Design

REST is a stateless architectural style that leverages standard HTTP methods to interact with resources. RESTful APIs rely on a simple, well-structured system of endpoints, which represent resources like users, products, or orders.

Endpoints should be designed to be intuitive, concise, and predictable. RESTful APIs follow a clear pattern:

GET for reading data without modifying the state of any underlying resource.

POST for creating new resources. POST is not idempotent (sending the same request multiple times could result in multiple resources being created).

PUT for updating existing resources. PUT is idempotent, meaning sending the same request multiple times will produce the same result.

DELETE for removing resources.

Each resource has a unique URI that clearly identifies it. For example, if you are working on an e-commerce platform, the following would be typical endpoints:

GET /products → Fetch all products.
GET /products/{id} → Fetch a specific product by its ID.
POST /products → Add a new product.
PUT /products/{id} → Update an existing product.
DELETE /products/{id} → Remove a product.

Request and Response Structure

The API's request and response structure is the contract between the client and the server. It should be simple, consistent, and predictable.

Request Formats

Most modern APIs use JSON (JavaScript Object Notation) as the standard format for requests and responses due to its human-readable nature and lightweight. However, you should also consider supporting other formats like XML if necessary.

Example Request body for creating a new user:

```
{
“username”: “johndoe”,
“email”: “johndoe@example.com”,
“password”: “securePassword”
}
```

This request is straightforward and contains all necessary data for user creation.

Response Formats

Responses should return the requested data or appropriate feedback on the operation's success or failure. Successful responses often include the created resource, a status message, and any other relevant information.

Example Response for fetching a user's details:

```
HTTP1.1 200 OK
Content-Type: application/vnd.api+json
  {
   “data”: [ {
   “userId”: “123456”,
```

```
    “username”: “goyalshalini”,
    “email”: “goyalxyzmail@mymail.com”,
    “createdAt”: “2024-09-30T12:32:56Z”
  }]
}
```

For a failed operation, always include error codes and helpful messages.

Example Error Response for an invalid request:

```
  {
    “error”: {
    “code”: 400,
    “message”: “Invalid request: Missing required ‘email’ field”
    }
  }
```

Query Parameters and Filtering

Many APIs require the ability to filter data, sort it, or paginate results. Use query parameters for these purposes:

Filtering: Filter response by criteria e.g. products where category is “electronics” and brand is “apple”

GET /products?category=electronics&brand=apple

Sorting: Sort results by a specific field e.g. sort result by price (low to high).

GET /products?sort=price&order=asc

Pagination: Retrieve data in manageable chunks e.g. chunk size is 20 records per page and get the second chunk i.e. record no 21 to 40 (or less).

GET /products?limit=20&page

5.3 Security Considerations

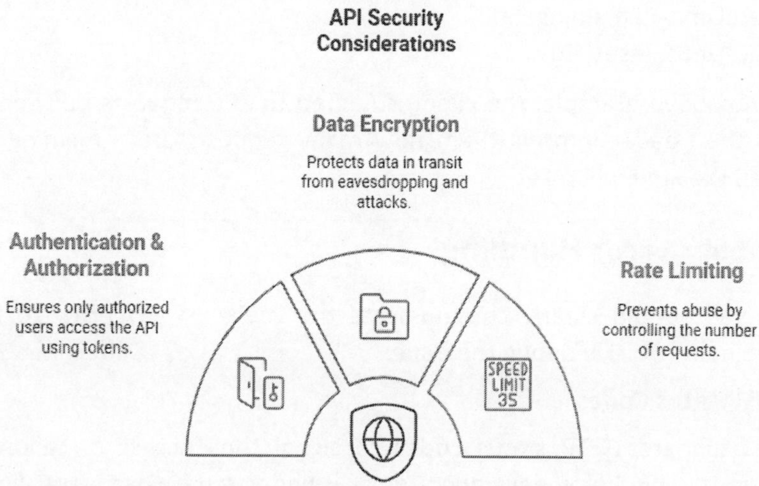

Figure – 5.3

Security should be at the forefront of API design. There are several layers of security that need to be implemented to protect your API and the data it handles.

Authentication and Authorization

OAuth2 (Resources Library > System Design > Building Blocks # 26) is the most commonly used standard for securing APIs. It allows users to authenticate once and receive an access token, which they use for subsequent requests. **JWT (JSON Web Tokens)** are also commonly used for stateless authentication.

Example of a request with a token:

Authorization: Bearer <access_token>

Data Encryption

Ensure that all sensitive data transmitted over the network is encrypted using SSL/TLS. This prevents eavesdropping and man-in-the-middle attacks. Chapter-13 talks about the concept in details.

Rate Limiting

To prevent abuse and ensure fair usage, implement rate limiting on your API. This limits the number of requests a client can make in a given time frame, protecting your server from being overwhelmed.

Example:

X-RateLimit-Limit: 100
X-RateLimit-Remaining: 50
X-RateLimit-Reset: 60

In the above example, the client is limited to 100 requests per minute, and the header informs them how many requests are remaining and when the limit will reset.

5.4 Error Handling

The API should clearly communicate the cause of any error to help developers quickly debug the issue.

HTTP Status Codes

Use standard HTTP status codes to signal the success or failure of requests. This helps developers quickly understand what went wrong. Some commonly used status codes are:

200 OK: The request was successful.
201 Created: The request was successful, and a resource was created.
400 Bad Request: The request was invalid (e.g., missing required parameters).
401 Unauthorized: Authentication failed or was not provided.
404 Not Found: The requested resource does not exist.
500 Internal Server Error: A generic server error occurred.

Each of these codes should be used consistently and paired with clear error messages.

Error Response Format

Error responses should provide enough information for developers to understand the issue and resolve it quickly. An effective error response contains an error code, a descriptive message, and possibly a link to the relevant section of the documentation.

Example:

```
{
 “error”: {
 “code”: 404,
 “message”: “User not found”
 }
}
```

5.5 Backward Compatibility (API Versioning)

The process of managing modifications to an API (Application Programming Interface) over time while preserving compatibility; and offering customers a smooth experience is the goal of API versioning. Older features may be deprecated or altered as APIs develop, necessitating a systematic method to support several versions for different clients. Versioning makes it possible for different API versions to coexist, guaranteeing backward compatibility and causing the least amount of inconvenience to users who rely on older versions.

Developing a good understanding around API versioning might be useful in case an interviewer is looking for an approach to enhance an API with additional functionality to it. In such case API versioning ensures that your API can evolve without breaking existing clients.

The Significance of API Versioning

Backward compatibility: guarantees that updates to the API don't interfere with already-running apps that use earlier iterations.

Incremental updates: allow for the progressive introduction of new features or modifications without requiring immediate acceptance by all users.

User Flexibility: Clients have flexibility over when to update by selecting which version of the API to use.

API Lifecycle Management: It supports continuous development while offering a clear route for retiring older versions.

Common Strategies

There are several strategies for API versioning:

URI Versioning: Include the version in the endpoint URI.

GET /v1/users

Query Parameter Versioning: Pass the version in the query string.

GET /users?version=1

Header Versioning: Specify the version in HTTP headers.

GET /users

Header: Accept-version: v1

Best Practices for Versioning APIs

- Begin by versioning: Versioning your API early on helps ensure that it is future-proof for modifications, even if it is still in its initial iteration.
- Policies for Deprecation: When a version will no longer be supported, make sure to make that clear. Before deprecating earlier versions, give users enough notice.
- Cut Down on Breaking Changes: To reduce disruption, if feasible, implement new features or modifications in a backward-compatible manner.
- Records: Make sure every version of the API has enough documentation so users can plan upgrades and comprehend version changes.
- Alignment of Versioning Strategies: Select a versioning approach that fits your product objectives and user base. While more sophisticated techniques (like header or media type versioning) may be appropriate for internal or enterprise APIs, simpler methods (like URI versioning) may be better for external, public-facing APIs.
- Graceful Migration: Provide tools, guides, and support to help users migrate from older versions to newer ones.

Note : When learning about API versioning, an understanding of “Canary” and “Blue-Green” deployment can be useful as it might help you during some further conversation with interviewers at a later stage.

Chapter 06

Database Design and Data Management

In any small or large-scale system design, databases play a pivotal role. They store, organize, and retrieve data essential for running applications. The focus of this chapter is to develop an understanding on its type, how to choose the right database, design schemas, and scale your database.

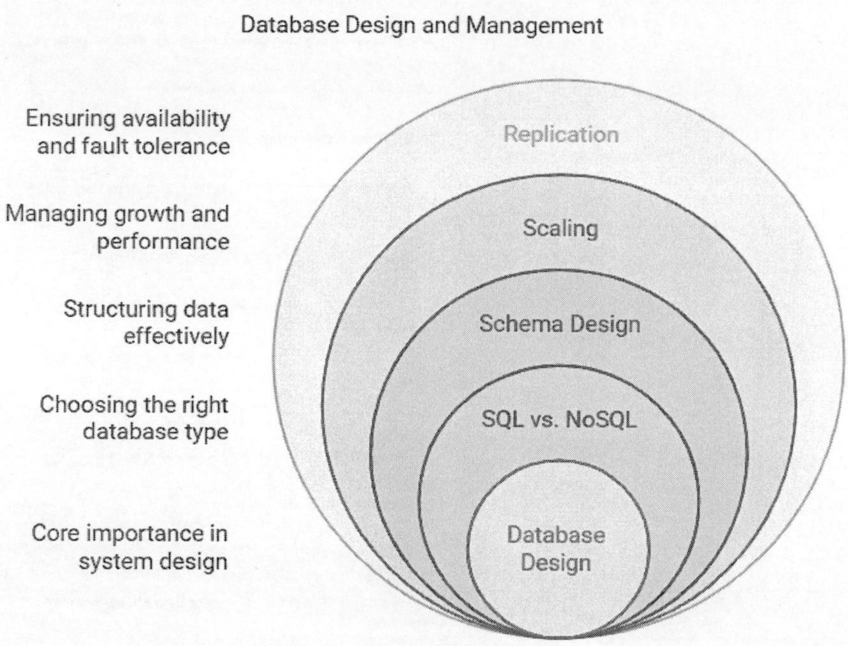

Figure – 6.1

Designing a database is not just about knowing the technical details of them but also understanding trade-offs, performance bottlenecks, and how it can be scaled over time.

6.1 SQL vs. NoSQL

An extremely popular discussion in system design interview is whether to use a relational (SQL) or a non-relational (NoSQL) database. Each comes with advantages and trade-offs, and the right choice depends on the specific needs of your system.

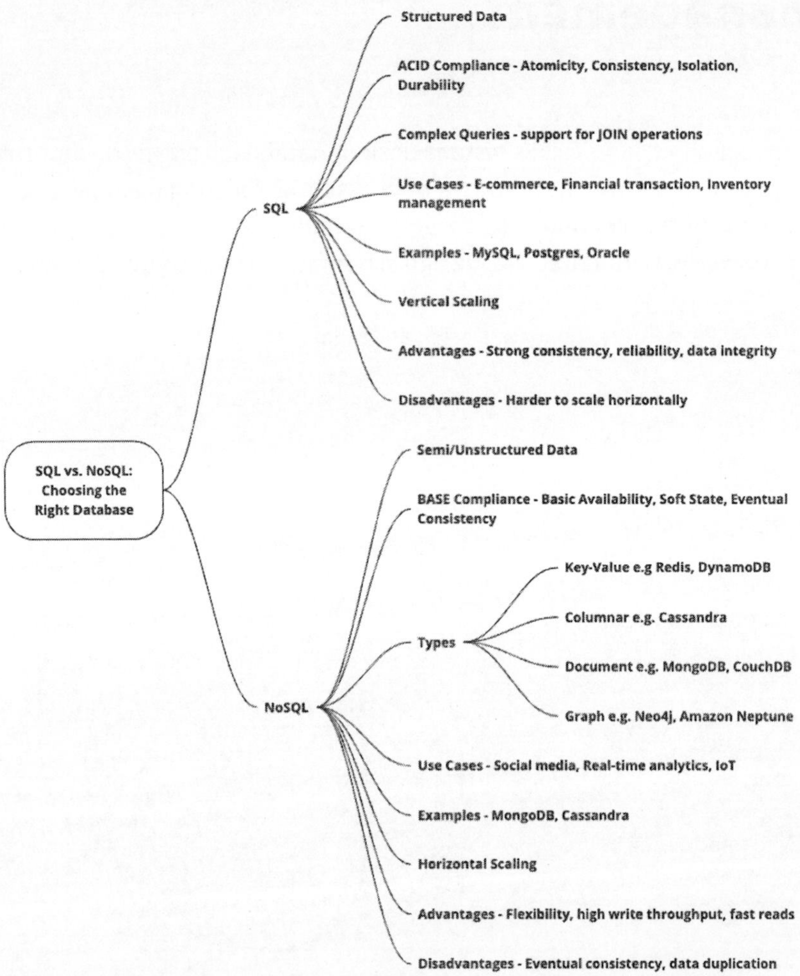

Figure – 6.2

► SQL Databases

SQL databases are relational databases (RDBMS) that organize data into tables with fixed schemas. Each table contains rows (records) and columns (fields), and relationships between tables are defined by foreign keys. Examples include MySQL, Postgres, SQL Server, DB2, and Oracle.

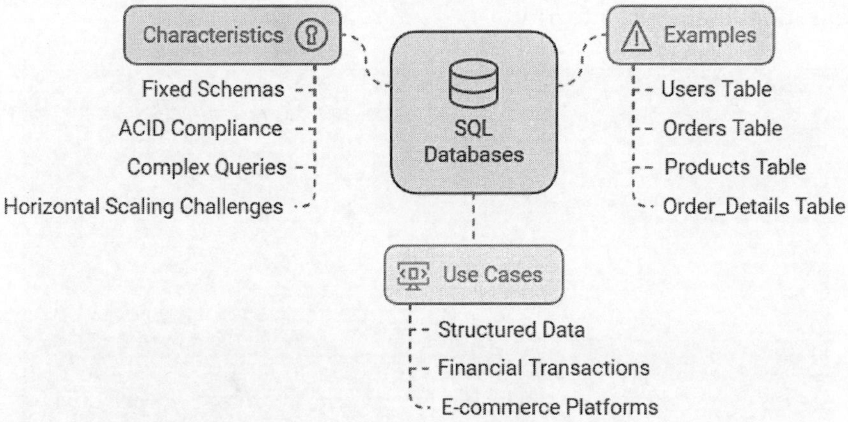

Figure – 6.3

Use Cases: SQL databases are best suited for applications that deal with structured data, such as e-commerce platforms where orders, products, and users have clear relationships.

Characteristics: SQL databases provide atomicity, consistency, isolation, and durability(ACID), ensuring data reliability, especially in financial transactions or systems requiring strict data integrity. SQL databases excel at performing complex JOIN operations, aggregating data, and handling queries across multiple tables

Challenges: SQL databases are not a great choice when it comes to horizontal partitioning, sharding. There still are mechanism to achieve it but they are quite complex.

<u>Examples of SQL Use Case</u>

For a retail application, you may have a 'users' table with columns for user ID, name, email, and password. Another table, 'orders', links each order to a specific user via a foreign key. You might also have a 'products' table for managing inventory, and an 'order_details' table to track which products are included in each order.

In this setup:

Users can place multiple Orders.

Each Order contains multiple Products.
The Orders and Products tables are linked via an order_details table.

This structure is highly normalized, minimizing data redundancy and ensuring referential integrity.

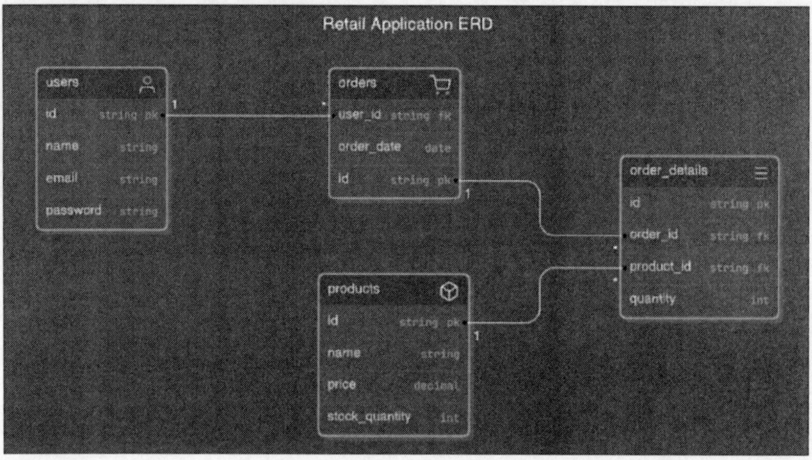

Figure – 6.4

▶ NoSQL Databases

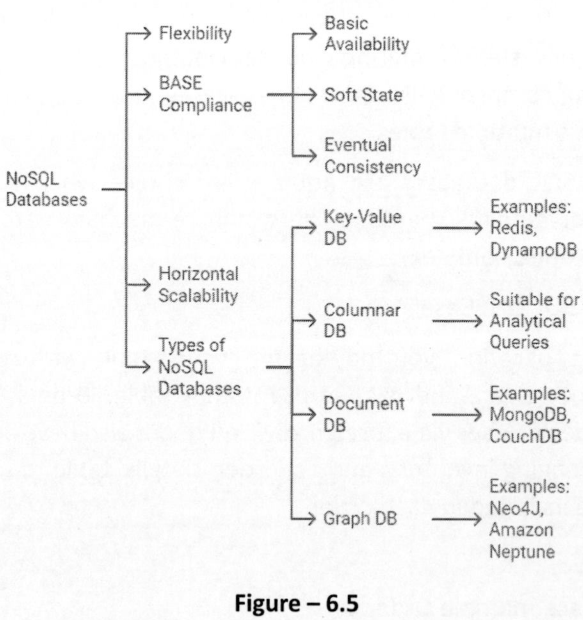

Figure – 6.5

NoSQL (these days known as "not only SQL") Databases, in contrast, offer flexibility by allowing for unstructured or semi-structured data. They do not rely on fixed schemas, and relationships between data are not always explicitly defined. As NoSQL means Not-Only-SQL, standard SQL language can also be used to perform insert/ update/ delete operations, with a few syntax changes. Examples include MongoDB, DynamoDB, Cassandra, and Couchbase.

Use Cases: NoSQL Databases are best for use cases involving massive amounts of unstructured data or where schema flexibility is required. They are also preferred in applications requiring high scalability and performance, such as social networks, real-time analytics, and content management systems.

BASE Compliance: BASE stands for **B**asic **A**vailability, **S**oft State and **E**ventual Consistency. While SQL databases prioritize strong consistency, NoSQL Databases are often known for basic availability and partition tolerance (CAP theorem), making them ideal for distributed systems where data is spread across multiple locations.

Horizontal Scalability: NoSQL Databases are designed for horizontal scaling, making them suitable for applications with growing data and traffic volumes. Sharding and replication are often built-in features.

"BASE" acronym breaks down:

Basic **A**vailability: The database appears to work most of the time.

Soft-state: Write operations are not reflected to all of the replicas immediately meaning there can be a small time gap before they all achieve consistency.

Eventual consistency: Stores exhibit consistency at some later point (e.g., lazily at read time).

Types of NoSQL databases

Key-Value DB: A key-value database uses a simple key-value method to store data. It stores data as a collection of key-value pairs in which a key normally serves as a unique identifier. Both keys and values can be anything, ranging from simple objects to complex compound objects. Example: Redis, Amazon's DynamoDB.

Columnar DB: A columnar database stores data by columns rather than by rows, which makes it suitable for analytical query processing, and thus for data warehouses also.

Document DB: NoSQL document databases are based on a model that does not require SQL and tables. Instead of using tables with the data types, columns, rows, schemas, and tabular relations used in SQL databases, DocumentDB uses documents with data type descriptions and values. Example: MongoDB, CouchDB.

Graph DB: In the Graph database, the entity is stored as a node with the relationship as edges. An edge gives a relationship between nodes. Every node and edge have a unique identifier. Compared to a relational database where tables are loosely connected, a Graph database is multi-relational in nature. The behavior makes it a suitable choice for social media type of use-cases. Example: Neo4J, Amazon Neptune.

<u>Example of NoSQL Use Case</u>

In a social media platform, you might use a document-based NoSQL database like MongoDB. Each user's profile, including their posts, followers, and comments, can be stored in a single document. This denormalization allows you to retrieve a user's entire profile in one query, without needing complex JOINs like in SQL DB.

A document in MongoDB might look like this:

- User details (name, email, etc.).
- An embedded array of posts (text, timestamp).
- An embedded array of followers (names or IDs).

This denormalized structure allows for fast reads and writes at the cost of data duplication, which is acceptable for systems prioritizing performance over normalization.

Example:

```
json
{
  "_id": "user12345",
  "name": "Shalini Goyal",
  "email": "goyalxyzmail@mymail.com",
  "profile_picture": "https://www.linkedin.com/in/goyalshalini.jpg",
```

```
"bio": "Technology Leader with a love for leadership and engineering.",
"posts": [
 {
  "post_id": "post001",
  "text": "Had a great day writing!",
  "timestamp": "2024-10-21T14:00:00Z",
  "likes": 45,
  "comments": [
   {
    "comment_id": "comment101",
    "user": "alok_sharan",
    "text": "Sounds amazing, Alok!",
    "timestamp": "2024-10-21T15:00:00Z"
   },
   {
    "comment_id": "comment102",
    "user": "Maria_Pinto",
    "text": "Wish I could join you next time!",
    "timestamp": "2024-10-21T15:30:00Z"
   }
  ]
 },
 {
  "post_id": "post002",
  "text": "Just finished a challenging problem. Feeling accomplished!",
  "timestamp": "2024-10-25T18:00:00Z",
  "likes": 30,
  "comments": [
  {
   "comment_id": "comment103",
   "user": "tech_leader",
   "text": "Great work! Keep it up!",
   "timestamp": "2024-10-25T18:30:00Z"
  }
 ]
}
],
```

```
"followers": [
  {
   "follower_id": "follower001",
   "name": "Sam Alter"
  },
  {
   "follower_id": "follower002",
   "name": "John Walker"
  },
  {
   "follower_id": "follower003",
   "name": "Emily Grey"
  }
],
"following": [
 {
  "following_id": "following001",
  "name": "David Green"
 },
 {
  "following_id": "following002",
  "name": "Sara Black"
 }
],
 "account_created_at": "2023-01-05T12:00:00Z",
 "last_login": "2024-11-01T09:00:00Z"
}
```

Explanation:

1. User Details: Basic information like name, email, profile_picture, and bio.
2. Posts: Embedded array of posts with attributes like post_id, text, timestamp, likes, and comments. Each post contains an array of comments, with fields for user details, comment text, and timestamp.
3. Followers and Following: Lists of followers and people the user follows, stored as embedded arrays with unique IDs and names.

4. Account Metadata: Fields like account_created_at and last_login to track user activity.

This denormalized structure enables fast retrieval of user profiles and posts without needing to execute multiple complex JOIN operations, which can be expensive in SQL-based systems. It's ideal for scenarios like social media platforms, where performance is prioritized and updates are mostly done at the document level.

6.2 Choosing the right Database

Selecting a database is a critical decision that depends on the nature of the data and its intended usage. SQL databases (like MySQL, PostgreSQL) are ideal for structured data with well-defined relationships, requiring consistency and reliability. They use a fixed schema, which is beneficial when the data structure is unlikely to change, and are ACID compliant, making them suitable for financial transactions or inventory management.

NoSQL databases (like MongoDB, Cassandra) are better suited for unstructured or rapidly evolving data. They offer flexible schema designs, allowing developers to store different types of data without predefined structures, which makes them ideal for content management, social media, and IoT applications. NoSQL databases are designed for horizontal scaling, meaning you can easily add servers to accommodate increased data, making them highly scalable for large applications.

Use-Case contains ↓	**SQL**	**NoSQL**
Data	Structured	Semi or Unstructured
Extraction	Complex joins and ad-hoc queries support	Too hard to achieve complex joins and run ad-hoc queries
Scaling	Vertical scaling is fit for the use case	Horizontal scaling is better for the use case
Data volume	Data does not grow exponentially and hence chances of hitting the limit (depending upon hardware) is miniscule	Intended use is to deal with very large volume of data

Use-Case contains ↓	SQL	NoSQL
Default	Suitable for most of the use cases during interview	Consider as first choice for distributed data where partition tolerance is important
Performance	Good performance that can be enhanced using indexing and caching techniques. Caching might require additional hardware and maintenance overhead	Very low data retrieval latency with inbuilt caching support
Consistency & Reliability	Strong requirement of overall ACID behavior	Eventual Consistency is just enough

Table – 6.1

Use SQL when you need complex relationships, strong consistency, and structured data. Choose NoSQL if your application requires scalability, flexibility in schema, or high write throughput. The choice should be guided by the specific needs of your project, keeping in mind the trade-offs in scalability, consistency, and complexity.

6.3 Database Schema Design

Once you've chosen your database, the next step is designing the schema. Schema design varies significantly between SQL Vs NoSQL Databases, and understanding these differences is crucial.

In SQL databases, data is organized into tables, and each table has a fixed structure with defined relationships between tables (typically through foreign keys). The goal is to normalize data, reducing redundancy and maintaining data integrity.

Normalization

Normalization involves organizing data to minimize duplication and dependency. This is typically done by dividing large tables into smaller ones and defining relationships between them. The process of normalization often follows these forms:

1st Normal Form (1NF): Eliminate duplicate rows and ensure that each column contains atomic values.

2nd Normal Form (2NF): Ensure that all non-key attributes are fully dependent on the primary key.

3rd Normal Form (3NF): Eliminate transitive dependencies, ensuring that non-key attributes do not depend on other non-key attributes.

For example, in a student management system, instead of storing all student and course data in a single table, you would break it down into multiple tables:

1. A students table for storing basic information.
2. A courses table for the available courses.
3. An enrollments table that links students to the courses they are enrolled in.

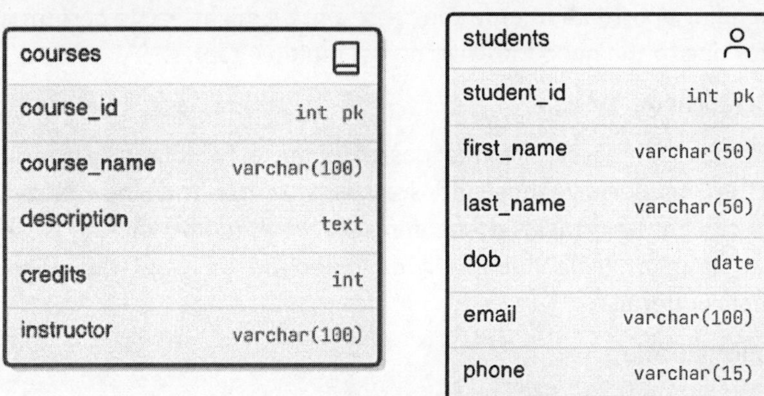

Figure – 6.6

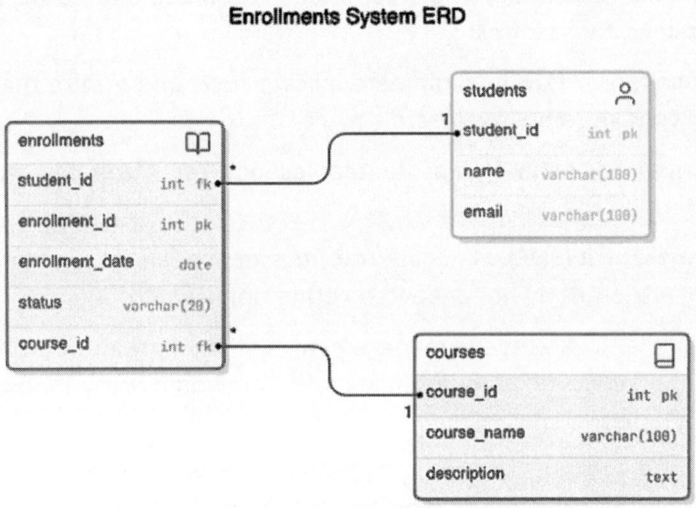

Figure – 6.7

This structure reduces redundancy and ensures data integrity but depending upon data volume and constraints, it might lead to performance issues due to the need for JOINs across multiple tables.

NoSQL Schema Design

In NoSQL Databases, schema design is more flexible, and the focus is often on performance and scalability rather than normalization. Data can be denormalized, meaning that related information is stored together in a single document or collection to avoid the need for complex queries.

Denormalization

Denormalization involves embedding related data within a single document or collection, making it faster to read at the cost of data duplication. In a NoSQL schema, you might store all details of an order, including the customer and products, within a single document.

For example, in an e-commerce application:

A single document might store the order ID, customer details, and an embedded list of products with quantities and prices.

This denormalized structure allows you to retrieve an entire order in one read, making the system highly performant for read-heavy operations.

However, this structure increases the risk of data inconsistency, as changes to one part of the data (e.g., product details) might not automatically reflect in all documents containing that product.

Trade-offs in NoSQL Schema Design

The trade-offs in NoSQL schema design include:

Faster reads: Since related data is stored together, reads are faster and simpler.

Data duplication: While performance is improved, data duplication can lead to larger storage requirements and potential inconsistencies.

Schema flexibility: You can change document structure without worrying about its impact on existing data. There is no schema update required (as needed in case of SQL database) making NoSQL database ideal for systems that evolve over time.

6.4 Scaling

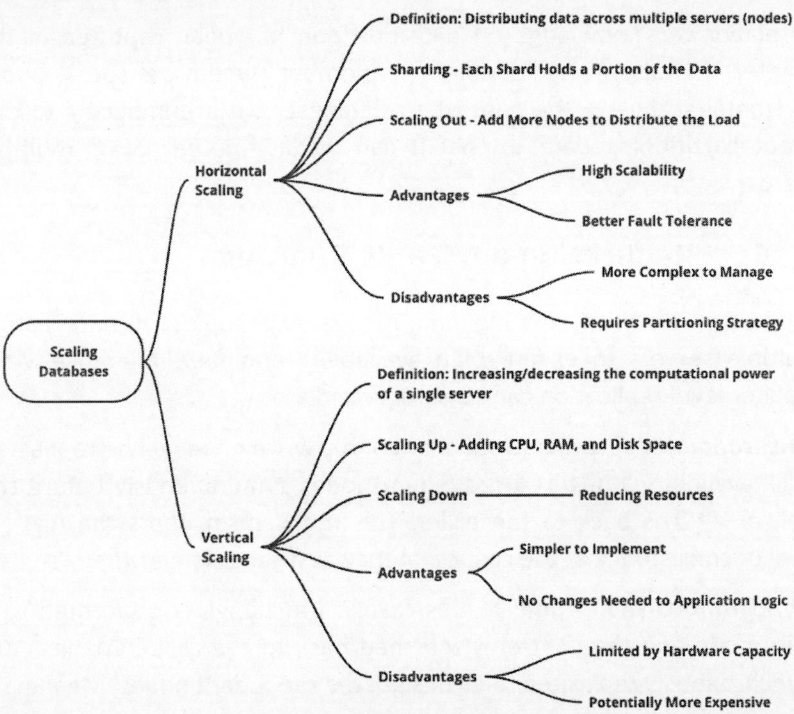

Figure – 6.8

As your system grows, you'll need to scale your database to handle more data and traffic. There are two primary methods for scaling: vertical scaling and horizontal scaling. The scaling mechanism can be implemented for components residing at other layers within your overall design as well but here we are learning it in context to databases.

Vertical Scaling

Vertical scaling involves increasing or decreasing the computational power of a single server by adding or removing resources such as CPU, RAM, and disk space. When we increase the computational power, it is known as "scaling up". While decreasing is called "scaling down". Generally, when we use the term vertical scaling, we are talking about scaling-up.

Horizontal Scaling (Sharding)

Horizontal scaling involves distributing data across multiple servers (or nodes), also known as **sharding**. Each shard contains a portion of the data, allowing the system to scale out by adding more nodes.

An elaborated knowledge on data partition has been captured in the chapter "Database Partitioning" (Remember, when we speak about horizontal scaling in the context to database, we are implicitly talking about partitioning data so that it can be distributed across multiple shards)

6.5 Replication and Fault Tolerance

Replication involves creating and maintaining copies of data across multiple servers to ensure high availability and fault tolerance. At a broader level replication can be categorized as -

Synchronous replication: Data change to a write node will be replicated to all available/configured redundant nodes simultaneously before the control returns back to the caller. This mechanism offers the highest level of consistency at the cost of latency as it takes longer time.

Asynchronous replication: In this case, data change is performed to a write node and the control is returned back to the caller. Changes are asynchronously replicated to all designated redundant nodes. Meaning it offers the highest speed at the cost of eventual consistency.

There are a few ways through which replication can be achieved in the real world. This topic is elaborated in chapter "Data Replication" within this book.

6.6 Estimating Storage and Query Handling

In system design interviews, you're often asked to estimate storage requirements and handle queries efficiently. These estimations help interviewers understand how well you can design systems to scale and how prepared you are to deal with real-world constraints like traffic peaks, user growth, and storage limitations. Let's go into more detail on how you can approach these calculations.

Query Handling Estimation

Estimating the number of queries per second (QPS) is vital for designing a system that can handle the expected traffic, especially during peak times. This involves understanding how often users interact with the system and how many queries each interaction generates.

Steps for Query Handling Estimation

1. Understand User Behavior:
    - Estimate how often users will interact with the system (e.g., for social media example how many times they post, like, or share content daily).
    - Identify the different types of queries your system will handle (e.g., reads, writes, updates, deletes).
2. Determine Peak Traffic:
    - Systems often experience traffic spikes during certain times (e.g., events, promotions). Your design should proactively account for peak load, not just average traffic.
    - Estimate how many users are active simultaneously during peak times (e.g., 10% of users might be online at once).
3. Classify Queries:
    - Read-heavy systems: Most interactions involve fetching data (e.g., social media timelines, search results).
    - Write-heavy systems: More data is being created than retrieved (e.g., logging systems, IoT).

4. Calculate Queries Per Second (QPS):
    - Based on user behavior, estimate how many read and write queries are generated.
    - Multiply the estimated queries by the number of users active at any given time.
5. Factor in Latency and Response Time:
    - Consider acceptable response times for each query type and the system's overall latency tolerance.
    - Aim for sub-second response times in high-traffic systems (e.g., a social media platform).

<u>Example 1: Social Media Platform Query Estimate</u>

For a social media platform with 10 million users, where each user makes 5 posts per day and likes 20 posts, let's estimate the QPS for:

Write Requests:

Posts per day = 10,000,000 users 5 posts = 50,000,000 posts/day
Posts per second = 50,000,000 posts per day / 86,400 seconds/day ≈ 578 posts/second

Read Requests (viewing a timeline): If each user views their timeline 10 times per day, fetching 50 posts per view:

Timeline views per day = 10,000,000 users 10 views = 100,000,000 views/day
Queries per second = 100,000,000 views per day / 86,400 seconds/day ≈ 1,157 queries/second

Like Operations: If each user likes 20 posts per day:

Likes per day = 10,000,000 users 20 likes = 200,000,000 likes/day
Likes per second = 200,000,000 likes per day / 86,400 seconds/day ≈ 2,314 likes/second

Total QPS for the platform:

578 (posts) + 1,157 (reads) + 2,314 (likes) ≈ 4,049 queries per second (QPS).

<u>Example 2: E-Commerce Platform Query Estimate</u>

For an e-commerce platform with 1 million users, where each user performs the following actions:

- Views products: 5 times per day
- Adds products to cart: 2 times per day
- Places an order: 1 time per week

Product Views (Read-heavy):

Views per day = 1,000,000 users 5 views = 5,000,000 views/day
Queries per second = 5,000,000 views per day / 86,400 seconds/day ≈ 58 reads/second

Add to Cart (Moderate writes):

Add to Cart per day = 1,000,000 users 2 additions = 2,000,000 actions/day
Queries per second = 2,000,000 actions per day / 86,400 seconds/day ≈ 23 writes/second

Orders Placed (Write-heavy but less frequent):

Orders per week = 1,000,000 users / 1 order/week = 1,000,000 orders/week
Orders per second = 1,000,000 orders per week / 604,800 seconds/week ≈ 1.65 orders/second

Total QPS for the e-commerce platform:

58 (reads) + 23 (add to cart) + 1.65 (orders) ≈ 82.65 QPS.

Chapter 07

Database Partitioning

Database partitioning is a strategy used to divide a large database into smaller, more manageable segments (partitions) to improve performance, scalability, and maintenance. By distributing the data across multiple partitions, the system can handle larger datasets more efficiently and ensure quicker access to relevant data.

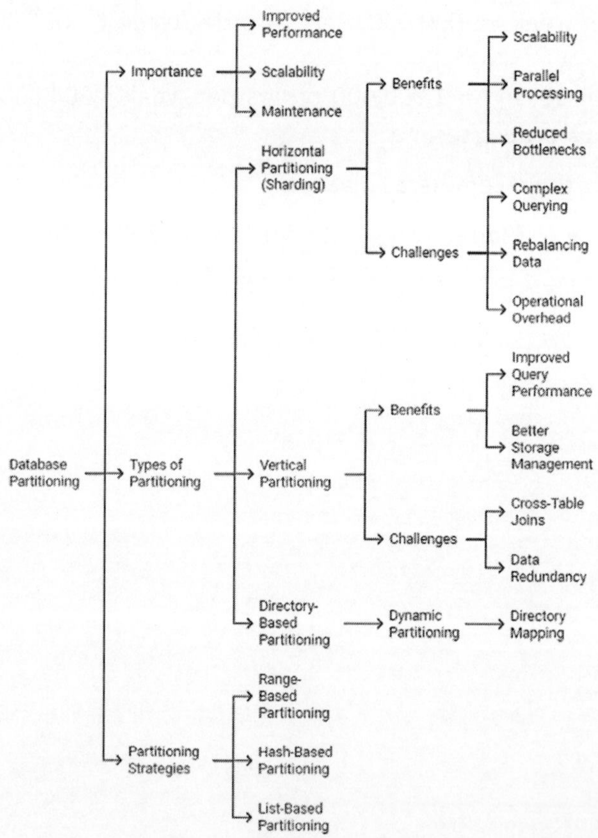

Figure – 7.1

Why Database Partitioning is Important:

Improved Performance: By spreading data across partitions, the system can reduce query response time, as it processes a smaller portion of data at a time.

Scalability: Partitioning enables the system to scale horizontally, accommodating more data as needed without overwhelming a single server.

Maintenance: With partitioning, tasks like backups, archiving, and indexing can be done on smaller datasets, reducing downtime and resource usage.

7.1 Types of Partitioning

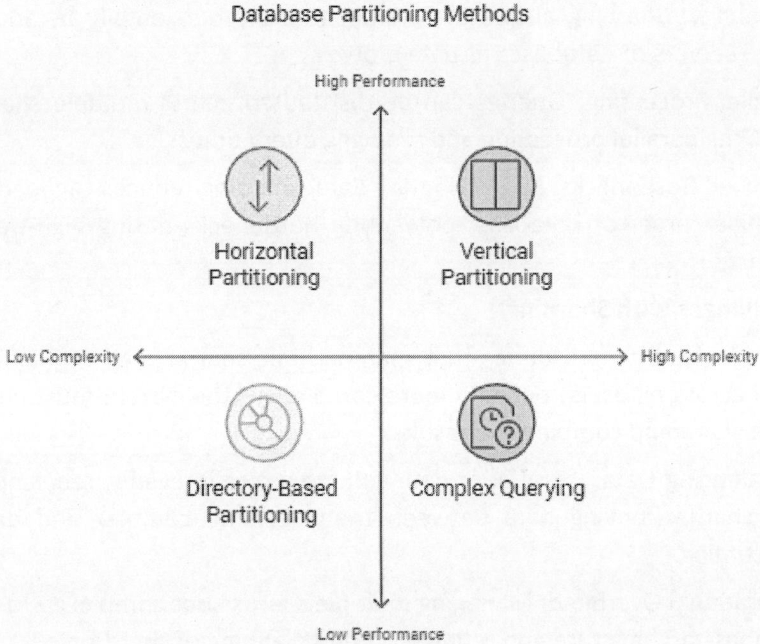

Figure – 7.2

▶ Horizontal Partitioning (Sharding)

Horizontal partitioning, also known as sharding, involves distributing data across different databases or servers. Each partition (shard) contains a subset depending upon the partitioning strategy e.g. shard key in case of shard partitioning (such as user ID or geographic region).

How Sharding Works

If you have a user table with millions of users, you can distribute the data to multiple shards by userID if we consider key based partitioning strategy. Users with IDs 1-500,000 may go to one shard, and users with IDs 500,001-1,000,000 may go to another. Each shard contains the same schema but different rows.

Example:

For a social media platform with users worldwide, you could shard the user table by geographic region, ensuring that users from North America are stored in one shard and users from Europe are stored in another.

Key Benefits of Horizontal Partitioning (Sharding)

Scalability: Sharding allows the system to scale horizontally by adding more servers or databases as data grows.

Parallel Processing: Queries can be distributed across multiple shards, enabling parallel processing and reducing query times.

Reduced Bottlenecks: By distributing data, sharding reduces the load on a single server or database, preventing bottlenecks during high-traffic events.

Challenges with Sharding

Complex Querying: Queries that span multiple shards (e.g., aggregating data across all users) become more complex, as the system must query each shard and combine the results.

Rebalancing Data: If traffic or data volume grows unevenly, rebalancing the shards (moving data between them) can be complex and time-consuming.

Operational Overhead: Managing multiple shards adds complexity to the database architecture and requires careful planning of shard keys.

► Vertical Partitioning

In vertical partitioning, columns of a table are split into different tables or databases. This is useful when certain columns are accessed more frequently than others. By storing frequently accessed columns separately, the system can retrieve data faster.

How Vertical Partitioning Works

Consider a user table with many columns, such as user_id, name, email, password_hash, address, profile_picture, and bio. Columns like name and email might be accessed more frequently than columns like profile_picture or bio. In vertical partitioning, you can store frequently accessed columns in one table and rarely accessed columns in another.

Example:

For a blogging platform, frequently accessed columns like title, author, and created_at can be stored separately from large columns like content and comments.

Key Benefits of Vertical Partitioning

Improved Query Performance: Queries that access only frequently used columns will execute faster, as the database reads from a smaller, more optimized table.

Better Storage Management: Vertical partitioning allows for better control over storage. Large data (like images or long text) can be stored separately, optimizing disk usage.

Challenges with Vertical Partitioning

Cross-Table Joins: Queries that need data from both partitioned tables may require complex joins, increasing query execution time.

Data Redundancy: Some columns may need to be duplicated across partitions, leading to potential data redundancy and increased storage requirements.

► Directory-Based Partitioning

Directory-based partitioning is a more dynamic form of partitioning. Instead of relying on predefined rules (like ranges or hash-based partitioning), the system uses a directory or lookup service to determine where data should be stored.

How It Works

A directory-based system maintains a mapping of data records to their respective partitions. When a new record is added, the directory is consulted to determine which partition will store the record. Similarly, when a query is made, the directory is checked to locate the partition containing the data.

Example

A cloud-based storage service like Dropbox could use directory-based partitioning to store user files across different geographic locations. The directory maps each file to a specific storage cluster based on factors like data access patterns and file size.

7.2 Partitioning Strategies

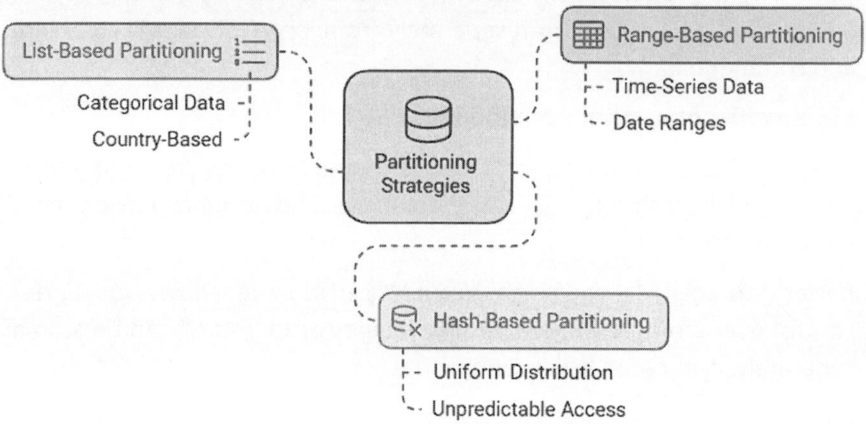

Figure – 7.3

Partitioning can be done using several different strategies. Choosing the right strategy depends on the nature of the data and the specific requirements of the system.

▶ Strategies

Range-Based Partitioning

In range-based partitioning, data is divided based on predefined ranges of values. For example, if you are partitioning a table by date, records from January might go into one partition, while records from February go into another.

Use Case:

Range-based partitioning is ideal for time-series data (such as logs or analytics data) where queries are often made based on time ranges.

Hash-Based Partitioning

In hash-based partitioning, a hash function is applied to a column (e.g., user ID), and the result determines which partition the data will go into. This method distributes data more evenly across partitions, preventing hot spots.

Use Case:

Hash-based partitioning is useful for applications where data access is unpredictable and uniform distribution is important, such as an online marketplace where users are randomly distributed across servers.

List-Based Partitioning

In list-based partitioning, data is divided based on predefined lists of values. For example, you might partition a customer table based on country, where customers from the US are in one partition, customers from the UK are in another, and so on.

Use Case:

This method is useful for applications where data is naturally divided by categories, such as a multi-national company with different business operations in each country.

► Dealing with Rebalancing

As data grows and usage patterns change, partitions may become unbalanced, leading to performance issues. Rebalancing involves redistributing data across partitions to maintain optimal performance.

Rebalancing Strategies

Adding New Partitions: As data grows, new partitions can be added to distribute the load. However, this often requires reassigning some existing data to new partitions.

Splitting Partitions: Large partitions can be split into smaller ones to reduce query time and improve overall performance.

Challenges in Rebalancing

Downtime: Rebalancing can lead to downtime if data needs to be moved between servers.

Complexity: It requires careful planning and execution to ensure data integrity during the rebalancing process.

▶ Example: Partitioning in a NoSQL Database

Let's take an example of a NoSQL database like Cassandra, which uses a distributed architecture to handle massive amounts of data. Cassandra partitions data using consistent hashing, a hash-based partitioning strategy that distributes data evenly across the nodes in a cluster.

In Cassandra, each node in the cluster is assigned a token range, and data is partitioned based on these ranges. When a new node is added to the cluster, Cassandra automatically rebalances the partitions by redistributing the token ranges, ensuring that no node is overloaded.

Use Case

A global e-commerce platform might use Cassandra to partition customer data by geographic region, ensuring that users in different countries can access their data quickly, while still maintaining global consistency.

Chapter 08

Data Replication

Replication is a cornerstone of modern distributed systems. It refers to the process of duplicating data across multiple servers or data centers to ensure that the system remains operational in the event of failures, increases its read performance, and can scale to handle a growing number of users. In an environment where users expect services to be available 24/7, replication is indispensable. Whether it's a social media platform, a global e-commerce service, or a banking application, replication ensures that data is always available, even in the event of server crashes or network failures.

High Availability: When you replicate data across multiple servers, you prevent a single point of failure from taking down your entire system. If one server goes offline, another replica can immediately take over, ensuring uninterrupted service.

Example: Netflix uses data replication extensively to ensure that if a data center in one region fails, viewers in that region can still stream shows from a different data center.

Fault Tolerance: Replication allows systems to be resilient to faults by storing copies of the data across different geographic locations. This way, if one location is compromised by a natural disaster or technical malfunction, the system can continue operating from other locations.

Load Balancing: Replication helps reduce the load on the primary server by distributing read traffic across multiple replicas. This becomes particularly useful for systems that handle large amounts of read queries, such as online news platforms or social networks.

Disaster Recovery: Replication ensures that the system can recover from catastrophic events like data corruption, hardware failures, or hacking attempts. By maintaining replicas in different regions or availability zones, organizations can recover data quickly and restore services after an outage.

Types of Replication

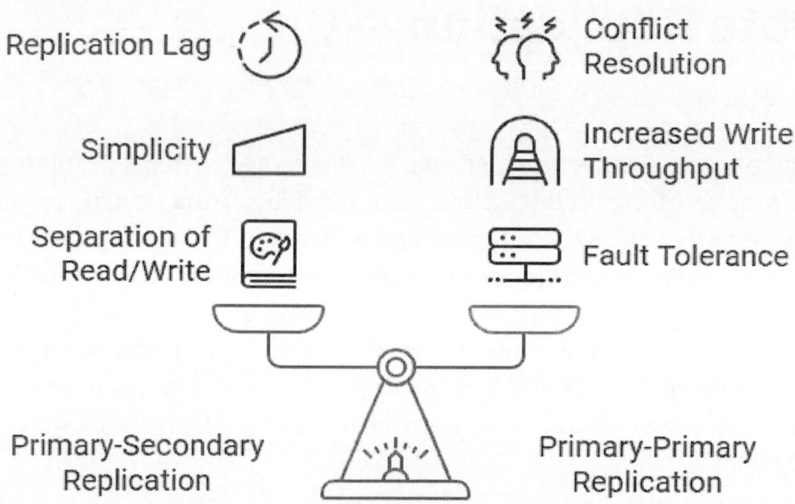

Comparing replication models' tradeoffs.

Figure – 8.1

There are several replication models, each with its strengths and weaknesses depending on the system's requirements.

► Primary-Secondary Replication

In Primary-Secondary Replication, the primary server handles all write operations, and the secondary servers replicate the data from the primary server to handle read operations. This model is widely used for systems that have a much higher ratio of reads to writes.

Primary Node: This server manages all data changes, such as inserts, updates, and deletes. Every time a change is made, the primary server replicates the updated data to its secondary servers.

Example: MySQL uses primary-secondary replication extensively in web applications. For instance, an e-commerce site may use the primary server for processing transactions (writes) while secondary servers handle product catalog browsing (reads).

Secondary Nodes: These nodes maintain copies of the data from the primary and typically handle read queries. In high-traffic systems, read queries are distributed across multiple secondary nodes to prevent overloading the primary.

Advantages

Separation of Read/Write Operations: Since reads and writes are handled by different nodes, overall system performance is improved.

Simplicity: This model is relatively easy to implement and maintain.

Disadvantages

Replication Lag: In asynchronous replication, changes made on the primary may take time to replicate to the secondary servers, leading to eventual consistency rather than immediate consistency.

Single Point of Failure: If the primary server goes down, writes cannot be processed until a new primary server is promoted.

▶ Primary-Primary Replication

Primary-Primary Replication allows multiple servers to act as primary. This means that both read and write operations can be performed on any of the servers, and the changes are propagated to the other primary nodes. This replication model is often used in systems where high availability is critical, and the system cannot afford to have a single point of failure.

Multi-Primary Setup: In this configuration, all primary servers can handle both reads and writes, and updates are synchronized across all nodes. Example: MongoDB supports multi-primary replication, which is useful in scenarios where data needs to be written in multiple locations simultaneously, such as in globally distributed applications.

Advantages

Fault Tolerance: If one primary server goes down, other primary servers can continue to handle writes, making the system highly available.

Increased Write Throughput: Writes can be distributed across multiple primary servers, which reduces the load on any single node.

Disadvantages

Conflict Resolution: Since multiple primary servers can perform writes simultaneously, conflicts may occur if two primary servers try to update the same record at the same time.

Increased Complexity: Managing data consistency across multiple primary servers is more challenging than in a primary-secondary model.

Replication Categories

When replicating data, the timing of when the data is replicated plays a critical role. There are two primary methods: synchronous and asynchronous replication.

- **Synchronous Replication:** In this method, the system waits for all replicas to acknowledge the write operation before considering the transaction complete. This ensures that all replicas have the latest data at the same time, guaranteeing consistency.

Advantages

- Strong Consistency: Since all replicas are updated at the same time, there is no risk of reading outdated data.
- No Data Loss: Synchronous replication ensures that data is not lost during failures.

Disadvantages

- Increased Latency: Because the system must wait for all replicas to acknowledge the write, it can introduce delays, especially in distributed systems where the replicas are located far apart.
- Reduced Write Throughput: The additional overhead of confirming every write across all replicas can slow down the system.

- **Asynchronous Replication**: Here, the master writes the data and immediately considers the transaction complete. The data is propagated to the replicas later. This approach is faster but can lead to **eventual consistency**, where replicas might temporarily have outdated information.

Advantages:

- Lower Latency: As the system doesn't need to wait for replicas, the write operations are faster.
- Better Performance: More suited for systems with high write volumes or those that prioritize speed over immediate consistency.

Disadvantages:

- Data Inconsistency: There is a risk of data being inconsistent across replicas, especially during failure scenarios.

- Potential Data Loss: If the Primary fails before the data has been propagated, the changes might not be replicated, resulting in data loss.

8.1 Designing a Replication System

Designing a robust replication system requires balancing performance, consistency, and availability. Different systems prioritize these factors differently, depending on the use case.

Handling Replication Lags

Replication lag is a common issue in asynchronous systems, where updates on the primary may take time to reach the secondary nodes. This delay can cause inconsistencies, especially in applications where real-time data accuracy is critical (e.g., financial services or stock trading platforms).

Techniques to Minimize Lag

- Parallel Replication: Increases the speed of replication by processing multiple updates simultaneously.
- High-Speed Networks: Ensuring that replication traffic occurs over low-latency, high-bandwidth networks can minimize lag.
- Efficient Replication Algorithms: Algorithms that prioritize the replication of critical data or group updates together can help reduce lag times.

Example: Facebook uses techniques like replication lag monitoring and dynamic load balancing between replicas to ensure that updates to user data propagate quickly across their global network.

Ensuring Data Consistency with Eventual Consistency Models

In systems using asynchronous replication, eventual consistency is the norm. Eventual consistency means that, while the system may not guarantee immediate consistency across all replicas, it ensures that, given enough time, all replicas will converge to the same state.

Eventual Consistency Models:

- Quorum-Based Systems: Some systems use quorum-based read and write operations to ensure that a majority of replicas agree on the state of data before returning a result.

- Conflict-Free Replicated Data Types (CRDTs): These are data structures that ensure eventual consistency by merging updates from different replicas in a mathematically sound way.

Example: Amazon DynamoDB is an example of a system that implements eventual consistency, offering both eventual and strong consistency options depending on the application's requirements.

8.2 Common Challenges

While replication provides many benefits, it also introduces several challenges that must be addressed.

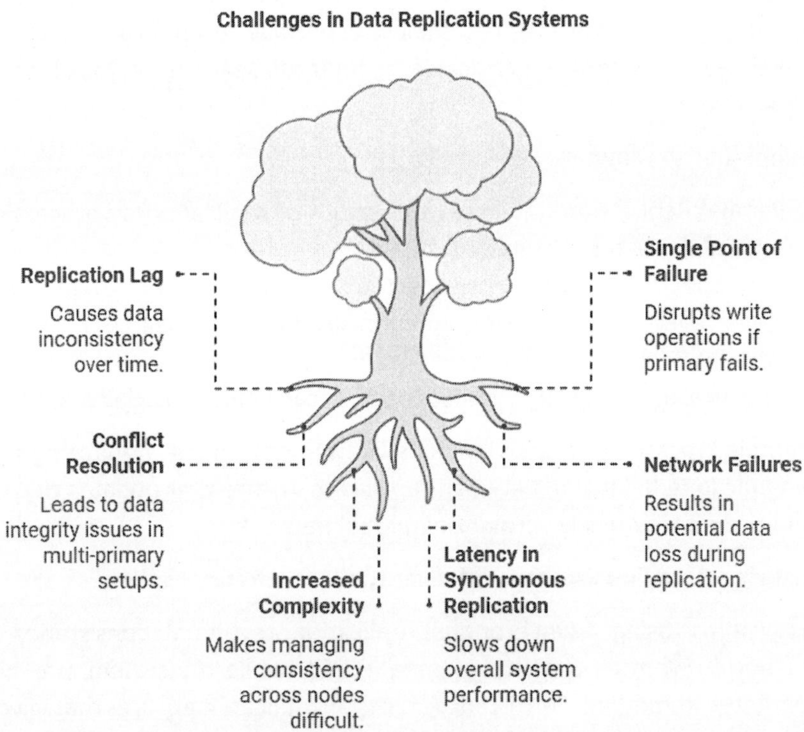

Figure – 8.2

Managing Conflicts in Multi-Primary Replication

In multi-primary replication setups, conflicts occur when two primary servers update the same record concurrently. Handling these conflicts is crucial to maintaining data integrity.

Conflict Resolution Strategies

- Last Write Wins (LWW): In this simple method, the most recent write (based on a timestamp) is accepted, and other conflicting writes are discarded. However, this can lead to data loss.
- Application-Specific Logic: Some systems use business rules to merge conflicting updates. For example, in a collaborative editing application, changes from different users can be merged intelligently rather than overwriting each other.

Example: CouchDB uses a combination of revision tracking and conflict resolution to handle conflicts in its multi-primary replication model.

Handling Replication Failures

Replication failures can lead to data loss or inconsistency if not handled properly. These failures may occur due to network issues, hardware failures, or software bugs.

Techniques for Handling Failures

- Retry Logic: The system should automatically retry failed replication attempts to ensure that updates eventually propagate to all replicas.
- Automatic Failover: In case of a failure, the system should promote a slave node to primary to maintain service availability without manual intervention.
- Write-Ahead Logging (WAL): This ensures that updates are logged before they are applied. In the event of a failure, the log can be replayed to restore the system to its last consistent state.

Example: PostgreSQL uses write-ahead logging to ensure that changes are not lost during crashes, and replicas can be brought back to a consistent state after recovery.

Chapter 09

Scalability

Scalability defines the ability of a system to adapt or respond (in terms of cost and performance) to changes in demands—whether it's user traffic, data volume, or the complexity of operations. Systems that are poorly designed for scalability can experience performance degradation, data loss, or complete failure under load. Thus, understanding how to make systems scalable is a fundamental skill in system design.

To keep the understanding simple, a system scalability can be achieved by considering each and every layers in a layered architecture i.e. Web, Application, and Database. Additionally, use of appropriate caching e.g. CDN can also help us achieve this goal. The primary consideration for scalability will be by enabling hardware redundancy. Let's dive down a bit more into it by learning some common ways to achieve this -

Vertical and Horizontal scaling: As already covered at length in database (chapter-6) of the book, Vertical scaling is the mechanism where you will right-size your hardware by appropriating its power (e.g. CPU, Memory) to match the demand whereas Horizontal scaling is where you will right-size the redundant count of a hardware to match your demand. In that chapter we discussed the concept in context to databases but the same can be applied to your web-servers as well as application servers.

Load Balancers: Load balancers are great tools to achieve scalability but remember, they can not achieve this task alone. They will require underlying hardware (e.g. web, application, or database servers). In essence, a load balancer ensures that the traffic requirement is appropriately distributed across all connected resources. For a detailed understanding refer to chapter "Load Balancing" of this book.

Caching: A great way to give a boost to increase in demand. Depending upon the nature of demand and content in use, a caching implementation (e.g. simple data, complex data structure, CDN) can be implemented for the purpose. For a detailed understanding refer to chapter "Caching" of this book.

9.1 Vertical and Horizontal Scaling

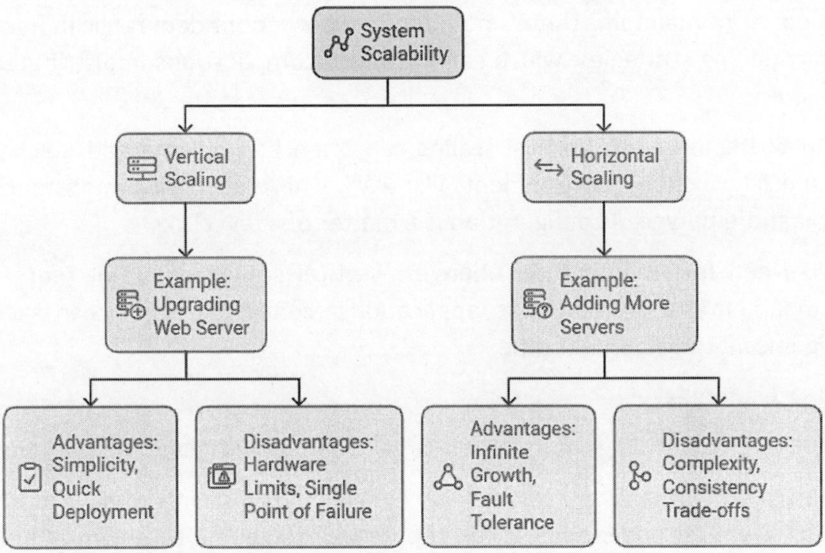

Figure – 9.1

► Vertical Scaling

Consider a web-based video streaming service where users can watch and upload videos. As the service gains popularity, user traffic increases exponentially, causing performance issues such as slower loading times and buffering. To address these issues, the company decides to scale vertically by upgrading their web application server with additional CPUs, more RAM, and faster storage.

This upgrade significantly enhances the server's ability to handle more concurrent user requests, improves streaming quality, and reduces buffering. The benefit here is that the company does not have to make significant changes to the software or the system's architecture—it's simply a matter of upgrading the hardware

Advantages

Simplicity: One of the key reasons vertical scaling is attractive is because of its simplicity. You don't need to redesign your system architecture or deal with the complexities of distributed systems. You simply upgrade your server hardware.

Consistency: Since everything is hosted on a single server, consistency is easier to maintain. There's no need to worry about data replication or partitioning strategies, which can introduce complications in distributed systems.

Quick Deployment: Vertical scaling can often be implemented quickly, especially in cloud environments like AWS, where upgrading an instance to a more powerful configuration is a matter of a few clicks.

No Need for Architectural Changes: Vertical scaling does not require fundamental changes to the application architecture, which can save significant development time.

Disadvantages

While vertical scaling has its benefits, it also comes with several limitations.

Hardware Limits: Every server has physical limits in terms of how much CPU, memory, and storage it can support. Once you hit these limits, you can't scale vertically any further. For instance, even the largest servers available today can only handle a certain number of transactions before they reach their maximum capacity.

Single Point of Failure: When you scale vertically, all your data and operations are on a single server. If that server crashes or experiences downtime, your entire system goes down with it. This makes vertical scaling less fault-tolerant compared to horizontal scaling.

Cost Inefficiency: High-end hardware required for vertical scaling can be extremely expensive. A top-tier server with the latest CPU and massive amounts of RAM costs significantly more than several mid-tier servers combined. The cost increases exponentially with the size of the resources you add.

Diminishing Returns: At a certain point, adding more hardware might not give you a proportional increase in performance. For instance, adding more RAM to a server might not improve response times if your bottleneck is CPU performance.

When to Use

Vertical scaling is a good option when:

- You have a monolithic application that isn't designed for distributed systems.
- Your system experiences low-to-moderate traffic and can be managed on a single machine.
- You need strong consistency, especially for transactional systems like banking applications.
- You want a quick solution to performance bottlenecks without re-architecting your system.

Vertical Scaling in Cloud Environments

In modern cloud computing platforms like AWS, Azure, and Google Cloud, vertical scaling can be done quickly by upgrading to a more powerful instance. For example, on AWS, you can start with a t2.medium instance and later upgrade to a t3.2xlarge instance if your traffic increases. This flexibility makes vertical scaling more accessible for small-to-medium-sized systems.

AWS Example

On AWS, you can upgrade an EC2 instance to a more powerful one by stopping the instance, modifying its instance type, and restarting it. For example, you can scale from a t3.small instance to a t3.2xlarge instance with more vCPUs and memory. This allows you to handle more traffic without making any changes to your application's architecture.

Auto Scaling with Cloud Providers

While vertical scaling is typically done manually, cloud providers like AWS and Google Cloud offer auto-scaling features that can dynamically adjust resources based on load. For example, if your server is running out of memory or CPU, the cloud platform can automatically upgrade your instance to a more powerful one to maintain performance. This is especially useful for handling traffic surges in a cost-efficient way.

Real-World Example: Vertical Scaling in Action

Use Case: SaaS Application

Let's consider a Software-as-a-Service (SaaS) application providing analytics for businesses. Initially, the application runs on a single midrange server that handles user requests and processes large datasets. As more businesses sign up for the service, the server starts to struggle with the increased number of queries and data processing.

Instead of redesigning the system to run on multiple servers, the team decides to scale vertically by upgrading to a server with more CPU cores and memory. This allows the system to process more requests simultaneously, reducing response times and improving the user experience. Because the system architecture is monolithic, vertical scaling is the most efficient solution in this case.

Impact of Vertical Scaling

After upgrading the server, the SaaS application can now handle up to 10x the number of users without any significant slowdowns. The user experience improves, and the company avoids the costs and complexities of re-architecting the system for horizontal scaling. However, the team recognizes that this approach has limits and that they may need to consider horizontal scaling in the future as the business continues to grow.

► Horizontal Scaling: Scalability Without Limits

While vertical scaling is constrained by hardware limits, horizontal scaling, or **scaling out**, allows you to add more servers to your system to distribute the load. This approach is often used in cloud-native and distributed systems, where you can scale your application by adding more instances instead of upgrading a single server.

How Horizontal Scaling Works

In horizontal scaling, multiple servers, or **nodes**, work together to handle the increased load. As the traffic or data grows, more servers are added to the system, each handling part of the load. This enables almost limitless growth, as the system can keep scaling as long as more nodes are added.

For example, consider a web application that handles 1,000 users on a single server. If traffic grows to 10,000 users, instead of upgrading the server (vertical scaling), you add 9 more servers to share the load. Each server now handles 1,000 users, distributing the workload across the system.

Real-World Example: Horizontal Scaling in Cloud Applications

Amazon, Netflix, and Facebook use horizontal scaling to handle millions of users. These companies don't rely on a single powerful server; instead, they distribute their services across thousands of servers worldwide. This allows them to handle huge amounts of data and traffic simultaneously without overwhelming any single server.

For instance, Netflix uses a **microservices architecture**, where different services (like video streaming, user authentication, recommendations, etc.) are handled by different sets of servers. Each service can scale independently by adding more servers as needed.

Advantages

Infinite Growth Potential: One of the biggest advantages of horizontal scaling is that there is no limit to how much you can scale. You can keep adding more servers to the system as needed.

Fault Tolerance: In a horizontally scaled system, if one server goes down, others can continue to handle the load. This makes the system much more resilient and fault-tolerant than vertical scaling, where the failure of a single server would bring down the entire system.

Cost Efficiency: Horizontal scaling can be more cost-effective than vertical scaling. Instead of investing in expensive high-end servers, you can use multiple mid-tier or commodity servers to handle the load.

Better Load Distribution: Horizontal scaling allows you to distribute different parts of your application (e.g., user authentication, content delivery) across multiple servers, optimizing performance for each service.

Disadvantages

Increased Complexity: Horizontal scaling introduces complexity, especially in terms of data management and synchronization. Managing data consistency across multiple servers requires additional strategies, like replication and sharding.

Consistency Trade-offs: In a distributed system, maintaining strong consistency can be difficult, especially when data is replicated across multiple nodes. Horizontal scaling often involves making trade-offs between **availability** and **consistency**, as explained in the **CAP theorem**.

Network Latency: When servers are distributed across multiple regions or data centers, network latency can become an issue. Communication between servers can introduce delays, especially in read-heavy applications.

When to Use

Horizontal scaling is ideal when:

- You need to handle large-scale traffic or data volumes that exceed the capacity of a single server.
- You're working with a distributed system or a microservices architecture.
- Your application requires high availability and needs to continue running even if some servers fail.
- You expect the system to grow significantly over time, making vertical scaling impractical.

Horizontal Scaling in Cloud Environments

Cloud environments like AWS and Google Cloud make horizontal scaling easier with services like auto-scaling groups. Auto-scaling automatically adds or removes servers based on demand, ensuring that your system scales dynamically without manual intervention.

For example, during peak hours, AWS auto-scaling can automatically spin up additional instances to handle the traffic surge. Once the traffic subsides, it scales down by terminating instances to save costs. This is particularly useful for e-commerce platforms that experience heavy traffic during specific periods like sales events or promotions. Additionally, services like Kubernetes allow for container-based scaling, where individual components of an application can scale independently based on their needs.

Another example is Google Cloud's Load Balancer, which automatically routes traffic to healthy instances spread across different regions, ensuring high availability and fault tolerance. As more users access the application, the system can dynamically scale horizontally without any manual intervention.

9.2 CAP Theorem

The CAP Theorem: Balancing Consistency, Availability, and Partition Tolerance

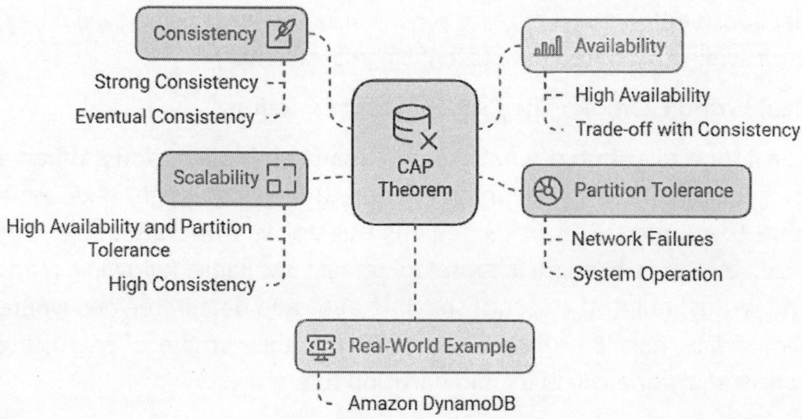

Figure – 9.2

The CAP theorem is a fundamental concept in designing distributed systems and plays a crucial role in scalability decisions. It states that a distributed system can only guarantee two out of three of the following properties:

- Consistency: Every read receives the most recent write or an error.
- Availability: Every request receives a response, without a guarantee that it contains the most recent data.
- Partition Tolerance: The system continues to operate despite arbitrary partitioning due to network failures.

In the context of scalability:

- Systems designed for high availability and partition tolerance often sacrifice consistency, providing eventual consistency instead of strong consistency.
- Systems designed for high consistency might become unavailable during network partitions.

Consistency-Availability Trade-off

In a globally distributed system, it's often impossible to maintain strict consistency across all nodes while also ensuring high availability. For example, when a network partition occurs, one node might not be able to immediately sync its data with another node. The system has to choose between waiting for synchronization (sacrificing availability) or providing outdated data (sacrificing consistency).

Real-World Example: The CAP Theorem in Action

Consider a distributed database that spans multiple regions. When a user updates their profile in one region, the change might take some time to propagate to other regions due to network latency. In this case, the system might choose to remain available (allowing reads and writes) but at the cost of showing outdated data in regions where the update hasn't propagated yet. This is an example of sacrificing consistency for availability and partition tolerance.

Eventual Consistency

Eventual consistency is a popular solution in distributed systems. It guarantees that, given enough time, all nodes will eventually have consistent data, but there may be moments when data is temporarily inconsistent across the system.

For example, Amazon DynamoDB offers eventual consistency for reads by default. This allows the system to provide faster responses and maintain high availability even during network partitions or heavy traffic.

9.3 Scalability Challenges

Even though scalability sounds promising, implementing it effectively comes with its challenges. Some of the common scalability issues include:

Data Consistency: As mentioned earlier, ensuring data consistency across multiple nodes in a distributed system is a major challenge. Replication lag, network partitions, and system failures can all lead to inconsistent data.

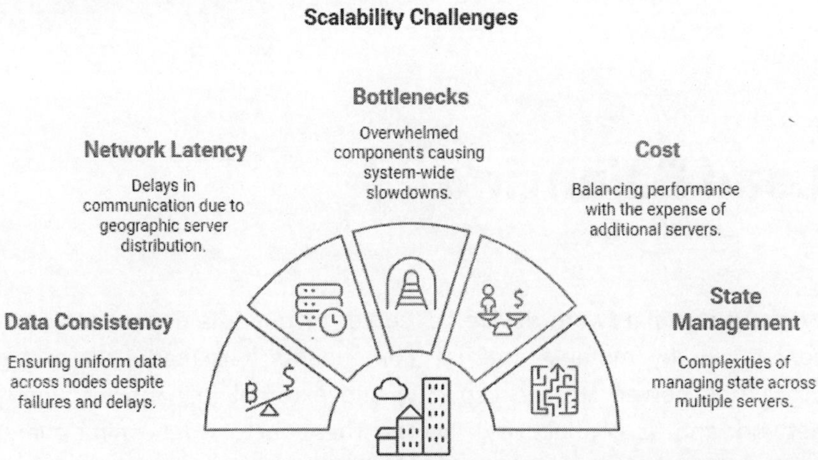

Figure – 9.3

Network Latency: In a distributed system, servers may be located in different geographic regions. This can lead to delays when servers need to communicate with each other, affecting system performance.

Bottlenecks: Even in horizontally scaled systems, certain components may become bottlenecks. For example, if all nodes rely on a single database, that database can become overwhelmed, causing system-wide slowdowns.

Cost: Scaling horizontally requires more servers, which increases costs. While cloud platforms offer pay-as-you-go models, organizations need to carefully balance the trade-off between performance and cost.

State Management: Stateless components (e.g., web servers) are easy to scale horizontally, but stateful components (e.g., databases) are much harder to scale. Managing state across multiple servers can become complex and requires strategies like sharding, replication, and session management.

Chapter 10

Load Balancing

Working of a hardware device i.e. server or node, is dependent on or constrained by multiple internal (components it is made out of e.g. processing power, storage capacity) and external (e.g. power supply, network and its connectivity) factors. These factors determine overall response rendering capabilities of the node including its performance, availability.

A load balancer acts as a traffic manager that distributes incoming network traffic/workloads across multiple redundant servers (or nodes) in a system. The goal is to prevent any single server from becoming a bottleneck, ensuring that all requests are handled smoothly and efficiently.

Why Load Balancing Is Important

To improve business continuity, usually a redundant copy of a server is deployed in the real world scenario. Managing the traffic or workload distribution among such deployed server(s) is achieved through a load-balancer. In a system without load balancing, all incoming traffic is directed to a single server. As traffic increases, this server becomes overwhelmed, leading to increased response times, request failures, or even server crashes.

For example, consider an e-commerce website during a holiday sale. If the traffic spikes and all requests are directed to a single server, that server will likely slow down or crash, causing customers to experience delays or errors. Now consider adding an additional redundant server for the site. In this case we will incorporate load balancing so that the traffic is distributed across two servers, allowing the website to handle at least double the load without any issues. Similarly, we can add more redundant servers in our system depending on traffic or workload volume expectation.

Moreover, a load-balancer also helps improve the overall security posture for an organization by reducing the attack surface of its back-end applications by distributing traffic to multiple nodes. This is an effective approach to minimize the impact that can arise in case of a distributed denial of services (DDoS) attack.

High Availability and Fault Tolerance

As per Wikipedia –

"High availability (HA) is a characteristic of a system that aims to ensure an agreed level of operational performance, usually uptime, for a higher than normal period".

"Fault tolerance is the ability of a system to maintain proper operation despite failures or faults in one or more of its components".

Meaning, Fault tolerance attracts more strict requirement over High availability. Load balancing enhances high availability and fault tolerance. By distributing traffic across multiple servers, the system can continue functioning even if one or more servers fail. This redundancy ensures that the system remains available and responsive even during hardware maintenance or failures.

For instance, if one server in a load-balanced group goes down, the load balancer automatically redirects traffic to the remaining healthy servers. This ensures uninterrupted service to users and prevents downtime.

Technology to Implement Load Balancer

A load balancer can be hardware based, software based, or virtual (with cloud technology). Here we are going to discuss the first two because of their relevance.

► **Hardware Based**

Hardware load balancers are dedicated physical devices that sit in front of the servers and distribute traffic based on pre-configured rules. They are typically used in large enterprise environments with high-performance requirements.

Advantages

- High Performance: Hardware load balancers offer extremely low latency and are capable of handling large amounts of traffic efficiently.

- Reliability: They are highly reliable and are often used in mission-critical applications where downtime is not an option.

Disadvantages

- Cost: Hardware load balancers are expensive to purchase and maintain, making them a costly solution for smaller organizations.
- Limited Flexibility: Unlike software load balancers, hardware load balancers are less flexible and harder to scale dynamically.

▶ Software Based

Software load balancers run on standard servers or cloud instances and distribute traffic based on configurable algorithms. They are more flexible than hardware load balancers and are widely used in cloud-based and modern distributed systems.

Advantages

- Cost-Effective: Software load balancers are cheaper and easier to deploy compared to hardware solutions. They can be scaled dynamically in cloud environments.
- Flexibility: Software load balancers can be easily reconfigured, allowing for quick adjustments based on changing traffic patterns or infrastructure needs.

Disadvantages

- Performance Overhead: Software load balancers may introduce more latency compared to hardware load balancers, especially in high-traffic environments.

Examples of popular software load balancers

- Nginx: A widely used open-source software that functions as a web server, reverse proxy, and load balancer.
- HAProxy: Another open-source load balancer known for its high performance and low resource consumption.

10.1 Types of Load Balancers

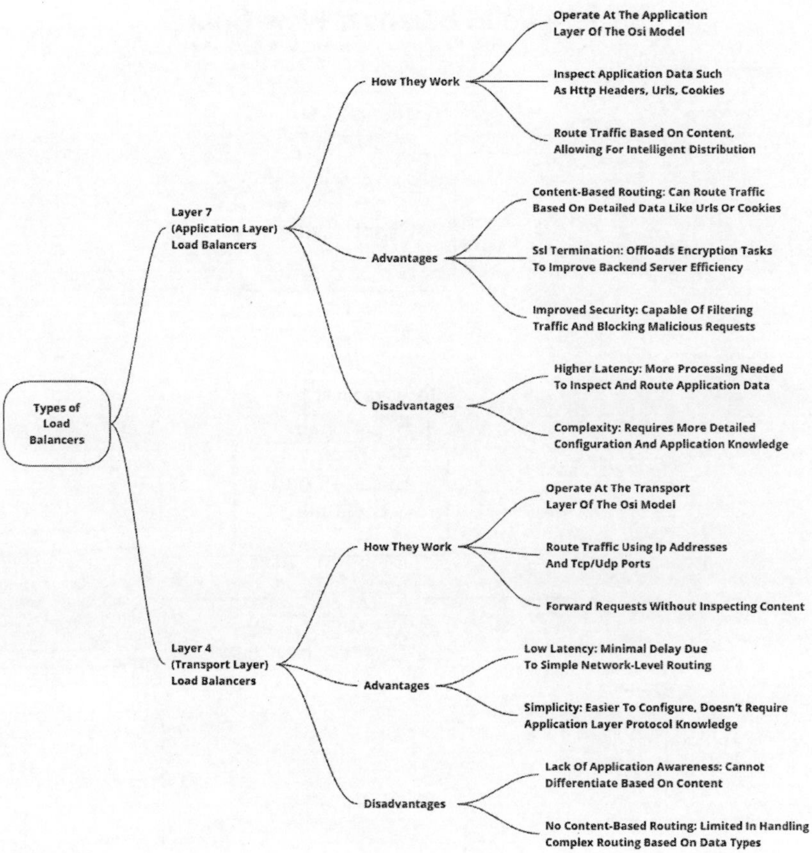

Figure – 10.1

There are several types of load balancers, each suited for different needs. The most common types include:

1. Layer 4 (Transport Layer) Load Balancers
2. Layer 7 (Application Layer) Load Balancers

Let's dive into each type in more detail.

► Layer 4 Load Balancers (Transport Layer)

Layer 4 load balancers operate at the transport layer of the OSI model, routing traffic based on network information such as IP addresses and TCP/UDP ports. They make routing decisions without considering the content of the traffic.

How Layer 4 Load Balancers Work

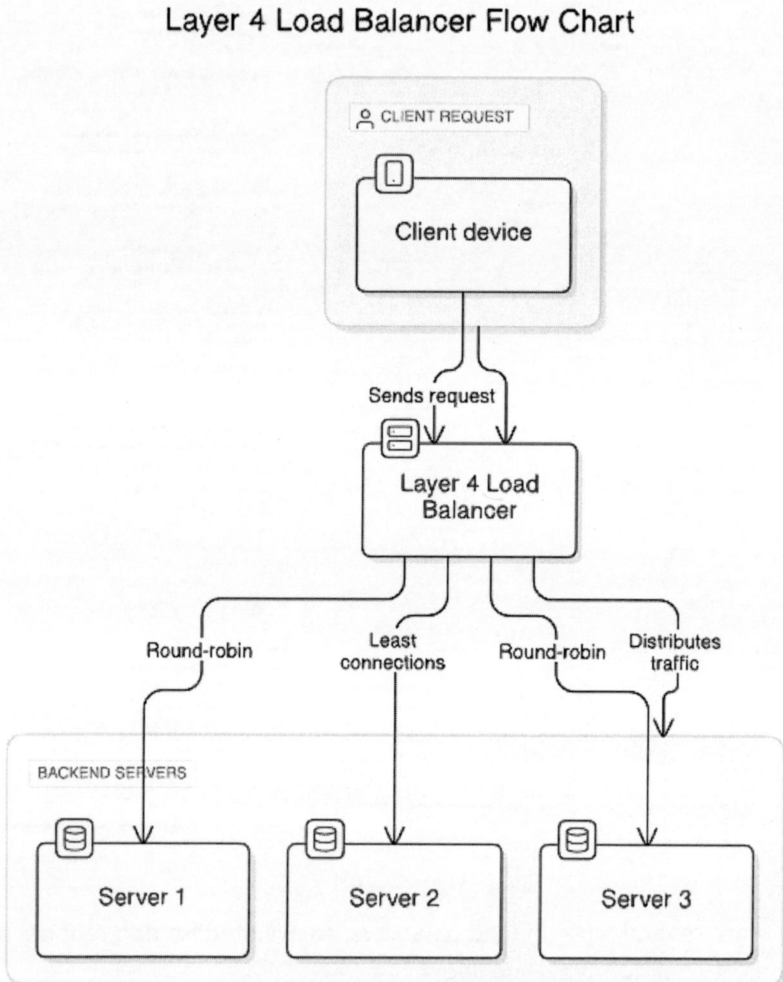

Figure – 10.2

Layer 4 load balancers use basic networking information like IP addresses and ports to direct traffic. When a client makes a request, the load balancer forwards that request to one of the available servers based on the defined load-balancing algorithm.

For example, if a client requests a web page, the load balancer doesn't inspect the HTTP request; it simply forwards the request to the next server based on network-layer information. This makes Layer 4 load balancers efficient and fast, as they don't need to process the application data.

Advantages of Layer 4 Load Balancers

- Low Latency: Since Layer 4 load balancers work at the network level, they introduce minimal latency. They simply forward traffic based on IP addresses and ports without inspecting the actual application data.
- Simplicity: These load balancers are relatively simple to configure and operate. They don't need to understand the application layer protocols, which makes them easier to manage.

Disadvantages of Layer 4 Load Balancers

- Lack of Application Awareness: Layer 4 load balancers cannot make decisions based on the content of the request. For example, they can't distinguish between a user requesting a login page and one requesting a static asset like an image.
- No Content-Based Routing: They can't perform tasks like routing traffic based on URLs, cookies, or HTTP headers, limiting their flexibility in complex application architectures.

► Layer 7 Load Balancers (Application Layer)

Layer 7 load balancers operate at the application layer, allowing them to make more intelligent routing decisions based on the content of the request. They inspect application data such as HTTP headers, cookies, and URLs to determine how to distribute traffic.

How Layer 7 Load Balancers Work

When a client sends a request, the Layer 7 load balancer inspects the content of the request, such as the URL or HTTP method, before deciding which server should handle the request. This allows the load balancer to perform more advanced routing, such as directing traffic based on the type of content being requested.

For example, in a web application, the load balancer might direct requests for /login to one set of servers that handle authentication and requests for /images to a different set of servers optimized for serving static content.

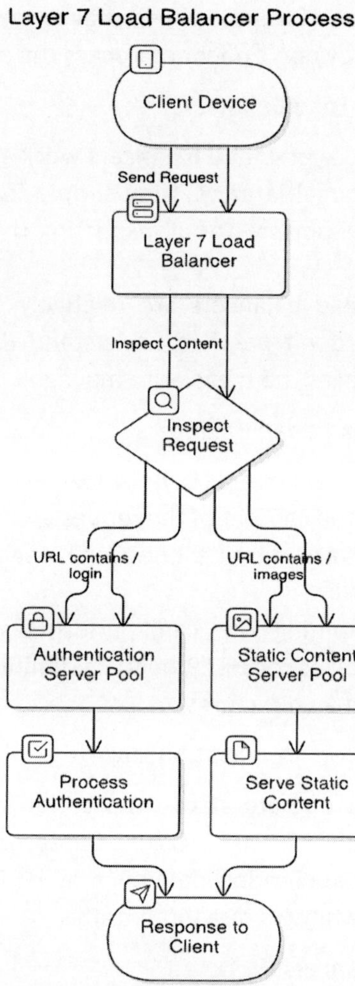

Figure – 10.3

Advantages of Layer 7 Load Balancers

- Content-Based Routing: Layer 7 load balancers can make decisions based on application data, allowing for more sophisticated routing strategies. For example, they can route users based on specific URLs, cookies, or user-agent headers.
- SSL Termination: Layer 7 load balancers often handle SSL termination (SSL Termination or SSL Offloading is the process of decrypting; SSL encrypted traffic), which offloads the task of encrypting and decrypting HTTPS traffic from the backend servers. This reduces the processing load on the servers and speeds up response times.

- Improved Security: These load balancers can inspect traffic at the application layer, allowing them to block malicious requests, filter certain types of traffic, and provide enhanced security features like DDoS protection.

Disadvantages of Layer 7 Load Balancers

- Higher Latency: Because they inspect application-layer data, Layer 7 load balancers introduce more latency than Layer 4 load balancers. However, this is often offset by the improved flexibility and functionality they offer.
- Complexity: Layer 7 load balancers are more complex to configure and manage. They require a deep understanding of the application and its traffic patterns to be used effectively.

10.2 Load Balancing Algorithms

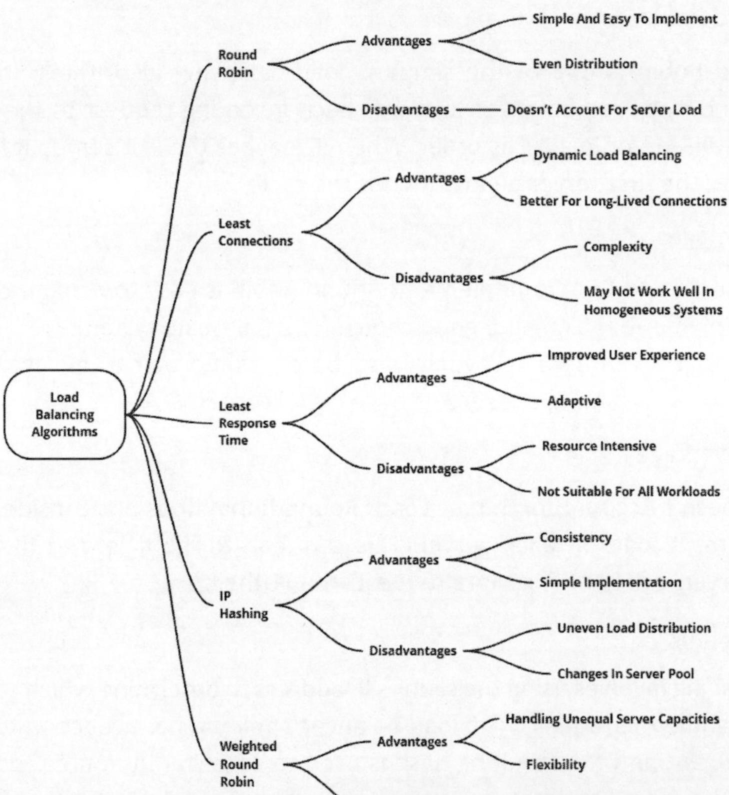

Figure – 10.4

Load balancing algorithms are divided into two main categories -

Static load balancing : Works on fixed or pre-configured rules and does not account for a server's current state within the group. Examples of static load balancing are - Round Robin, Weighted Round Robin, IP Hash

Dynamic load balancing : Load balancing is performed by considering the current state of each server within the group that makes it adaptable. Examples are - Least connection, Least response time, Weighted least connection, and Resource based.

The choice of algorithm depends on the use case and the type of system being deployed. Here are some of the most common load-balancing algorithms:

▶ Static Load Balancing

Round Robin

Round Robin is one of the simplest load-balancing algorithms. In this method, the load balancer forwards each incoming request to the next available server in a cyclic order. When it reaches the last server, it loops back to the first server and continues the cycle.

Advantages

- Simple and Easy to Implement: Round Robin is easy to configure and implement, making it a good choice for small-scale systems.
- Even Distribution: It evenly distributes traffic across all available servers, assuming the servers have equal capacity.

Disadvantages

- Doesn't Account for Server Load: Round Robin does not consider the current load on each server. This can lead to inefficiencies if some servers are handling more requests than others.

IP Hashing

IP Hashing involves using the client's IP address to determine which server will handle the request. The load balancer applies a hash function to the IP address, and the resulting hash is used to consistently route requests from the same IP address to the same server.

Advantages

- Consistency: IP Hashing ensures that the same client (identified by their IP address) is always routed to the same server. This can be useful for systems that require session persistence, where a user's session data needs to remain on a specific server.
- Simple Implementation: Once the hash function is set up, it's a straightforward method that doesn't require constant monitoring of server performance.

Disadvantages

- Uneven Load Distribution: IP Hashing can result in uneven load distribution, especially if some clients generate significantly more traffic than others. This can lead to overloading certain servers while others remain underutilized.
- Changes in Server Pool: If a server is added or removed from the pool, the hash distribution changes, potentially routing existing clients to new servers and breaking session persistence.

Weighted Round Robin

Weighted Round Robin is an extension of the basic Round Robin algorithm. It assigns a weight to each server based on its capacity or performance. Servers with higher weights receive more requests, while those with lower weights receive fewer requests.

Advantages

- Handling Unequal Server Capacities: This algorithm is useful when servers have different capacities. For example, if one server is more powerful than others, it can be assigned a higher weight to handle more traffic.
- Flexibility: You can adjust the weights dynamically based on the performance of each server, making this method adaptable to changing workloads.

Disadvantages

- Not Ideal for Constant Traffic: In scenarios where all servers have similar capacity or traffic remains constant, Weighted Round Robin might not offer significant advantages over simpler methods like Round Robin or Least Connections.

► Dynamic Load Balancing

Least Connections

The Least Connections algorithm directs traffic to the server with the fewest active connections. This ensures that servers that are already handling more traffic don't get overloaded.

Advantages

- Dynamic Load Distribution: This algorithm is ideal for systems where the traffic load varies greatly across servers. It balances the load dynamically by directing new requests to underutilized servers.
- Better for Long-Lived Connections: Systems that manage long-lived connections, such as video streaming or chat applications, benefit from this method because it avoids overloading specific servers.

Disadvantages

- Complexity: Least Connections is more complex to implement compared to Round Robin because it requires constant monitoring of the number of active connections on each server.
- May Not Work Well in Homogeneous Systems: In systems where all requests have similar resource demands, this algorithm may not offer significant advantages over simpler methods like Round Robin.

Least Response Time

The Least Response Time algorithm routes traffic to the server with the lowest response time for health monitoring requests. It considers both the number of active connections and the current response time of each server to decide which server should handle the next request.

Advantages

- Improved User Experience: By directing traffic to the server that responds the fastest, this algorithm can improve the overall user experience by minimizing latency and response times.
- Adaptive: It adapts dynamically to the performance of each server, ensuring that the most responsive server gets the next request.

Disadvantages

- Resource Intensive: This algorithm requires the load balancer to continuously monitor the response times of all servers, which can consume additional resources and increase complexity.

- Not Suitable for All Workloads: In cases where response time isn't the most important factor (e.g., batch processing systems), this algorithm may not provide significant benefits.

10.3 Use Cases for Load Balancing

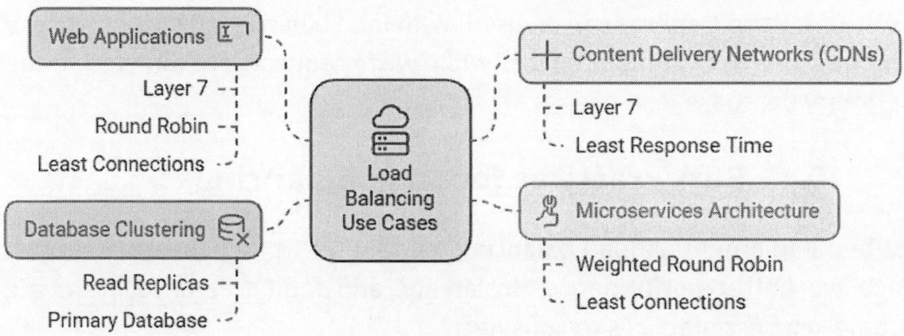

Figure – 10.5

Different use cases require different load-balancing strategies, and understanding when to use a specific algorithm or method is critical for ensuring optimal system performance. Below are some common use cases for load balancing:

Web Applications

For web applications that handle user requests and deliver dynamic content, load balancing helps distribute traffic across multiple web servers. A common approach is using a **Layer 7** load balancer with Round Robin or Least Connections, allowing the system to dynamically route user requests based on current load.

Content Delivery Networks (CDNs)

CDNs use load balancers to serve static content (like images and videos) from servers that are geographically closer to users. Layer 7 load balancers with **Least Response Time** algorithms are often used to ensure that users receive content with minimal latency.

Microservices Architecture

In a microservices architecture, load balancers distribute traffic across multiple services, each responsible for a different part of the application.

Load balancers ensure that traffic is routed to the appropriate service, and **Weighted Round Robin** or **Least Connections** can be used to balance the load between different instances of each service.

Database Clustering

In database systems with multiple replicas or shards, load balancers can distribute queries across different database nodes. For read-heavy systems, **Read Replicas** can be used, with load balancers distributing read requests across multiple replicas while write requests are directed to the primary database instance.

10.4 Best Practices for Load Balancing

When implementing load balancing, certain best practices can help you achieve better performance, scalability, and fault tolerance. Here are some key best practices to consider:

Health Checks

Configure regular health checks for each server in the load balancer's pool. These checks monitor the status of each server, ensuring that only healthy servers receive traffic. If a server becomes unresponsive or fails a health check, the load balancer can automatically redirect traffic to other servers.

SSL Termination

For applications using SSL/TLS for secure communication, it's a good practice to configure SSL termination at the load balancer. This means the load balancer handles the encryption and decryption of traffic, offloading this resource-intensive task from backend servers, improving their performance.

Session Persistence (Sticky Sessions)

For some applications, it's necessary to ensure that all requests from the same client are directed to the same server, especially in cases where session data is stored locally on the server. Session persistence, also known as sticky sessions, can be configured in the load balancer to achieve this.

Scalability and Auto Scaling

When using cloud platforms, enable auto-scaling features alongside load balancing. Auto-scaling automatically adds or removes servers based on real-time traffic, ensuring that the system can handle surges in demand without manual intervention.

Redundancy

For high-availability systems, ensure that your load balancer is redundant. This involves setting up multiple load balancers in different regions or availability zones to avoid a single point of failure. In case one load balancer fails, the other can take over and maintain service continuity.

Chapter 11

Caching

In a large-scale systems, where millions of requests might hit the server per minute, accessing the data from its origin e.g. database for every request can be costly.

Caching is a mechanism to temporarily store and render copies of data subset, mastered in a different storage, so that future requests can be served faster. Cached data reduces the load on databases and other services, improves response times, and enhances user experience.

Caching can be applied at various layers of technology including Operating system, Web applications, Database, and Networking that covers CDN (Content delivery networks) and DNS (Domain name services) layers.

11.1 Common Caches

CPU Level cache

It includes L1, L2 & L3 caching where L1 demonstrates highest speed but lowest data storage and L3 demonstrates lowest speed, compared to other L caches, but more storage in the group.

In-Memory Caches

In-memory caches, like Redis or Memcached, store data in RAM for quick access. These are fast and efficient because they leverage the speed of main memory to serve requests, reducing the need for disk I/O or network round trips.

- **Redis**: An in-memory key-value store that supports various data structures like strings, hashes, lists, and sets.

- **Memcached**: A simpler in-memory caching system, primarily used for storing key-value pairs in a fast, distributed manner.

Use Case

In-memory caches are ideal for scenarios like storing session data, user authentication tokens, or frequently accessed database queries (e.g., product catalog data in e-commerce).

Distributed Caches and Local Caches

- **Local Cache**: Local caches reside on the same server where the application is running. They are fast but limited in size, and since they are not shared across instances, they can't scale well in distributed systems. Example: Java's Guava library provides local caching capabilities.
- **Distributed Cache**: Distributed caches are shared across multiple application instances and nodes, enabling scalability. They store data centrally, which is accessible to all the servers in a cluster. Example: Redis can be used as a distributed cache across multiple web servers to ensure consistency and improve cache hit rates.

Use Case

Distributed caches are beneficial when you have multiple application servers and need to maintain a consistent cache state across all instances.

Browser Caching and Content Delivery Networks (CDNs)

- **Browser Cache**: Browsers can store static assets (CSS, JavaScript, images) locally on a user's machine. This reduces the need to download these assets from the server every time a user visits the site, improving load times and saving bandwidth.
- **Content Delivery Networks (CDNs)**: CDNs cache static content like images, videos, and scripts at various geographical locations. CDNs serve cached content to users from the nearest edge server, reducing latency and speeding up content delivery.

Use Case

CDNs are widely used for high-traffic websites, video streaming platforms, and applications that serve large amounts of static data, ensuring faster load times for users regardless of their geographic location.

Caching In a Web-Journey

The following diagram (Figure 11.1) illustrates a high-level overview of components and their typical interactions within a web journey. It highlights the implementation of caching at various layers of use.

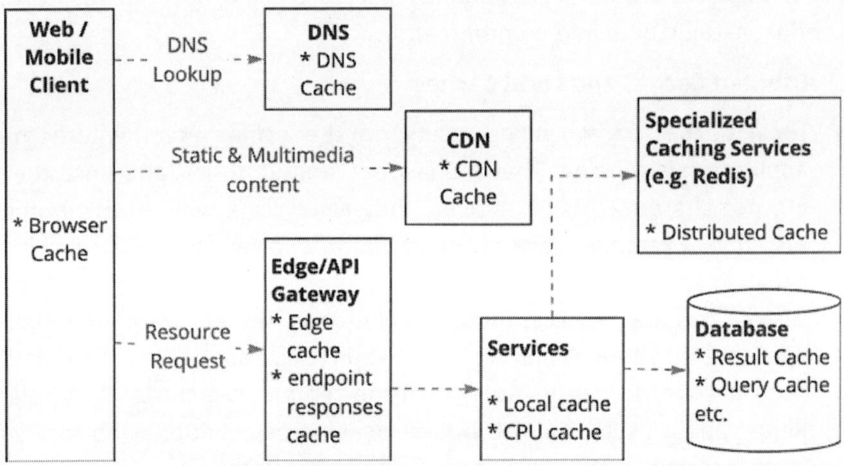

Figure – 11.1

11.2 Caching Strategies

Caching strategies help determine how data is cached and updated. Implementing the right strategy ensures optimal performance and consistency of cached data.

Write-Through Caching: In this strategy, data is written to both the cache and the underlying storage (database) at the same time. This ensures that the cache is always up-to-date with the latest data.

Advantage: Ensures data consistency as both the cache and database are updated simultaneously.

Disadvantage: Slightly slower write operations because of the dual writes (cache and database).

Write-Back Caching: Here, data is written to the cache first and updated to the underlying storage (database) later, usually in a batch process. This approach offers faster writes but at the risk of losing data if the cache crashes before the write-back to the database occurs.

Advantage: Faster write performance as data is written to the cache first.

Disadvantage: Potential data loss if the cache fails before updating the database.

Cache-Aside Pattern

In the cache-aside pattern, the application first checks the cache for the requested data. If the data is found (cache hit), it is returned immediately. If not (cache miss), the application retrieves the data from the database, stores a copy in the cache, and then returns the data.

Use Case

This strategy is widely used in systems where the cache is expected to store frequently accessed but relatively static data. For example, a product catalog that rarely changes can benefit from this approach.

Read-Through Cache

In the read-through caching pattern, the cache itself queries the underlying data store when a cache miss occurs. The application doesn't need to manually query the database; instead, the cache is responsible for fetching and storing the data automatically.

Use Case

This is useful for systems that require seamless access to data without the application managing the caching logic, such as content management systems (CMS) with dynamic content.

11.3 Cache Eviction Policies

Eviction policies dictate when cached data should be removed from the cache to make room for new data. Below are common cache eviction strategies:

Least Recently Used (LRU)

LRU removes the least recently accessed data when the cache is full. This approach assumes that recently accessed data is more likely to be accessed again, while older data can be discarded.

Use Case

LRU is ideal for systems where recently accessed data is more likely to be accessed again, such as user session management.

First-In-First-Out (FIFO)

In FIFO, the oldest data (the one that was added first) is evicted from the cache when space is needed for new data. It treats cached data in the order of arrival, without considering access frequency.

Use Case

FIFO is used in systems where data access patterns are predictable and time-bound, such as event logs.

Time-to-Live (TTL) or Expiry-Based Eviction

In this strategy, cached data is automatically evicted after a set period (TTL). This ensures that stale data is removed, keeping the cache updated with fresh content.

Use Case

TTL is useful for caching dynamic content, such as news articles, where old content can become irrelevant after a certain period.

11.4 Designing a Cache System

Designing an effective caching system involves careful planning of where and how caches are placed in the overall system architecture.

Cache Placement

Where to place the cache in a system depends on the specific use case:

- Client-Side Caching: Useful for reducing network traffic between the client and the server by storing static assets (e.g., images, CSS files) on the client-side.

- Server-Side Caching: Used to reduce the load on databases and backend services by storing frequently accessed data in memory (e.g., session data).
- Database Caching: Placing a cache layer between the application and the database can significantly improve query performance by storing frequently requested data.

Key Metrics to Monitor

- Cache Hit Rate: The percentage of requests that are served from the cache. A higher hit rate indicates that the cache is effective.
- Latency: The time taken to serve a request from the cache. Lower latency is crucial for improving user experience.
- Eviction Rate: The frequency at which items are evicted from the cache due to capacity limits.

11.5 Common Caching Pitfalls

While caching can significantly improve performance, improper use can lead to issues.

Over-Caching and Stale Data

Over-caching can result in stale data being served to users if the cache isn't properly invalidated or updated. For instance, if user profile information is cached but not updated when the user changes their details, it could lead to inconsistency between the cached and actual data.

Cache Consistency Issues

In distributed systems, ensuring cache consistency across multiple nodes is challenging. In scenarios where caches are not synchronized, different nodes may serve stale or inconsistent data. To mitigate this, proper **cache invalidation** strategies must be implemented.

Example: Implementing a Cache for a Web Application

Let's consider the case of an e-commerce platform that uses caching to improve performance. The platform implements:

- **In-memory caching** (Redis) to store product catalog data, reducing database lookups.

- **Browser caching** for static assets like CSS and JavaScript to reduce page load times.
- **CDN caching** for images and videos, ensuring fast delivery to users worldwide.

By leveraging multiple caching strategies, the platform significantly reduces database load, improves page load times, and ensures a smooth user experience, even during high-traffic events like Black Friday sales.

Chapter 12

Messaging Queues

Messaging queues decouple services and allow different parts of a system to communicate asynchronously, enabling better scalability, fault tolerance, and load management. By using queues, producers (services that generate messages) and consumers (services that use those messages) don't need to be available at the same time, making the system more resilient to fluctuations in load and failures.

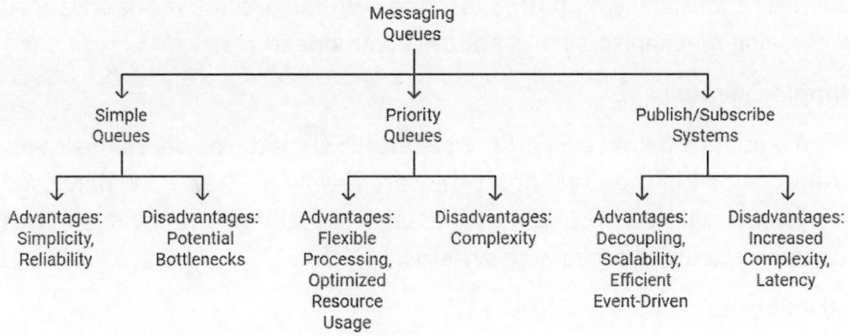

Figure – 12.1

Why to Use Messaging Queues

Decoupling: One of the most significant advantages of messaging queues is that they decouple the producer and consumer of the message. The producer can continue its operation without waiting for the consumer to process the message. This approach is especially useful in microservices architectures where different services may have varying processing times.

Load Levelling: Messaging queues act as buffers that help distribute workload evenly across consumers. If the incoming requests spike, the queue can store messages until consumers are ready to process them, preventing overloading any single consumer or service.

Reliability: Queues store messages persistently, ensuring that they are not lost even if the consumer is temporarily unavailable. This guarantees that no data is lost, which is crucial for applications requiring strong reliability guarantees, such as financial transaction systems.

Real-World Example: Consider a ridesharing application like Uber. When a user requests a ride, the system generates multiple events: checking nearby drivers, calculating ride fares, sending notifications, etc. Using messaging queues allows the system to handle each of these tasks independently, preventing any single component from becoming a bottleneck.

12.1 Types of Messaging Queues

There are various types of messaging queues, each tailored for specific use cases. The two primary types are simple queues and priority queues. Additionally, publish/subscribe systems provide more advanced messaging mechanisms for event-driven architectures.

Simple Queues

Simple queues follow a First-In-First-Out (FIFO) pattern, where messages are processed in the exact order they are received. They are widely used in systems where the order of message processing is critical, such as e-commerce order processing systems.

Advantages

- Simplicity: Simple queues are easy to implement and manage, making them ideal for straightforward tasks where maintaining message order is important.
- Reliability: Since the messages are processed sequentially, there's less chance of race conditions or disordering.

Disadvantages

- Potential Bottlenecks: If one message takes longer to process, subsequent messages are delayed, which can create bottlenecks in high-traffic systems.

Real-World Example: In an online store, a simple queue might be used to process orders. The system processes each order sequentially, ensuring that customers are billed in the same order their requests are received.

Priority Queues

In contrast to simple queues, priority queues allow messages to be processed based on their priority levels rather than the order in which they are received. This is useful for systems where some tasks are more critical than others, and delays in processing them could lead to significant issues.

Advantages

- Flexible Processing: Priority queues enable high-priority tasks to be processed faster, even if other lower-priority tasks are queued up.
- Optimized Resource Usage: Resources are allocated more effectively since critical tasks are handled promptly, reducing the risk of system failures.

Disadvantages

- Complexity: Implementing priority queues requires additional logic to assign and manage priorities, making the system more complex.

Real-World Example: In a hospital management system, patient data updates could be queued as normal tasks, while critical alerts (like emergencies) would be processed immediately due to their higher priority.

Publish/Subscribe Systems

Publish/Subscribe (Pub/Sub) systems take a more sophisticated approach to messaging by enabling one-to-many (fan-out), many-to-one (fan-in), and many-to-many communication between producers and consumers. Rather than directly sending messages to a single queue, publishers broadcast messages to "topics", and consumers (subscribers) receive those messages.

Advantages

- Decoupling of Producers and Consumers: Producers don't need to know the details of the consumers, and consumers can subscribe to multiple topics.
- Scalability: Pub/Sub models scale well in distributed systems as the number of subscribers can increase without affecting the performance of the producer.

- Efficient Event-Driven Architectures: This system works well for event-driven architectures, where events (messages) need to be consumed by multiple services or components.

Disadvantages

- Increased Complexity: Pub/Sub systems are more complex to design and manage, requiring attention to message filtering, topic management, and routing.
- Latency: Due to the broadcasting of messages to multiple subscribers, Pub/Sub can introduce latency in environments with high volumes of events.

Real-World Example: In a stock trading platform, a Pub/Sub system could be used where stock price changes (publishers) are broadcasted to multiple interested subscribers (such as mobile apps, trading algorithms, or notification services).

12.2 Popular Queue Systems

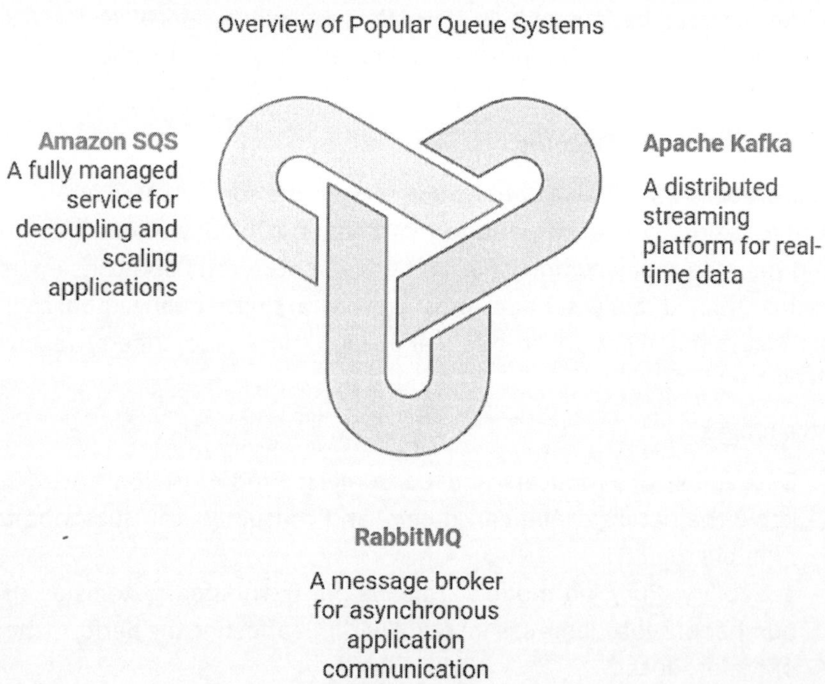

Figure – 12.2

There are several messaging queue systems available, each with its unique features and suited for different use cases. In this section, we'll explore some of the most popular queue systems: Apache Kafka, RabbitMQ, and Amazon SQS.

Apache Kafka

Apache Kafka is a distributed streaming platform often used for building real-time data pipelines and streaming applications. Kafka is known for handling high-throughput, fault-tolerant messaging at scale.

Key Features

- Scalability: Kafka is designed to handle millions of messages per second by distributing them across multiple nodes and partitions.
- Durability: Messages are stored on disk and replicated across the Kafka cluster, ensuring fault tolerance.
- Partitioning: Kafka uses partitions to parallelize message consumption, enabling high performance and scalability.
- Stream Processing: Kafka supports stream processing, allowing real-time transformations and aggregations of message data.

Use Cases

- Real-Time Data Streaming: Kafka is used by companies like LinkedIn and Netflix to power real-time analytics and recommendation engines.
- Event Sourcing: Kafka's ability to store ordered logs of events makes it an excellent choice for event-driven architectures.

Example: LinkedIn uses Kafka to handle billions of events per day, ensuring that data streams for user interactions, job recommendations, and notifications are processed in real-time.

RabbitMQ

RabbitMQ is a message broker that enables applications to communicate asynchronously. It is highly configurable, supporting various messaging patterns like direct exchange, fanout exchange, and topic exchange. It is important to know that Producers and consumers interact differently in RabbitMQ and Kafka. In RabbitMQ, the producer sends and monitors if the message reaches the intended consumer. On the other hand, Kafka producers publish messages to the queue regardless of whether consumers have retrieved them.

Key Features

- Flexible Routing: RabbitMQ supports advanced message routing techniques, allowing for greater control over how messages are delivered to consumers.
- Reliability: It guarantees message delivery by storing messages in queues and ensuring acknowledgments from consumers.
- Plugins and Extensions: RabbitMQ offers a variety of plugins to extend its functionality, such as clustering and monitoring tools.
- Acknowledgments and Retries: RabbitMQ ensures messages are processed exactly once, with support for retry mechanisms if consumers fail to process them.

Use Cases

- Task Queues: RabbitMQ is widely used in background task processing systems. For example, in an e-commerce platform, it could handle tasks like sending confirmation emails or processing orders asynchronously.
- Microservices Communication: RabbitMQ is commonly used in microservices architectures to handle asynchronous communication between services.

Example: Instagram uses RabbitMQ for internal communication between its services, ensuring that millions of user-generated events (such as likes, follows, and photo uploads) are processed reliably.

Amazon SQS

Amazon Simple Queue Service (SQS) is a fully managed message queuing service provided by AWS. It enables developers to decouple and scale microservices, distributed systems, and serverless applications.

Key Features

- Fully Managed Service: AWS handles the underlying infrastructure, allowing developers to focus on building applications rather than managing queues.
- Scalability: SQS can handle a virtually unlimited number of messages, automatically scaling to meet demand.
- Message Retention: Messages can be retained for up to 14 days, ensuring that no data is lost even if the consumer is unavailable for an extended period.

- Integration with AWS Ecosystem: SQS integrates seamlessly with other AWS services like Lambda, SNS, and EC2, making it a preferred choice for cloud-native applications.

Use Cases

- Decoupling Microservices: SQS is often used in microservices architectures to buffer and route messages between loosely coupled services.
- Asynchronous Processing: SQS can be used to offload long-running tasks, such as image processing or video transcoding, from the main application thread.

Example: Amazon itself uses SQS internally to power services like order processing system. Orders are placed into an SQS queue and processed by backend services asynchronously.

12.3 Designing for Messaging Queues

Designing a messaging queue system is a complex task that requires careful consideration of factors such as scalability, reliability, and fault tolerance. Below are best practices and design considerations for implementing messaging queues, especially in microservices architectures.

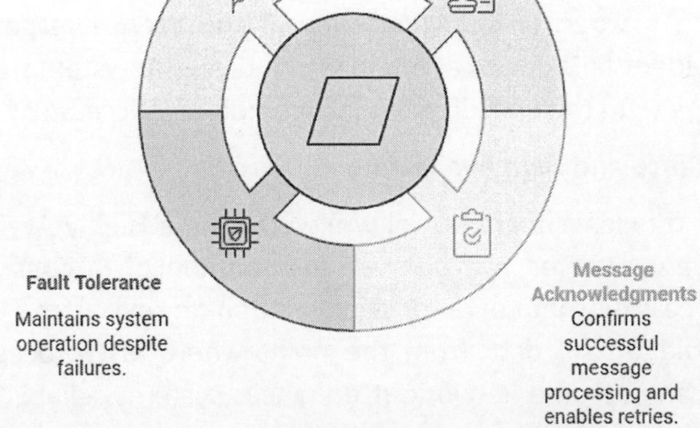

Figure – 12.3

Idempotency in Messaging Queues

One of the most critical aspects of designing a robust messaging queue system is ensuring idempotency. In distributed systems, messages may be delivered multiple times due to retries or failures. Ensuring that consumers can handle duplicate messages without adverse effects is crucial.

Idempotent Operations: An operation is idempotent if it can be applied multiple times without changing the result beyond the initial application. For instance, deducting an item from inventory should only happen once, even if the message is processed multiple times.

Example: In a payment processing system, a message to charge a customer's credit card must be idempotent. If the charge is processed multiple times, it should only result in a single debit.

Message Acknowledgments and Retries

Messaging queues must have mechanisms for ensuring that messages are processed successfully. This involves acknowledging the receipt of a message and retrying if processing fails.

Message Acknowledgments: The consumer must acknowledge a message once it has been successfully processed. If no acknowledgment is received, the message remains in the queue and is retried after a timeout.

Retries: If a message fails to be processed (e.g., due to a transient error), the system should retry the message. However, it is essential to limit retries to prevent an endless loop of failed messages.

Example: In a video encoding pipeline, if the service responsible for encoding videos fails due to a temporary outage, the system should retry the message until the encoding process completes successfully.

Fault Tolerance and High Availability

Messaging queues is a great tool while creating a Highly Available and Fault Tolerant system. In a pub-sub environment, if a consumer fails before processing some data for reasons then on revival, the consumer can get hold of the data from the point where last processing was successful and resume its work. It enhances systems reliability in case of fail-over.

Key Considerations

- Replication: Queue data should be replicated across multiple servers or data centers to ensure that no messages are lost if one server goes down.
- Failover Mechanisms: If a consumer fails, another instance should be able to take over processing without interrupting the system.

Example: In a financial system processing real-time transactions, RabbitMQ might be configured in a highly available mode, where messages are replicated across multiple brokers to ensure that no transactions are lost if a broker fails.

Scalability in Messaging Queues

As traffic grows, the messaging queue system must be able to scale to meet increasing demand. This involves both vertical scaling (increasing the capacity of individual nodes) and horizontal scaling (adding more nodes to the system).

- Horizontal Scaling: Most modern messaging systems, such as Kafka and SQS, support horizontal scaling, where additional nodes or partitions can be added to distribute the load.
- Sharding: In systems like Kafka, messages can be partitioned or sharded across multiple nodes. Each partition handles a subset of messages, allowing the system to process messages in parallel.

Example: Spotify uses Kafka to manage a massive stream of user activity data. By horizontally scaling Kafka across many nodes and partitioning the data, Spotify ensures that it can process millions of events per second, providing real-time insights and recommendations.

Chapter 13

Security

As modern systems become more interconnected, they also become increasingly vulnerable to attacks, data breaches, and unauthorized access. Security isn't just about protecting data but is also about ensuring the overall integrity, availability, and confidentiality of a system.

Proper security implementation must be an integral part of system design, not an afterthought. It ensures that systems are resilient against a variety of threats, including:

Data Breaches: Unintended exposure of sensitive data (personal information, financial records, etc.).

Unauthorized Access: Attackers gaining access to systems they shouldn't have access to.

Denial of Service (DoS) Attacks: Overloading systems to the point where legitimate users cannot access services.

Malware and Exploits: Malicious software and vulnerabilities that can compromise a system's integrity.

Security must be considered at multiple layers such as - network, application, and data - to safeguard against a wide array of threats.

Why Security is Critical in System Design

- **Data Privacy Regulations**: With laws such as GDPR (General Data Protection Regulation) and CCPA (California Consumer Privacy Act), organizations can face legal consequences if they fail to remain compliant.
- **User Trust**: Users expect their data to be handled securely. A security breach can destroy trust and cause irreversible damage to a company's reputation.
- **Financial Impact**: Security breaches often result in fines, legal fees, and the cost of mitigating the attack.

13.1 Common Security Practices in Applications

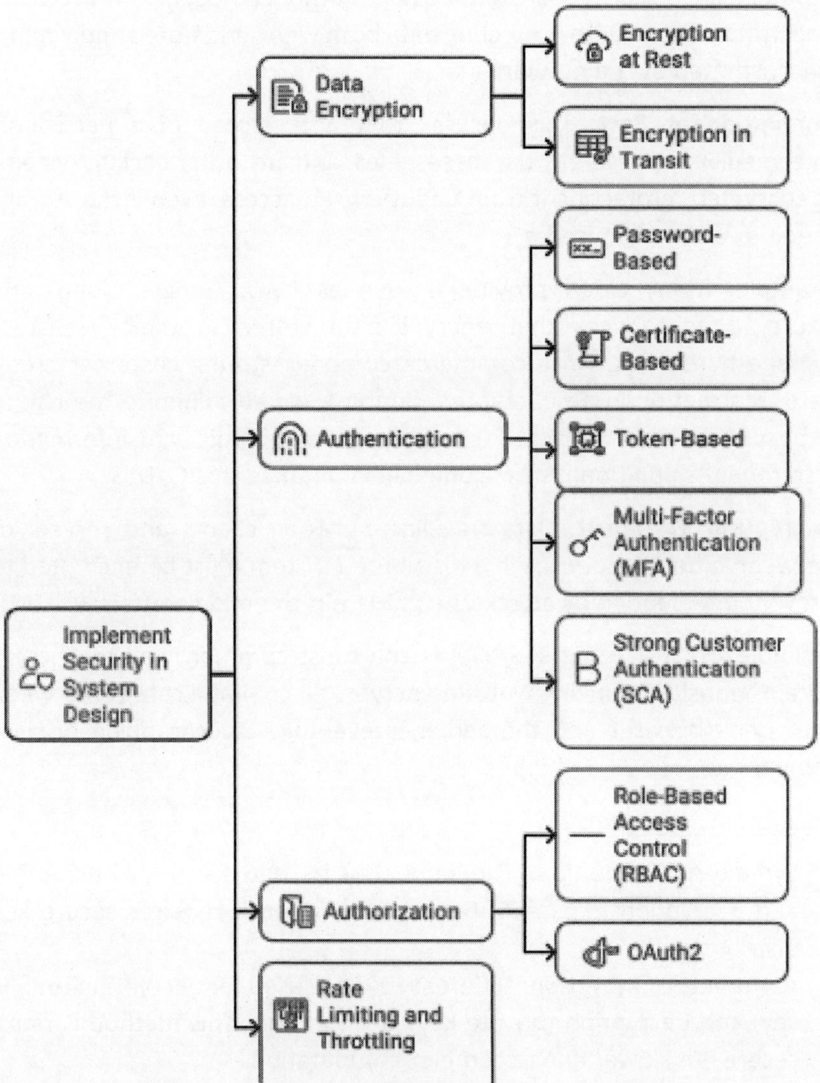

Figure – 13.1

Implementing security in system design involves a variety of practices. Some of the most critical areas include data encryption, authentication and authorization, and rate limiting and throttling.

Data Encryption (At Rest, In Transit)

Data encryption is the process of converting data from plain text into an unreadable format, ensuring that only authorized users can access it. Encryption is critical to protecting data both when it is stored and when it is transmitted over a network.

Encryption at Rest: This ensures that data stored in a persistent/ intermediary storage e.g. databases, files, and any other backup systems is encrypted, protecting it from unauthorized access, even if the storage medium is compromised.

Example: Many cloud providers, such as AWS, Google Cloud, and Azure, offer services that encrypt data stored in their persistent storage by default. An e-commerce company storing customer credit card information in an encrypted database would minimize the risk of exposure during a breach. Remember, storing credit card information also requires additional strict compliance outlined by PCI/DSS.

Encryption in Transit: Data traveling between clients and servers or between different services in a distributed system must be encrypted to prevent interception by attackers e.g. Man-in-the-middle-attack (MITM).

Example: HTTPS (using TLS/SSL) is the most common way to encrypt data in transit. A banking website encrypts all communications between the user's browser and the server, preventing eavesdropping or data tampering.

<u>Encryption Algorithms</u>

- Symmetric Encryption: The same key is used for both encryption and decryption (e.g., AES, DES). While faster, it requires secure key distribution.
- Asymmetric Encryption: Different keys are used for encryption (public key) and decryption (private key), such as RSA. This method is more secure but slower due to complex computation.

Authentication and Authorization

These are two pillars of access control in security systems. It is essential to understand the details for both and the related methods that can be used to achieve them.

▶ **Authentication**: This verifies that a user or system is who they claim to be. Strong authentication practices ensure that unauthorized entities are kept out.

Common Authentication Methods: Authentication methods vary in their approach and security level, each providing distinct advantages based on context and risk. Here are key types commonly implemented to secure systems.

1. Password-Based Authentication

- **Description**: Users authenticate by providing a password. Password-based systems must enforce strong password policies, such as requiring complexity (length, special characters) and secure storage.
- **Security**: Passwords should be hashed using algorithms like bcrypt or PBKDF2 to prevent easy decryption in case of data breaches.
- **Limitations**: Vulnerable to brute force attacks and phishing without additional security measures.

2. Certificate-Based Authentication

- **Description**: Utilizes digital certificates for verification. Each user is issued a unique certificate, which is validated by a trusted certificate authority.
- **Application**: Commonly used in secure applications like VPNs, corporate systems, and SSL/TLS for server authentication.
- **Security**: Offers high security as it's difficult to forge certificates, but it requires robust certificate management.

3. Token-Based Authentication

- **Description**: Users log in using tokens generated by a physical device (e.g., smartphone, security key, or smart card). Tokens can serve as a passwordless solution or part of multi-factor authentication (MFA).
- **Operation**: Users verify their credentials once and receive a time-limited token, reducing the need for repeated logins.
- **Advantages**: Reduces password dependency and enables secure access across devices.
- **Example**: Mobile authenticator apps like Google Authenticator generate tokens valid for 30 seconds.

4. Multi-Factor Authentication (MFA)

- **Description**: Increases security by requiring at least one additional form of authentication beyond the password.
- **Authentication Factors**:
  - Something you know: A password or PIN.
  - Something you have: A device, token, or security key.
  - Something you are: Biometrics like fingerprint or facial recognition.

Example: Google 2FA, where users enter a password followed by a one-time code sent to their phone.

5. Strong Customer Authentication (SCA) (Specific to the Financial Sector)

- **Requirement**: SCA an authentication method. It is a regulatory requirement in the European Union under the Payment Services Directive 2 (PSD2), designed to increase the security of online payments and reduce fraud. Mandated by the Revised Payment Services Directive (PSD2), SCA is designed to protect against online payment fraud.
- **Authentication Factors**:
  - Knowledge (e.g., PIN or password)
  - Possession (e.g., a device or token)
  - Inherence (e.g., biometric verification)
- **Security Enhancements**:
  - Transaction Risk Analysis: Detects fraudulent patterns in real-time.
  - Dynamic Linking: Authenticates transactions by linking the authorization code to the payment amount and recipient.
  - Independent Elements: Ensures that compromising one factor doesn't affect others, strengthening overall security.

► **Authorization**: Once authenticated, authorization determines what actions a user can perform on the available resources. It enforces least privilege principles, ensuring users only access what they need.

Common Authorization Protocols

- Role-Based Access Control (RBAC): Users are assigned roles, and roles are given permissions to access certain resources. This is commonly used in corporate environments where different teams need different levels of access to company systems.

- OAuth2: A widely used protocol that allows applications to request limited access to a user's account without exposing credentials. For example, when you log into a third-party app using your Google or Facebook account, OAuth2 is often used to authorize access.

Example: In a banking system, a customer service agent might be authorized to view customer profiles but not modify financial data. Similarly, OAuth2 is used in many APIs to provide secure third-party access to services without exposing sensitive information.

Rate Limiting and Throttling

Rate limiting and throttling help prevent misuse of system resources by limiting the number of requests a client can make in a specified time window. This practice prevents Denial of Service (DoS) attacks, protects against excessive usage, and ensures fair use of resources.

Rate Limiting: Sets a hard cap on the number of requests allowed during a period. For instance, a user might only be able to make 100 API requests per minute. Exceeding the limit results in rejected requests.

Example: APIs from services like Twitter and GitHub implement rate limiting to prevent abuse. If a user tries to access the API more than the allowed number of times per minute, they will receive an HTTP 429 "Too Many Requests" response.

Throttling: A technique that manages incoming requests by gradually reducing the response rate or quality of service as usage approaches a defined limit. Unlike rate limiting, which strictly blocks requests beyond a set threshold, throttling allows for controlled, gradual adjustments. This helps to prevent sudden drops in performance and ensures a smoother experience, especially under heavy load, by slowing down responses or prioritizing essential requests rather than fully denying access.

Example: Cloudflare uses throttling to manage sudden traffic spikes. If a website experiences a surge in traffic, Cloudflare might throttle access for non-critical users to ensure the core functionality remains available.

13.2 Secure API Design

APIs are a common point of attack in many modern systems, as they often expose a direct interface to sensitive data or services. Designing secure APIs is critical to safeguarding data and preventing unauthorized access.

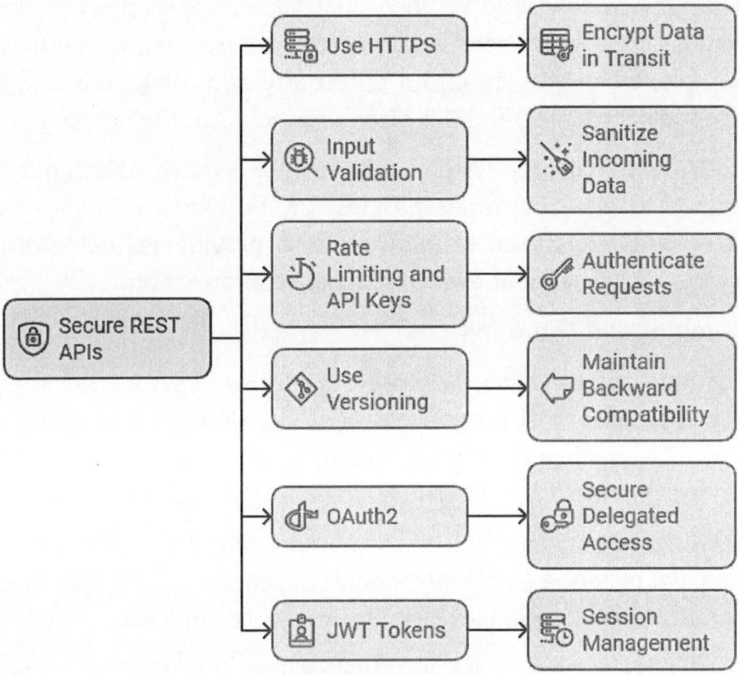

Figure – 13.2

Best Practices for Securing REST APIs

REST APIs are widely used due to their simplicity and scalability, but they can introduce vulnerabilities if not secured properly. Below are some best practices:

- **Use HTTPS**: Always secure your API endpoints with HTTPS to ensure data is encrypted in transit. HTTP communication can be intercepted, exposing sensitive data such as API keys, tokens, and user data.

  Example: Most modern APIs, like Google Maps API or Stripe's payment API, only accept HTTPS requests.

- **Input Validation**: Validate and sanitize all incoming data. Never trust user input, as this is a common vector for injection attacks like SQL injection or cross-site scripting (XSS).

  Example: Use libraries like OWASP ESAPI (Open Web Application Security Project - Enterprise Security API) to ensure all input data is sanitized, preventing attacks that could manipulate the API by passing malicious payloads.

- **Rate Limiting and API Keys**: Implement rate limiting, and require API keys for authenticating requests. This ensures that only authorized users can access the API and that services cannot be abused by malicious actors.
- **Use Versioning**: Implementing API versioning (e.g., v1, v2) is a key practice to avoid disrupting existing clients when updating your API. By designating versions, you ensure that clients relying on older features or structures can continue functioning seamlessly, while new versions introduce enhancements or changes. This approach prevents breaking changes from impacting all users at once and provides flexibility for gradual client migration to updated versions.

  Example: GitHub's API uses versioning in its URL structure to ensure backward compatibility and secure upgrade paths.

OAuth2 and JWT Tokens

OAuth2 (Open Authorization) and JWT (JSON Web Tokens) are critical for modern API security. They provide secure ways to manage access control and authorization, allowing users to authenticate once and then access multiple resources securely.

OAuth2: In essence it is an authorization protocol, a popular open standard for token-based authentication and authorization. OAuth2 enables secure, delegated access to resources, allowing users to authenticate with one service (e.g., Google) and grant access to a third-party application.

Example: When a user logs into an app using their Facebook or Google account, OAuth2 is often used to handle the secure authentication and authorization flow without sharing user credentials.

JWT Tokens: JWT tokens are compact, URL-safe tokens that represent claims about a user. These tokens can be passed around as credentials and are used for session management in stateless applications.

How it works

- After the user authenticates, the server generates a JWT containing claims (user ID, roles, expiration time).
- The JWT is signed using a secret or public/private key pair, ensuring that it cannot be tampered with.
- The client stores the token (usually in local storage or cookies) and sends it with each request to access protected resources.

Example: A JWT token might be issued to a user who logs into an e-commerce website. The token is then used to authenticate subsequent requests, such as adding items to a cart or placing an order.

13.3 Handling Data Breaches

Even with robust security measures, data breaches remain a possibility. A prepared response plan can help minimize damage and expedite recovery. This section covers essential practices for managing data breaches effectively.

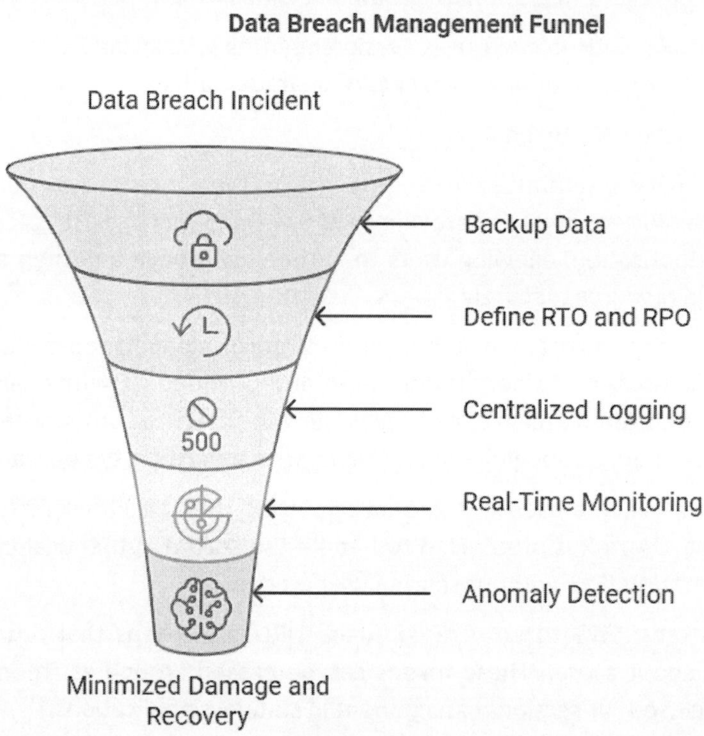

Figure – 13.3

Regular Backups: Maintaining regular backups is essential to ensure data can be quickly restored if needed. Backups should be encrypted and stored securely, ideally off-site or in a different geographic location, to prevent data loss in a breach.

Example: AWS provides automated snapshot services for their cloud databases. These snapshots can be configured for regular intervals and are stored in multiple availability zones, ensuring secure and reliable recovery options if data is compromised.

Disaster Recovery Plans: A disaster recovery plan (DRP) outlines the steps for restoring systems and data in the event of a breach. Two critical parameters in a DRP are the Recovery Time Objective (RTO) and Recovery Point Objective (RPO)

- **RTO:** The maximum time allowed for restoring systems to operational status after failure.
- **RPO:** The maximum acceptable data loss measured in time, a guiding element to determine how often backups should be taken. E.g. if RPO is 10mins then the system must ensure a mechanism to retain data older than 10 mins from current time (say delta backup every 10mins).

Example: After Target's 2013 data breach, which compromised over 40 million credit card records, the company overhauled its DRP to prioritize data integrity, encryption standards, and timely recovery. As part of these improvements, they set RTO and RPO goals to minimize downtime and data loss.

Centralized Logging: Centralized logging collects logs from all system components, creating a single source of truth for security monitoring. Tools like the ELK Stack (Elasticsearch, Logstash, Kibana) make it possible to monitor, search, and visualize logs in one place, enhancing the efficiency of incident response.

Example: Netflix leverages ELK Stack and Grafana to centralize and visualize logs in real time. This setup enables security teams to monitor suspicious events and respond rapidly to any potential breach.

Real-Time Monitoring and Alerts: Real-time monitoring tools such as Prometheus, Nagios, and Datadog are essential for spotting unusual activity as it happens. These tools trigger alerts for patterns indicative of breaches, enabling prompt action to mitigate threats.

Example: A company employing Datadog may detect an unusual volume of login attempts, which could signal a brute-force attack. The monitoring system alerts security teams immediately, enabling swift containment and investigation.

Anomaly Detection: Machine learning algorithms applied to logs and user behavior data can help in anomaly detection by identifying deviations from normal patterns. This approach can reveal potential breaches that might otherwise go unnoticed.

Example: AWS GuardDuty uses machine learning and threat intelligence to detect abnormal behavior and flag it. For instance, if it detects that sensitive data is being accessed from an unusual location or under unusual conditions, it can alert administrators for further investigation.

By defining RTOs, RPOs, and using tools like AWS GuardDuty, organizations can create a layered, resilient approach to detecting and managing potential data breaches. This ensures both a rapid response and an ongoing enhancement of security measures.

PART 2

BEHAVIORAL INTERVIEWS

Chapter 14

Introduction to Behavioral Interviews

Applying for a new job involves more than your just technical proficiency. Employers are equally interested in your ability to handle practical difficulties and professional settings.

This section of the book has been created relevant to companies that follow the pattern as used by major tech organizations such as FAANG (Facebook, Amazon, Apple, Netflix, and Google). Everything from comprehending the goal of behavioral interviews to becoming proficient with the S.T.A.R. method—a potent approach for organizing your responses—will be covered.

Beyond that, we will also covers typical scenarios you can run into and ways for responding to them. You'll discover how to modify your answers so that they align with the company's principles and culture as well as stress management strategies for interviews and how to be well-prepared.

This guide gives you the self-assurance and resources you need to ace behavioral interviews, whether you're wanting to start your career or have already experienced it. Let's get started by going over the essentials of these interviews and how to be well-prepared.

Figure – 14.1

You'll encounter a variety of questions during a job interview, but the behavioral interview can be the trickiest. Let's start by answering - what does that actually mean?

The purpose of behavioral interviews is to evaluate your past performance in handling real-world scenarios. In cases where you have not worked in any organization, your experience from education time should be used. These interviews are not meant to be about make-believe situations or your technical skills alone; rather, they are meant to uncover how you have overcome obstacles, worked with colleagues, and resolved issues in real-world work settings. The concept is simple: your previous experience and actions give you important insight into your future performance potential.

Example: Instead of asking, "Do you know how to manage a team?" a behavioral interviewer might ask, "Can you tell me about a time when you led a team to achieve a specific goal?"

This shift in questioning helps employers gauge your problem-solving abilities, teamwork, leadership skills, and how you handle stress or conflict.

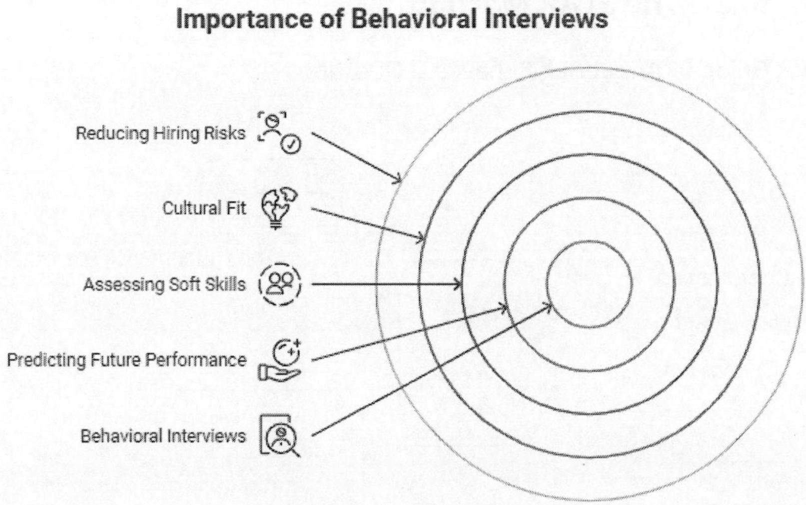

Figure – 14.2

14.1 Importance

Here are a few reasons why employers place significant emphasis on behavioural interview:

1. Predicting Future Performance: By looking at how you've handled situations in the past, employers can make informed guesses about how you'll perform in similar scenarios in their company.
2. Assessing Soft Skills: Technical skills are crucial, but soft skills like communication, adaptability, and teamwork are equally important. Behavioral interviews help assess these attributes.
3. Cultural Fit: Employers want to ensure that you'll fit well within their company's culture. Your responses can reveal your values, work ethic, and how you interact with others.
4. Reducing Hiring Risks: Hiring is a cost intensive process. A suitable people match provides long term stability for the company from hiring perspective. It is a win-win for both a company and a staff. Behavioral interviews help minimize this risk by providing deeper insights into a candidate's capabilities and compatibility.

Think of it this way, Technical tests can show you know how to code, but behavioral interviews show how you'll collaborate with your team, handle deadlines, and navigate workplace challenges.

14.2 The STAR Method

Your Guide to Answering Behavioral Questions

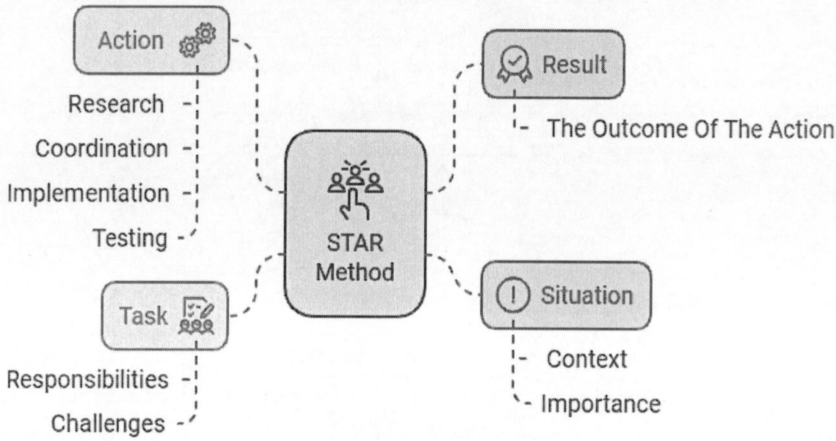

Figure – 14.3

One of the most effective and powerful ways to navigate behavioral interviews is by using the S.T.A.R. method. This structured approach helps you provide clear and comprehensive answers, ensuring you cover all the essential aspects of your experience.

STAR stands for:

Situation (S): Start by setting the context. Describe the scenario you were in i.e. where this happened and why it was important. This helps the interviewer understand the background of your story.

Example: "In my previous role as a software developer at XYZ Company, we were working on a major update for our flagship product."

Task (T): Explain your responsibility or the challenge you faced. What was expected of you in that situation?

Example: "I was tasked to lead the integration of a new payment gateway to improve transaction speeds and user experience."

Action (A): Detail the specific steps you took to address the task or challenge. Focus on what you did, not what the team did. Share how you made progress.

Example: "I began by researching various payment gateways to find one that met our technical requirements. After selecting the most suitable option, I coordinated with the design and backend teams to implement the integration. I also developed a testing protocol to ensure the new system worked seamlessly."

Result (R): Share the outcome of your actions. Whenever possible you must use quantifiable metrics to demonstrate the impact. It can be cost savings related, related to time to market, quality or efficiency improvement in percentages or customer satisfaction increase.

Example: "As a result of the integration, transaction speeds increased by 25%, and we saw a 15% boost in user satisfaction scores. This update also reduced payment-related support tickets by 30%."

Why Use the STAR Method?

- Clarity: It provides a clear structure, making your answers easy to follow.
- Completeness: Ensures you cover all necessary aspects of your experience.
- Relevance: Helps you stay focused on the question, avoiding unnecessary details.
- Impact: Highlights the positive outcomes of your actions, showcasing your effectiveness.

<u>Example of a STAR-Based Answer:</u>

Question: "Can you describe a time when you had to handle a difficult project?"

Answer:

- Situation: "In 2024, at ABC Corp, we had a tight deadline to launch a new feature for our mobile app."
- Task: "I was responsible for coordinating the development and ensuring timely delivery."
- Action: "I organized daily stand-up meetings to monitor progress, identified potential bottlenecks early, and reallocated resources where necessary. I also facilitated open communication between the design and development teams to address any issues promptly."
- Result: "We successfully launched the feature two days ahead of the schedule, which was well-received by users and led to a 20% increase in app downloads."

Tips for Using the STAR Method

1. Prepare in Advance: Think of several experiences from your past roles that showcase different skills and qualities. Practice structuring them using STAR.
2. Be Specific: Avoid vague statements. Provide enough detail to make your story compelling and believable.
3. Focus on Your Role: Even if you were part of a team, emphasize what *you* specifically did to contribute to the outcome.
4. Quantify Results: Numbers provide concrete evidence of your achievements. Include metrics to showcase the impact you made.
5. Stay Relevant: Tailor your stories for the job you're applying for. Highlight experiences that demonstrate the skills and qualities the employer is seeking.

14.3 Common Behavioral Interview Questions

To help you prepare, here are some common behavioral interview questions you might encounter, along with guidance on how to approach them using the STAR method:

1. Tell me about a time when you had to solve a complex problem.

   Situation: Describe the problem.
   Task: Explain your responsibility in addressing it.
   Action: Detail out the steps you took to solve it.
   Result: Share the outcome and what you learned.

2. Describe a situation where you had to work as part of a team.

   Situation: Set the scene of the team project.
   Task: Explain your role within the team.
   Action: Detail out how you collaborated with team members.
   Result: Share the success of the project and your contribution to it.

3. Can you share an example of a time when you had to adapt to a significant change at work?

   Situation: Outline the change.
   Task: Explain your role in adapting to it.
   Action: Detail out the steps you took to manage the change.
   Result: Share the positive outcome and any improvements made.

4. Tell me about a time when you received critical feedback. How did you handle it?

   Situation: Context of the feedback.
   Task: Explain your responsibility to respond.
   Action: Detail out how you processed and acted on the feedback.
   Result: Share improvements made and how it benefited your work.

5. Describe a time when you went above and beyond your job responsibilities.

   Situation: Describe the scenario where you took extra steps.
   Task: Explain what was expected of you.
   Action: Detail out the additional actions you took.
   Result: Share the impact of your extra efforts.

Preparing Your Own Stories

- **Reflect on Past Experiences:** Many of us have executed most of the mentioned situations (without noticing) while at work. These could include challenges, successes, teamwork, leadership, conflict resolution, and more. Think about all such various situations you've encountered in your career. That will help you put the stories into a correct frame.
- **Diversify Your Examples:** Have a range of stories ready that showcase different skills and qualities. This ensures you're prepared for a variety of questions.
- **Practice Out Loud:** Rehearse your STAR responses to gain confidence and ensure fluency during the actual interview.

14.4 Adapting to Different Interview Styles

While the STAR method is highly effective, it's essential to remain flexible. Some interviewers might prefer a more conversational approach or ask follow-up questions to delve deeper into your experiences. Here's how to stay adaptable:

1. **Be an Active Listener:** Pay attention to the interviewer's questions and any hints about the depth of detail they expect.
2. **Be Concise Yet Detailed:** Strive for a balance between brevity and providing enough information to make your story compelling.

3. **Engage with the Interviewer:** Be prepared to elaborate on parts of your story if the interviewer shows interest or asks for more details.
4. **Stay Calm:** If a question catches you off guard, take a moment to gather your thoughts. It's perfectly acceptable to ask for clarification or a moment to think before responding.

Example of an Adaptable STAR Response for Software Engineers

Question: "Tell me about a time when you had to manage multiple priorities."

Answer

- Situation: "At XYZ Company, I was simultaneously working on three critical features for a product release, each with tight deadlines and dependencies on different teams."
- Task: "My responsibility was to ensure all features were developed, tested, and deployed on time without causing any delays in the release schedule."
- Action: "I created a priority list based on business impact and technical complexity. I broke down each feature into smaller tasks and allocated time for code reviews and testing. I also collaborated closely with cross-functional teams (QA, Product, and Design) to make sure there were no bottlenecks and that dependencies were addressed early. To manage my workload, I automated repetitive tasks like deployment and testing where possible."
- Result: "All three features were completed ahead of schedule, with minimal bugs, and contributed to a successful product release. The product team praised the efficient collaboration, and the automation of tasks reduced deployment time by 20%."

Follow-Up Engagement

Interviewer: "How did you decide which tasks to delegate?"

Answer: "I evaluated each team member's expertise and workload, assigning specific parts of the features that matched their strengths. For instance, I delegated some of the testing tasks to a team member with strong test automation skills, which helped speed up the QA process. This approach not only ensured efficiency but also provided opportunities for team members to take ownership of critical tasks."

Final Thoughts

By understanding the purpose of behavioral interview and mastering the STAR method, you can effectively showcase your experiences and skills. Remember to prepare diverse stories, practice your responses, and stay adaptable during the interview. The following chapters will delve deeper into preparing for interviews, tackling common questions, and specific strategies for FAANG companies. With thorough preparation and the right mindset, you'll be well-equipped to excel in your next behavioral interview.

Chapter 15

The Essentials of Interview Prep

Preparing for a behavioral interview requires more than just brushing up on your past experiences. It's about understanding the company, the role you're applying for, and how your skills align with the job requirements. This chapter will guide you through a comprehensive preparation process to ensure you're fully equipped for your interview.

15.1 Researching the Company Culture

Understanding the company culture gives you valuable insights into what the company values in its employees, how it operates, and what kind of work environment you can expect. It allows you to tailor your interview responses to align with their values and shows that you've done your homework and are genuinely interested in becoming part of their team. It also helps you determine whether the company is a good fit for you, which is just as important as you being a good fit for them.

Start with the Company Website

Begin your research on the company's official website. Pay close attention to the 'About Us', 'Mission', 'Impact' and 'Careers' sections. These pages usually provide a wealth of information about the company's values, goals, and the type of people they are looking to hire. Look for any specific mention of the qualities or attributes they value in their employees.

Explore Social Media and Blogs

Next, check out the company's social media profiles—LinkedIn, Twitter, Facebook, Instagram—and their blogs if they have one. These platforms can give you a more casual insight into the company's culture. Pay attention to the tone of their posts, the kind of content they share, and how they interact with their audience and employees. This can give you a sense of the company's personality and priorities.

Employee Reviews on Sites Like Glassdoor

Websites like Glassdoor and Indeed feature employee reviews that can provide unfiltered insights into the company's culture. Look for patterns in what employees say about work-life balance, management styles, and overall satisfaction. While individual reviews can be subjective, common themes in reviews can give you a reliable picture of the company's work environment.

Look for News Articles and Press Releases

Search for recent news articles, interviews with company executives, and press releases. These sources can give you a sense of the company's latest initiatives, achievements, and challenges. Often, these elements are closely tied to the company's cultural and strategic priorities.

Network with Current or Former Employees

If possible, reach out to current or former employees of the company on LinkedIn. To make it easy, try to find people who are already your 1st or 2nd connection on LinkedIn. A brief chat can provide first-hand insights that are not available through public sources. Ask them about their daily work life, how the company responds to challenges, project scope, team dynamics, success metrics and what they enjoy most about working there.

Attend Company Events and Webinars

Attending public events or webinars hosted by the company can also give you a feel for the company's culture. How they handle these events, the type of content they present, and the way they interact with participants can reflect their cultural priorities and operational style.

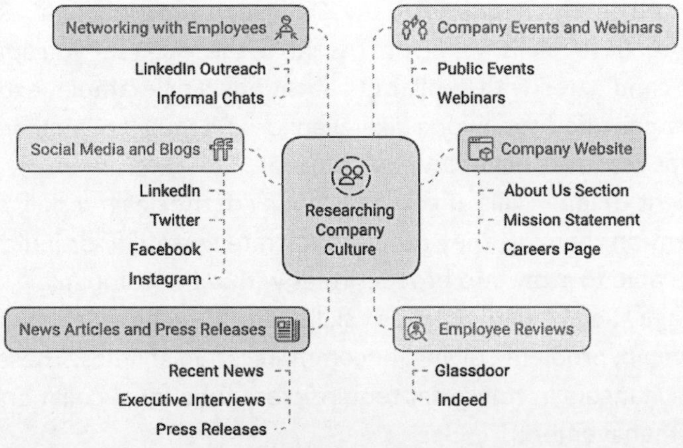

Figure – 15.1

15.2 Understanding the Role and Its Responsibilities

Before stepping into an interview, you must have a comprehensive understanding of the role you're applying for. This ensures that you can effectively communicate how your skills and experiences align with the company's needs. It also allows you to present yourself as the perfect candidate and shows the interviewer that you are serious about the position and have taken the time to prepare thoroughly.

1. Study the Job Description Thoroughly

- Read Every Detail: Absorb every detail in the job posting, focusing on the listed responsibilities and required competencies. This will give you a clear idea of what the employer is looking for.
- Highlight Key Phrases: Pay attention to recurring skills or qualities emphasized in the job description (JD). These are likely the most desired aspects of the role so highlight them for yourself to focus more on them.

2. Analyze Essential Skills and Qualifications

- Essential Qualifications: Look for specific degrees, professional certifications, or technical skills mentioned in the JD. Ensure you can discuss these during the interview.
- Experience Requirements: Pay attention to the experience level requested, such as "entry-level" or "5+ years of experience." Tailor your discussion points to match these requirements.

3. Desired Skills and Qualifications

- Preferred but Not Required: Many JDs include a section for "Desired" or "Nice-to-Have" skills. While not essential, these can set you apart from other candidates with similar qualifications. For example, experience with a specific framework (like Django or React) or familiarity with DevOps practices might give you an edge.
- Highlight Unique Skills: If you possess any of the desired skills, be sure to mention them, as they can demonstrate versatility or indicate that you're able to grow into broader roles within the company.
- Leverage Soft Skills: Desired skills often include attributes like leadership, problem-solving, or communication abilities. These can be game-changers in roles that require cross-functional collaboration or team management.

4. Research Similar Roles

- Investigate Job Titles: Look into similar roles both within the company and across the industry to get a sense of broader expectations. Keep in mind, however, that the same job title can have varying responsibilities depending on the company's needs. While this research can give you a general idea, do not to rely solely on the title for understanding the role.
- Look at Career Paths: Use LinkedIn to explore professionals in similar roles. This can give you insights into the skills, qualifications, and achievements that stand out in the field. However, make sure to cross-check these profiles with the JD to ensure you're aligning with the company's specific needs.

5. Prepare Relevant Examples

- Match Experiences with Job Needs: Reflect on your professional history to find examples where you've demonstrated the key skills needed for the position Here's how you can do that effectively:
  - Identify Key Skills: Start by reviewing the JD and identifying the core skills the company is looking for, such as technical expertise, teamwork, problem-solving, or leadership abilities.
  - Reflect on Relevant Experiences: Think back on your career and find instances where you've demonstrated these key skills. These could be from previous jobs, internships, or even academic projects. Focus on experiences that closely align with the job requirements.
  - Provide Concrete Examples: Once you've identified the relevant experiences, frame them using specific examples. Highlight situations where you used these skills to achieve a positive result. This not only shows that you have the necessary qualifications but also that you can apply them effectively in real-world scenarios.
  - Customize for the Role: Tailor your examples to match the job's context. For instance, if the position requires project management experience, highlight times when you successfully managed a project, detailing how you handled challenges, collaborated with teams, and met deadlines.
- Scenario-Based Preparation: Consider preparing detailed stories using the STAR method that relate directly to the JD (Refer to 'The Star Method' in the previous chapter).

15.3 Reviewing the Job Description

A JD is more than just a list of duties; it's a roadmap for your interview preparation. By carefully reviewing the JD, you can identify the key areas to focus on and tailor your responses accordingly.

As discussed above, you should list the primary responsibilities and emphasized asks. Here's an example how to put these both in action

Job Published : Software Engineer at ABC Corp

Main Duties:

- Writing clean, maintainable code in Java and Python.
- Collaborating with cross-functional teams (Product, Design, and QA) to deliver new features.
- Participating in code reviews and providing feedback to peers.
- Identifying and fixing bugs in a timely manner.

Here the role involves a mix of coding, collaboration, and troubleshooting. It mentions "writing clean, maintainable code", "collaborating with cross-functional teams to deliver new features" and "fixing bugs". These tasks are likely core to the role, meaning the company expects you to spend a significant amount of time coding and working closely with other departments.

By identifying core tasks, you understand that mastering both clean coding practices and teamwork are critical to success in this role. You can then prepare examples that highlight your strengths in these areas for the interview.

Identify Desired Skills and Competencies

Desired Skills, while they may not be mandatory for the role, can significantly set you apart from other candidates who only meet the Required Skills. These desired skills often show that you bring added value to the team, making you a more versatile and adaptable hire. Here's a breakdown of why and how they differ:

- Required Skills are the essential qualifications or experiences needed to perform the job's core responsibilities. For example, if the job is for a software engineer, required skills might include proficiency in specific programming languages like Python or Java.
- Desired Skills are additional skills that the company would like but doesn't require. These could be more advanced technical expertise,

industry knowledge, or even soft skills like leadership or creative problem-solving. They are often mentioned in the JD as "nice-to-have", "desired", or "preferred."

<u>Example</u>

Job Published : Software Engineer at ABC Corp

Desired Skills (Nice-to-Have)

- Familiarity with cloud services like AWS or Google Cloud.
- Experience in DevOps and CI/CD pipelines.
- Leadership experience or mentoring junior developers.

In this case, the *Desired Skills* provide an opportunity for you to stand out if you have experience with AWS or DevOps, or if you've led teams in the past. While not mandatory, these skills can set you apart by demonstrating a broader skill set and showing potential for future growth in the role, like leading projects or implementing cloud-based solutions.

Understand Required Experience

When looking at JDs, you need to grasp the level of expertise and type of work the role requires. Here's how to break it down:

► Years of Experience

Look for any specific experience requirements such as "3+ years of software development experience" or "entry-level role." This shows the level of proficiency expected for the position.

► Project Types

If the JD mentions types of projects or industries (e.g., "experience in building e-commerce platforms" or "worked in healthcare tech"), it helps you align your past work with what the company needs.

Example: If a company is hiring for a Senior Backend Developer and mentions "experience building microservices for scalable platforms," you should reference any relevant projects where you've built microservices. This could be the kind of work they expect you to handle regularly.

Certifications

If the job mentions certifications like "AWS Certified Solutions Architect" or "PMP certification," and you have them, it's important to show how those certifications have prepared you to succeed in the role.

Example: Let's say you're applying for a Data Analyst role and the preferred qualifications mention "experience with data visualization tools like Tableau." Even if it's not required, having Tableau experience can set you apart, especially if you've used it to drive insights in a previous role.

Analyze Language and Tone

The language and tone of the JD can offer insight into the company culture and values. Paying attention to this helps you tailor your approach.

► Cultural Hints

A JD written in a casual, conversational tone might suggest a more flexible and laid-back work environment, while a formal tone could indicate a traditional corporate culture. Knowing this allows you to adjust how you present yourself.

► Values

Pay attention to recurring keywords like "collaboration," "innovation," or "customer focus." These are signals of what the company values most and should guide how you frame your skills and experiences in the interview.

Example: If the JD frequently mentions "collaboration," emphasize your experience working in cross-functional teams and highlight any projects where teamwork played a key role in your success.

15.4 Reflecting on Past Experiences

Reflecting on your past experiences is a basic need for preparing strong responses in a behavioral interview. It allows you to draw upon real examples that demonstrate your qualifications and fit for the role. It also helps you assess your career progression and articulate your value proposition clearly. This way, you will be ready to discuss your background in a way that resonates with the employer's needs.

1. Structure Responses Using the STAR Method

- **Use STAR:** When preparing your examples, structure them using the **STAR Method** (Situation, Task, Action, Result). [Refer to 'The Star Method' in the previous chapter] for a more detailed explanation of the STAR method and how to effectively apply it during interviews.
- **Craft Compelling Stories:** Develop concise, clear stories around your key experiences. Ensure you have a variety of examples that highlight

different skills, such as leadership, problem-solving, or teamwork. This will prepare you to answer a wider range of questions.

2. Reflect on Challenges

- **Overcoming Obstacles:** Think about times you faced challenges and how you overcame them, focusing on your problem-solving and resilience.
- **Growth Opportunities:** Consider experiences that led to personal or professional growth. These stories can be particularly compelling as they demonstrate your ability to learn and improve.

3. Assess Achievements

- **Identify Major Achievements:** Focus on the accomplishments you are most proud of, especially those that made a significant impact on your previous employers. This could include successfully completed projects, efficiency improvements, or innovations that benefited the team or organization.
- **Highlight Recognitions:** Include any recognitions or awards you have received, as these serve as powerful indicators of your skills, performance, and contributions. These could come from leadership, peers, or external organizations.
- **Certifications**: If you hold relevant certifications, be sure to highlight these as well. Certifications, especially those that your employer values or emphasizes, can add credibility and further validate your qualifications. These can demonstrate your commitment to continuous learning and staying updated in your field.

15.5 Creating a Portfolio of Personal Success Stories

One of the most powerful tools you can bring to a behavioral interview is a portfolio of personal success stories. These are well-prepared examples of your past work that demonstrate that you are capable of clear, structured communication.

1. **Select Impactful Stories:** Include a diverse set of examples that showcase different competencies, such as technical skills, problem-solving, teamwork, or leadership. This variety prepares you to answer a wider range of questions. Create a grid with common

behavioral questions on one axis and your key experiences on the other. This helps you see which stories can be used to answer multiple questions. For each question, identify which experience or story you would use to answer it

2. **Structure Stories Clearly:** Reference the STAR format for telling stories as we introduced earlier. Provide enough context to make the story compelling, but don't overwhelm the listener with unnecessary information. Focus on the key actions and outcomes to maintain interest.
3. **Anticipate Probing:** Be prepared for the interviewer to ask follow-up questions to dig deeper into your story. Think about what additional details they might want to know and how you would answer. Ensure that all parts of your story are consistent and that you can back up your claims with evidence if asked.
4. **Practice Delivery:** Practice telling your stories out loud to ensure you can convey them confidently and succinctly. Rehearsing helps you get comfortable with your delivery and ensures you don't stumble over key points. **In addition,** don't underestimate the value of practicing with family members or peers. They can offer helpful feedback, even if they aren't in your field, and help you refine both your presentation and your storytelling.

Final Thoughts

Preparing for a behavioral interview is a multifaceted process that goes beyond simply reviewing your resume. It involves deep research into the company culture, a thorough understanding of the role, and a reflective analysis of your past experiences. By creating a portfolio of personal success stories, practicing your STAR responses, and planning for common behavioral questions, you can walk into your interview fully prepared to impress. The next chapters will dive deeper into specific behavioral questions, techniques for tailoring your responses to different companies, and strategies for mastering the interview process.

Chapter 16

Mastering Common Questions and Approaches

In this chapter, we'll explore a range of common behavioral interview questions, providing detailed guidance on how to approach each one. Mastering these questions will give you a significant advantage in your interviews, helping you to stand out as a confident and well-prepared candidate.

16.1 Categories of Behavioral Questions

Behavioral interview questions generally fall into several broad categories. Understanding these categories will help you recognize the type of question being asked and prepare an appropriate response.

Problem-Solving and Critical Thinking

- These questions assess your ability to analyze situations, identify problems, and develop solutions.
- Example Question: "Tell me about a time when you identified a significant problem at work and how you resolved it."

Leadership and Initiative

- These questions focus on your leadership qualities and your ability to take charge or make decisions when necessary.
- Example Question: "Describe a situation where you took the lead on a project. What was the outcome?"

Teamwork and Collaboration

- These questions evaluate how well you work with others, including your communication, cooperation, and conflict-resolution skills.

- Example Question: "Give an example of a time when you had to work closely with a team to achieve a goal."

Adaptability and Flexibility

- These questions measure your ability to adapt to change, manage stress, and stay effective in unpredictable situations.
- Example Question: "Can you describe a time when you had to adapt to significant changes at work?"

Time Management and Prioritization

- These questions assess how well you manage your time, prioritize tasks, and handle multiple responsibilities.
- Example Question: "Tell me about a time when you had to manage competing priorities. How did you handle it?"

Communication and Interpersonal Skills

- These questions explore how effectively you communicate with others, both in writing and verbally.
- Example Question: "Describe a situation where you had to explain a complex concept to a non-technical audience."

Handling Conflict and Difficult Situations

- These questions test your ability to navigate conflicts, manage disagreements, and maintain professionalism under pressure.
- Example Question: "Tell me about a time when you had to resolve a conflict within your team."

Achievement and Motivation

- These questions delve into your past achievements, your drive to succeed, and how you stay motivated in challenging situations.
- Example Question: "What is an accomplishment you're particularly proud of, and how did you achieve it?"

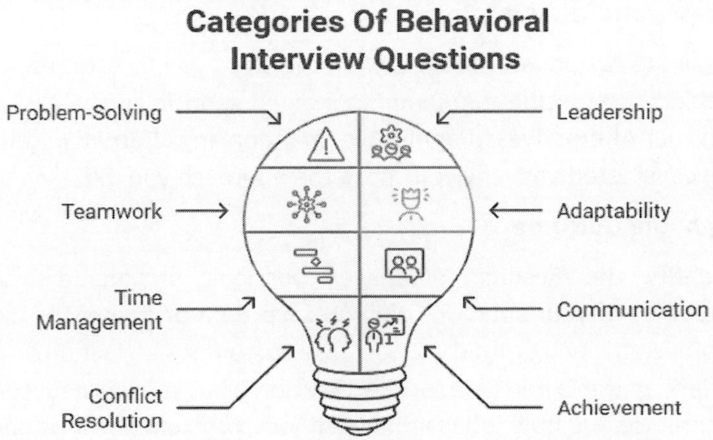

Figure – 16.1

In the next section, we'll see how you can approach each of these categories.

16.2 Problem-Solving and Critical Thinking

Problem-solving and critical thinking are highly valued skills in any workplace. Employers want to see that you can identify issues, analyze them effectively, and develop practical solutions. Here's how to approach these questions:

Understand the Problem

- Clarify the Question: Make sure you fully understand the problem being asked about. Don't hesitate to ask for clarification if needed.
- Identify the Core Issue: Break the problem down to its core components. What was the main challenge? What factors contributed to it?

Demonstrate Your Analytical Skills

- Step-by-Step Analysis: Walk the interviewer through your thought process. Explain how you identified the problem, what factors you considered, and how you prioritized them.
- Tools and Methods: Mention any specific tools, methodologies, or frameworks you used to analyze the problem (e.g., SWOT analysis, root cause analysis).

[Link for SWOT analysis - https://www.wordstream.com/blog/ws/2017/12/20/swot-analysis]

Showcase Your Solution

- Detail the Actions You Took: Explain the steps you took to resolve the problem. Be specific about your role and responsibilities.
- Consider Alternatives: If applicable, mention any alternative solutions you considered and why you chose the approach you did.

Highlight the Outcome

- Quantify the Results: Whenever possible, provide measurable outcomes of your solution. Did you save time or money, or did you improve efficiency, or did you increase customer satisfaction?
- Reflect on the Experience: Briefly mention what you learned from the experience and how it has influenced your problem-solving approach in subsequent situations.

Example STAR Response

Question: "Can you tell me about a time when you identified a significant problem at work and how you resolved it?"

Situation: "In my previous role as a project manager, I noticed that our team was consistently missing deadlines due to unclear communication and misaligned expectations."

Task: "I was responsible for identifying the root cause of these delays and finding a solution to improve our workflow."

Action: "I conducted a thorough review of our project management processes and discovered that there was no standard protocol for communication and task delegation. I introduced a new system that included regular status meetings, clear documentation of roles and responsibilities, and a shared project management tool that everyone could access."

Result: "As a result of these changes, our team's on-time delivery rate improved by 40% within three months, and overall project efficiency increased significantly."

16.3 Leadership and Initiative

Leadership isn't just about managing people; it's about taking initiative, making decisions, and driving projects forward. When responding to leadership questions, focus on demonstrating your ability to influence others, make strategic decisions, and lead by example.

Set the Scene

- Context is Key: Start by setting the context for your leadership experience. Was it a formal leadership role or an instance where you stepped up without an official title?
- Team Dynamics: Briefly describe the team or group you were leading, including any relevant challenges or dynamics.

Demonstrate Initiative

- Identify the Need for Leadership: Explain why leadership was needed in this situation. Was there a lack of direction? A critical decision that needed to be made?
- Take the Lead: Describe how you took the initiative to lead. Did you volunteer for the role, or were you asked to step up?

Showcase Your Leadership Style

- Decision-Making: Explain the decisions you made and why. Highlight how you considered different perspectives or gathered input from your team.
- Communication: Discuss how you communicated your vision or plan to the team. How did you ensure everyone was on the same page?

Highlight the Impact

- Team Success: Focus on the positive outcomes of your leadership. Did your team meet its goals? Overcome challenges?
- Personal Reflection: Reflect on what you learned from this leadership experience and how it has shaped your approach to leading others in the future.

<u>Example STAR Response</u>

Question: "Describe a situation where you took the lead on a project. What was the outcome?"

Situation: "In 2022, at my previous company, we were tasked with launching a new product line, but the project was behind schedule, and team morale was low."

Task: "As the most experienced member of the team, I took it upon myself to lead the project and get it back on track."

Action: "I started by re-aligning the team with clear goals and timelines. I held daily stand-up meetings to track progress and address any roadblocks.

I also delegated tasks based on each team member's strengths and ensured open communication throughout the project."

Result: "Under my leadership, we successfully launched the product on time, and it became one of our best-selling lines. The team also reported higher satisfaction and a stronger sense of collaboration."

16.4 Teamwork and Collaboration

Teamwork and collaboration are essential in almost every role. Employers want to see that you can work well with others, contribute to group efforts, and help resolve conflicts. Here's how to approach these questions:

Emphasize Collaboration

- Highlight Team Efforts: Make it clear that you value teamwork and understand the importance of collaborating with others to achieve a common goal.
- Your Role in the Team: Explain your specific role within the team and how you contributed to the group's success.

Focus on Communication

- Effective Communication: Discuss how you ensured clear and effective communication within the team. Did you facilitate meetings or provide updates or resolve misunderstandings?
- Listening and Supporting: Highlight how you listened to others' ideas and supported your teammates when needed.

Showcase Conflict Resolution Skills

- Addressing Conflicts: If there were any conflicts or disagreements within the team, explain how you helped resolve them. What steps did you take to ensure a positive outcome?
- Maintaining Professionalism: Emphasize your ability to maintain professionalism and keep the team focused on the goal, even during challenging situations.

Highlight the Outcome

- Team Success: Describe the team's accomplishments and how your collaboration contributed to the success of the project.
- Personal Reflection: Reflect on what you learned about teamwork and how you apply these lessons in future collaborative efforts.

Example STAR Response

Question: "Give an example of a time when you had to work closely with a team to achieve a goal."

Situation: "In my role as a marketing coordinator, our team was tasked with launching a new advertising campaign for a key client."

Task: "I was responsible for coordinating the efforts of the design, content, and sales teams to ensure the campaign was cohesive and aligned with the client's objectives."

Action: "I organized weekly meetings to keep everyone informed and on track. I also created a shared project timeline to ensure all teams were aware of their deadlines and deliverables. When a disagreement arose between the design and content teams over the creative direction, I facilitated a meeting to discuss the pros and cons of each approach and helped the team reach a consensus."

Result: "The campaign was launched successfully, resulting in a 25% increase in client engagement and a 15% boost in sales. The client was thrilled with the results, and the team was recognized for their collaborative effort."

16.5 Adaptability and Flexibility

In today's fast-paced work environments, adaptability and flexibility are critical. Employers want to know that you can handle change, manage stress, and remain effective when the unexpected happens. Here's how to approach these questions:

Set the Scene

- Describe the Change: Start by explaining the change or unexpected event that required you to adapt. This could be a shift in project scope, a new team dynamic, or a sudden challenge.
- Initial Reaction: Briefly mention your initial reaction to the change and how you began to assess the situation.

Demonstrate Your Adaptability

- Step-by-Step Response: Walk the interviewer through the steps you took to adapt to the change. How did you prioritize your tasks? What strategies did you use to stay focused and productive?

- Problem-Solving: Highlight any problem-solving skills you used to manage the change effectively. Did you develop a new approach or seek input from others?

Showcase Flexibility

- Willingness to Pivot: Emphasize your willingness to pivot and take on new responsibilities or roles as needed. Did you volunteer to help in a new area? Learn a new skill?
- Positive Attitude: Discuss how you maintained a positive attitude and kept the team motivated during the transition.

Highlight the Outcome

- Successful Adaptation: Focus on the successful outcome of your adaptability. Did the project succeed despite the challenges? Did your flexibility lead to new opportunities or improvements?
- Personal Reflection: Reflect on what you learned from the experience and how it has improved your ability to handle change in the future.

Example STAR Response

Question: "Can you describe a time when you had to adapt to significant changes at work?"

Situation: "In my previous job as a software developer, our company underwent a major restructuring, and my team was merged with another department with a completely different focus."

Task: "I was responsible for adapting to this new team dynamic while continuing to meet my project deadlines."

Action: "I took the initiative to learn about the other department's processes and tools, which were unfamiliar to me. I also made an effort to build relationships with the new team members by setting up one-on-one meetings and offering to help with their projects where I could. To manage the added workload, I re-prioritized my tasks and adjusted my schedule to accommodate the new demands."

Result: "Despite the significant changes, I successfully delivered my projects on time and even helped streamline some of the new team's processes. My manager praised my adaptability, and I was able to contribute to the overall success of the department during the transition."

16.6 Time Management and Prioritization

Effective time management and prioritization are essential in any job, particularly in roles with multiple responsibilities or tight deadlines. Employers want to see that you can manage your time well, prioritize tasks effectively, and stay organized under pressure.

Set the Scene

- Describe the Workload: Start by explaining the context in which you had to manage your time or prioritize tasks. Was it a particularly busy period? Were there multiple projects with competing deadlines?
- Identify the Challenges: Briefly outline the main challenges you faced in managing your workload.

Demonstrate Time Management

- Organizational Tools: Discuss any tools or methods you used to manage your time, such as to-do lists, project management software, or time-blocking techniques.
- Prioritization Criteria: Explain how you prioritized tasks. What criteria did you use to determine which tasks were most important or urgent?

Showcase Your Decision-Making

- Balancing Priorities: Highlight how you balanced competing priorities. Did you delegate tasks? Negotiate deadlines? Adjust your schedule?
- Flexibility: Emphasize your ability to stay flexible and adjust your plan as needed while still meeting deadlines.

Highlight the Outcome

- Successful Task Completion: Focus on how your time management and prioritization led to the successful completion of tasks or projects.
- Efficiency Gains: If applicable, mention any efficiency gains or improvements in productivity that resulted from your approach.

<u>Example STAR Response</u>

Question: “Tell me about a time when you had to manage competing priorities. How did you handle it?”

Situation: “In my role as a project coordinator, I was managing two major projects that were both due within the same week, and both had critical deadlines that couldn’t be moved.”

Task: "My task was to ensure that both projects were completed on time and to the highest standard."

Action: "I started by creating a detailed timeline for each project, identifying key milestones and deadlines. I then prioritized tasks based on urgency and importance, and delegated smaller tasks to team members who had the capacity to help. I also communicated with both project stakeholders to keep them informed of progress and manage their expectations. To ensure I stayed on track, I used project management software to monitor progress and make adjustments as needed."

Result: "Both projects were completed on time and exceeded client expectations. My ability to manage competing priorities was recognized by my manager, and I was later promoted to a more senior project management role."

16.7 Communication and Interpersonal Skills

Strong communication and interpersonal skills are critical in almost any role, as they impact your ability to work effectively with colleagues, clients, and other stakeholders. Employers want to see that you can communicate clearly, listen actively, and build positive relationships with others.

Set the Scene

- Describe the Situation: Start by explaining the context in which your communication skills were critical. Was it a team project? A client presentation? A conflict resolution situation?
- Identify the Communication Challenge: Briefly outline the main communication challenge you faced in this situation.

Demonstrate Effective Communication

- Clear and Concise Communication: Discuss how you ensured your communication was clear and concise. Did you use visual aids? Tailor your message to the audience?
- Active Listening: Highlight how you listened actively to others' input or concerns. Did you ask clarifying questions? Provide feedback?

Showcase Interpersonal Skills

- Building Relationships: Explain how you built or maintained positive relationships with colleagues, clients, or stakeholders. Did you use empathy? Show appreciation?

- Conflict Resolution: If applicable, discuss how you resolved any conflicts or misunderstandings through effective communication.

Highlight the Outcome

- Positive Communication Outcome: Focus on the positive outcomes of your communication efforts. Did you successfully deliver a message? Resolve a conflict? Strengthen a relationship?
- Reflection: Reflect on what you learned from the experience and how you apply these communication skills in your current role.

Example STAR Response

Question: "Describe a situation where you had to explain a complex concept to a non-technical audience."

Situation: "In my role as a software engineer, I was asked to present a new technical solution to a group of senior managers who didn't have a technical background."

Task: "My task was to ensure that the managers understood the solution and its benefits so that they could make an informed decision."

Action: "I prepared a presentation that simplified the technical details and focused on the benefits and potential impact of the solution. I used visual aids, such as diagrams and charts, to help illustrate the key points. During the presentation, I made sure to avoid technical jargon and encouraged the managers to ask questions if anything was unclear."

Result: "The presentation was well-received, and the managers appreciated the clarity of the explanation. They approved the solution, and it was successfully implemented, resulting in a significant improvement in system performance."

16.8 Conflict Resolution

Conflict is inevitable in any workplace, and how you handle it can significantly impact team dynamics and project outcomes. Employers want to see that you can manage disagreements professionally and find constructive solutions. Here's how to approach these questions:

Set the Scene

- Describe the Conflict: Start by explaining the context of the conflict. Who was involved? What was the disagreement about?

- Identify the Stakes: Briefly outline why resolving the conflict was important. How could it have impacted the team or project?

Demonstrate Conflict Resolution Skills

- Approach to Resolution: Discuss the steps you took to resolve the conflict. Did you facilitate a discussion? Mediate between parties? Find a compromise?
- Communication and Empathy: Highlight how you used communication and empathy to understand both sides of the issue and find a solution that worked for everyone.

Showcase Professionalism

- Maintaining Professionalism: Emphasize your ability to remain calm and professional throughout the conflict. How did you ensure that the situation didn't escalate?
- Focus on the Goal: Discuss how you kept the team focused on the overall goal, despite the disagreement.

Highlight the Outcome

- Positive Resolution: Focus on the positive outcome of the conflict resolution. Was the issue resolved amicably? Did the team become stronger as a result?
- Reflection: Reflect on what you learned from the experience and how it has influenced your approach to handling conflicts in the future.

Example STAR Response

Question: "Tell me about a time when you had to resolve a conflict within your team."

Situation: "In my previous role, there was a significant disagreement between two team members about the best approach to complete a critical project."

Task: "My task was to mediate the conflict and find a solution that would allow the project to move forward without delay."

Action: "I arranged a meeting with both team members to discuss their concerns and perspectives. I listened carefully to each side and acknowledged their valid points. I then facilitated a brainstorming session to explore potential compromises. We agreed on a hybrid approach that incorporated elements from both perspectives, which allowed the project to continue smoothly."

Result: "The conflict was resolved, and the project was completed on time. Both team members appreciated the compromise and were able to work together more effectively in the future. The experience reinforced the importance of communication and collaboration in achieving team success."

16.9 Achievement and Motivation

Questions about your achievements and motivation provide an opportunity to showcase your drive, determination, and the impact of your work. Employers want to see that you are motivated to succeed and can deliver tangible results. Here's how to approach these questions:

Set the Scene

- Describe the Achievement: Start by explaining the context of your achievement. What was the project or goal? Why was it important?
- Identify the Challenge: Briefly outline any challenges or obstacles you faced in achieving this goal.

Demonstrate Your Motivation

- Internal and External Motivators: Discuss what motivated you to achieve this goal. Was it a personal drive for success? A desire to help your team or company? Recognition from others?
- Overcoming Obstacles: Highlight how your motivation helped you overcome any obstacles or challenges along the way.

Showcase Your Accomplishment

- Detail the Achievement: Provide specific details about your accomplishment. What did you do? How did you go above and beyond?
- Quantify the Results: Whenever possible, provide measurable outcomes of your achievement. Did you increase sales? Improve efficiency? Win an award?

Highlight the Impact

- Positive Impact: Focus on the positive impact of your achievement on the team, company, or clients. How did it contribute to the overall success of the organization?
- Reflection: Reflect on what this achievement taught you about yourself and how it has influenced your approach to work in the future.

Example STAR Response

Question: "What is an accomplishment you're particularly proud of, and how did you achieve it?"

Situation: "In my role as a sales manager, I was tasked with turning around a struggling sales region that had consistently underperformed for several quarters."

Task: "My goal was to increase sales in the region by at least 20% within six months."

Action: "I started by conducting a thorough analysis of the region's sales data and identified key areas for improvement. I then implemented a new sales strategy that focused on targeted marketing, improved customer outreach, and enhanced training for the sales team. I also set clear, achievable targets for each sales representative and provided ongoing support and feedback."

Result: "Within six months, sales in the region increased by 25%, exceeding my target. The team's morale and performance improved significantly, and the region became one of the top-performing areas in the company. This accomplishment taught me the importance of strategic planning, team motivation, and continuous improvement."

Final Thoughts

Mastering behavioral interview questions is a crucial step in preparing for your interviews. By understanding the different categories of questions and learning how to approach each one with the STAR method, you can effectively showcase your skills, experiences, and qualifications. The next chapter will highlight specific strategies for tailoring your responses to different companies, particularly FAANG companies, to ensure you present yourself as the ideal candidate for any role.

With these detailed approaches, you're well on your way to excelling in behavioral interviews and making a strong impression on potential employers. Remember, preparation is key, and with thorough practice and reflection, you can confidently navigate even the toughest behavioral questions.

Chapter 17

Decoding FAANG Interviews

When preparing for behavioral interviews with FAANG (or alike) companies - **F**acebook (now Meta), **A**mazon, **A**pple, **N**etflix, and **G**oogle - you need to understand that these companies have high expectations and a unique set of values. The behavioral interview questions at these companies are not only designed to assess your skills and experiences but also to determine if you fit into their distinct cultures. This chapter brings the specific behavioral questions often asked at FAANG companies and provide detailed guidance on how to tailor your responses to meet their expectations.

Figure – 17.1

17.1 Drivers for the process

These companies seek a candidate who can demonstrate a great balance of top technical talent as well as aligned with their unique cultures and values. Here's why behavioral interviews are a staple in their hiring:

1. Emphasis on Leadership and Innovation: FAANG companies thrive on innovation and leadership. Behavioral questions help identify

individuals who can contribute positively to their corporate culture by leading projects, thinking creatively and driving change.

2. Team Collaboration: These companies often work on large, collaborative projects. Understanding how you work within a team, handle conflicts, and contribute to group goals is crucial.
3. Adaptability: The tech industry is fast-paced and ever-changing. All the big tech companies value employees who can adapt to new challenges, learn quickly, and pivot when necessary.
4. Customer-Centric Approach: Understanding customer needs and striving to exceed them is fundamental. Behavioral interviews help assess your ability to prioritize and deliver customer satisfaction.
5. Cultural Fit: Each FAANG company has a distinct culture. For example, Google's culture emphasizes creativity and openness, while Amazon focuses on customer obsession and operational excellence. Behavioral interviews help ensure candidates will thrive within these environments.

17.2 Understanding Cultures

Before diving into the questions, it's essential to understand the cultural differences among FAANG companies. Each company has its own set of values and priorities, and your responses should reflect an alignment with these.

Facebook (Meta) (https://www.metacareers.com/culture/)

- **Core Values:** Focus on openness, boldness, and building a community. Facebook values individuals who can take initiative, think creatively, and collaborate effectively.
- **Interview Focus:** Expect questions about how you handle challenges, work in teams, and contribute to a mission-driven environment.

Amazon (https://www.amazon.jobs/content/en/our-workplace/leadership-principles)

- **Core Values:** Customer obsession, ownership, and a focus on results. Amazon emphasizes leadership principles such as delivering results, thinking big, and having a bias for action.
- **Interview Focus:** Prepare for questions that probe your ability to take ownership of projects, make data-driven decisions, and prioritize customer needs.

Apple (https://www.apple.com/careers/uk/shared-values.html)

- **Core Values:** Innovation, simplicity, and attention to detail. Apple looks for individuals who are passionate about their work, pay close attention to details, and can innovate.
- **Interview Focus:** Expect questions that explore your passion for technology, your ability to innovate, and how you maintain high standards in your work.

Netflix (https://jobs.netflix.com/culture)

- **Core Values:** Freedom, responsibility, and a focus on results. Netflix values independence and accountability, as well as a commitment to delivering high-quality work.
- **Interview Focus:** Be prepared to discuss how you manage your responsibilities, work independently, and contribute to a high-performance culture.

Google (https://about.google/intl/ALL_us/commitments/)

- **Core Values:** Innovation, transparency, and a focus on user experience. Google values creativity, collaboration, and a commitment to making a positive impact.
- **Interview Focus:** Expect questions that assess your problem-solving abilities, creativity, and how you contribute to a collaborative work environment.

17.3 Common Questions & Sample Answers

Now that you understand the cultural priorities at FAANG companies, let's explore some common behavioral questions you might encounter there. These questions are designed to assess various aspects of your professional experience, including leadership, teamwork, problem-solving, and adaptability.

Facebook (Meta) Behavioral Questions

Facebook's interview process is designed to identify candidates who can thrive in a fast-paced, mission-driven environment. The questions often focus on your ability to collaborate, innovate, and handle challenges. Here's how to approach some of the most common questions:

1. Tell me about a time when you worked on a project that didn't go as planned. How did you handle it?

- What They're Looking For: Facebook wants to see how you handle setbacks and whether you can stay motivated and find solutions in challenging situations.
- How to Answer: Focus on your problem-solving abilities and resilience. Describe a specific project, explain what went wrong, and detail the steps you took to address the issue. Emphasize how you stayed positive and found a way to move forward.

<u>Example STAR Response</u>

- Situation: "I was working on a new feature for our app, but halfway through the project, we discovered a significant bug that threatened to delay the launch."
- Task: "My task was to find a solution to the bug without compromising the project timeline."
- Action: "I collaborated with the development team to identify the root cause of the bug and then worked overtime to implement a fix. I also kept the project stakeholders informed of our progress."
- Result: "We were able to resolve the bug within a week, and the feature launched on time with no further issues. The project was well-received by users, and I learned valuable lessons about risk management."

2. Describe a situation where you had to work with a team to achieve a goal.

- What They're Looking For: Collaboration is key at Facebook. They want to know how well you work with others, especially in cross-functional teams.
- How to Answer: Provide an example that highlights your teamwork skills, your ability to communicate effectively, and how you contributed to the team's success.

<u>Example STAR Response</u>

- Situation: "Our team was tasked with launching a new marketing campaign for a product, and we had to coordinate with the sales and design teams."

- Task: "I was responsible for ensuring that the messaging was consistent across all channels and that the campaign met our deadlines."
- Action: "I set up regular check-ins with the sales and design teams to ensure we were all aligned and that any issues were addressed promptly. I also facilitated communication between the teams and kept everyone focused on our shared goals."
- Result: "The campaign launched successfully and exceeded our sales targets by 20%. The collaborative effort was praised by all departments involved."

3. Can you tell me about a time when you had to make a decision with limited information?

- What They're Looking For: Facebook values decisiveness and the ability to make informed decisions quickly, even when not all the data is available.
- How to Answer: Highlight your ability to assess a situation, gather as much relevant information as possible, and make a decision confidently.

<u>Example STAR Response</u>

- Situation: "During a product development cycle, we faced a decision about whether to pivot our approach due to a potential change in market demand."
- Task: "I needed to decide whether to proceed with the original plan or adjust our strategy based on the limited data we had."
- Action: "I consulted with key stakeholders, reviewed the available market research, and weighed the risks and benefits of each option. After careful consideration, I decided to pivot our approach to better align with the emerging market trends."
- Result: "The decision to pivot resulted in a successful product launch that met the new market demand and received positive feedback from customers."

Amazon Behavioral Questions

Amazon's interview process is heavily influenced by their Leadership Principles. Questions are designed to assess how well you align with these principles, especially in areas like ownership, customer obsession, and delivering results. Here's how to tackle some of the most common questions:

4. Tell me about a time when you took ownership of a project.

- What They're Looking For: Amazon wants to see that you can take full responsibility for a project and drive it to success, even when challenges arise.
- How to Answer: Focus on a situation where you took charge of a project, managed it from start to finish, and ensured its success.

Example STAR Response

- Situation: "I was assigned to lead a new product development project that was critical to our company's growth strategy."
- Task: "My task was to manage the entire project, from initial concept to final delivery, ensuring that it met all deadlines and quality standards."
- Action: "I took ownership of the project by setting clear goals, creating a detailed project plan, and coordinating with cross-functional teams. I also regularly updated senior management on our progress and addressed any challenges that arose."
- Result: "The project was completed ahead of schedule and under budget, and the product was successfully launched to strong market reception. My leadership was recognized with an internal award for excellence."

5. Give me an example of a time when you made a difficult decision without enough data.

- What They're Looking For: Amazon values leaders who can make informed decisions quickly, even when faced with uncertainty.
- How to Answer: Discuss a scenario where you had to make a tough decision with limited information, and how you managed the risks associated with it.

Example STAR Response

- Situation: "During a critical phase of a project, we faced a decision about whether to continue with a specific vendor or switch to a new one due to potential reliability issues."
- Task: "I needed to make a decision quickly to avoid delays in the project timeline."

- Action: "I reviewed the vendor's performance history, consulted with my team for their input, and considered the potential risks of switching vendors. Despite the limited data, I decided to move forward with a new vendor that offered better reliability."
- Result: "The decision to switch vendors prevented potential delays, and the project was completed successfully. The new vendor also proved to be a valuable long-term partner."
- Describe a situation where you had to deal with a difficult customer.
- What They're Looking For: Customer obsession is one of Amazon's key principles. They want to see that you prioritize customer needs and can handle difficult situations effectively.
- How to Answer: Provide an example where you resolved a challenging customer issue, focusing on your problem-solving and customer service skills.

Example STAR Response

- Situation: "A high-profile customer was unhappy with the delivery delays on a critical order, and the issue was escalating quickly."
- Task: "My task was to resolve the issue to the customer's satisfaction while also addressing the root cause of the delay."
- Action: "I immediately contacted the customer to apologize for the inconvenience and assured them that we were working on a solution. I expedited the order and provided a discount on future purchases as a gesture of goodwill. I also worked with our logistics team to identify and fix the issue that caused the delay."
- Result: "The customer was satisfied with the resolution and continued to do business with us. The logistics issue was resolved, preventing future delays and improving overall customer satisfaction."

Apple Behavioral Questions

Apple's interview process is designed to identify candidates who are passionate about innovation, attention to detail, and maintaining high standards. Here's how to approach some of the most common questions:

6. Describe a time when you had to innovate to solve a problem.

- What They're Looking For: Apple values creativity and innovation. They want to see that you can think outside the box and develop creative solutions to problems.

- How to Answer: Focus on a situation where you identified a unique solution to a problem and how it positively impacted the outcome.

Example STAR Response

- Situation: "While working on a new product design, we encountered a significant challenge with the materials we were using, which were not meeting our quality standards."
- Task: "My task was to find an innovative solution that would maintain our high standards while staying within budget."
- Action: "I researched alternative materials and worked closely with our suppliers to develop a new composite material that met our quality requirements. I also led a series of tests to ensure that the new material performed as expected."
- Result: "The innovative use of the new material not only met our quality standards but also reduced production costs by 15%. The product was launched successfully and received positive feedback from customers."

7. Can you tell me about a time when you had to pay close attention to detail to ensure quality?

- What They're Looking For: Apple's commitment to quality is unwavering. They want to see that you have a keen eye for detail and are committed to delivering high-quality work.
- How to Answer: Provide an example where your attention to detail ensured the success of a project or product.

Example STAR Response

- Situation: "During the development of a new software feature, I noticed some inconsistencies in the user interface design that could have affected the user experience."
- Task: "My task was to ensure that the final product met Apple's high standards of quality and consistency."
- Action: "I meticulously reviewed the design specifications and identified the areas that needed improvement. I worked closely with the design team to make the necessary adjustments and conducted multiple rounds of testing to ensure that the issues were resolved."
- Result: "The final product was flawless, and the feature received praise from both internal teams and users for its seamless user

experience. My attention to detail was recognized during the project's post-launch review."

8. Tell me about a time when you had to manage a project under a tight deadline.

- What They're Looking For: Apple values efficiency and the ability to deliver high-quality work under pressure. They want to see how you manage time-sensitive projects without compromising on quality.
- How to Answer: Highlight your time management skills and your ability to stay focused and maintain quality under pressure.

<u>Example STAR Response</u>

- Situation: "I was leading a product launch that had an immovable deadline, and we encountered some unexpected technical issues just weeks before the launch."
- Task: "My task was to ensure that the product launch went ahead as planned without any compromises on quality."
- Action: "I immediately organized the team to work on a solution, prioritizing tasks based on their impact on the launch. I also arranged for additional resources to address the technical issues and set up daily progress meetings to keep everyone aligned."
- Result: "Despite the challenges, we met the launch deadline, and the product was released on time with no quality issues. The launch was a success, and the product received positive feedback from both customers and the media."

Netflix Behavioral Questions

Netflix's culture is built on freedom, responsibility, and a focus on results. The interview questions often explore how you manage your responsibilities, make decisions, and contribute to a high-performance culture. Here's how to approach some of the most common questions:

9. Tell me about a time when you had to work independently to achieve a goal.

- What They're Looking For: Netflix values independence and accountability. They want to see that you can take ownership of your work and deliver results without needing constant supervision.
- How to Answer: Highlight your ability to work independently, manage your responsibilities, and achieve your goals.

Example STAR Response

- Situation: "I was assigned to lead a new marketing campaign for one of our key products, and I was given full responsibility for its execution."
- Task: "My task was to develop and execute the campaign strategy independently, ensuring it met our targets."
- Action: "I conducted market research, developed the campaign strategy, and managed all aspects of the execution, from creative development to media placement. I regularly reviewed the campaign's performance and made adjustments as needed to optimize results."
- Result: "The campaign exceeded our targets, achieving a 30% increase in brand awareness and a 20% increase in sales. My ability to manage the project independently was recognized by senior management."

10. Describe a situation where you had to make a difficult decision that went against the consensus.

- What They're Looking For: Netflix encourages independent thinking and values individuals who can make tough decisions, even when they go against the grain.
- How to Answer: Discuss a scenario where you made a decision based on your judgment, despite opposition, and how it ultimately led to a positive outcome.

Example STAR Response

- Situation: "During a project review meeting, the majority of the team favored a particular approach to solving a problem, but I believed that a different approach would be more effective."
- Task: "My task was to convince the team to consider my approach and make the best decision for the project."
- Action: "I presented my analysis, highlighting the potential risks and benefits of both approaches. I also provided data and case studies to support my argument. After thorough discussion, I stood by my decision to pursue the alternative approach."
- Result: "My approach was eventually implemented, and it resulted in a more efficient solution that saved the project time and

resources. The team acknowledged that my decision was the right one, and it reinforced the importance of critical thinking in our processes."

11. Can you tell me about a time when you had to deliver results under pressure?

- What They're Looking For: Netflix is a results-driven company. They want to see how you handle high-pressure situations and deliver outstanding results.
- How to Answer: Focus on a scenario where you successfully managed a high-pressure situation and achieved your goals.

Example STAR Response

- Situation: "I was leading a major product launch that had a very tight deadline due to a last-minute change in the release schedule."
- Task: "My task was to ensure that the launch was successful despite the time constraints."
- Action: "I quickly reorganized the project plan, prioritizing critical tasks and reallocating resources to meet the new deadline. I also maintained constant communication with the team to keep everyone focused and motivated."
- Result: "The product launch was a success, with the product being released on time and receiving excellent reviews. The team's ability to deliver results under pressure was recognized by senior leadership."

Google Behavioral Questions

Google's interview process focuses on innovation, collaboration, and problem-solving. The questions often explore how you approach challenges, work with others, and contribute to the company's mission. Here's how to approach some of the most common questions:

12. Tell me about a time when you had to solve a complex technical problem.

- What They're Looking For: Google values innovative problem-solving and wants to see how you approach complex challenges.
- How to Answer: Provide an example where you used your technical skills and creativity to solve a difficult problem.

Example STAR Response

- Situation: "We were developing a new algorithm for a search feature, but we encountered a significant challenge with the performance and scalability of the algorithm."
- Task: "My task was to find a solution that would improve the algorithm's performance while maintaining its accuracy."
- Action: "I conducted a detailed analysis of the algorithm's performance bottlenecks and identified areas for optimization. I also collaborated with my team to brainstorm alternative approaches. After several iterations, we developed a new version of the algorithm that significantly improved performance."
- Result: "The optimized algorithm was successfully implemented, resulting in a 40% improvement in performance and a 25% increase in search accuracy. The project was recognized as a key innovation by the company."

13. Describe a time when you had to work with a team to achieve a common goal.

- What They're Looking For: Google values collaboration and teamwork. They want to see how well you work with others and contribute to group efforts.
- How to Answer: Provide an example where you worked effectively with a team to achieve a shared goal.

Example STAR Response

- Situation: "Our team was tasked with developing a new feature for our platform that required close collaboration between the engineering, design, and product teams."
- Task: "My task was to ensure that the engineering team's work was aligned with the design and product teams' vision and goals."
- Action: "I facilitated regular cross-functional meetings to ensure clear communication and alignment. I also worked closely with the design team to incorporate their feedback into the development process and collaborated with the product team to prioritize features based on user needs."
- Result: "The feature was successfully launched, and it received positive feedback from users. The project was a great example of

effective cross-functional collaboration, and it helped strengthen relationships between the teams."

14. Can you tell me about a time when you had to adapt to a rapidly changing project requirement?

- What They're Looking For: Google operates in a fast-paced environment where change is constant. They want to see how you adapt to new challenges and stay effective under pressure.
- How to Answer: Discuss a scenario where you successfully adapted to changing requirements and still delivered results.

Example STAR Response

- Situation: "While working on a mobile app project, the client requested several last-minute changes to the app's user interface design."
- Task: "My task was to incorporate these changes without delaying the project's launch."
- Action: "I quickly organized a meeting with the design and development teams to assess the feasibility of the changes and their impact on the timeline. We agreed on a revised plan that prioritized the most critical changes while staying on track for the launch."
- Result: "The changes were implemented successfully, and the app was launched on time. The client was pleased with the final product, and the team's ability to adapt to the changing requirements was praised."

17.4 Approach to Craft Responses

When crafting your responses, remember to:

1. **Align with Company Values:** Tailor your responses to reflect the values and priorities of the company you're interviewing with. Use language that resonates with their mission and culture.
2. **Use the STAR Method:** Structure your answers using the STAR method (Situation, Task, Action, Result) to provide clear and concise responses that are easy to follow.
3. **Be Specific:** Provide specific examples from your past experiences that demonstrate your skills and qualifications. Avoid vague or general statements.

4. **Quantify Results:** Whenever possible, include quantifiable outcomes to highlight the impact of your actions.
5. **Practice and Prepare:** Practice your responses to common questions in advance, focusing on delivering them confidently and naturally during the interview.

Final Thoughts

Preparing for behavioral interviews at FAANG companies requires a deep understanding of each company's culture, values, and expectations. By aligning your responses with these priorities and demonstrating your skills through specific examples, you can present yourself as a strong candidate who is well-prepared to contribute to their success. Next, we will explore pro level strategies for mastering the behavioral interview process, including handling curveball questions, managing interview stress, and making a lasting impression.

Chapter 18

Pro-Level Strategies

Many a times behavioral interviews demand you to respond some challenging questions, especially if you are going for a senior position or appearing for a high-tech company. To get yourself prepared for any unexpected or challenging situation, you need to learn a few advanced level strategies that are covered in this chapter. The strategies include handling curveball questions, manage stress during the interview, and leave a lasting impression on your interviewers.

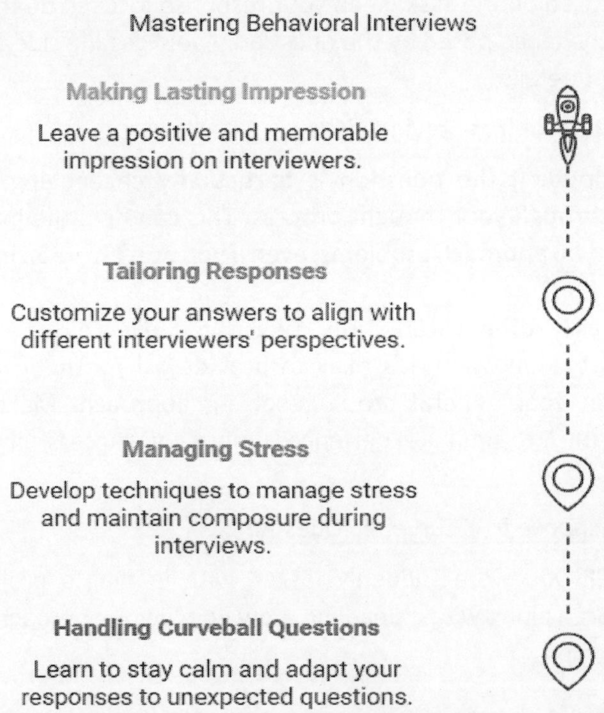

Figure – 18.1

18.1 Handling Curveball Questions

Even with thorough preparation, you may encounter questions that catch you off guard. These type of questions are designed to test your ability to think on your feet and adapt to unexpected situations.

Stay Calm and Collected

- Pause and Reflect: If you're faced with a question that seems difficult or out of the ordinary, take a moment to gather your thoughts. A brief pause can help you formulate a coherent response.
- Clarify if Needed: Don't hesitate to ask for clarification if the question is unclear. This shows that you're thoughtful and attentive to detail.

Use the STAR Method as a Framework

- Adapt Your Examples: Even if the question is unexpected, you can often adapt one of your prepared STAR examples to fit the scenario. Focus on the core skills or experiences, the question is probing.
- Stay Focused on the Task: Keep your response focused on the specific task or challenge posed by the question. Avoid getting side tracked by irrelevant details.

Demonstrate Problem-Solving Skills

- Think Aloud: If the question is particularly challenging, consider talking through your thought process. This can help the interviewer see how you approach problems, even if you don't have an immediate answer.
- Provide a Hypothetical Solution: If you don't have a direct experience that fits the question, it's okay to provide a hypothetical solution based on your general problem-solving approach. Make sure to relate it back to similar experiences where you successfully resolved issues.

<u>Example Response to a Curveball Question</u>

Question: "If you were suddenly tasked with leading a project in an unfamiliar area along with a deadline, how would you approach it?"

Response Sample

- Situation: "In a previous role, I was asked to lead a project that involved a technology I wasn't initially familiar with, and a delivery was due in 3 months' time."

- Task: "My task was to quickly get up to speed and ensure the project stayed on track."
- Action: "I started by conducting thorough research on the technology and reaching out to colleagues who had more experience in the area. I also attended relevant training sessions and workshops to build my knowledge. To ensure the project's success, I leveraged the expertise of my team members who were more familiar with the technology and coordinated their efforts effectively. I reviewed the tasks that were due in the given time and ensured the resources alignment to achieve that."
- Result: "Despite the initial challenge, the project was completed successfully, and I gained valuable expertise in a new area. This experience taught me the importance of being adaptable and resourceful when facing unfamiliar challenges."

18.2 Managing Stress During the Interview

Stress is a natural part of the interview process, especially when interviewing for high-stakes positions at top companies. Learning how to manage stress effectively can make a significant difference in your performance.

Preparation Is Key

- Thorough Preparation: The more prepared you are, the less likely you are to feel overwhelmed during the interview. Review common questions, practice your STAR responses, and research the company thoroughly.
- Mock Interviews: Conduct mock interviews with a friend, mentor, or coach to simulate the interview environment. This can help you get used to the pressure and refine your responses.

Mindfulness and Breathing Techniques

- Deep Breathing: Practice deep breathing exercises before and during the interview to help calm your nerves. Inhale deeply through your nose, hold for a few seconds, and exhale slowly through your mouth.
- Mindfulness: Stay present during the interview. Focus on the question being asked rather than worrying about previous answers or what might come next. This helps you respond thoughtfully and confidently.

Positive Visualization

- Visualize Success: Before the interview, spend a few minutes visualizing a successful outcome. Imagine yourself answering questions confidently, engaging with the interviewers, and receiving positive feedback. This can boost your confidence and reduce anxiety.
- Affirmations: Use positive affirmations to reinforce your self-belief. Remind yourself of your strengths, achievements, and the value you bring to the table.

Control Your Body Language

- Maintain Good Posture: Sit up straight with your shoulders back. This not only projects confidence but also helps you feel more in control.
- Controlled Movements: Be mindful of nervous habits like fidgeting or tapping your feet. Keep your hands steady and make deliberate gestures to emphasize key points.

Stay Hydrated and Energized

- Drink Water: Stay hydrated before and during the interview. A dry mouth can make speaking difficult, and dehydration can increase stress levels.
- Healthy Snacks: Have a light, healthy snack before the interview to maintain your energy levels. Avoid heavy meals that can make you feel sluggish.

18.3 Tailoring Your Responses

During the interview process, you may meet with multiple interviewers, each with their own perspective and priorities. Tailoring your responses to suit each interviewer can help you make a stronger connection and leave a positive impression.

Research Your Interviewers

- LinkedIn Profiles: Before the interview, look up your interviewers on LinkedIn to learn about their background, role, and areas of expertise. This can give you insights into what they might focus on during the interview.
- Company Bio: If available, review the interviewer's bio on the company's website. This may provide additional information about their role and responsibilities.

Understand Their Perspective

- Technical vs. Non-Technical Interviewers: Tailor your responses based on the interviewer's background. For example, a technical interviewer may be more interested in your problem-solving process and technical skills, while a non-technical interviewer may focus on your teamwork and communication abilities.
- Hiring Managers: If you're speaking with a hiring manager, emphasize how your skills and experience align with the specific needs of the team or department they manage.

Adjust Your Communication Style

- Formal vs. Casual: Some interviewers may prefer a more formal communication style, while others may be more casual. Pay attention to the interviewer's tone and adjust your communication style accordingly.
- Detail vs. Big Picture: Technical interviewers may appreciate detailed explanations of your work, while higher-level managers might be more interested in the big picture and overall impact.

Highlight Relevant Experiences

- Tailored Examples: Choose examples from your experience that are most relevant to the interviewer's role or the department they represent. This shows that you understand their priorities and are well-suited for the team.
- Specific Achievements: If you know that an interviewer values certain skills or experiences, make sure to highlight specific achievements that demonstrate those qualities.

<u>Example of Tailoring a Response</u>

Scenario: You're interviewing with both a technical lead and a hiring manager during the same interview process.

Response to **the Technical Lead**

- Situation: "In my previous role, while developing a new feature, we encountered a significant performance bottleneck."
- Task: "My task was to identify and resolve the bottleneck to improve the feature's performance."
- Action: "I conducted a detailed analysis of the codebase, optimized key functions, and implemented caching strategies to reduce load times."

- Result: “The optimization led to a 30% improvement in performance, which was critical for meeting our project deadlines.”

Response to the **Hiring Manager or someone in HR**

- Situation: “In my previous role, I was responsible for leading the development of a key product feature.”
- Task: “My task was to ensure the feature was delivered on time and met our quality standards.”
- Action: “I managed the project timeline, coordinated with cross-functional teams, and addressed any technical challenges that arose.”
- Result: “The feature was successfully launched on schedule, and it contributed to a 20% increase in user engagement. My ability to lead the project effectively was recognized by both the team and senior management.”

18.4 Making a Lasting Impression

Leaving a strong, lasting impression is crucial in any interview. It’s not just about answering questions well—it’s also about demonstrating your enthusiasm for the role, your alignment with the company’s values, and your ability to contribute to the team’s success.

Ask Thoughtful Questions

- Show Your Interest: Asking insightful questions demonstrates your genuine interest in the role and the company. It also allows you to gather important information to determine if the role is the right fit for you.
- Focus on the Future: Ask about the company’s future goals, upcoming projects, or team dynamics. This shows that you’re thinking about how you can contribute to their long-term success.

Examples of Thoughtful Questions

- “Can you tell me more about the team I would be working with and how this role fits into the overall structure?”
- “What are the biggest challenges the team is currently facing, and how can I contribute to overcoming them?”
- “How do you see this role evolving over the next few years?”

Reiterate Your Enthusiasm

- Express Your Excitement: Make sure to express your enthusiasm for the role and the company. Let the interviewers know why you're excited about the opportunity and how it aligns with your career goals.
- Connect Your Experience: Highlight how your experience and skills make you an ideal candidate for the role. Reinforce the value you can bring to the team.

Example of Reiterating Enthusiasm

- "I'm really excited about the possibility of joining your team. The work you're doing aligns perfectly with my experience in [specific area], and I'm eager to contribute my skills to help achieve the company's goals."

Be Authentic

- Stay True to Yourself: Authenticity is key to making a lasting impression. Be genuine in your responses and let your personality shine through. Interviewers appreciate candidates who are honest and sincere.
- Share Personal Insights: Don't be afraid to share personal insights or experiences that connect to the role or the company's values. This can help you stand out and make a memorable impression.

Example of Authenticity

- "One of the reasons I'm particularly interested in this role is because of [specific aspects of the company's mission or culture]. It really resonates with my personal values, and I'm excited about the opportunity to contribute to something I'm passionate about."

Final Thoughts

Mastering behavioral interviews requires a combination of thorough preparation, strategic thinking, and the ability to adapt to different situations. By handling curveball questions with confidence, managing stress effectively, tailoring your responses to different interviewers, and making a lasting impression, you can set yourself apart as a top candidate. In the next chapter, we'll explore the importance of post-interview strategies, including following up, reflecting on your performance, and leveraging feedback to improve your interview skills. With these advanced strategies, you'll be well-equipped to navigate even the most challenging behavioral interviews and move one step closer to landing your dream job.

Chapter 19

Post-Interview Strategies

The interview process doesn't end when you walk out of the interview room. How you handle the post-interview phase can be just as important as your performance during the interview. This chapter focuses on the actions you should take after the interview to leave a lasting positive impression, learn from your experience, and prepare for future opportunities.

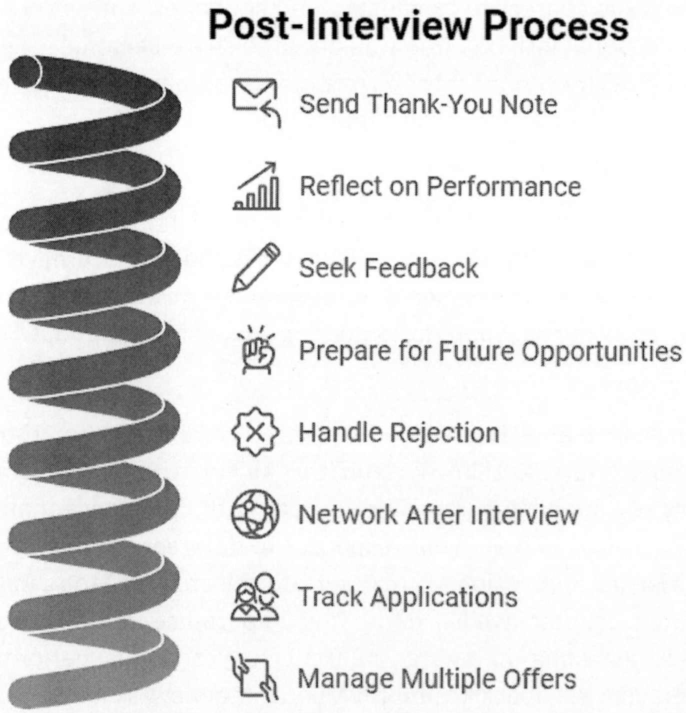

Figure – 19.1

19.1 Sending a Thank-You Note

Importance of a Thank-You Note

Sending a thank-you note after your interview is a simple yet powerful way to show appreciation for the opportunity and reinforce your interest in the position. It's a professional courtesy that can set you apart from other candidates.

▶ What to Include in Your Note

Your thank-you note should be concise, genuine, and personalized. Here's what you should include

- Express Gratitude: Start by thanking the interviewer for their time and the opportunity to interview for the role. For example, "Thank you for taking the time to meet with me today. I appreciate the opportunity to discuss how I can contribute to your team."
- Highlight Key Points: Briefly mention something specific from the interview that resonated with you, whether it was a discussion point, a challenge that was presented, or something about the company culture that excites you. For instance, "I particularly enjoyed our discussion about the challenges your team faces with scaling the new product. I'm excited about the possibility of contributing my experience in [specific skill] to help address those challenges."
- Reaffirm Your Interest: End with a statement that reaffirms your enthusiasm for the role and your eagerness to contribute to the team. For example, "I'm very enthusiastic about the prospect of joining [Company Name] and applying my skills to help your team achieve its goals."
- Keep It Short: The note should be short and to the point, generally not more than 4-5 lines. Your goal is to remind the interviewer of your strengths and keep yourself on top of their mind.

▶ When to Send the Note

The timing of your thank-you note is crucial. Aim to send it within 24 hours of your interview. This shows that you are prompt and thoughtful, and it keeps the positive impression fresh in the interviewer's mind.

▶ Follow Up Politely

If you haven't heard back after a week or two, it's okay to send a polite follow-up email. No response can be a sign of delay in the process instead of your rejection. Express your continued interest and inquire about the next steps in the hiring process.

Example Follow-Up Email: "Dear Sharon, I hope you're doing well. I wanted to follow up on my recent interview for the Engineering Manager position. I remain very interested in the opportunity to join Amazon and contribute to your team. I would appreciate any updates you can provide regarding the next steps in the process. Thank you again for your time and consideration. Best regards, Ann".

19.2 Reflecting on Your Performance

Importance of Reflection

Reflecting on your interview experience is essential for continuous improvement. It allows you to assess what went well, what could have been better, and how you can prepare more effectively for future interviews. Reflection is a critical part of the learning process and helps you to grow as a professional.

► Questions to Ask Yourself

After the interview, take some time to ask yourself the following questions

- What Went Well? Identify the parts of the interview where you felt confident and performed well. Was it your ability to explain your thought process? Did you solve a problem efficiently? Recognizing your strengths will help you build on them in future interviews.
- What Could Have Been Better? Reflect on the areas where you struggled. Did you stumble on a specific type of problem or fail to explain something clearly? Understanding your weaknesses is the first step toward improving them.
- Did You Ask the Right Questions? Consider whether you asked insightful questions during the interview. This not only shows your interest in the role but also helps you gauge if the company is the right fit for you.
- How Was Your Communication? Evaluate how well you communicated your thoughts and solutions. Did you articulate your ideas clearly and confidently? Was there any point where you felt misunderstood?

Writing a Reflection Journal

Consider keeping a journal where you document your reflections after each interview. This can help you track your progress over time and identify patterns in your performance. Write down what you did well, what you struggled with, and any feedback you received. This journal will be a valuable resource as you continue to refine your interview skills.

19.3 Seeking Feedback

Why Feedback Matters

Asking for feedback after an interview, regardless of the outcome, is a great way to learn and improve. Constructive feedback can provide insights into how you were perceived by the interviewer and highlight areas where you can enhance your skills or approach.

How to Ask for Feedback

When reaching out for feedback, be polite and appreciative. Here's how you can structure your request

- Express Gratitude: Start by thanking the interviewer again for their time and consideration. For example, "Thank you once again for the opportunity to interview for the software engineering position."
- Request Feedback: Politely ask if they could provide any feedback on your performance. You could say, "I'm always looking to improve, and I would greatly appreciate any feedback you could provide about my interview performance."
- Be Open-Minded: Make it clear that you're open to constructive criticism. For instance, "I'm very open to constructive feedback as I continue to refine my skills and approach."

Handling Negative Feedback

Receiving negative feedback can be tough, but it's an invaluable tool for growth. When you receive feedback:

- Stay Positive: Keep in mind that the purpose of feedback is to help you get better. Don't take it personally; instead, view it as an opportunity to learn.
- Analyze and Apply: Carefully consider the feedback and think about how you can apply it to future interviews. For example, if the feedback

mentions that you struggled with a specific type of problem, dedicate more time to practicing that area.

- Follow Up: If appropriate, you can follow up with a brief note thanking the interviewer for their feedback and letting them know how you plan to address the points they raised. This shows that you are proactive and committed to self-improvement, and can possibly open the door for other opportunities with the firm in future.

19.4 Preparing for the Next Opportunity

Continuous Learning

The interview process, whether successful or not, should be seen as a learning experience. Use each interview as a steppingstone to improve your skills, refine your approach, and better prepare for future opportunities.

Updating Your Study Plan

Based on your reflections and the feedback you've received, update your preparation plan. Focus on the areas where you need the most improvement, whether it's technical skills, problem-solving techniques, or communication.

- Focus on Growth Areas: Identify the areas where you struggled during the interview and prioritize them in your study plan. For example, if you had trouble with dynamic programming, allocate more time to practice problems in that area.
- Revisit Strong Areas: Don't neglect your strengths. Regularly revisit topics you're confident in to ensure you maintain your edge. This balanced approach will help you build a comprehensive skill set.

Setting Up Mock Interviews

- Find a Partner: Identify a friend, mentor, or coach who can conduct mock interviews with you. Choose someone who can provide honest and constructive feedback.
- Simulate the Interview Environment: Treat the mock interview as if it was the real thing. Dress appropriately, set up a quiet space, and time your responses. This will help you get comfortable with the interview setting.

- Record and Review: If possible, record your mock interviews. Reviewing the recording can help you spot areas for improvement in your delivery, body language, and clarity of responses.

Utilizing Online Platforms

- Practice with AI Tools: Use AI-powered platforms that offer mock interview simulations. These tools can provide immediate feedback on your answers, helping you refine your responses and improve your performance. Examples:
  Google Warmup : https://grow.google/certificates/interview-warmup/
  Remasto : https://remasto.com/
- Engage in Online Communities: Join online forums and communities focused on interview preparation. Engage in discussions, share your experiences, and learn from others who have gone through similar processes.

Continuous Learning

- Stay up to date on Industry Trends: Keep yourself informed about the latest trends and developments in your industry. This knowledge can help you answer industry-specific questions more confidently.
- Expand Your Skill Set: Consider taking online courses, attending workshops, or earning certifications to enhance your qualifications. This not only improves your resume but also boosts your confidence in interviews.

Staying Motivated

Job searching and interviewing can be a long and challenging process. It's important to stay motivated and keep your end goal in mind. Celebrate small victories along the way, such as nailing a particularly difficult problem or receiving positive feedback. Remember, each interview is a step closer to landing the job you want.

19.5 Dealing with Rejection

Accepting Rejection Gracefully

Rejection is a natural part of the job search process, but it's how you handle it that matters. Accepting rejection gracefully shows professionalism and resilience. Remember that a rejection isn't a reflection of your worth or abilities; it's just part of the journey toward finding the right fit.

Learning from Rejection

Each rejection provides an opportunity to learn and grow. Reflect on what might have gone wrong and how you can improve for next time. Consider reaching out to the interviewer for feedback to gain insights into areas where you can improve.

Moving Forward

Don't dwell on rejection; instead, use it as fuel to keep moving forward. Update your resume, refine your interview skills, and keep applying for roles that excite you. The right opportunity will come along, and when it does, you'll be even more prepared.

19.6 Networking After the Interview

Building Relationships

Even if you don't get the job, building relationships with the people you meet during the interview process can be valuable. Networking with professionals in your field opens doors for future opportunities and allows you to stay connected with industry trends.

- How to Network: Connect with your interviewers and other company representatives on LinkedIn. When sending a connection request, include a personalized message thanking them for the opportunity and expressing your interest in staying connected.

Example Expression of Continued Interest: "Dear Jack, I wanted to express my continued interest in opportunities at Alibaba. While this particular role wasn't the right fit, I believe my skills and experience could contribute to your team in the future. Please keep me in mind for any upcoming positions that align with my background. Best regards, Ron".

- Maintaining the Relationship: Periodically engage with their posts, share relevant industry news, or reach out for advice or insights on industry-related topics. This helps keep you on top of their mind for future openings or opportunities they might know of.

Leveraging Alumni Networks

If any of your previous company has a strong alumni network, consider joining it if applicable. Alumni networks often provide support, job leads, and valuable connections that can help you in your job search or career growth.

- How to Engage: Attend alumni events, participate in discussions, and contribute to the community by sharing your knowledge and experiences. This not only helps you build your network but also positions you as an active and engaged member of the community.

19.7 Tracking Your Applications

Importance of Keeping Track

Keeping track of your job applications is essential for staying organized and managing follow-ups effectively. This ensures that you don't miss any opportunities and can follow up in a timely manner.

Using a Job Tracker

Create a job application tracker using a spreadsheet or a dedicated app. Include columns for the company name, position, application date, interview dates, contact information, and follow-up status. This tracker will help you monitor your progress and ensure you're staying on top of your job search.

Analyzing Trends

Periodically review your job tracker to identify patterns in your job search. For example, if you notice that you're getting to the final interview stage but not receiving offers, it might indicate a need to refine your closing strategy or ask better questions about the role and company.

19.8 Handling Multiple Offers

How to Manage Multiple Offers

If you're fortunate enough to receive multiple job offers, it's important to handle them professionally. Evaluate each offer based on factors such as scope of work, salary, benefits, total compensation, work-life balance, company culture, travel and long-term career growth.

- Making a Decision: Compare the offers using a pros and cons list, considering both immediate and long-term career goals. Think about which role aligns best with your values, skills, and aspirations.
- Communicating Your Decision: Once you've made your decision, promptly inform the other companies of your choice. Thank them for the offer and express your appreciation for their consideration, keeping the door open for future opportunities.

Negotiating the Best Offer

Negotiation is a normal part of the job offer process. If you feel that an offer could be improved, don't hesitate to negotiate. This could involve discussing salary, benefits, or other aspects of the job offer.

- How to Negotiate: Approach the negotiation professionally, presenting your case with data to support your request. For instance, "Based on my research and experience level, I believe a salary in the range of [amount] would be more aligned with industry standards. I'm excited about the opportunity to contribute to [Company Name] and would love to discuss how we can bridge this gap."
- Why It's Important: Successful negotiation can lead to better compensation and job satisfaction, setting a positive tone for your future relationship with the company.

19.9 Preparing for Onboarding

Getting Ready for Your New Role

Once you've accepted a job offer, preparing for onboarding is your next step. This involves familiarizing yourself with the company's tools, culture, and expectations before your first day.

Learning About Company Tools and Processes

Reach out to your new employer to inquire about any tools or processes you should be familiar with before starting. This could include company software, communication platforms, or internal procedures.

- Why It's Important: Being prepared for your first day shows initiative and helps you hit the ground running. Understanding the company's tools and processes beforehand allows you to focus on building relationships and contributing from day one.

Setting Goals for Your First 90 Days

Set clear goals for what you want to achieve in your first 90 days in the new role. These goals should be aligned with the company's objectives and help you establish yourself as a valuable team member quickly.

- Example Goals: These could include learning specific tools, meeting key stakeholders, and contributing to an important project. Discuss these goals with your manager to ensure alignment and get their support.

Chapter 20

60 Key Questions with Sample Answers

To help you prepare thoroughly for any behavioral interview, here's a comprehensive list of 60 common behavioral interview questions, each accompanied by a well-crafted STAR-based response for maximum impact.

1. Tell me about a time you faced a significant challenge at work. How did you handle it?

Situation: In my role as a senior software engineer in 2022, I was working on a critical project to launch a new feature for a client. We were nearing the end of development when our lead backend engineer left unexpectedly due to personal reasons. This occurred just two weeks before the project deadline, leaving us short-staffed and behind schedule. The remaining team, though talented, was overwhelmed by the sudden workload.

Task: My task was to find a way to redistribute the work, ensure the backend portion of the feature was completed, and still deliver the project on time. I also needed to maintain the morale and motivation of the team, who were feeling the pressure of the deadline and the sudden departure.

Action: I immediately organized a meeting with the team to discuss the situation and understand everyone's capacity. I took over some of the most complex backend tasks myself since I had prior experience with backend development. I reassigned the remaining tasks to team members based on their strengths and expertise. To ensure consistent progress, I implemented daily check-ins where we could address blockers quickly and track progress. Additionally, I communicated the situation to the project manager and product owner to manage expectations and prepare for any potential delays.

Result: Despite the unexpected challenge, we were able to finish the backend work one day ahead of the deadline. The project was delivered on time, and the client was satisfied with the results. The experience not only allowed me to step up as a leader but also strengthened my relationship with the team. My proactive approach helped maintain team morale and keep everyone focused on the end goal, demonstrating my ability to handle pressure and lead effectively during challenging situations.

---

2. Describe a situation where you had to work under pressure.

Situation: I was responsible for managing a critical system deployment for a large client during one of the highest traffic periods of the year 2023. Everything was going according to plan, but just two hours before deployment, the QA team discovered a critical bug that affected the stability of the system. The pressure was on, as the deployment had been heavily publicized, and any delay would negatively affect the company's reputation and cause financial losses.

Task: My task was to resolve the issue as quickly as possible and ensure the deployment could still proceed within the original window, all while coordinating with the QA, DevOps, and development teams. I also needed to keep the project stakeholders updated without causing unnecessary panic.

Action: I immediately gathered the relevant teams for a quick stand-up meeting to assess the situation. The first step was identifying the root cause of the bug, which turned out to be an overlooked edge case in the code handling customer data inputs. I worked closely with the developer who had implemented the feature to write a hotfix. Simultaneously, I coordinated with QA to ensure that they were ready to test the fix as soon as it was committed. I also informed the stakeholders about the situation, explaining that there might be a 30-minute delay but ensuring them we had everything under control.

Result: We successfully deployed the hot-fix within 45 minutes of discovering the bug, and the system deployment proceeded with only a slight delay. The issue did not affect the end-users, and the event went smoothly. This experience showcased my ability to stay calm under pressure, effectively prioritize tasks, and lead a team through a high-stakes situation. It also reinforced the importance of strong communication and collaboration during critical moments.

---

3. Can you give an example of a time when you had to take the lead on a project?

Situation: 3 months ago, I was part of a software development team working on an important project to deliver a new feature for a flagship product. Halfway through the project, our project manager had to take an unexpected leave due to a family emergency. With no immediate replacement and only three weeks until the deadline, the team faced uncertainty, and progress slowed as the leadership void created confusion around priorities.

Task: I volunteered to step in as the interim project manager, despite it being outside my typical responsibilities as a senior software engineer. My task was to take over project management duties, keep the team focused, and ensure we delivered the feature on time.

Action: I began by reviewing the project timeline and identifying the remaining tasks. I reorganized the project workflow, breaking down large tasks into smaller, manageable chunks, and reassigned responsibilities based on each team member's strengths. I scheduled daily stand-ups to track progress and address any blockers quickly. I also maintained close communication with the product team and key stakeholders to keep them informed of our progress and any potential risks. Additionally, I made sure that my team had all the resources they needed, and I provided additional support where necessary, balancing both my development work and leadership role.

Result: Under my leadership, the team regained focus, and we successfully completed the project on time. The feature was launched with positive feedback from both users and stakeholders. This experience not only showcased my leadership abilities but also demonstrated my capacity to step up when needed and manage a project from both a technical and organizational perspective.

---

4. Tell me about a time when you had to resolve a conflict within your team.

Situation: In 2022, while working on a major product update, our development and design teams had a conflict over how to implement a new feature. The design team insisted on a particular layout that would require significant changes to the existing codebase, while the developers argued that the design was not technically feasible within the current timeline and would introduce complexity to the code structure.

Task: As the tech lead, my task was to mediate the conflict and find a solution that would satisfy both teams while ensuring the project stayed on track. I also needed to maintain team cohesion and avoid any further delays.

Action: I organized a meeting with both teams to facilitate an open discussion. I encouraged both sides to explain their reasoning and listened carefully to their concerns. After hearing both perspectives, I proposed a compromise: we would implement a simplified version of the design for the current release, allowing us to meet the deadline, while scheduling the more complex elements for a future sprint. I also worked with the design team to adjust the layout slightly, making it easier to implement without compromising the user experience.

Result: Both teams accepted the compromise, and the project proceeded without further delays. The feature was successfully launched, and the end-users appreciated the new design. This experience highlighted my ability to mediate conflicts and foster collaboration between cross-functional teams, ensuring that the project remained on track while maintaining a positive team dynamic.

---

5. Describe a time when you had to adapt to a significant change at work.

Situation: 3 years back, at my previous company, we underwent a major restructuring that involved a shift from a monolithic architecture to microservices. This required significant changes to the development process, tools, and workflows. Many team members, including myself, were unfamiliar with microservices architecture, and there was initial resistance from some developers who were comfortable with the old system.

Task: My task was to not only adapt to the new architecture but also ensure that my team was equipped to migrate the components we were responsible for, successfully. We had to complete this transition without disrupting ongoing projects and meet deadlines for new feature developments.

Action: I took the initiative to attend several training sessions on microservices and started experimenting with building microservices-based components on a smaller scale. I also encouraged my team to embrace the new architecture by organizing knowledge-sharing sessions where we discussed the benefits of microservices and how they aligned with our long-term goals. To ease the transition, I created documentation and a set of best practices that our team could follow as we migrated our codebase. Additionally, I collaborated with DevOps to ensure the deployment pipeline was adjusted to support the new architecture.

Result: The transition to microservices was completed smoothly, and the team quickly adapted to the new development process. The new architecture allowed us to deliver features faster, scale more efficiently, and improve the maintainability of the codebase. This experience demonstrated my ability to embrace change, lead a team through transitions, and ensure successful outcomes in the face of significant technical challenges.

---

6. Can you share an example of a time when you exceeded expectations on a project?

Situation: 3 months back, I was tasked with optimizing the performance of a backend service that was experiencing slow response times during peak usage. The service was critical to the company's e-commerce platform, and improving its performance was a high priority for the business. The initial goal was to reduce the response time by at least 20%, which was considered an ambitious but achievable target.

Task: My task was to analyze the bottlenecks, refactor the code, and improve the overall performance of the service without disrupting the existing functionality or introducing new bugs.

Action: I began by profiling the service using performance monitoring tools to identify the key bottlenecks. After discovering several inefficient database queries and redundant processing steps, I rewrote parts of the service to optimize these queries and implement caching for frequently accessed data. Additionally, I collaborated with the DevOps team to ensure that the infrastructure was configured optimally for performance, making adjustments to the load balancing and server allocation.

Result: The response time of the service improved by 45%, far exceeding the original goal of a 20% reduction. The improvement led to a significant decrease in customer complaints about slow load times and contributed to a noticeable increase in user retention and conversions. The leadership team praised my initiative and technical expertise, and the optimization became a best practice example for future projects. This experience demonstrated my ability to not only meet expectations but to exceed them by delivering exceptional results.

---

7. Tell me about a time when you had to learn something new quickly.

Situation: I had recently been promoted to a team lead position when I was assigned to a project that required the use of a cloud platform I had little experience with. This cloud platform was critical for deploying our microservices, and the project timeline was already tight. I needed to get up to speed quickly with the platform to ensure that our team could deliver on schedule.

Task: My task was to learn the cloud platform rapidly, become proficient in deploying services, and support the rest of my team in implementing the solution. I also needed to ensure that the project stayed on track despite my initial unfamiliarity with the platform.

Action: I dedicated the first few days to studying the platform's documentation and using online resources, including tutorials and training courses. I also reached out to a colleague who had prior experience with the platform and scheduled a few one-on-one sessions where they walked me through the key concepts and best practices. To accelerate my learning, I set up a sandbox environment where I could experiment with deploying simple services and testing configurations. I made sure to share my learnings with the team through detailed documentation and internal presentations.

Result: Within a week, I became proficient in the cloud platform and successfully deployed our services as planned. The project progressed without delays, and my quick learning allowed me to provide valuable guidance to the team as we implemented the solution. The successful delivery of the project was a testament to my adaptability and ability to quickly master new technologies.

---

8. Describe a time when you made a mistake at work. How did you handle it?

Situation: 5 years back, while managing a system update for one of our core services, I accidentally merged a feature branch that contained incomplete code into the main production branch. This mistake caused the system to behave unpredictably, affecting several users and leading to a brief service disruption. The issue was detected shortly after the update was deployed to production.

Task: My task was to address the error immediately, fix the production branch, and communicate the issue to the relevant stakeholders. I also needed to implement measures to prevent similar mistakes from happening in the future.

Action: As soon as I realized the mistake, I immediately rolled back the deployment to revert the system to its previous stable state. I then conducted a quick investigation to pinpoint the root cause of the issue, which was the premature merging of the feature branch. I fixed the incomplete code, ran additional tests, and ensured that the feature was ready before redeploying. After the situation was under control, I took full responsibility for the error in a team meeting and communicated the steps I had taken to prevent a recurrence. I proposed implementing stricter branch protection rules and enhancing our code review process to ensure that incomplete features couldn't be merged into production without thorough testing.

Result: The system was restored within an hour, and the users affected by the brief disruption were quickly informed. My proactive response and transparent communication helped maintain trust within the team and with stakeholders. The new branch protection measures were adopted, and similar mistakes were avoided in future deployments. This experience taught me the importance of attention to detail and taking responsibility for errors.

---

9. Can you tell me about a time when you had to deal with a difficult client or stakeholder?

Situation: While working as the lead developer on a client project about 6 months back, we were tasked with delivering a custom solution for a key feature. Midway through development, the client began requesting several scope changes, many of which were out of alignment with the original requirements. The frequent changes not only disrupted the development flow but also put the project's timeline at risk.

Task: My task was to manage the client's expectations, ensure that we stayed on schedule, and deliver a product that met their business needs. I also needed to maintain a good relationship with the client while navigating these challenges.

Action: I scheduled a one-on-one meeting with the client to understand their changing priorities and the reasons behind the scope adjustments. I explained the impact these changes were having on the project timeline and suggested a more structured approach to managing requests. I proposed creating a formal change request process where each new requirement would be reviewed, estimated, and scheduled based on its priority and the available timeline. Additionally, I communicated that certain lower-priority features might need to be deferred to a later phase if they continued to introduce delays.

Result: The client agreed to the change request process, and we were able to regain control of the project timeline. By setting clear expectations and managing the scope effectively, we successfully delivered the product within the agreed-upon time frame. The client was satisfied with the final outcome, and our working relationship improved as a result of the clearer communication. This experience reinforced the importance of setting boundaries and managing client expectations while maintaining a collaborative and positive working relationship.

---

10. Describe a time when you had to manage competing priorities.

Situation: 2 years back at one point, I was simultaneously managing two high-priority development projects: one involved implementing a new feature for our flagship product, while the other required urgent fixes to address performance issues in our legacy system. Both projects had overlapping deadlines, and each was critical to the company's success.

Task: My task was to ensure that both projects progressed on schedule, without compromising the quality of the work, while balancing the demands of multiple stakeholders who expected results from each project.

Action: I began by assessing the scope and timelines of both projects to identify which tasks were most urgent and could have the biggest impact. I broke the work into smaller, manageable chunks and delegated tasks based on my team members' strengths and availability. I communicated with stakeholders from both projects to manage their expectations, explaining that some lower-priority tasks might be delayed to ensure the highest-priority work was completed on time. I also made sure to have daily sync meetings with the team to track progress, address blockers, and make adjustments as necessary.

Result: Both projects were completed successfully and on time. The new feature was launched without issues, and the legacy system performance improvements significantly reduced downtime and improved user satisfaction. This experience highlighted my ability to balance multiple high-priority projects and effectively manage competing priorities while delivering quality results.

---

11. Tell me about a time when you had to influence others to achieve a goal.

Situation: Last month, I was part of a cross-functional team tasked with improving the performance of a critical customer-facing application. The application had been running slowly, and user complaints were increasing. However, not all team members were aligned on how to address the issue—some wanted to implement quick fixes, while others (including myself) believed in a more robust, long-term solution involving significant refactoring of the codebase.

Task: My task was to influence the team, particularly the project stakeholders and the product manager, to commit to a more sustainable solution, even though it would take longer to implement than quick fixes.

Action: I began by gathering data to demonstrate the long-term benefits of refactoring the codebase, including performance benchmarks, potential reductions in technical debt, and the long-term cost of maintaining quick fixes. I presented this data to the team in a meeting, showing the clear advantages of investing time upfront for a more permanent solution. Additionally, I shared examples of past projects where quick fixes led to more problems down the road. I also engaged one-on-one with key team members and the product manager to address their concerns and ensure they felt heard and involved in the decision-making process.

Result: After seeing the data and understanding the long-term value, the team agreed to prioritize the codebase refactor. We implemented the changes over the next few sprints, which significantly improved the application's performance and reduced future maintenance issues. This experience showed the power of using data and clear communication to influence others and achieve the best outcome for the team and the product.

---

12. Describe a time when you had to handle a difficult decision.

Situation: Last year during a major system migration project, we were hit with an unexpected issue: our chosen third-party tool for database migration turned out to be incompatible with some of our legacy systems. The issue became evident halfway through the project, and we had already invested significant time and resources into the tool. The team was split between abandoning the tool and restarting the migration process, or finding a workaround that would allow us to continue with the same tool.

Task: My task was to evaluate both options and make a decision that would minimize disruption and ensure the successful completion of the project within the tight timeline.

Action: I organized a meeting with the team to thoroughly assess the impact of each option. I asked the engineers to estimate the time and effort required to switch tools versus implementing a workaround. I also reached out to the third-party vendor to see if there were any updates or patches that could resolve the issue. After gathering all the information, I made the difficult decision to abandon the tool and switch to an alternative that had full compatibility, even though it meant redoing some of the work we had already completed. I communicated this decision to the team and stakeholders, explaining that it was the best choice for long-term project success, despite the short-term setbacks.

Result: Although the switch caused a slight delay, the new tool allowed us to complete the migration without further compatibility issues. In the end, we delivered the project within a reasonable timeframe, and the solution proved to be more stable and reliable. This experience reinforced my ability to make tough decisions that prioritize the long-term success of a project over short-term convenience.

---

13. Tell me about a time when you received critical feedback. How did you respond?

Situation: During a performance review last year, my manager provided feedback that my code reviews were too focused on syntax and formatting rather than on the overall design and logic of the code. This feedback surprised me because I had always taken pride in my attention to detail during reviews, but I realized I was missing the bigger picture in some instances.

Task: My task was to improve the depth and value of my code reviews by focusing not just on code style but on the architecture, scalability, and maintainability of the code being submitted.

Action: I took the feedback seriously and decided to enhance my approach to code reviews. First, I spent time studying best practices for code review, especially focusing on evaluating software architecture and design patterns. I also asked more experienced engineers on the team for advice on how they conduct thorough code reviews. I then began applying these new strategies in my reviews, providing more constructive feedback on how the code could be improved for performance, scalability, and maintainability. In addition, I started including more detailed explanations in my feedback, rather than simply pointing out issues.

Result: Over time, my code reviews became more comprehensive, and the quality of my feedback improved. My manager noted the improvement in my next performance review, and my peers appreciated the more in-depth discussions that followed from my feedback. This experience taught me the importance of listening to constructive criticism and continually improving my skills.

---

14. Can you give an example of a time when you took a risk and it didn't pay off? How did you handle it?

Situation: In 2020, I was working as a senior software engineer on a high-stakes project that required us to select a new database solution. Our team was under pressure to scale our application, and I decided to take a calculated risk by choosing a relatively new, cutting-edge database technology that promised better performance and scalability than the traditional options we had been using.

Task: My task was to integrate this new database into our system, with the goal of improving performance and handling a higher load of user data. We needed to ensure that the database was stable, fast, and could support future growth while still meeting the project's deadlines.

Action: After researching the technology, I led the initiative to implement the new database. I worked closely with the DevOps team to set up the environment and integrate the database with our existing architecture. However, after several weeks of development and testing, we encountered numerous unexpected issues, including frequent downtimes, difficult debugging processes, and inadequate documentation. Despite these problems, we pushed forward, trying to resolve the issues on the fly.

Result: Eventually, it became clear that the new database was not ready for production in our specific use case. The instability it introduced led to more delays and technical debt, and we were forced to revert to our previous, more stable database system. While the risk didn't pay off, I quickly shifted gears by leading the rollback to the previous technology, ensuring minimal disruption to the project timeline. I conducted a postmortem to analyze what went wrong and shared my findings with the team. This experience taught me to be more cautious when adopting unproven technologies in mission-critical projects and to run smaller pilot tests before making such significant architectural changes.

---

15. Tell me about a time when you went above and beyond your job responsibilities.

Situation: In 2022 at my previous employer, I was working as a software engineer when I noticed that many of our internal teams were struggling with the inefficiencies of our existing deployment pipeline. This wasn't part of my responsibilities at the time, but I realized that improving the pipeline would benefit the entire company, including my own team.

Task: My task was to streamline and automate the deployment process, even though this wasn't part of my official job description. I wanted to reduce the amount of manual effort required and eliminate the frequent delays that occurred due to human error.

Action: On my own initiative, I started by analyzing the current deployment process and identifying the main pain points. I collaborated with the DevOps team to explore automation tools and best practices for continuous integration and continuous deployment (CI/CD). I then created a proof-of-concept that demonstrated how automated scripts could reduce the manual steps involved in deployments. Once the concept was approved, I worked overtime to fully implement the automated pipeline, testing it thoroughly before rolling it out to the rest of the engineering team. I also created documentation and conducted training sessions to ensure that everyone understood how to use the new system.

Result: The automated pipeline significantly improved the efficiency of the deployment process, reducing deployment times by 50% and eliminating errors caused by manual interventions. The success of the project was recognized across the company, and I was commended for taking the initiative to improve a critical part of the development workflow. This experience reinforced my belief in going above and beyond to add value to the team and the organization as a whole.

---

16. Describe a time when you had to motivate a team to achieve a difficult goal.

Situation: In 2023, I was leading a team of software engineers on a complex feature development project for a new product launch. Midway through the project, we encountered unexpected technical challenges that delayed progress, and it became clear that the team was feeling demotivated by the mounting pressure and looming deadlines.

Task: My task was to reignite the team's motivation, keep everyone focused, and ensure that we met the upcoming deadline without sacrificing the quality of the work.

Action: I began by organizing a team meeting where I acknowledged the challenges we were facing and reassured everyone that we had the skills to overcome them. I broke the larger project down into smaller, more manageable milestones so that the team could feel a sense of accomplishment as we hit each one. I also worked closely with each team member, offering one-on-one support to those who were struggling with specific tasks. Additionally, I set up a reward system where we celebrated small wins with shout-outs and recognition during our daily stand-ups.

Result: The team's morale improved significantly, and we began making steady progress again. By focusing on small achievements and offering support, we were able to complete the project on time. The new feature launched successfully and was well-received by both stakeholders and customers. This experience taught me that sometimes the key to achieving difficult goals is maintaining motivation and breaking down overwhelming tasks into smaller, more achievable steps.

---

17. Can you tell me about a time when you had to handle a project with limited resources?

Situation: 2 years back, I was assigned to lead the development of a new software tool for an internal process at my company. However, due to the budget constraints and competing priorities, I had only a small team and limited resources to work with. Additionally, I needed to complete the project within a tight timeframe.

Task: My task was to deliver a fully functional software tool that met the project's requirements while working within the constraints of limited resources, both in terms of personnel and budget.

Action: I started by carefully analyzing the project scope and identifying the most critical features that had to be included in the first release. I communicated this prioritization to the stakeholders, explaining that some non-essential features would need to be deferred to a later phase. I also leveraged open-source tools and frameworks to reduce costs and development time. I closely monitored progress through agile sprints, regularly reassessing the workload and reassigning tasks as needed to ensure we stayed on track. To make up for the smaller team size, I encouraged team members to take ownership of multiple areas of the project and provided additional support to fill in any gaps.

Result: Despite the limited resources, we delivered the software tool on time, and it met the key requirements of the internal teams. The stakeholders were impressed with how we managed to create a solution that exceeded expectations, even under constrained circumstances. This experience reinforced my belief that resource constraints can be overcome with careful planning, prioritization, and leveraging available tools effectively.

---

18. Tell me about a time when you had to make a decision without all the information you needed.

Situation: 3 months back, while working on a product feature that was critical to the success of an upcoming release, we encountered a situation where our data analytics system wasn't providing enough insight into how users would interact with the feature. We had a limited amount of user data, and time constraints meant that we couldn't wait for more testing or feedback.

Task: My task was to decide whether to move forward with the current implementation or make adjustments to the feature, all without having complete data to fully back up the decision.

Action: I convened a meeting with the development and product teams to review the data we had. We discussed potential user scenarios, identified the most likely outcomes based on past user behavior, and conducted a risk assessment. I decided to move forward with the current implementation, but to mitigate the risk, I included an A/B testing mechanism that would allow us to gather more user data once the feature was live. I also ensured that we had a rollback plan in place, in case the feature didn't perform as expected.

Result: After the feature went live, the A/B testing revealed positive user engagement, and no rollback was necessary. The feature contributed to the product's overall success, and the ability to make a decision under uncertainty proved valuable. This experience taught me the importance of balancing risk with action, even when you don't have all the information you need.

---

19. Describe a time when you had to learn from a failure.

Situation: Last year I was leading a project to implement a new customer relationship management (CRM) system across multiple departments in the company. Despite thorough planning, the initial rollout of the system was met with significant resistance from the end users, and the adoption rates were far lower than expected. The new system disrupted established workflows, which caused frustration among employees, and the training provided was insufficient.

Task: My task was to understand why the implementation failed, take responsibility, and make the necessary changes to ensure the successful adoption of the CRM system.

Action: I initiated feedback sessions with key stakeholders and end users to understand their specific concerns and pain points. It became clear that the training provided wasn't tailored to the different departments' needs and that some of the system's functionalities didn't align well with their established workflows. I collaborated with the CRM provider to make necessary adjustments to the system and created a series of targeted training sessions for each department. Additionally, I introduced a phased rollout plan, starting with one department at a time, so that we could gather feedback and make improvements before expanding to the rest of the company.

Result: After making these adjustments, the adoption rate increased significantly, and the system became an essential tool for managing customer interactions across departments. The phased rollout allowed us to address issues as they arose, and the more tailored training sessions helped employees become comfortable with the new system. This experience taught me the importance of gathering feedback, listening to users, and being flexible when it comes to implementation.

---

20. Can you give an example of a time when you had to deal with a difficult team member?

Situation: 2 years back, I was leading a software development team on a tight deadline when one of the team members began missing deadlines and delivering subpar work. Their performance was affecting the overall progress of the project and creating frustration among other team members, but I knew the team member had the potential to perform better.

Task: My task was to address the team member's performance issues while maintaining a positive team environment and ensuring the project stayed on track.

Action: I scheduled a one-on-one meeting with the team members to discuss their performance issues in a private and supportive setting. I began by acknowledging their past contributions and asking if there were any personal or professional challenges they were facing that might be affecting their work. The team member confided that they were struggling to balance the project with personal issues and were feeling overwhelmed by the workload. Together, we came up with a plan to temporarily redistribute some of their responsibilities to other team members, while I provided additional support and mentorship to help them regain their confidence and improve their work quality.

Result: The team member's performance improved significantly over the next few weeks. They were able to meet their deadlines, and their contributions helped the team deliver the project on time. This experience reinforced the importance of empathy and open communication in managing team dynamics and ensuring that everyone can perform at their best.

---

21. Tell me about a time when you had to handle a sensitive situation at work.

Situation: Last year, while working on a major project for a key client, I discovered a significant issue with the code during the testing phase that had the potential to delay the project. The issue was related to data privacy, and if left unresolved, it could have led to serious compliance violations. However, the client was expecting the project to be delivered on time, and they were unaware of this internal problem.

Task: My task was to address the technical issue immediately, communicate the potential delay to the client in a way that maintained their trust, and ensure that the team could resolve the problem without compromising on quality or data privacy standards.

Action: I first collaborated with the engineering team to thoroughly investigate the issue and determine a realistic timeline for fixing it.

Once we had a clearer understanding of the problem and the solution, I communicated the situation to the client. I explained the nature of the issue without going into technical details, reassuring them that our team was working diligently to resolve it. I proposed a revised timeline for the delivery and emphasized that addressing this issue was critical to ensuring the security and privacy of their users. I also worked closely with the team to provide support and guidance to ensure the solution was implemented as quickly as possible.

Result: The client appreciated our transparency and accepted the revised timeline. The issue was resolved without any breaches of data privacy, and the project was delivered with all the necessary compliance requirements in place. This experience reinforced the importance of clear communication, honesty, and maintaining client trust in sensitive situations.

---

22. Describe a time when you had to work with limited guidance.

Situation: Early in my career, I was assigned to lead the development of a new feature for one of our core applications. My manager was unavailable for a few weeks due to the other commitments, and I was given only a rough outline of the feature's requirements. I had no one to immediately turn to for guidance, and the success of the feature was crucial for an upcoming release.

Task: My task was to take full ownership of the feature development, ensure it aligned with the overall product strategy, and deliver it on time without detailed instructions or oversight.

Action: I began by conducting my own research to fully understand the feature's potential impact on the product and the user base. I consulted with product managers and customer support teams to gather more insights into how the feature could best serve user needs. Once I had a clear understanding, I created a detailed project plan and started development. I made sure to document all my decisions and continuously tested the feature to ensure it aligned with the project goals. To compensate for the lack of guidance, I communicated regularly with stakeholders to ensure that I was on the right track and made adjustments based on their feedback.

Result: I successfully delivered the feature on time, and it became one of the most-used tools in the application. The feature received positive feedback from both users and stakeholders. This experience taught me the importance of self-reliance, proactivity, and decision-making when working with limited guidance.

---

23. Can you tell me about a time when you had to handle a difficult customer situation?

Situation: 6 months back, I was working as a software engineer when a key customer reported a critical bug in our application that caused intermittent data loss during transactions. The customer was a high-value client who relied heavily on our product for their business operations, and after experiencing repeated issues, they were frustrated and considering switching to a competitor. The problem had been reported several times, but previous fixes had not fully resolved the issue.

Task: My task was to identify and fix the bug as quickly as possible to prevent further data loss, restore the customer's confidence in our product, and ensure they didn't leave for a competitor.

Action: I immediately escalated the issue within the engineering team and took personal ownership of debugging the problem. I reviewed the previous fixes and identified that the root cause of the issue was deeper in the transaction processing module than initially thought. I isolated the problem to a race condition that occurred under specific circumstances during peak usage. I worked closely with the DevOps team to replicate the production environment and test the fix thoroughly. To ensure the issue was fully resolved, I coordinated with the QA team to simulate various stress scenarios. Additionally, I communicated directly with the customer to keep them informed of our progress, explaining the technical challenges we were addressing and giving them realistic timelines for resolution.

Result: After deploying the fix, the customer experienced no further issues with data loss, and we continued monitoring their system to ensure stability. The customer appreciated the transparency and proactive communication throughout the process. Their confidence in our product was restored, and they decided to stay with us. This experience reinforced the importance of thorough debugging, cross-team collaboration, and clear communication when dealing with critical customer issues under pressure.

---

24. Tell me about a time when you had to adapt to a rapidly changing situation at work.

Situation: 6 months back, I was working on a software development project when halfway through, the client requested major changes to the scope of the project. These changes involved significant adjustments to both the user interface and backend architecture, which would impact the overall timeline and resource allocation. The new requirements came unexpectedly, and the team had already completed a significant portion of the original plan.

Task: My task was to adapt to the new project requirements, ensure that the team could incorporate the changes without causing too much delay, and maintain communication with the client about the new timeline and potential challenges.

Action: I immediately held a meeting with the team to assess the impact of the requested changes. We revisited our timeline and resource allocation to determine which parts of the original scope could be deprioritized or modified. I then created a new project plan that incorporated the client's changes and shared it with them, being transparent about the implications for the timeline and potential risks. I worked closely with the team to implement the changes efficiently, setting up daily stand-ups to address any blockers or unexpected issues.

Result: Although the changes extended the project timeline by a few weeks, we were able to successfully integrate all of the client's new requirements. The client was happy with the final product, and the flexibility and adaptability of the team were acknowledged. This experience taught me how to remain flexible and respond quickly to shifting project demands without losing sight of the overall objectives.

---

25. Describe a time when you had to take on a task outside your job description.

Situation: This was about 6 months ago when during a critical product release at my company, our DevOps engineer unexpectedly went on medical leave. This left the team without the necessary support to manage the infrastructure and deployment processes, which were crucial for the upcoming release. Although my primary role was as a software engineer focused on feature development, I knew that without someone stepping up to handle the DevOps tasks, the release would be significantly delayed.

Task: My task was to temporarily take over the DevOps responsibilities, ensuring that the infrastructure was properly maintained, and the deployment processes continued smoothly without impacting the release timeline.

Action: Although DevOps was not my core expertise, I quickly familiarized myself with our CI/CD pipelines, server infrastructure, and the deployment scripts. I spent time reviewing documentation, consulting with other engineers who had some DevOps experience, and engaging with external support from our cloud provider. I managed deployments, monitored system performance, and addressed any issues that arose during the release cycle. I also kept thorough documentation of all changes and processes so that the DevOps engineer could easily resume their work when they returned.

Result: The release went ahead as scheduled, with no major downtime or deployment issues. My willingness to step in and handle the DevOps responsibilities during a critical time was recognized by both the engineering team and management. This experience taught me the value of adaptability and how stepping outside of your comfort zone can help keep a project on track when unexpected challenges arise.

---

26. Can you give an example of a time when you had to make a quick decision?

Situation: 6 months back, while managing a live demo for a potential client, the application we were showcasing suddenly crashed. This demo was critical for closing a high-value contract, and the client was ready to evaluate our product against competitors. Time was of the essence, and the client was already on the call, expecting the demo to proceed smoothly.

Task: My task was to make an immediate decision about how to handle the situation, either by finding a quick solution to get the demo back on track or rescheduling the meeting, which could jeopardize the deal.

Action: I quickly assessed the situation, realizing that a full restart of the application would take too long. Instead, I decided to pivot by focusing on a different, pre-recorded demo video that highlighted the same key features, but without the risk of another crash. I explained the situation to the client, framing it as an opportunity to view the product's capabilities in action. I also assured them that our team was already working on fixing the issue and that we could follow up with a live demo later if needed.

Result: The client appreciated the quick pivot and remained engaged throughout the demo. Afterward, they expressed interest in moving forward with our product. We later fixed the application issue and scheduled another session, but the client was already convinced of the product's value by then. This experience reinforced the importance of quick decision-making and adaptability in high-pressure situations.

---

27. Tell me about a time when you had to manage a team through a difficult period.

Situation: During an economic downturn in 2022, our company had to implement budget cuts, resulting in the downsizing of my software development team. This put extra pressure on the remaining team members, who had to take on additional responsibilities while continuing to meet tight deadlines.

Task: My task was to manage the team's morale, help them navigate the increased workload, and ensure that we continued to meet our project deadlines despite the reduced manpower.

Action: I held a team meeting to acknowledge the challenges we were facing and to reassure everyone that we could overcome them with a collaborative approach. I focused on setting clear, achievable goals and adjusted our workflow to prioritize the most critical tasks. I also encouraged open communication, ensuring that any frustrations or concerns were addressed quickly. To alleviate some of the pressure, I implemented flexible work schedules and distributed the workload more evenly. I made sure to regularly check in with individual team members to offer support and recognize their hard work.

Result: Despite the difficult circumstances, the team successfully delivered on all key projects. Morale improved over time as the team adapted to the new structure, and productivity levels remained high. This experience taught me the importance of leadership, empathy, and clear communication during challenging times.

---

28. Describe a time when you had to handle multiple deadlines at once.

Situation: Last year as a project manager, I was overseeing three major projects, all of which had overlapping deadlines. Each project was critical to the company's quarterly revenue goals, and failure to meet any of the deadlines would result in significant setbacks.

Task: My task was to ensure that all three projects were completed on time without sacrificing quality, despite the competing deadlines and resource constraints.

Action: I began by creating a detailed timeline for each project, identifying the most critical tasks and any potential bottlenecks. I then prioritized the tasks based on their urgency and impact on the overall project timelines. I delegated specific responsibilities to team members based on their strengths, ensuring that no one was overwhelmed. To keep everything on track, I held daily stand-ups with each project team and regularly communicated with stakeholders to manage their expectations. I also built in buffer time to handle any unforeseen issues and made adjustments to the plan as needed.

Result: All three projects were completed on time and met the company's quality standards. The successful delivery of these projects contributed significantly to the company's quarterly revenue targets. This experience demonstrated my ability to manage multiple high-priority tasks simultaneously and reinforced the importance of clear planning and delegation.

---

29. Can you tell me about a time when you had to lead a cross-functional team?

Situation: 9 months back, I was tasked with leading the development of a new feature that required close collaboration between the software development, design, and marketing teams. Each team had its own priorities, and there were concerns about how to integrate their work-streams efficiently.

Task: My task was to bring these cross-functional teams together to ensure that the feature was developed, designed, and marketed in a cohesive way, while meeting the project's deadlines.

Action: I started by setting up regular cross-functional meetings where each team could share their progress and identify any blockers. I made sure that everyone understood the overall goals of the project and how their individual contributions fit into the larger picture. I also worked to mediate any disagreements between teams, focusing on finding solutions that worked for everyone. For instance, when the design team's proposed layout caused delays for the development team, I worked with both sides to adjust the design while keeping the user experience intact. I also created a shared project timeline that allowed for better alignment across teams.

Result: The feature was successfully developed, with all teams contributing seamlessly. The collaboration led to a well-designed, functional feature that was marketed effectively, resulting in strong customer engagement post-launch. This experience taught me the importance of facilitating communication and collaboration across different departments to achieve shared goals.

---

30. Tell me about a time when you had to present a complex idea to a non-expert audience.

Situation: Last year, I was tasked with presenting the technical details of a new software integration to the company's board of directors. The board was made up of non-technical members, and I needed to explain the benefits and functionality of the integration in a way that was easy for them to understand, without diving too deep into technical jargon.

Task: My task was to communicate the complexity of the integration clearly and concisely, highlighting the key benefits and addressing potential concerns from a business perspective.

Action: I started by identifying the core elements of the integration that would be most relevant to the board, focusing on how it would improve the company's operational efficiency and reduce costs. I created a visual presentation that used diagrams and analogies to explain the technical concepts in a way that was accessible to non-experts. For example, instead of explaining the specifics of API integration, I compared it to connecting different systems like "bridging two separate islands." Throughout the presentation, I emphasized the tangible benefits to the business, such as faster response times and improved customer satisfaction, and left technical details to the Q&A session.

Result: The board members appreciated the clarity of the presentation and approved the integration with full confidence. My ability to simplify complex technical ideas for a non-technical audience contributed to the project's success. This experience reinforced the importance of tailoring communication to the audience's level of expertise.

---

31. Describe a time when you had to change your approach to achieve a goal.

Situation: I was leading a development team working on a feature release for a client, and we initially planned to use a specific framework that aligned with the client's tech stack. However, halfway through the project, we encountered performance bottlenecks that we hadn't anticipated. Our original approach was no longer feasible, and we risked missing the deadline if we continued down that path.

Task: My task was to find an alternative solution that would allow us to deliver the feature on time without sacrificing performance, even if it meant changing the core approach midway through development.

Action: I paused the current development work and gathered the team for a brainstorming session to evaluate other frameworks that could better meet the performance requirements. After researching and testing a few alternatives, we decided to switch to a different framework that was more suited to handle high-performance tasks but required some initial setup and refactoring. I communicated the change to the client, explaining the reasons for the shift and how it would ultimately benefit the project. I also reorganized the project timeline to account for the transition period and reassigned tasks based on the new framework.

Result: Despite the mid-project pivot, we delivered the feature on time, and it exceeded the client's performance expectations. The client was impressed with our ability to adapt quickly to changes without impacting the overall delivery. This experience taught me the importance of flexibility and knowing when to change course to achieve the best possible outcome.

---

32. Can you give an example of a time when you had to take a calculated risk?

Situation: I was leading a product development team when we identified an opportunity to add a new feature that was not originally part of the product roadmap. This feature had the potential to significantly differentiate our product from competitors, but it required reallocating resources from another high-priority project.

Task: My task was to assess the potential benefits of the new feature and make a decision about whether to pursue it, knowing that it could impact the progress of other ongoing projects.

Action: I conducted a thorough market analysis to evaluate the demand for the feature and how it could provide a competitive advantage. I then worked closely with the team to estimate the development effort and the potential risks involved, such as delaying the other project and stretching resources thin. After gathering this information, I presented a detailed business case to the leadership team, outlining the risks and rewards. I recommended moving forward with the feature but suggested a phased rollout to mitigate the risks, allowing us to continue progress on the other project while dedicating some resources to the new feature.

Result: The leadership team approved the phased approach, and we successfully developed and launched the feature. It became a standout element of the product, leading to a 20% increase in customer acquisition within the first quarter. The other project also stayed on track due to the phased allocation of resources. This experience reinforced the value of taking calculated risks when supported by data and strategic planning.

---

33. Tell me about a time when you had to mentor a colleague.

Situation: A junior developer on my team was struggling with understanding some advanced coding concepts, particularly when it came to debugging complex issues. The developer's performance was being impacted, and they were starting to lose confidence in their abilities.

Task: My task was to mentor this colleague, help them improve their technical skills, and ensure they regained their confidence to contribute effectively to the team.

Action: I began by setting up regular one-on-one sessions with the developer to identify the specific areas they were struggling with. I used these sessions to walk them through real-world examples of debugging scenarios, explaining my thought process and approach to solving complex issues. I also provided them with additional resources, such as coding challenges and online courses, to help reinforce their learning. Over time, I gradually involved the developer in more challenging tasks, providing support when necessary but encouraging them to take ownership of their work. I also made sure to give positive feedback when they showed progress, which helped boost their confidence.

Result: Over the course of a few months, the junior developer's skills improved significantly. They became more comfortable with debugging and were able to handle more complex tasks independently. The quality of their work increased, and they expressed gratitude for the mentorship. This experience highlighted the importance of investing time in mentoring others and how it can benefit both the individual and the team as a whole.

---

34. Describe a time when you had to handle a tight deadline.

Situation: I was tasked with delivering a critical software update for a client, but due to the delays in the initial development phase, the deadline was only a week away, leaving very little time for testing and final adjustments. Missing the deadline would result in penalties and damage the relationship with the client.

Task: My task was to ensure that the update was delivered on time without compromising quality, despite the tight deadline.

Action: I immediately assessed the situation and prioritized the remaining tasks based on their criticality. I implemented a more aggressive but structured testing approach, where we focused on the most critical functionality first and ran parallel tests for different components. I also coordinated with the team to work in shifts, ensuring that there was continuous progress without overworking any individual. Additionally, I communicated with the client to manage their expectations and assured them that we were on track for delivery.

Result: We successfully delivered the software update on time, with minimal issues reported by the client. The client was impressed with the quick turnaround and the quality of the update. This experience reinforced my ability to work efficiently under pressure and the importance of clear prioritization and communication during tight deadlines.

---

35. Can you give an example of a time when you had to navigate a complex organizational structure to achieve a goal?

Situation: While working on a project to integrate a new software tool into our company's operations, I needed to collaborate with several departments, each with its own processes and priorities. Getting approval and alignment from all the stakeholders involved was challenging, as each department had its own agenda.

Task: My task was to navigate the complexities of the organizational structure, align all the key stakeholders, and ensure the successful implementation of the software tool.

Action: I started by identifying the key stakeholders in each department and scheduling one-on-one meetings to understand their specific needs and concerns. I used these meetings to build relationships and gather insights into how the software tool could benefit each department. I then organized a cross-departmental meeting where I presented a unified plan that addressed the concerns of each group while aligning with the company's overall goals. I facilitated open discussions to ensure that all stakeholders felt heard and that any conflicts were resolved collaboratively. Throughout the process, I maintained clear and consistent communication, providing regular updates to keep everyone on the same page.

Result: The software tool was successfully integrated, with each department feeling satisfied with the outcome. The cross-departmental collaboration led to smoother adoption, and the tool improved overall operational efficiency. This experience taught me the importance of relationship-building and communication when working in a complex organizational structure.

---

36. Tell me about a time when you had to overcome a significant obstacle to achieve a goal.

Situation: A couple of years back, I was leading the development of a mobile app for a client who wanted the app to launch in multiple regions with different language options. However, halfway through the project, we ran into a major issue: the localization framework we had chosen wasn't compatible with some of the languages we needed to support. This meant that the app wouldn't be able to meet the requirements for a global launch.

Task: My task was to find a solution that would allow us to support all necessary languages without delaying the project or compromising the user experience in different regions.

Action: I immediately called a meeting with the team to explore alternatives. We researched several other localization frameworks and identified one that could handle the required languages, but it would involve rewriting parts of the app's code to integrate it. I made the decision to temporarily pause feature development so we could prioritize this integration. I also worked closely with the product manager to revise the project timeline and kept the client informed about the changes and how they would impact the launch. The team worked extra hours to ensure that the new framework was implemented smoothly, and we allocated additional resources to test the app thoroughly in each language.

Result: We successfully integrated the new localization framework without significant delays, and the app launched globally as planned. The client was impressed with our ability to overcome the obstacle and deliver on their vision. This experience taught me the importance of adaptability and problem-solving when faced with unexpected challenges.

---

37. Describe a time when you had to balance conflicting priorities.

Situation: I was leading two major product releases simultaneously—one for a new feature and one for a critical security update. Both projects had overlapping deadlines, and stakeholders from each side were pushing for their projects to be prioritized.

Task: My task was to balance the conflicting priorities and ensure that both projects were delivered on time without compromising quality.

Action: I started by assessing the potential impact of delaying either project. The security update was critical to protecting user data, so I decided that it needed to take precedence. I communicated this decision to the product team, explaining the reasons behind the prioritization. To ensure that the feature release wasn't delayed significantly, I reallocated resources from other lower-priority tasks and adjusted the development schedule. I also worked closely with both teams to identify any tasks that could be completed in parallel to save time.

Result: The security update was delivered on time, ensuring that user data remained protected. The feature release was delayed by only a few days, but the stakeholders appreciated the transparency and the rationale behind the decision. Both projects were ultimately successful, and this experience reinforced the importance of clear prioritization and effective communication when managing conflicting demands.

---

38. Can you give an example of a time when you had to implement a significant change in your organization?

Situation: As a senior engineer, I was tasked with leading the transition from a monolithic architecture to a microservices-based system. This was a significant change for the entire engineering department, as most of the team had only worked with monolithic systems before, and the new approach required adopting new tools and methodologies.

Task: My task was to manage this transition smoothly, ensuring that the team understood the benefits of microservices, and that the new architecture was implemented without causing disruptions to ongoing projects.

Action: I began by organizing a series of training sessions to educate the team about microservices architecture, its benefits, and how it would impact our existing workflows. I collaborated with the DevOps team to set up the necessary infrastructure and created detailed documentation to guide the team through the transition. I also implemented a phased approach, where we would start by migrating less critical services to microservices while continuing to maintain the monolithic system for high-priority features. Throughout the process, I maintained open communication with both the engineering team and senior management, providing regular updates on the progress of the transition.

Result: The transition to microservices was successful, and we saw immediate improvements in scalability and deployment speed. The team adapted well to the new architecture, and it became a core part of how we developed and maintained services moving forward. This experience reinforced the importance of planning, training, and communication when implementing significant organizational changes.

---

39. Tell me about a time when you had to work with a difficult supervisor.

Situation: In a previous role, I had a supervisor who had very high expectations but was often unclear about what they wanted. This led to confusion within the team, as we were frequently asked to make changes to projects late in the process without clear direction, which caused delays and frustration.

Task: My task was to find a way to work productively with this supervisor while managing my own workload and ensuring the team could meet deadlines despite the unclear instructions.

Action: I took the initiative to schedule regular one-on-one meetings with my supervisor to clarify expectations before starting any new project. In these meetings, I asked specific questions to understand their vision more clearly and confirmed project goals in writing. I also encouraged the team to document all communications and changes so that we had a clear record of instructions. Additionally, I proactively anticipated potential issues and brought them up early in our discussions to avoid last-minute surprises.

Result: By establishing clearer communication channels, the working relationship with my supervisor improved, and the team experienced fewer last-minute changes. We were able to meet deadlines more consistently, and the overall project quality improved. This experience taught me the importance of taking the lead in establishing clarity when working with challenging supervisors.

---

40. Describe a time when you had to lead a team through a period of change.

Situation: A couple of years back, my company was undergoing a significant rebranding initiative, which required changing our core product's look, feel, and functionality. This was a major shift, as the product had been established in the market for years, and the changes needed to be implemented within a tight timeframe.

Task: My task was to lead the engineering team through the rebranding, ensuring that we met the deadlines while integrating the new design and functionality without affecting the product's existing user base.

Action: I organized a series of meetings with the product, design, and marketing teams to ensure that everyone was aligned on the rebranding goals. I worked with my team to break down the project into manageable sprints, assigning tasks based on individual strengths and priorities. To ensure that the rebranding didn't affect the product's usability, I set up a parallel testing environment where we could validate the new changes before rolling them out to users. I also maintained regular communication with the team to address any concerns and adjust the timeline as needed.

Result: The rebranding was completed on time, and the new design and functionality were well-received by users. The smooth transition helped reinforce the product's position in the market, and the team felt proud of their contribution to the successful rebrand. This experience taught me the importance of leadership and clear communication during periods of significant change.

---

41. Can you give an example of a time when you had to resolve a complex problem?

Situation: While working as a systems engineer, our web application was experiencing sporadic downtime that was affecting user experience and costing the company potential revenue. The problem was intermittent, making it difficult to diagnose and resolve quickly. The entire team was under pressure to fix the issue, but no clear cause had been identified.

Task: My task was to identify the root cause of the downtime, fix the issue, and ensure that the application's performance was stabilized without further interruptions.

Action: I started by gathering data from the application's logs and monitoring systems to look for patterns that could point to the underlying issue. I also worked closely with the DevOps and database teams to investigate whether server configuration or database queries were contributing to the problem. After conducting a deep dive into the logs, I discovered that the downtime was caused by memory leaks in one of the services, which led to resource exhaustion during peak usage times. I quickly proposed a fix by optimizing the code to better manage memory allocation and implemented more frequent garbage collection. I also suggested increasing our server monitoring alerts to catch similar issues early.

Result: Once the fix was deployed, the application's performance stabilized, and there were no further incidents of downtime. The solution not only resolved the immediate problem but also improved the overall efficiency of the application. This experience reinforced the importance of thorough problem analysis and collaboration with cross-functional teams to solve complex technical issues.

---

42. Tell me about a time when you had to manage a project with a tight budget.

Situation: I was assigned to lead a project to develop a new internal tool for our company's operations team. The project had a very limited budget due to other ongoing priorities, and we needed to develop the tool without overspending.

Task: My task was to ensure that the tool was developed efficiently, within budget constraints, while still meeting the key requirements of the operations team.

Action: I began by reviewing the project scope and identifying which features were absolutely essential for the tool's functionality. I worked with the operations team to prioritize these features and eliminated any non-critical requests that would increase costs. I also leveraged open-source software and libraries wherever possible to avoid licensing fees. Instead of hiring external developers, I redistributed tasks within my team to handle the development work in-house. Throughout the project, I closely tracked expenditures and regularly updated stakeholders on our progress to ensure that we stayed within budget.

Result: We successfully developed and deployed the tool within the allocated budget, and it met all of the key requirements set by the operations team. The tool improved operational efficiency, and stakeholders were pleased with how we managed the project despite the financial constraints. This experience taught me the value of resource management and prioritization in budget-sensitive projects.

---

43. Describe a time when you had to persuade someone to see things your way.

Situation: 3 months back, I was working on a product development team as an engineering manager, and we were debating whether to implement a new feature that I believed would improve user engagement. However, the product manager was hesitant, arguing that the feature would take up too many resources and potentially delay other higher-priority tasks.

Task: My task was to persuade the product manager that the feature would ultimately benefit the product and the company's long-term goals, while demonstrating how we could implement it without significant resource drain.

Action: I gathered data on user behavior that supported the need for the new feature, showing how it could increase user engagement and retention. I also created a rough prototype to demonstrate how the feature would work, using existing resources to minimize the impact on development time. In addition, I proposed an incremental rollout plan, where we could start with a limited version of the feature to test its impact before committing to a full release. I presented this plan to the product manager, addressing their concerns about resource allocation and explaining how the feature aligned with the company's broader goals.

Result: After seeing the data and the prototype, the product manager agreed to move forward with the feature. We implemented the initial version, which was well-received by users and resulted in a noticeable increase in engagement. This experience taught me the importance of backing up ideas with data and offering flexible solutions to persuade stakeholders.

---

44. Can you give an example of a time when you had to work with a limited timeframe?

Situation: I was part of a software development team tasked with implementing a critical feature for a client who had an upcoming product demo. However, due to delays in earlier phases of development, we were left with only one week to complete the feature and ensure it was fully functional before the demo. This was a key project milestone, and missing the deadline could have jeopardized the client relationship.

Task: My task was to help the team deliver the feature within the tight deadline, ensuring that it met the client's requirements and was stable enough for the demo.

Action: Given the limited timeframe, I prioritized the core functionalities that were critical to the demo and collaborated closely with the team to break down the tasks into smaller, manageable pieces. We organized the work into sprints, with daily stand-ups to track progress and identify any potential blockers immediately. To save time, we used automated testing tools to speed up the quality assurance process and ran code reviews in parallel to development. I also worked extra hours, coordinating with other engineers and staying in constant communication with the client to manage expectations and adjust the scope where necessary.

Result: Despite the tight deadline, we successfully delivered the core feature on time. The client's demo went smoothly, and they were impressed with the functionality we delivered. The success of this project reinforced the importance of strategic prioritization, teamwork, and clear communication when working under intense time constraints.

---

45. Tell me about a time when you had to manage a project with significant risks.

Situation: I was managing a large-scale software development project for a major client when we discovered that a critical third-party API we relied on was being deprecated, which posed a significant risk to the project timeline and functionality.

Task: My task was to mitigate this risk by finding an alternative solution that wouldn't delay the project or compromise the client's expectations, all while keeping the client informed and managing their concerns.

Action: I immediately gathered my team to brainstorm alternatives. We researched several new APIs and found one that could replace the deprecated service, though it required modifications to our codebase. I created a risk mitigation plan that included adjusting our development timeline and allocating additional resources to integrate the new API. I also communicated transparently with the client, explaining the situation and providing them with options on how we could proceed. Throughout the integration process, I kept the client updated on our progress and ensured that the new API was thoroughly tested before deployment.

Result: We successfully integrated the new API without significantly impacting the project timeline, and the client was satisfied with our proactive approach. The final product met their expectations, and the risk was effectively managed. This experience demonstrated the importance of risk management and transparent communication in delivering successful projects.

---

46. Describe a time when you had to lead by example.

Situation: During a critical product launch, my team was facing mounting pressure due to tight deadlines and high expectations from stakeholders. Several team members were feeling overwhelmed, and productivity was beginning to dip as stress levels rose.

Task: As the team lead, my task was to motivate the team, keep everyone focused, and ensure that we met our deadlines without burning out. I needed to set the tone and lead by example to foster resilience and determination within the group.

Action: I made a point of staying calm and maintaining a positive attitude, even in the face of setbacks. I took on additional tasks to help lighten the load for the rest of the team, staying late when needed and being present to troubleshoot issues quickly. I also actively participated in our daily stand-ups, offering support and brainstorming solutions to blockers. To keep morale high, I encouraged open communication and celebrated small wins throughout the process. My goal was to show through my actions that we could overcome the challenges if we stayed focused and worked together.

Result: The team followed suit, adopting a more positive and proactive mindset. We delivered the product on time, and the launch was a success. Team members expressed their appreciation for the support and leadership I provided during the stressful period. This experience reinforced the importance of leading by example and demonstrating a hands-on approach when managing high-pressure situations.

---

47. Can you give an example of a time when you had to develop a new process?

Situation: While working as a software engineer at a fast-growing startup, I noticed that our code review process was inefficient. Reviews were taking too long, and often, code quality issues were slipping through the cracks, leading to bugs in production. The process relied heavily on manual effort, and there was no clear structure, which slowed down development.

Task: My task was to develop a more efficient, structured process for code reviews that would reduce errors, improve quality, and speed up the overall development cycle.

Action: I started by analyzing our existing workflow to identify bottlenecks and frequent pain points. I researched best practices for code reviews and collaborated with senior engineers to get their input. I then proposed a new process that involved automatic linting and testing as part of our CI pipeline, setting clear guidelines for what needed to be reviewed in each pull request, and establishing a rotating review schedule so that no one person was overburdened. I also set up a tracking system to measure review times and code quality improvements.

Result: The new process led to a significant reduction in review times and a marked improvement in code quality. We experienced fewer bugs in production, and engineers were able to merge their code faster, without compromising quality. This process was eventually adopted across multiple teams in the company. This experience highlighted the value of refining internal processes to improve productivity and quality.

---

48. Tell me about a time when you had to manage a difficult conversation.

Situation: Last year, one of the team members I was managing had been underperforming for several months. Their work quality was inconsistent, and they missed multiple deadlines. As the team lead, it was my responsibility to address these issues in a constructive way without damaging the team member's morale.

Task: My task was to have a difficult conversation with the employee about their performance, provide constructive feedback, and help them improve without demoralizing them or creating a negative atmosphere within the team.

Action: I scheduled a private meeting with the employee to discuss their performance. I approached the conversation with empathy, starting by acknowledging their strengths and past contributions to the team. I then provided specific examples of where their performance had fallen short and explained the impact it was having on the project. I asked if there were any challenges they were facing that might be affecting their work and listened carefully to their response. Together, we developed a performance improvement plan that included setting clear expectations, providing additional training, and scheduling regular check-ins to monitor progress.

Result: The employee responded positively to the feedback and worked diligently to improve their performance. Over the next few weeks, their work quality improved significantly, and they regained their confidence. This experience taught me the importance of empathy and clear communication when handling difficult conversations, and how addressing issues early can lead to positive outcomes.

---

49. Describe a time when you had to make a difficult financial decision.

Situation: As a senior software engineer, I was managing a project that involved choosing between two third-party libraries for a critical feature. One was a highly reliable, well-supported but expensive enterprise solution, while the other was an open-source alternative with limited support but no direct costs. We were working within a constrained budget, and choosing the enterprise solution would require cutting funding from other parts of the project.

Task: My task was to evaluate the trade-offs and recommend a solution that fit our budget while ensuring that the project met its technical requirements and long-term scalability needs.

Action: I conducted a detailed analysis of both options, considering factors like performance, security, scalability, and the potential future maintenance costs. I ran performance tests and consulted with the engineering team about the implications of each choice. After gathering this data, I presented both options to the leadership team, clearly outlining the risks and benefits. I ultimately recommended going with the open-source solution but proposed allocating part of the budget to hire additional engineers for maintenance and customization, mitigating the risks of limited support.

Result: The leadership team approved the open-source solution with the additional engineering support. We successfully integrated the library, staying within budget and meeting our performance goals. The project was delivered on time, and the open-source solution proved stable in the long term, with the additional support ensuring quick resolution of any issues. This experience taught me the importance of balancing technical needs with financial constraints and finding creative solutions that optimize both.

---

50. Can you give an example of a time when you had to deliver bad news to a team or client?

Situation: I was managing a software development project for a client when we encountered a major technical issue that delayed the project timeline by several weeks. The client was expecting the project to be delivered on time, and I knew they would be disappointed with the news.

Task: My task was to communicate the delay to the client in a way that maintained their trust and confidence in our team's ability to deliver the project.

Action: I scheduled a meeting with the client as soon as the issue was identified. I approached the conversation with transparency and honesty, explaining the nature of the technical issue and why it had impacted the timeline. I provided them with a revised project plan, outlining the steps we were taking to resolve the issue and ensure it didn't happen again. I also reassured them that we would dedicate additional resources to get the project back on track. To mitigate their disappointment, I offered a discounted rate on the final invoice as a gesture of goodwill.

Result: Although the client was initially disappointed, they appreciated the transparency and the proactive steps we were taking to resolve the issue. The project was eventually completed successfully, and the client continued to work with us on future projects. This experience taught me the importance of honesty and proactive communication when delivering bad news.

---

51. Tell me about a time when you had to lead a remote team.

Situation: During the COVID-19 pandemic, my company transitioned to remote work, and I was assigned to lead a software development team that was now fully distributed across different time zones. This was a new experience for the team, and there were concerns about maintaining productivity and communication while working remotely.

Task: My task was to ensure that the team remained productive, collaborative, and focused on delivering projects despite the challenges of remote work.

Action: I set up a structured system of regular virtual meetings, including daily stand-ups, weekly sprint planning, and retrospectives to keep the team aligned. To accommodate different time zones, I scheduled meetings at times that worked for everyone, and I encouraged asynchronous communication using tools like Slack and Trello. I also implemented shared project tracking systems so that everyone could easily see what was being worked on and what was next in the pipeline. To maintain team morale, I organized virtual team-building activities and encouraged one-on-one check-ins to address any personal challenges or concerns.

Result: The team adapted well to remote work, and we maintained high levels of productivity throughout the pandemic. We successfully delivered all projects on time, and the team felt supported and connected, despite the physical distance. This experience reinforced my ability to lead and manage distributed teams effectively, ensuring strong collaboration and output in a remote environment.

---

52. Describe a time when you had to innovate to solve a problem.

Situation: While working on a critical feature for a client, we encountered a performance bottleneck in our backend system. The existing architecture wasn't designed to handle the high volume of concurrent requests that the client needed, and redesigning the entire system would take too long given the project timeline.

Task: My task was to find an innovative solution to improve performance without a full architectural overhaul, ensuring we could meet the client's requirements within the deadline.

Action: I researched possible performance enhancements and identified that a queue-based approach could help manage the load more efficiently. Instead of processing requests synchronously, I proposed implementing a message queue that would allow us to process the tasks asynchronously, smoothing out the load spikes. I worked with the DevOps team to implement this solution and introduced lightweight optimizations in our database queries to reduce query execution time. This approach allowed us to handle more requests concurrently without rearchitecting the entire system.

Result: The implementation significantly improved system performance, allowing us to meet the client's concurrency requirements without exceeding the project timeline. The client was pleased with the result, and the innovation became a standard practice for other high-traffic projects. This experience highlighted the importance of creative problem-solving and adapting quickly to technical challenges.

---

53. Can you give an example of a time when you had to handle a crisis at work?

Situation: During a high-profile product launch, our application experienced a critical outage due to a bug in the codebase. The outage occurred just a few hours before the product launch event, which was attended by important stakeholders and clients. This could have damaged our reputation if not resolved immediately.

Task: My task was to lead the team in identifying the root cause of the outage, implementing a fix, and ensuring that the system was stable in time for the launch.

Action: I quickly gathered the engineering team and initiated a crisis management protocol. We identified the bug as a race condition in the backend services that only appeared under heavy load. I divided the team into smaller groups, assigning one group to investigate the issue and another to work on a temporary rollback solution to get the application up and running. Simultaneously, I communicated regularly with stakeholders, keeping them informed of our progress and reassuring them that the issue was being handled. Once we identified the root cause, we implemented a fix and ran intensive testing to ensure stability under load.

Result: The issue was resolved just in time for the product launch, and the application remained stable throughout the event. Stakeholders appreciated the transparency and rapid response, and the launch proceeded successfully. This experience reinforced the importance of remaining calm under pressure and quickly mobilizing the team to handle critical crises.

---

54. Tell me about a time when you had to make a decision that was unpopular.

Situation: At the time I was working at XYZ company as a team leader, I made the decision to implement a new process for peer code reviews, requiring all team members to review each other's work before pushing to production. Some of the team members were resistant to the change, as they felt it added extra time to their workflow and wasn't necessary for smaller tasks.

Task: My task was to implement the new peer review process in a way that addressed team concerns while ensuring that code quality and collaboration improved.

Action: I held a team meeting to explain the rationale behind the new process, focusing on how it would improve code quality, catch bugs earlier, and help team members learn from each other. I also shared data from other teams who had successfully implemented peer reviews, showing that it led to fewer bugs in production and faster issue resolution. To accommodate the team's concerns about workflow, I introduced a flexible approach where smaller, low-risk changes could go through a faster review process, while more complex code required thorough review. I also scheduled a trial period to gather feedback and refine the process if needed.

Result: While there was initial resistance, the team quickly saw the benefits of the new process. Code quality improved, and the number of bugs in production decreased significantly. After the trial period, the team fully adopted the peer review process, and it became a standard practice. This experience showed me that even unpopular decisions can succeed with clear communication, data to support the change, and a willingness to listen to feedback.

---

55. Describe a time when you had to collaborate with a team from a different department.

Situation: I was working on a new feature for a mobile app, and its success depended on data from our analytics team. However, there was a delay in getting the necessary analytics data due to a lack of alignment between the engineering and analytics teams.

Task: My task was to facilitate better collaboration between the two teams to ensure the data was provided on time, and that the feature was developed with accurate insights.

Action: I scheduled a series of cross-team meetings to understand the analytics team's challenges and to explain the engineering team's requirements and timelines. We agreed on a shared plan and set clear deadlines for each team's deliverables. I also introduced a shared project management tool to improve visibility into both teams' progress, allowing for easier communication and ensuring that any blockers were quickly addressed.

Result: The improved collaboration allowed the analytics team to provide the necessary data ahead of the deadline, and we were able to integrate the feature as planned. The collaboration between the departments became more efficient, and the process was adopted for future cross-functional projects. This experience taught me the importance of clear communication and structured collaboration when working with teams from different departments.

---

56. Can you give an example of a time when you had to take the initiative to solve a problem?

Situation: A few weeks back, I noticed that our customer support team was receiving a high volume of tickets related to the same technical issue, which was frustrating both customers and staff. The issue wasn't being resolved quickly enough because of a gap in communication between the development and support teams.

Task: My task was to take the initiative to bridge the gap between the two teams and find a more efficient way to resolve these recurring technical issues.

Action: I started by analyzing the tickets to identify the root cause of the technical problem and then met with both the development and support teams to discuss the issue. I facilitated communication between the teams, ensuring that the developers understood the scope of the problem from the customers' perspective and that the support team had the tools and knowledge to handle the issue effectively. I also worked with the development team to implement a long-term fix and provided the support team with a knowledge base article that they could use to assist customers in the meantime.

Result: The communication between the teams improved, and the technical issue was resolved. The number of support tickets related to the problem dropped significantly, and customer satisfaction improved, as a result. This experience highlighted the importance of taking the initiative to solve problems that affect multiple departments and ensuring that teams work together effectively.

---

57. Tell me about a time when you had to delegate tasks effectively.

Situation: Last year, I was managing a large project with a tight deadline and realized that I wouldn't be able to complete all the tasks on my own. The team was capable, but some members were new and hesitant to take on more responsibility.

Task: My task was to delegate responsibilities effectively, ensuring that everyone on the team contributed while maintaining quality and meeting the project deadline.

Action: I began by assessing each team member's strengths and expertise. I delegated tasks based on their individual skills, ensuring that each person was assigned work that suited their abilities and allowed them to grow. For the newer team members, I provided more detailed instructions and mentorship to help them build confidence in their roles. I also set clear expectations and deadlines for each task and held regular check-ins to monitor progress and offer support. By encouraging open communication, I ensured that team members felt comfortable asking for help when needed.

Result: The project was completed on time, and the quality of the work was high. The team members felt more confident and engaged in their roles, and the newer members expressed appreciation for the opportunity to take on more responsibility. This experience reinforced the importance of effective delegation and how it can lead to both individual growth and successful project outcomes.

---

58. Describe a time when you had to work with a difficult client.

Situation: In my last project, I was managing an account for a client who frequently requested last-minute changes to the project scope, causing delays and frustration within the team. The client had high expectations but didn't always communicate clearly, which made it difficult to meet their needs.

Task: My task was to manage the client's expectations while keeping the project on track and ensuring that the team didn't get overwhelmed by constant changes.

Action: I scheduled a meeting with the client to discuss their concerns and explain how the frequent changes were impacting the project timeline and the team's ability to deliver quality work. I provided a detailed project plan with clear milestones and deadlines, emphasizing the importance of sticking to the agreed-upon scope to meet their expectations. I also suggested setting up regular progress meetings to keep the client informed and address any issues before they escalated. Throughout the project, I maintained open communication and worked to build a positive relationship with the client.

Result: The client agreed to the project plan, and the scope of changes was significantly reduced, allowing us to complete the project on time.

The client was satisfied with the final product and appreciated the clear communication. This experience taught me the importance of managing client expectations and maintaining strong communication throughout the project.

---

59. Can you give an example of a time when you had to manage a project that was not going as planned?

Situation: 6 months back, I was leading a software development project when we encountered a major technical issue with a third-party integration that threatened to delay the entire project. The integration was critical to the functionality of the software, and the team was struggling to find a solution.

Task: My task was to find a way to resolve the technical issue without significantly delaying the project or compromising the quality of the software.

Action: I immediately convened a meeting with the development team to assess the situation and brainstorm potential solutions. We identified a workaround that would allow us to continue development while we worked on a permanent fix for the integration. I adjusted the project timeline and communicated the changes to stakeholders, ensuring that they were aware of the situation and our plan to resolve it. I also implemented additional testing and quality assurance measures to ensure that the workaround didn't impact the final product.

Result: The project was completed on time, and the final product met all quality standards. The workaround was successful, and the technical issue was resolved without impacting the user experience. This experience demonstrated my ability to manage unexpected challenges and keep projects on track.

---

60. Tell me about a time when you had to handle multiple responsibilities simultaneously.

Situation: A year ago, I was managing two major projects at the same time. One was a product launch and another one a company-wide initiative to improve process efficiency. Both required my full attention, and I was also responsible for leading my team through these changes while maintaining productivity.

Task: My task was to manage all responsibilities effectively, ensuring that both projects stayed on track and that my team remained supported during the process.

Action: I prioritized my tasks by creating a detailed schedule that allocated specific time blocks to each responsibility. I delegated responsibilities to my team members, empowering them to take ownership of key tasks, while I focused on high-level decision-making. I also implemented a system for regular check-ins to track progress on both projects, providing support where needed and adjusting timelines as necessary. Additionally, I made sure to communicate clearly with stakeholders about progress and any potential delays, keeping everyone aligned.

Result: Both projects were completed successfully, with the product launch being a success and the process efficiency initiative leading to measurable improvements. My ability to balance multiple responsibilities was recognized by senior management, and the team appreciated the clear communication and structure. This experience reinforced my skills in time management, delegation, and multitasking.

PART 3

CODING INTERVIEWS

Chapter 21

DSA Roadmap for Coding Interviews

The purpose of this Data Structures & Algorithms (DSA) roadmap is to provide you with a structured and comprehensive plan to master DSA over six months. This guide will help you systematically build your knowledge, starting with fundamental concepts and gradually moving towards complex topics. By following this roadmap, you'll develop the skills and confidence needed to excel in coding interviews and solve problems efficiently.

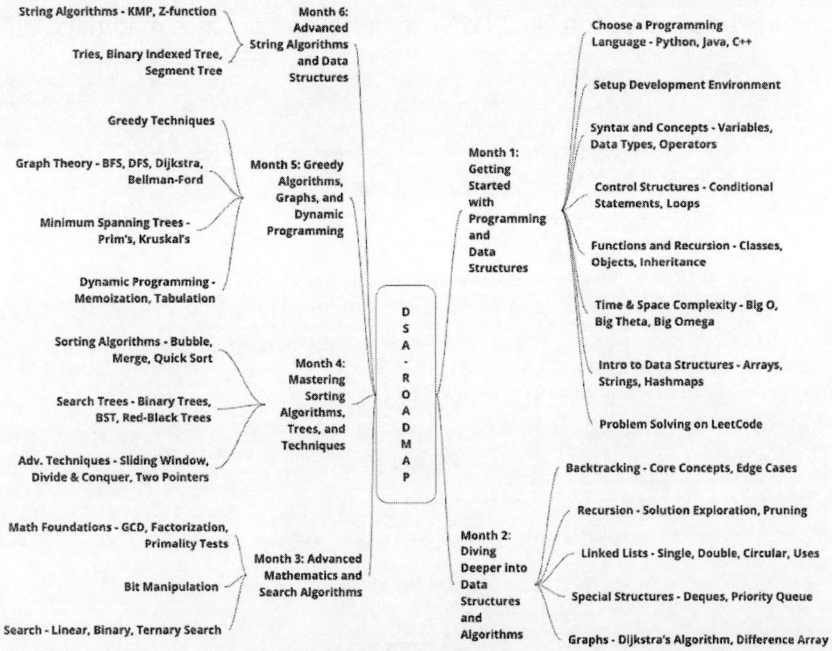

Figure — 21.1

How to Use this Roadmap

This roadmap is designed to be flexible, allowing you to adjust the pace according to your current skill level and schedule. Each month focuses on specific areas of DSA, with clear goals and recommended practices. To make the most of this guide, dedicate regular time to studying, practicing problems, and reviewing concepts. While the plan is structured for six months, extend or compress timelines based on your comfort level and progress.

21.1 Month One: Programming and Data Structures

The goal this month is to establish a solid foundation in programming and data structures. You'll begin by choosing a programming language and getting comfortable with its basic features. By the end of the month, you should have a grasp of essential programming concepts, data structures, and object-oriented programming (OOP).

Refer [Part 4: Resources For Interviews] section of the book. Go to 'Month-1' for video tutorials, DSA examples, and practice materials.

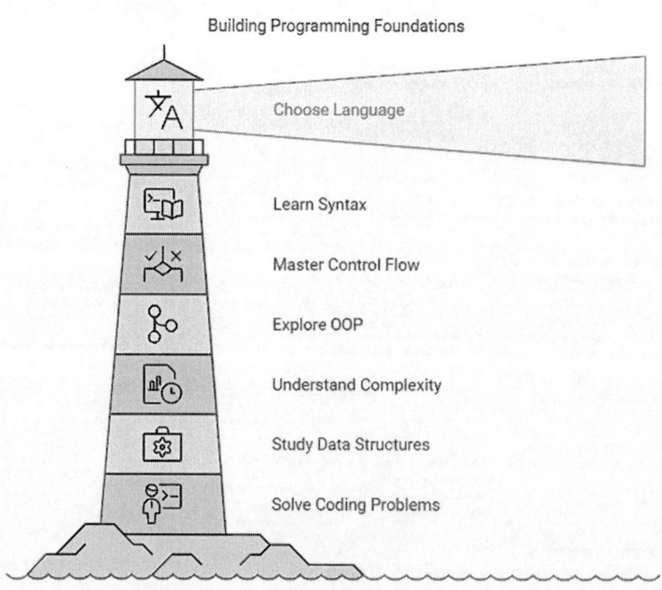

Figure – 21.2

▶ **Pick a Programming Language**

- Choose a language that suits your needs (e.g., Python, Java, C++).
- Set up the development environment with necessary tools like IDEs or compilers.
- Plan to stick with this language consistently throughout your journey.

▶ **Learn Basic Syntax, Data Types, Variables, and Operators**

- Understand the core syntax and write simple programs.
- Get familiar with primitive data types like integers, floats, and characters.
- Learn how to use operators like arithmetic, logical, and comparison operators in your code.

▶ **Master Conditional Statements, Loops, and Functions**

- Use conditional statements (if-else) to control the flow of your programs.
- Implement loops (for, while) to repeat actions based on conditions.
- Learn to write functions, understand parameters, return values, and reusability.

▶ **Explore Object-Oriented Programming (OOP)**

- Get introduced to OOP concepts like classes, objects, inheritance, polymorphism, encapsulation, and abstraction.
- Write simple OOP programs to practice creating and using classes and methods.

▶ **Introduction to Time & Space Complexity**

- Understand the basics of time complexity and how it affects algorithm efficiency.
- Learn about Big O, Big Ω, and Big Θ notations and how they describe algorithm performance.

▶ **Study Data Structures: Arrays, Strings, and Hashmaps**

- Work with arrays: Learn how to declare, initialize, and manipulate array elements.
- Explore strings: Practice string manipulations like concatenation, slicing, and searching.
- Understand hashmaps: Learn the concept of key-value pairs and basic operations such as insertion, deletion, and lookup.

► **Solve Coding Problems on LeetCode**

- Set up your LeetCode environment and start solving problems, focusing on beginner-friendly challenges.
- Begin with easy problems and progress to medium difficulty as you grow more confident.
- Don't hesitate to use the problem editorials or discussions if you get stuck.

Closing Thoughts for Month 1

By the end of Month 1, you should have a clear understanding of fundamental programming concepts, be comfortable working with essential data structures, and have started to develop problem-solving skills. Use this month to build good habits, write code daily, and understand the importance of both thinking and coding. Prepare for the more complex challenges ahead by solidifying your base.

Prerequisites Before Entering Month 2

To build a strong foundation before advancing to Month 2, familiarize yourself with LeetCode and begin honing your problem-solving skills. Here's a simple step-by-step guide that you can use if you are not using it already.

LeetCode Step-by-Step Guide

1. **Set Up Your LeetCode Environment**

- Home Base: Use the LeetCode Algorithms Problem Set (https://leetcode.com/problemset/algorithms/) as your starting point.
- Sort Problems: Sort problems from easiest to hardest by clicking the "Difficulty" header twice.
- Unsolved on Top: Sort unsolved problems to the top by clicking the empty header in the first column.

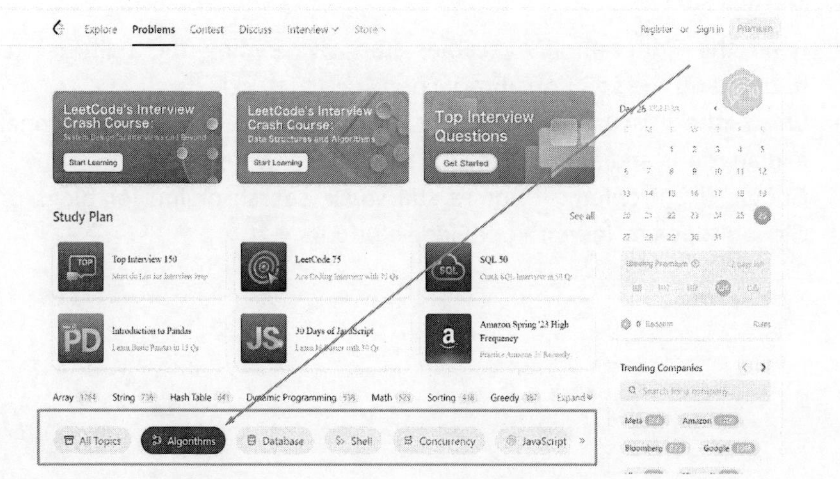

Figure – 21.3

2. **Begin Solving Problems**

- Start Easy: Focus on the easiest problems first and move on to harder ones as you progress.
- Use Editorials: Choose problems that have an editorial for guidance and well-explained solutions.
- Focus on Quality: Prioritize problems with good reviews, ideally with a 4:1 upvote-to-downvote ratio.

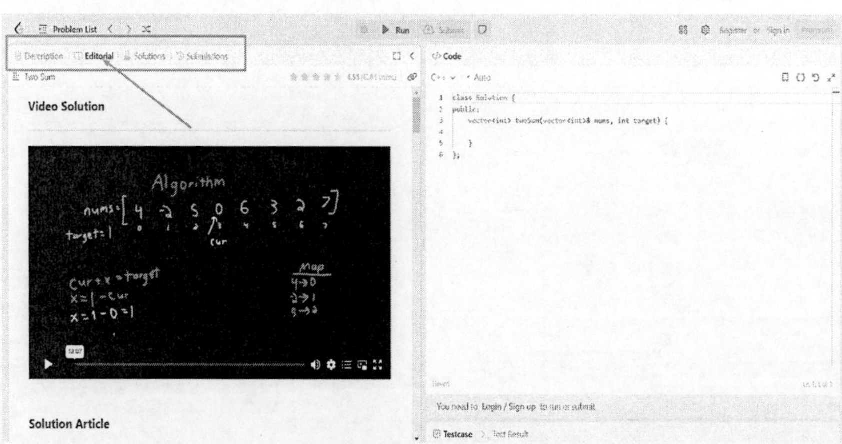

Figure – 21.4

3. **Getting Unstuck**

- Read the Editorial: If available, start by reading the editorial to understand the solution approach.
- Check the Discuss Tab: Explore the "Discuss" tab for additional explanations and alternative approaches.
- Google the Problem: If you're still stuck, search online for blogs or GitHub repositories with detailed solutions.

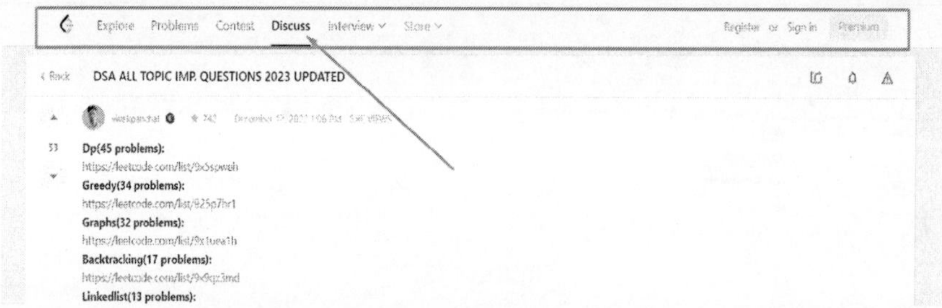

Figure – 21.5

4. **Refine Your Skills**

- Filter by Tags: If you need to improve in specific areas, filter problems by tags related to the algorithms or data structures you need to practice.

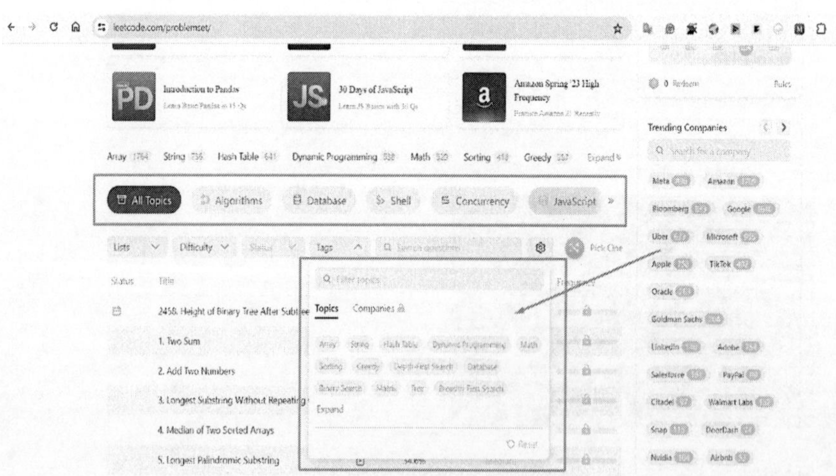

Figure – 21.6

- Optimize Solutions: Revisit older problems and refine your solutions for better runtime and memory efficiency.
- Participate in Contests: Weekly contests on LeetCode offer an excellent opportunity to test your skills under time pressure and see how you rank against others.

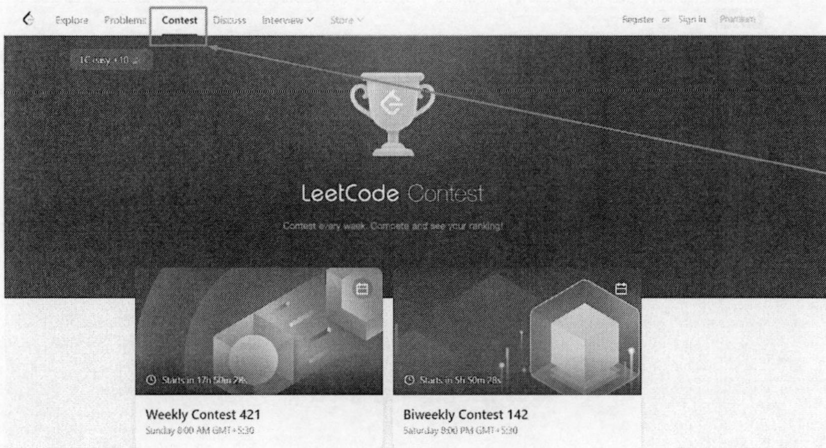

Figure – 21.7

Completing this guide will help you sharpen your problem-solving skills and get comfortable using LeetCode as a resource. Focus on building good habits and refining your approaches before moving on to the more advanced topics in Month 2.

21.2 Month Two: Diving Deeper into DSA

This month, you'll deepen your understanding of essential data structures and algorithms. You'll focus on recursion, backtracking, and various fundamental data structures. Additionally, you'll explore key algorithms like Kadane's algorithm and the difference array. By the end of this month, you'll have a strong grasp of these topics, which will create a decent building blocks for tackling more complex programming challenges.

Refer [Part 4: Resources For Interviews] section of the book. Go to 'Month-2' for video tutorials, DSA examples, and practice materials.

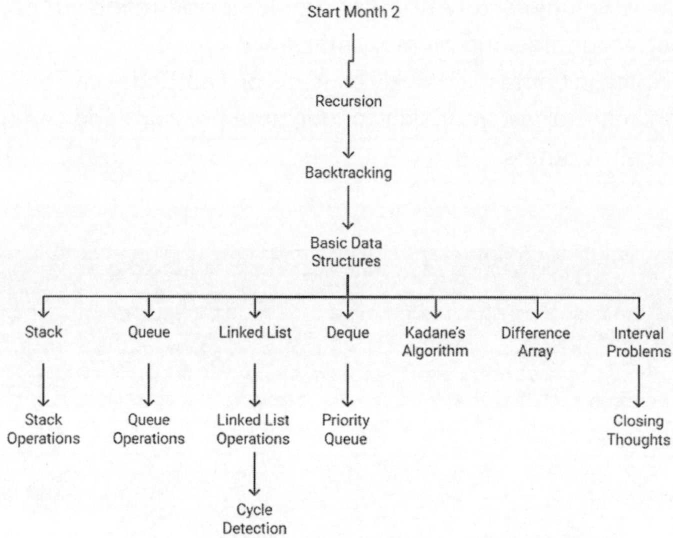

Figure – 21.8

Recursion

- Understand the core principles: Learn how recursive calls work and how to recognize base and recursive cases.
- Problem decomposition: Practice breaking down problems into smaller subproblems that can be solved recursively.
- Recursion depth: Recognize the impact of recursion depth and stack space limitations.
- Edge cases: Learn to handle edge cases carefully in recursive algorithms.

Backtracking

- Solution exploration: Learn to explore multiple solutions by trying out various possibilities and backtracking when constraints are violated.
- Efficiency: Focus on writing optimized backtracking solutions by pruning unnecessary branches early.
- Problem patterns: Recognize patterns that can be solved using backtracking, such as generating permutations and solving puzzles.

Basic Data Structures (Stack, Queue, Linked List)

- Stack: Master the LIFO principle, understanding when to use stacks in algorithms such as depth-first search (DFS), expression evaluation, and backtracking problems.

- Queue: Understand the FIFO principle and its applications in breadth-first search (BFS), task scheduling, and buffering.
- Linked List: Grasp the fundamentals of linked list operations such as insertion, deletion, and traversal, as well as common interview scenarios involving linked lists (e.g., detecting cycles, reversing lists).

Stack

- Understanding stack operations: Master push, pop, and peek operations, and their use in solving problems involving recursion and backtracking.
- Applications: Recognize where stacks are useful in algorithms like expression parsing, undo/redo functionality, and balanced parentheses checking.

Queue

- Queue operations: Master the basic enqueue and dequeue operations.
- Applications: Learn to apply queues in scenarios like BFS, task scheduling, and circular queues for resource management. Focus on implementing both basic and priority queues.

Linked Lists

- List operations: Understand how to implement linked lists, perform insertion, deletion, and traversal.
- Problem-solving: Focus on how linked lists can be applied in real-world problems like memory management and data organization.
- Cycle detection: Learn to detect loops in linked lists, an essential concept in many algorithmic problems.

Cycle Detection in Linked Lists

- Cycle detection algorithms: Master techniques like Floyd's Cycle-Finding Algorithm (Tortoise and Hare) to detect loops.
- Impact of cycles: Understand why detecting cycles is important in preventing infinite loops and deadlocks in programs.

Deque (Double-Ended Queue)

- Deque operations: Learn to implement deque operations such as inserting and removing elements from both ends.
- Sliding window problems: Focus on applying deques in problems involving sliding windows and maintaining order within a range.

Priority Queue

- Priority-based operations: Learn how priority queues work using heaps and how to efficiently insert and remove elements based on priority.
- Problem-solving: Focus on solving problems where elements need to be processed in a specific order, such as task scheduling and shortest path algorithms.

Kadane's Algorithm

- Maximizing subarrays: Master Kadane's algorithm for finding the maximum sum of contiguous subarrays, a frequent interview problem.
- Optimization: Focus on optimizing algorithms for maximum subarray problems by reducing time complexity from brute-force solutions.

Difference Array

- Range updates: Learn how difference arrays help perform efficient range updates in constant time.
- Efficiency: Master how to reduce complexity for problems involving interval-based modifications.

Interval Problems

- Interval handling: Focus on mastering algorithms that merge intervals, find overlaps, and solve problems that involve range-based operations.
- Practical applications: Apply interval problems to scheduling, allocation, and sorting tasks in competitive programming.

Closing Thoughts for Month 2

By the end of this month, you will have strengthened your understanding of advanced data structures and algorithms. The knowledge gained will equip you to tackle more complex coding challenges with confidence, especially in competitive programming or technical interviews.

21.3 Month Three: Advanced Mathematics and Search Algorithms

This month focuses on strengthening your mathematical foundations, learning advanced number theory concepts, and mastering search algorithms. You will explore topics such as bit manipulation, primality tests, binary and ternary search, and fundamental mathematical techniques to tackle competitive programming challenges.

Refer [Part 4: Resources For Interviews] section of the book. Go to 'Month-3' for video tutorials, DSA examples, and practice materials.

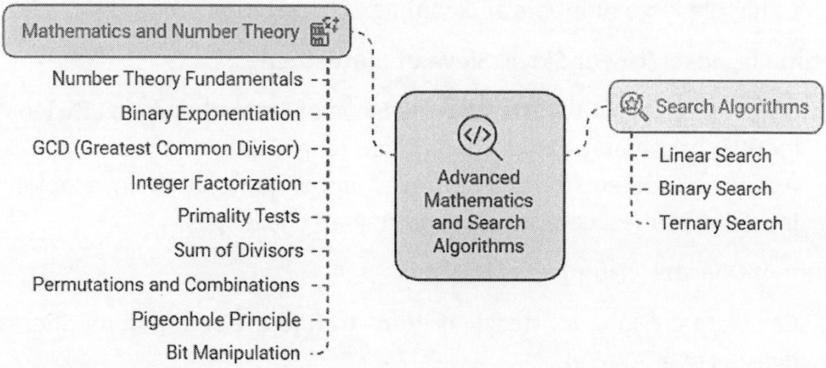

Figure – 21.9

Maths and Number Theory

- Focus on mathematical concepts: Learn number theory fundamentals, including divisibility, factorization, and modular arithmetic.
- Apply number theory: Solve problems related to prime factorization, common divisors, and number manipulation to reinforce your understanding.

Binary Exponentiation

- Master efficient exponentiation: Learn how to quickly compute large powers using the binary exponentiation method.
- Focus on optimization: Apply binary exponentiation to solve problems that involve repeated multiplication and modular arithmetic.

GCD (Greatest Common Divisor)

- Understand GCD computation: Master the Euclidean algorithm to calculate GCD efficiently.
- Solve GCD-based problems: Apply the GCD concept in modular arithmetic, fraction simplification, and other number-related problems.

Integer Factorization

- Factorize integers efficiently: Learn how to break down numbers into prime factors and apply these techniques in solving problems related to divisibility and factorization.
- Focus on advanced factorization methods: Utilize optimized approaches to handle large numbers and complex factorization scenarios.

Primality Tests (Linear Sieve, Sieve of Eratosthenes)

- Implement primality tests: Use the Sieve of Eratosthenes to efficiently identify prime numbers within a given range.
- Apply in problems: Utilize prime number generation in problems involving primes, composites, and related challenges.

Sum of Divisors / Number of Divisors

- Calculate divisors: Master algorithms to find the sum and number of divisors of a number.
- Apply to number theory problems: Solve problems involving divisor sums, factor counts, and divisor-based challenges.

Permutations and Combinations (Star and Bars, Inclusion-Exclusion Principle)

- Master combinatorics: Learn how to calculate permutations, combinations, and apply the inclusion-exclusion principle to solve combinatorial problems.
- Solve advanced combinatorics: Apply these techniques to complex problems involving arrangements and selections.

Pigeonhole Principle

- Apply the principle: Use the pigeonhole principle to prove existence results and solve problems that rely on counting arguments.
- Solve existence-based problems: Identify scenarios where the pigeonhole principle helps prove the existence of specific conditions.

Bit Manipulation

- Learn bit manipulation: Master bitwise operations, such as AND, OR, XOR, and bit shifts, to solve problems more efficiently.
- Apply in optimizations: Use bit manipulation to optimize solutions to problems that involve binary representations and operations.

Search Algorithms

Linear Search

- Understand basic searching: Implement linear search for unsorted data and analyze its performance.
- Solve search-based problems: Focus on identifying specific elements in arrays and matrices using linear search techniques.

Binary Search

- Master binary search: Implement binary search for efficiently finding elements in sorted arrays.
- Apply binary search: Solve problems that require quick lookups and use binary search in decision-making scenarios.

Ternary Search

- Learn ternary search: Understand how to apply ternary search to optimize the search for unimodal functions.
- Compare with binary search: Solve problems that benefit from the additional precision offered by ternary search.

Closing Thoughts for Month 3

This month you will have gained a deep understanding of essential mathematical techniques and search algorithms, equipping you with tools to tackle advanced programming problems.

This foundation will allow you to approach problems with confidence, especially those related to optimization and efficiency. The goal here is to learn the mathematical foundations and advanced number theory concepts essential for problem-solving in competitive programming.

You'll also dive into bit manipulation techniques and explore various search algorithms, including linear, binary, and ternary search.

21.4 Month Four: Sorting, Trees, and Advanced Techniques

This month, the focus shifts to mastering various sorting algorithms, understanding tree data structures, and delving into advanced techniques like sliding windows, divide and conquer, and two-pointer methods. By the end of the month, you will have a strong grasp of sorting mechanisms, tree structures, and strategies for optimizing solutions to complex challenges.

Refer [Part 4: Resources For Interviews] section of the book. Go to 'Month-4' for video tutorials, DSA examples, and practice materials.

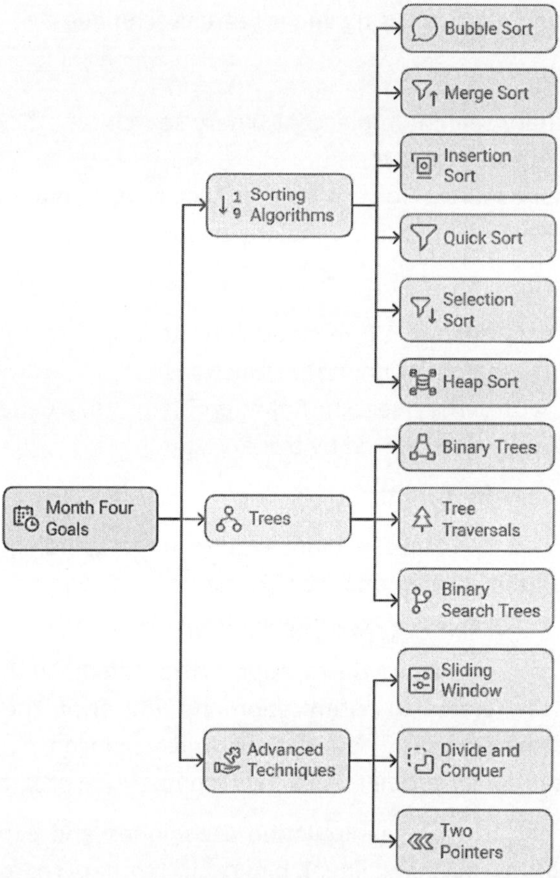

Figure – 21.10

Sorting Algorithms

Bubble Sort

- Understand how Bubble Sort works by repeatedly swapping adjacent elements to sort a list.
- Analyze its time complexity and identify when Bubble Sort is appropriate.

Merge Sort

- Master the divide and conquer approach in Merge Sort to break down arrays into smaller parts and merge them in sorted order.
- Learn how Merge Sort optimizes sorting for larger datasets.

Insertion Sort

- Understand how Insertion Sort works by picking elements and placing them in the correct position.
- Analyze its performance on small and partially sorted datasets.

Quick Sort

- Learn how Quick Sort uses partitioning to sort arrays.
- Focus on understanding the average vs. worst-case time complexities and when to use Quick Sort.

Selection Sort

- Understand how Selection Sort repeatedly selects the minimum element from unsorted parts and swaps it into position.
- Evaluate its performance for small datasets.

Heap Sort

- Learn how Heap Sort uses binary heaps to efficiently sort data.
- Compare its performance with other sorting algorithms, focusing on its space and time complexity.

Trees

Binary Trees

- Understand the structure and properties of binary trees.
- Practice implementing basic operations such as insertion, deletion, and traversal (in-order, pre-order, post-order).

Tree Traversals

- Learn and implement tree traversal techniques: in-order, pre-order, post-order, and level-order.
- Understand when to use each traversal method based on the problem.

Binary Search Trees (BST)

- Learn the unique properties of binary search trees and how they enable efficient searching, insertion, and deletion.
- Implement and practice BST operations in various coding problems.

Advanced Techniques

Sliding Window

- Understand the sliding window technique for solving problems related to subarrays or substrings.
- Practice implementing solutions that require continuous window updates and optimization.

Divide and Conquer

- Master the divide and conquer technique for breaking problems into smaller subproblems and solving them recursively.
- Apply this approach to problems like finding maximum subarrays or merging sorted lists.

Two Pointers

- Learn the two-pointer technique for efficiently solving array and string problems, such as finding pairs or subarrays with specific properties.
- Practice applying this method to problems involving partitioning or searching.

Closing Thoughts for Month 4

By the end of Month 4, you should have mastered multiple sorting algorithms, gained a solid understanding of tree-based data structures, and become comfortable with advanced techniques like sliding windows, divide and conquer, and two-pointers. These skills will be essential as you continue solving more complex problems in programming and competitive coding.

21.5 Month Five: Greedy Algorithms, Graphs, and Dynamic Programming

In this month, the focus will be on mastering greedy algorithms, understanding graph theory, and diving deep into dynamic programming (DP).

These topics will equip you with the essential tools to solve complex problems in competitive programming and system design. By the end of the month, you will be comfortable tackling a wide range of problems involving optimization, search, and dynamic problem-solving techniques.

Refer [Part 4: Resources For Interviews] section of the book. Go to 'Month-5' for video tutorials, DSA examples, and practice materials.

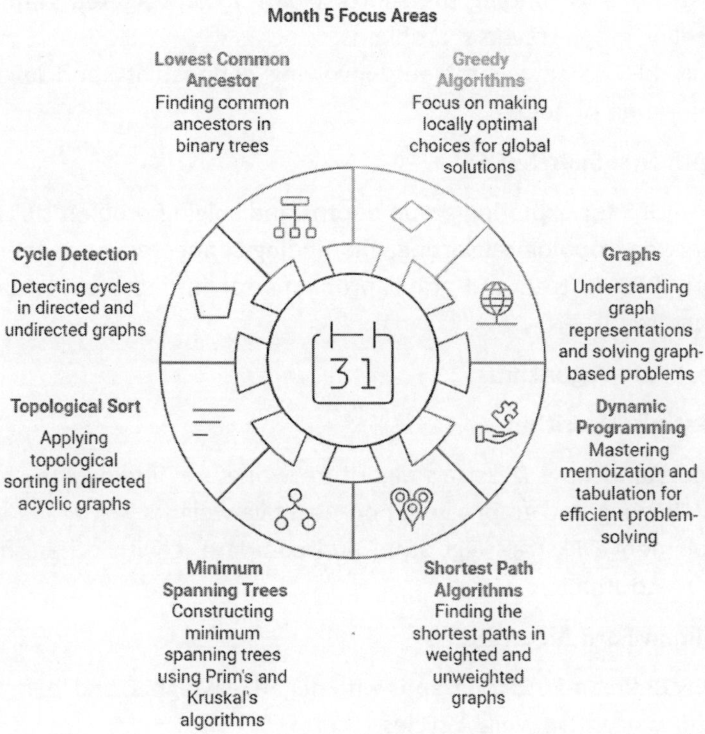

Figure – 21.11

Greedy Algorithms

- Grasp the core concept of greedy algorithms: make the locally optimal choice at each step with the hope of achieving a global optimum.
- Learn how to recognize and solve classic greedy problems such as the coin change problem, fractional knapsack problem, and job sequencing problem.

Graphs

- Understand different graph representations (adjacency matrix, adjacency list) and properties of graphs (directed, undirected, weighted, and unweighted).
- Learn to implement and work with these representations to solve graph-based problems.

Search Algorithms in Graphs

► Breadth First Search (BFS)

- Master BFS for finding the shortest path in unweighted graphs and handling graph traversal problems.
- Apply BFS to solve problems involving connectivity and level-wise exploration of nodes.

► Depth First Search (DFS)

- Learn DFS for exploring graph depths and solving problems like cycle detection, topological sorting, and finding connected components.
- Apply DFS to tree and graph problems for in-depth exploration of structures.

Shortest Path Algorithms

► Dijkstra's Algorithm

- Understand how Dijkstra's algorithm works for finding the shortest path in weighted graphs with non-negative weights.
- Implement Dijkstra's algorithm and compare it with other shortest path algorithms.

► Bellman-Ford Algorithm

- Study Bellman-Ford for graphs with negative weights, and learn how it handles negative weight cycles.
- Compare the time complexity and use cases of Bellman-Ford with Dijkstra's algorithm.

► Floyd-Warshall Algorithm

- Learn the Floyd-Warshall algorithm for finding shortest paths between all pairs of vertices.
- Implement it to solve problems involving dense graphs where all-pairs shortest path calculations are needed.

Minimum Spanning Tree Algorithms

► Prim's Algorithm

- Master Prim's algorithm for finding the minimum spanning tree in a graph, focusing on its greedy approach.
- Learn when to apply Prim's algorithm, particularly in network design problems.

▶ **Kruskal's Algorithm**

- Understand Kruskal's algorithm for constructing a minimum spanning tree by considering edge weights and avoiding cycles.
- Compare Kruskal's approach with Prim's to identify the most suitable algorithm for different scenarios.

Topological Sort

- Grasp the concept of topological sorting in directed acyclic graphs (DAGs) and learn to apply it in scheduling and dependency resolution problems.

Cycle Detection

- Learn algorithms for detecting cycles in both directed and undirected graphs, and understand their implications in graph traversal and algorithms like topological sort.

Lowest Common Ancestor (LCA)

Study the LCA problem in trees, focusing on binary trees and binary search trees, and learn to implement solutions that efficiently find the common ancestor of two nodes.

Dynamic Programming (DP)

▶ **Memoization**

- Master memoization, which stores results of expensive recursive function calls and reuses them to avoid redundant computations.
- Apply this technique to optimize recursive algorithms, making them more efficient.

▶ **Tabulation**

- Learn the tabulation method, a bottom-up approach to dynamic programming that solves subproblems iteratively and uses the results to build up to the solution of the overall problem.

DP Problem List (Topic-Wise)

▶ **Linear DP**

- Focus on mastering linear dynamic programming problems that involve sequential decision-making and optimization.

▶ **DP with Trees and Graphs**

- Learn how to apply dynamic programming techniques to tree and graph problems, especially those involving pathfinding and state transitions.

▶ **Knapsack-Based DP**

- Study variations of knapsack problems and learn how to apply dynamic programming to solve them efficiently.

▶ **DP with Bit Manipulation**

- Explore problems where dynamic programming is combined with bit manipulation to optimize state transitions.

▶ **DP on Math Problems**

- Solve mathematical problems using dynamic programming to improve your number theory skills.

▶ **Classical DP Problems**

- Master classical dynamic programming problems such as the longest increasing subsequence, coin change, and edit distance.

▶ **Grid-Based DP**

- Learn to apply dynamic programming to grid-based problems that involve pathfinding, counting paths, and optimizing movement in grids.

▶ **Multidimensional DP**

- Focus on multidimensional dynamic programming problems where the state space is more complex, and multiple variables need to be optimized simultaneously.

▶ **Digit Problems with DP**

- Explore digit-related dynamic programming problems, focusing on problems like finding specific digit patterns or counting numbers with certain properties.

▶ **Interval Problems with DP**

- Learn how to solve interval-related problems using dynamic programming, particularly when dealing with overlapping intervals and partitioning intervals.

Closing Thoughts for Month 5

By the end of Month 5, you should have a strong understanding of greedy algorithms, graph theory, and dynamic programming. These techniques will allow you to solve a variety of complex problems in a systematic and optimized manner. Keep practicing, and remember to solidify your understanding by solving a wide range of problems.

21.6 Month Six: Advanced String Algorithms and Data Structures

This month focuses on mastering advanced string algorithms and essential data structures that are commonly used in competitive programming and real-world applications.

You'll learn about string pattern matching, hashing techniques, and advanced tree-based data structures such as Binary Indexed Trees (BIT) and Segment Trees.

By the end of this month, you'll be proficient in solving complex string manipulation problems and efficiently handling large datasets with specialized data structures.

Refer [Part 4: Resources For Interviews] section of the book. Go to 'Month-6' for video tutorials, DSA examples, and practice materials.

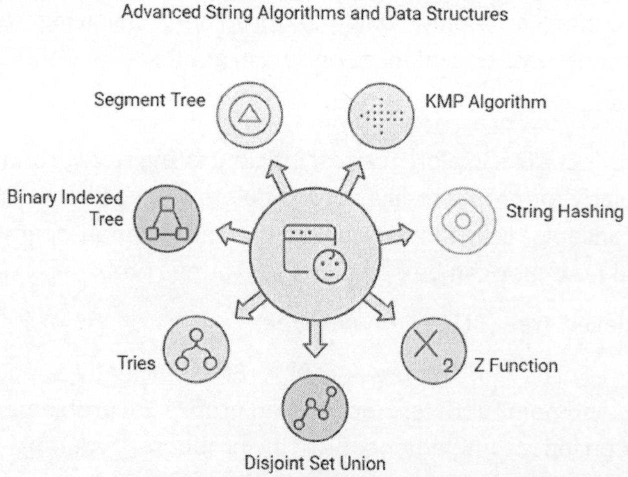

Figure – 21.12

KMP (Knuth-Morris-Pratt) Algorithm

- What to Focus On: Learn how the KMP algorithm works by pre-processing patterns into the longest prefix suffix (LPS) array to allow for efficient string matching.
- Core Concepts: Focus on understanding how the LPS array helps skip unnecessary comparisons and the scenarios where KMP is effective.

String Hashing

- What to Focus On: Learn the basics of string hashing for efficient string comparison, exploring hash functions, collisions, and methods to reduce them.
- Core Concepts: Understand how to implement hash functions and apply them to solve problems involving substring searches.

Z Function

- What to Focus On: Grasp the concept of the Z-function, which calculates the Z-array for strings to determine the longest substring from each position that matches the prefix.
- Core Concepts: Learn how the Z-function helps in pattern matching, string comparison, and string analysis.

Disjoint Set Union (DSU)

- What to Focus On: Master the union-find data structure and understand how path compression and union by rank improve efficiency.
- Core Concepts: Apply DSU to problems involving connected components, cycles, and merging sets in graphs.

Tries

- What to Focus On: Explore tries for efficient string storage and retrieval, particularly for problems like autocomplete and spell-checking.
- Core Concepts: Learn insertion, search, and deletion operations in a trie and how they can be optimized for various problems.

Binary Indexed Tree (BIT) / Fenwick Tree

- What to Focus On: Understand how BITs efficiently support range queries and point updates, focusing on prefix sum problems.
- Core Concepts: Implement BITs in problems requiring frequent updates and queries over a range of values.

Segment Tree

- What to Focus On: Learn how segment trees work for answering range queries and performing element updates in logarithmic time.
- Core Concepts: Focus on solving problems that require dynamic range queries, such as sum, minimum, or maximum queries.

Closing Thoughts for Month 6

By the end of Month 6, you'll be well-equipped to handle complex string and data structure problems efficiently. Mastery of these algorithms and data structures will provide a strong foundation for more advanced topics in the upcoming months, enabling you to tackle sophisticated competitive programming challenges with ease.

Chapter 22

Problem-Solving Strategies and Techniques

In the realm of problem - solving and decision making, Kidlin's law stands as a guiding principle that states that "If you write the problem clearly, then the matter is half solved."

This chapter covers key strategies to help you approach challenges systematically, from understanding the problem to choosing the best solution. Strengthening these techniques will boost both your interview performance and day-to-day coding skills.

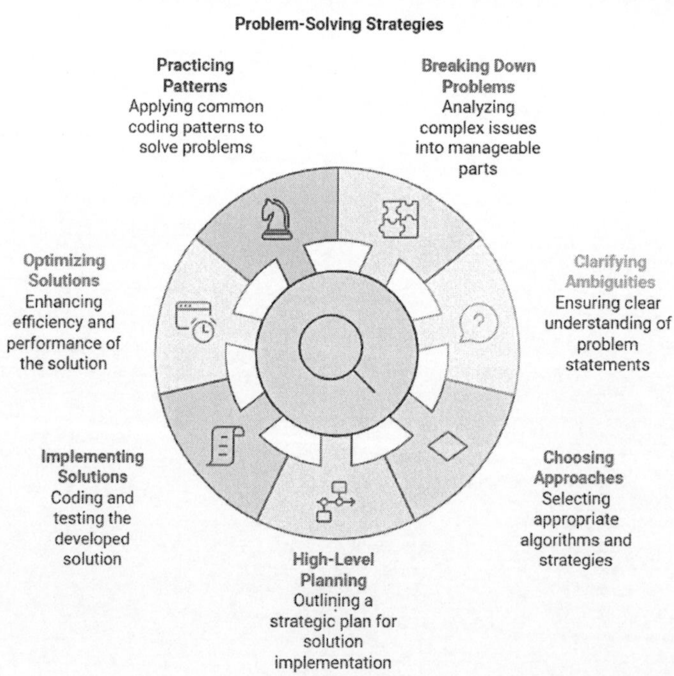

Figure – 22.1

22.1 Breaking Down the Problem

Understanding the problem is the most crucial step in problem-solving. A common mistake candidates make is rushing into coding without fully grasping the problem. This section will guide you through the process of breaking down the problem into its fundamental parts.

Reading the Problem Statement Carefully: Start by reading the problem statement thoroughly, not just once but multiple times. Each time you read, you may notice new details or nuances that you missed before. Pay attention to keywords that hint at the constraints or special cases, such as "at least," "no more than," "maximum," and "unique."

Identifying Inputs and Outputs: Clearly define what the inputs and outputs of the problem are. For example, in a problem where you need to find the longest palindrome in a string, the input is a string, and the output is the length of the longest palindrome. Make sure you understand the data types of inputs and outputs (e.g., integers, strings, arrays) and any constraints on their values.

Defining the Objective: The next step is to understand the core objective of the problem. Ask yourself, "What is the problem asking me to solve or optimize?" For instance, if the problem is about optimizing the scheduling of tasks, your objective might be to minimize the total time taken or to maximize the utilization of resources.

Breaking Down Complex Problems: For more complex problems, break them down into smaller, more manageable sub-problems. For example, if the problem involves multiple steps like sorting, searching, and filtering, identify each step and its role in the overall solution. This breakdown helps in organizing your thoughts and creating a clear roadmap for solving the problem.

22.2 Clarifying Ambiguities

Ambiguities in the problem statement can lead to incorrect solutions if not addressed early on. Here's how to deal with them:

Asking Clarifying Questions: If you're unsure about any part of the problem, don't hesitate to ask the interviewer for clarification. For example, if the problem involves processing a list of numbers, you might ask, "Can the list contain negative numbers?" or "Is the input list always sorted?"

Handling Edge Cases: Consider potential edge cases that may not be explicitly mentioned in the problem statement. Examples of edge cases include empty inputs, maximum or minimum possible values, and cases where no solution exists. Address these cases early to avoid surprises later in your implementation.

Verifying Constraints: Clarify any constraints on the input, such as size limits, time limits, or memory usage. Understanding these constraints is crucial for choosing the right algorithm and ensuring that your solution is both correct and efficient.

22.3 Choosing the Right Approach

Once you've understood the problem, the next step is to devise a plan for solving it. This involves selecting the most appropriate algorithm or strategy.

Algorithm Selection Based on Problem Type: Different types of problems often require different algorithms. For example:

- Sorting and Searching: For problems involving finding elements in sorted data or sorting data, consider algorithms like QuickSort, MergeSort, or Binary Search.
- Graph Problems: For problems involving networks or connections, consider graph algorithms like Dijkstra's algorithm for shortest paths or Depth-First Search (DFS) and Breadth-First Search (BFS) for exploring nodes.
- Dynamic Programming: For optimization problems or problems that involve making decisions over time, Dynamic Programming can be effective, such as in the knapsack problem or calculating Fibonacci numbers.

Choosing the Appropriate Data Structures: The choice of data structures can significantly impact the efficiency of your solution. For example:

- Arrays and Linked Lists: Good for problems involving sequences or when you need fast access to elements.
- Hash Maps and Sets: Ideal for problems requiring fast lookups or to avoid duplicates.

- Heaps/Priority Queues: Useful for problems where you need to access the smallest or largest elements quickly, like in a scheduling or optimization problem.

Considering Trade-offs: Sometimes, you might need to trade off between time complexity and space complexity. For instance, a dynamic programming solution might use more memory but solve the problem faster than a recursive solution. Discuss these trade-offs with the interviewer if they are relevant.

22.4 High-Level Planning

Plan Your Solution on a High Level: Instead of writing pseudocode, focus on a higher-level plan for your approach.

- Why It Matters: While pseudocode is often useful, some problems are better solved by having a well-defined high-level strategy rather than focusing too much on individual lines of code.
- How to Do It: Break down the problem into distinct stages (e.g., input validation, core logic, and result processing) and explain each stage in broad terms before diving into implementation. Use flowcharts or diagrams if necessary to visualize the flow of your solution.

Example: For a problem involving sorting and filtering a large dataset, the high-level plan might involve:

- Input Handling: Parse the input and convert it into a more usable format.
- Sorting: Apply an efficient sorting algorithm to organize the data.
- Filtering: Use logical checks or data structures to remove unnecessary items.
- Result Compilation: Format the final output according to the specifications.

22.5 Implementing the Solution

Code Efficiency Through Refactoring

After implementing a working solution, revisit your code to improve its efficiency and readability.

- Why It Matters: Often, your first solution might work but could be optimized further. Refactoring ensures that your code is both efficient and maintainable.
- How to Do It: Identify parts of the code that can be simplified or optimized. This could involve reducing nested loops, reusing variables, or breaking down complex logic into simpler functions. Look for patterns in your code that could be refactored into reusable functions or modules.

Example: If your code includes repetitive logic, consider creating helper functions that can be reused across multiple parts of your code. This reduces redundancy and makes your code cleaner.

Scenario-Based Testing

Instead of focusing only on simple and edge cases, approach testing with real-world scenarios that reflect how the problem might be used in practice.

- Why It Matters: Real-world scenarios provide a better sense of how your solution performs under practical conditions. They ensure that your solution isn't just theoretically sound but also robust in application.
- How to Do It: Think of scenarios where your code might be used in a live system. Consider different conditions, such as varying data sizes, unexpected inputs, and system constraints. Test your solution with a mix of standard inputs, edge cases, and performance-heavy conditions.

Example: For a problem that involves sorting user data, you might test scenarios where:

- The dataset includes a mix of regular and edge cases (e.g., missing data fields or special characters).
- The dataset size scales from a few entries to millions of records to simulate heavy system usage.

22.6 Optimizing the Solution

Analyzing Complexity

Understanding the complexity of your solution is essential for optimizing it and ensuring it's scalable.

Time Complexity: Evaluate the time complexity of your solution by analyzing how the number of operations grows with the size of the input. Common time complexities include O(1), O(log n), O(n), O(n log n), and O(n^2). For example, a nested loop that iterates over an array twice typically has a time complexity of O(n^2).

Space Complexity: Space complexity measures the amount of memory your solution uses. Consider both the input size and any additional space required by your algorithm, such as auxiliary arrays or recursion stacks. For example, a recursive algorithm that requires storing multiple function calls on the stack may have a higher space complexity than an iterative one.

Identifying Bottlenecks

After analyzing the complexity, look for parts of your code that could be optimized. Bottlenecks often occur in loops, recursive calls, or operations that require frequent data access.

Optimizing Loops: If your code contains nested loops, consider whether they can be combined or if an alternative approach (like using a hash map) could reduce the number of iterations. For example, instead of using a nested loop to check for duplicates in an array, use a hash set to track seen elements.

Improving Data Access: Accessing data efficiently is crucial, especially in large datasets. For example, if your solution involves frequent lookups in a list, consider using a dictionary or hash map instead, as these offer O(1) average time complexity for lookups compared to O(n) for lists.

Optimizing Recursion: Recursive solutions can often be optimized by converting them to iterative solutions, which may reduce space complexity. Alternatively, using memorization can prevent redundant calculations in recursive functions, significantly improving performance.

22.7 Practicing Common Coding Patterns

Two Pointers

The Two Pointers pattern involves using two pointers to process two elements simultaneously. These pointers typically start at different positions (e.g., the beginning and the end of an array) and move towards each other until they meet or a condition is satisfied. This technique is especially useful for problems involving sorted arrays or arrays that need to be processed in pairs.

Sample Questions

1. **Two Sum II - Input Array Is Sorted:** Find two numbers such that they add up to a specific target number. Return the indices of the two numbers.

- Link to problem : https://leetcode.com/problems/two-sum-ii-input-array-is-sorted/

2. **Container With Most Water:** Given n non-negative integers representing the height of each vertical line on a chart, find two lines that together with the x-axis forms a container that would hold the most water.

- Link to problem : https://leetcode.com/problems/container-with-most-water/

3. **Remove Duplicates from Sorted Array:** Remove the duplicates in-place such that each element appears only once and return the new length.

- Link to problem : https://leetcode.com/problems/remove-duplicates-from-sorted-array/

4. **Next Permutation:** Rearrange numbers into the lexicographically next greater permutation of numbers.

- Link to problem : https://leetcode.com/problems/next-permutation/

5. **Trapping Rain Water:** Given n non-negative integers representing an elevation map where the width of each bar is 1, compute how much water it can trap after raining.

- Link to problem : https://leetcode.com/problems/trapping-rain-water/

Fast and Slow Pointers

The Fast and Slow Pointers pattern, also known as the Tortoise and Hare algorithm, involves using two pointers that move through the data structure at different speeds. This technique is useful for detecting cycles in linked lists and finding the middle of a linked list.

Sample Questions

1. **Linked List Cycle:** Determine if a linked list has a cycle in it.

- Link to problem : https://leetcode.com/problems/linked-list-cycle/

2. **Middle of the Linked List:** Given a non-empty, singly linked list with head node head, return a middle node of the linked list.

- Link to problem : https://leetcode.com/problems/middle-of-the-linked-list/

3. **Palindrome Linked List:** Given a singly linked list, determine if it is a palindrome.

- Link to problem : https://leetcode.com/problems/palindrome-linked-list/

4. **Happy Number:** Write an algorithm to determine if a number n is "happy".

- Link to problem : https://leetcode.com/problems/happy-number/

5. **Circular Array Loop:** Given a circular array of integers, determine if there is a loop in the array.

- Link to problem : https://leetcode.com/problems/circular-array-loop/

Sliding Window

The Sliding Window pattern is a common technique for solving problems that involve arrays or strings. It involves maintaining a window that slides over the data structure to find a solution efficiently.

Sample Questions

1. **Longest Substring Without Repeating Characters:** Given a string, find the length of the longest substring without repeating characters.

- Link to problem : https://leetcode.com/problems/longest-substring-without-repeating-characters/

2. **Longest Repeating Character Replacement:** Given a string s that consists of only uppercase English letters, you can replace any letter in s with another letter at most k times. Find the length of the longest substring containing all repeating letters you can get after performing the above operations.

- Link to problem : https://leetcode.com/problems/longest-repeating-character-replacement/

3. **Sliding Window Maximum:** Given an array nums and a sliding window size k, find the maximum value in each sliding window.

- Link to problem : https://leetcode.com/problems/sliding-window-maximum/

4. **Permutation in String:** Given two strings s1 and s2, write a function to return true if s2 contains the permutation of s1.

- Link to problem : https://leetcode.com/problems/permutation-in-string/

5. **Fruit Into Baskets:** In a row of trees, you can pick at most two kinds of fruits. You want to collect the most fruits in each window.

- Link to problem : https://leetcode.com/problems/fruit-into-baskets/

Merge Intervals

The Merge Intervals pattern is used to solve problems that involve intervals or ranges that can overlap. It is used when the problem requires combining intervals that share a common overlap or intersection.

Sample Questions

1. **Merge Intervals:** Given a collection of intervals, merge all overlapping intervals.

- Link to problem : https://leetcode.com/problems/merge-intervals/

2. **Insert Interval:** Given a set of non-overlapping intervals, insert a new interval into the intervals (merge if necessary).

- Link to problem : https://leetcode.com/problems/insert-interval/

3. **Non-overlapping Intervals:** Given a collection of intervals, find the minimum number of intervals you need to remove to make the rest of the intervals non-overlapping.

- Link to problem : https://leetcode.com/problems/non-overlapping-intervals/

4. **Interval List Intersections:** Given two lists of closed intervals, each list of intervals is pairwise disjoint and in sorted order. Return the intersection of these two interval lists.

- Link to problem : https://leetcode.com/problems/interval-list-intersections/

Cyclic Sort

The Cyclic Sort pattern is used for solving problems when the input data lies within a fixed range. It is particularly useful for arranging elements of an array in a cyclic manner to achieve the desired order.

Sample Questions

1. **Kth Missing Positive Number:** Given an array of positive integers sorted in a strictly increasing order, return the Kth positive integer that is missing from this array.

- Linktoproblem:https://leetcode.com/problems/kth-missing-positive-number/

2. **Find All Numbers Disappeared in an Array:** Find all elements that do not appear in a given array of n integers where each integer is in the range [1, n].

- Link to problem : https://leetcode.com/problems/find-all-numbers-disappeared-in-an-array/

3. **Set Mismatch:** Given an array nums representing the data status of this set after the error, find the number that occurs twice and the number that is missing.

- Link to problem : https://leetcode.com/problems/set-mismatch/

4. **Find the Duplicate Number:** Given an array nums containing n + 1 integers where each integer is between 1 and n (inclusive), prove that at least one duplicate number must exist. Find the duplicate one.

- Link to problem : https://leetcode.com/problems/find-the-duplicate-number/

5. **Find All Duplicates in an Array:** Given an array of integers, 1 ≤ a[i] ≤ n (n = size of array), some elements appear twice and others appear once. Find all the elements that appear twice in this array.

- Link to problem : https://leetcode.com/problems/find-all-duplicates-in-an-array/

6. **Missing Number:** Given an array containing n distinct numbers taken from 0, 1, 2, ..., n, find the one that is missing from the array.

- Link to problem : https://leetcode.com/problems/missing-number/

Linked List In-Place Reversal

The Linked List In-Place Reversal pattern involves reversing the order of elements in a linked list in place without using extra memory or additional data structures.

Sample Questions

1. **Reverse Linked List:** Reverse a singly linked list.

- Link to problem : https://leetcode.com/problems/reverse-linked-list/

2. **Rotate List:** Given the head of a linked list, rotate the list to the right by k places.

- Link to problem : https://leetcode.com/problems/rotate-list/

3. **Reverse Linked List II:** Reverse a part of the linked list from position m to n.

- Link to problem : https://leetcode.com/problems/reverse-linked-list-ii/

4. **Reverse Nodes in k-Group:** Given a linked list, reverse the nodes of a linked list k at a time and return its modified list.

- Link to problem : https://leetcode.com/problems/reverse-nodes-in-k-group/

Two Heaps

The Two Heaps pattern is used to efficiently solve problems that involve managing two sets of data to allow quick access to the minimum or maximum values. Typically, it involves using a Min Heap and a Max Heap.

Sample Questions

1. **Find Right Interval:** For a given list of intervals, return the smallest start interval of the interval that starts after the end of this interval.

- Link to problem : https://leetcode.com/problems/find-right-interval/

2. **Find Median from Data Stream:** The median is the middle value in an ordered integer list. Write a program to find the median of a data stream.

   ○ Link to problem : https://leetcode.com/problems/find-median-from-data-stream/

3. **Sliding Window Median:** Given an array nums, there is a sliding window of size k which is moving from the very left of the array to the very right. Return the median array for each window.

   ○ Link to problem : https://leetcode.com/problems/sliding-window-median/

4. **IPO:** Suppose LeetCode will start its IPO soon. In order to sell a good price of its shares to Venture Capital, LeetCode would like to work on some projects to increase its capital before the IPO. Given several projects and a limited amount of capital, find the maximum number of projects that can be done.

   ○ Link to problem : https://leetcode.com/problems/ipo/

Breadth First Search (BFS)

The Breadth First Search (BFS) pattern is used for traversing or searching tree and graph data structures. It explores all nodes at the present depth before moving on to nodes at the next depth level.

<u>Sample Questions</u>

1. **Binary Tree Level Order Traversal:** Given a binary tree, return the level order traversal of its nodes' values.

   ○ Link to problem : https://leetcode.com/problems/binary-tree-level-order-traversal/

2. **Binary Tree Zigzag Level Order Traversal:** Given a binary tree, return the zigzag level order traversal of its nodes' values.

   ○ Link to problem : https://leetcode.com/problems/binary-tree-zigzag-level-order-traversal/

3. **Binary Tree Level Order Traversal II:** Given a binary tree, return the bottom-up level order traversal of its nodes' values.

   ○ Link to problem : https://leetcode.com/problems/binary-tree-level-order-traversal-ii/

4. **Minimum Depth of Binary Tree:** Given a binary tree, find its minimum depth.

- Link to problem : https://leetcode.com/problems/minimum-depth-of-binary-tree/

5. **N-ary Tree Level Order Traversal:** Given an n-ary tree, return the level order traversal of its nodes' values.

- Link to problem : https://leetcode.com/problems/n-ary-tree-level-order-traversal/

6. **Average of Levels in Binary Tree:** Given a non-empty binary tree, return the average value of the nodes on each level.

- Link to problem : https://leetcode.com/problems/average-of-levels-in-binary-tree/

7. **Flood Fill:** An image is represented by a 2D array of integers, each integer representing the pixel value of the image. Given a coordinate (sr, sc) representing the starting pixel, perform a flood fill algorithm.

- Link to problem : https://leetcode.com/problems/flood-fill/

8. **Find if Path Exists in Graph:** Given an undirected graph and two nodes, find if there is a path between them.

- Link to problem : https://leetcode.com/problems/find-if-path-exists-in-graph/

9. **Max Area of Island:** Given a non-empty 2D array grid of 0's and 1's, an island is a group of 1's connected 4-directionally. Find the maximum area of an island in the grid.

- Link to problem : https://leetcode.com/problems/max-area-of-island/

10. **Number of Islands:** Given a 2D grid consisting of '1's (land) and '0's (water), find the number of islands.

- Link to problem : https://leetcode.com/problems/number-of-islands/

11. **Rotting Oranges:** Given a grid of integers where each integer represents a different state of oranges, find the minimum time until there are no fresh oranges.

- Link to problem : https://leetcode.com/problems/rotting-oranges/

12. **Course Schedule:** There are a total of n courses you have to take, labeled from 0 to n-1. Some courses may have prerequisites, and you need to take these courses in a specific order.

- Link to problem : https://leetcode.com/problems/course-schedule/

Depth First Search (DFS)

The Depth First Search (DFS) pattern is used for traversing or searching tree and graph data structures. It starts from the root (or any arbitrary node in a graph) and explores as far as possible along each branch before backtracking.

Sample Questions

1. **Binary Tree Preorder, Inorder, Postorder Traversals:** Implement the preorder, inorder, and postorder traversals of a binary tree.

- Preorder Traversal : https://leetcode.com/problems/binary-tree-preorder-traversal/
- Inorder Traversal : https://leetcode.com/problems/binary-tree-inorder-traversal/
- PostorderTraversal:https://leetcode.com/problems/binary-tree-postorder-traversal/

2. **Number of Islands:** Given a 2D grid consisting of '1's (land) and '0's (water), find the number of islands.

- Link to problem : https://leetcode.com/problems/number-of-islands/

3. **Validate Binary Search Tree:** Given a binary tree, determine if it is a valid binary search tree.

- Link to problem : https://leetcode.com/problems/validate-binary-search-tree/

4. **Lowest Common Ancestor of a Binary Tree:** Given a binary tree, find the lowest common ancestor of two given nodes in the tree.

- Link to problem : https://leetcode.com/problems/lowest-common ancestor-of-a-binary-tree/

5. **Symmetric Tree:** Given a binary tree, check whether it is a mirror of itself.

- Link to problem : https://leetcode.com/problems/symmetric-tree/

6. **Binary Tree Maximum Path Sum:** Given a non-empty binary tree, find the maximum path sum.

   - Link to problem : https://leetcode.com/problems/binary-tree-maximum-path-sum/

7. **Invert Binary Tree:** Invert a binary tree.

   - Link to problem : https://leetcode.com/problems/invert-binary-tree/

8. **Diameter of Binary Tree:** Given a binary tree, find the length of the diameter of the tree.

   - Link to problem : https://leetcode.com/problems/diameter-of-binary-tree/

9. **Flatten Binary Tree to Linked List:** Given a binary tree, flatten it to a linked list in place.

   - Link to problem : https://leetcode.com/problems/flatten-binary-tree-to-linked-list/

10. **Kth Smallest Element in a BST:** Given a binary search tree, write a function to find the k-th smallest element in it.

    - Link to problem : https://leetcode.com/problems/kth-smallest-element-in-a-bst/

11. **All Nodes Distance K in Binary Tree:** Given a binary tree, find all the nodes that are at distance K from a target node.

    - Link to problem : https://leetcode.com/problems/all-nodes-distance-k-in-binary-tree/

12. **Clone Graph:** Given a reference of a node in a connected undirected graph, return a deep copy of the graph.

    - Link to problem : https://leetcode.com/problems/clone-graph/

Backtracking

Backtracking is an algorithmic technique for solving problems by incrementally building candidates to the solutions and abandoning a candidate as soon as it determines that the candidate cannot possibly be completed to a valid solution.

<u>Sample Questions</u>

1. **Subsets:** Given a set of distinct integers, return all possible subsets.

- Link to problem : https://leetcode.com/problems/subsets/

2. **Subsets II:** Given a collection of integers that might contain duplicates, return all possible subsets.

- Link to problem : https://leetcode.com/problems/subsets-ii/

3. **Permutations:** Given a collection of distinct integers, return all possible permutations.

- Link to problem : https://leetcode.com/problems/permutations/

4. **Permutations II:** Given a collection of numbers that might contain duplicates, return all possible unique permutations.

- Link to problem : https://leetcode.com/problems/permutations-ii/

5. **Combination Sum:** Given a set of candidate numbers and a target number, find all unique combinations in candidates where the candidate numbers sum to the target.

- Link to problem : https://leetcode.com/problems/combination-sum/

6. **Combination Sum II:** Given a collection of candidate numbers and a target number, find all unique combinations in candidates where the candidate numbers sum to the target.

- Link to problem : https://leetcode.com/problems/combination-sum-ii/

7. **Palindrome Partitioning:** Given a string, partition it such that every substring of the partition is a palindrome.

- Link to problem : https://leetcode.com/problems/palindrome-partitioning/

8. **Letter Combinations of a Phone Number:** Given a string containing digits from 2-9 inclusive, return all possible letter combinations that the number could represent.

- Link to problem : https://leetcode.com/problems/letter-combinations-of-a-phone-number/

Top K Elements

The Top K Elements pattern is a common algorithmic pattern used to find the top or bottom K elements in a collection of elements. It often involves using a Priority Queue (Heap).

Sample Questions

1. **Kth Largest Element in an Array:** Find the k-th largest element in an unsorted array.

- Link to problem : https://leetcode.com/problems/kth-largest-element-in-an-array/

2. **Top K Frequent Elements:** Given a non-empty array of integers, return the k most frequent elements.

- Link to problem : https://leetcode.com/problems/top-k-frequent- elements/

3. **K Closest Points to Origin:** Given an array of points, find the k closest points to the origin.

- Link to problem : https://leetcode.com/problems/k-closest-points-to-origin/

4. **Kth Largest Element in a Stream:** Design a class to find the k-th largest element in a stream.

- Link to problem : https://leetcode.com/problems/kth-largest-element-in-a-stream/

5. **Find K Closest Elements:** Given a sorted array and a target value, find the k closest elements to the target in the array.

- Link to problem : https://leetcode.com/problems/find-k-closest-elements/

6. **Least Number of Unique Integers after K Removals:** Given an array of integers, find the least number of unique integers after removing exactly k elements.

- Link to problem : https://leetcode.com/problems/least-number-of-unique-integers-after-k-removals/

7. **Reorganize String:** Given a string, rearrange the characters so that no two adjacent characters are the same.

- Link to problem : https://leetcode.com/problems/reorganize-string/

8. **Task Scheduler:** Given a char array representing tasks, find the least number of intervals required to finish all tasks.

- Link to problem : https://leetcode.com/problems/task-scheduler/

9. **Maximum Frequency Stack:** Implement a stack-like data structure that can push and pop the most frequent element.
   - Link to problem : https://leetcode.com/problems/maximum-fre quency-stack/

K-Way Merge

The K-Way Merge pattern is a technique used to merge k sorted arrays or lists into a single sorted array or list. This pattern is particularly useful for dealing with large datasets or streams of data that are already sorted and need to be combined efficiently.

Sample Questions

1. **Kth Smallest Number in a Sorted Matrix:** Given a matrix where each row and each column is sorted in ascending order, find the k-th smallest element.
   - Link to problem : https://leetcode.com/problems/kth-smallest-element-in-a-sorted-matrix/
2. **Merge k Sorted Lists:** Merge k sorted linked lists and return it as one sorted list.
   - Link to problem : https://leetcode.com/problems/merge-k-sorted- lists/
3. **Find K Pairs with Smallest Sums:** Given two integer arrays, find k pairs with the smallest sums.
   - Link to problem : https://leetcode.com/problems/find-k-pairs-with-smallest-sums/
4. **Smallest Range Covering Elements from K Lists:** Given k lists of sorted integers, find the smallest range that includes at least one number from each of the k lists.
   - Linktoproblem:https://leetcode.com/problems/smallest-range-covering-elements-from-k-lists/

Modified Binary Search

The Modified Binary Search pattern is used to optimize certain types of binary search problems. While traditional binary search typically involves searching for a target value in a sorted array by repeatedly dividing the search interval in half, the modified binary search pattern adapts this approach for different scenarios.

Sample Questions

1. **Binary Search:** Implement binary search for a target value in a sorted array.

- Link to problem : https://leetcode.com/problems/binary-search/

2. **Search Insert Position:** Given a sorted array and a target value, return the index if the target is found. If not, return the index where it would be if it were inserted in order.

- Link to problem : https://leetcode.com/problems/search-insert-position/

3. **Find Smallest Letter Greater Than Target:** Given a sorted list of characters, find the smallest character greater than a given target.

- Link to problem : https://leetcode.com/problems/find-smallest-letter-greater-than-target/

4. **Find First and Last Position of Element in Sorted Array:** Given a sorted array, find the starting and ending position of a given target value.

- Link to problem : https://leetcode.com/problems/find-first-and-last-position-of-element-in-sorted-array/

5. **Search in a Sorted Infinite Array:** Given an infinite sorted array, search for a target value.

- Link to problem : https://leetcode.com/discuss/interview-experience/1979273/infinite-sorted-array

6. **Search in Rotated Sorted Array:** Given a rotated sorted array, search for a target value.

- Link to problem : https://leetcode.com/problems/search-in-rotated-sorted-array/

Tries

The Trie (pronounced "try") coding pattern, short for retrieval tree or prefix tree, is a tree-like data structure used to efficiently store and retrieve a large set of strings or sequences. It's particularly useful for tasks involving searching for words, prefixes, or patterns in a dataset.

Sample Questions

1. **Implement Trie (Prefix Tree):** Implement a Trie with insert, search, and startsWith methods.

- Link to problem : https://leetcode.com/problems/implement-trie-prefix-tree/

2. **Search Suggestions System:** Given an array of product names and a search query, return a list of suggested products based on the search query.

- Link to problem : https://leetcode.com/problems/search-suggestions-system/

3. **Design Add and Search Words Data Structure:** Implement a data structure that supports adding new words and searching for a word that may contain a dot as a wildcard character.

- Link to problem : https://leetcode.com/problems/design-add-and-search-words-data-structure/

4. **Extra Characters in a String:** Given a string and a list of dictionary words, find the minimum number of extra characters in the string after splitting the string into dictionary words.

- Link to problem : https://leetcode.com/problems/extra-characters-in-a-string/

5. **Word Search II:** Given a board and a list of words, find all words in the board.

- Link to problem : https://leetcode.com/problems/word-search-ii/

6. **Implement Magic Dictionary:** Design a data structure that is initialized with a list of words and allows searching a word in the dictionary after modifying exactly one character.

- Link to problem : https://leetcode.com/problems/implement-magic-dictionary/

Chapter 23

Navigating Through the Interview Process

The coding interview is where all your preparation is put to the test. This is your chance to showcase your problem-solving abilities, coding skills, and how well you can perform under pressure.

This chapter will guide you through every stage of the coding interview, from the moment you introduce yourself to the final handshake (or virtual sign-off). By understanding what to expect and how to handle each part of the interview, you can approach it with confidence and clarity.

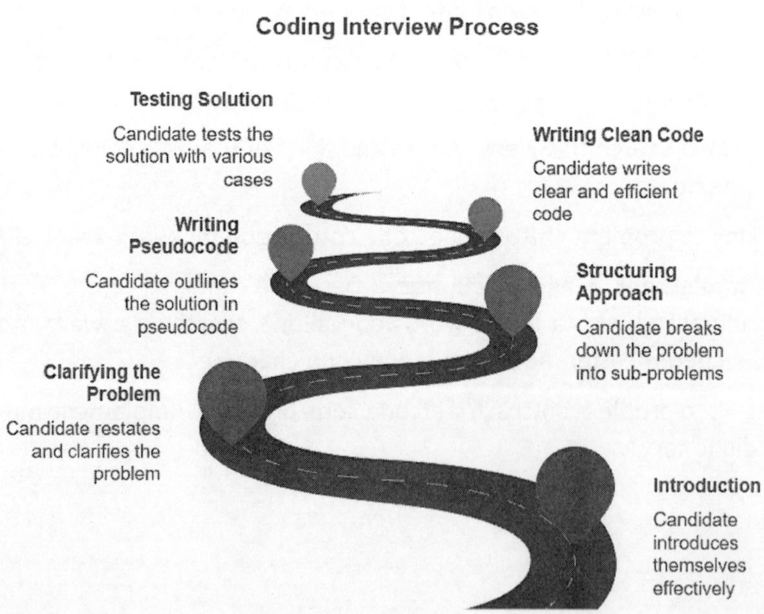

Figure – 23.1

23.1 Introduction

First Impression

The way you introduce yourself sets the tone for the rest of the interview. It's important to make a strong, positive impression right from the start.

Start with a Brief Introduction: Begin by stating your name, your current position, and a quick summary of your background. Keep it concise—about 30 seconds to one minute.

Example: "Hi, I'm [Your Name]. I'm currently a software engineer at [Your Company], where I've been working on developing scalable backend systems for the past three years. I'm passionate about problem-solving and have been focusing on improving my skills in data structures and algorithms to prepare for this interview."

Highlight Key Skills and Experience: Tailor your introduction to highlight the skills and experiences most relevant to the job you're interviewing for. Mention any specific technologies or projects that align with the company's needs.

Example: "In my current role, I've worked extensively with [relevant technologies, e.g., Java, Python, AWS], and I've led several projects that required optimizing algorithms for large-scale data processing. I'm excited about this opportunity because I see a strong alignment with the work your team is doing, particularly in [specific area related to the job]."

Show Enthusiasm: It's important to convey genuine interest in the role and the company. Your enthusiasm can make a big difference in how you're perceived.

Example: "I'm particularly excited about the chance to contribute to [Company Name] because I've always admired [specific aspects of the company, e.g., their innovative use of technology, their focus on user experience]. I'm eager to bring my experience and skills to your team."

23.2 Clarifying the Problem

Importance of Asking the Right Questions

Once you're given a problem to solve, the first thing you should do is ensure you fully understand it. Many candidates make the mistake of jumping straight into coding without clarifying the problem, which can lead to misunderstandings and mistakes.

Restate the Problem in Your Own Words: Begin by summarizing the problem back to the interviewer to confirm your understanding. This helps to ensure that you're on the right track and gives the interviewer a chance to correct any misunderstandings.

Example: "So, if I understand correctly, the problem is to find the longest substring without repeating characters in a given string. Is that right?"

Ask Detailed Questions: If any part of the problem is unclear, ask specific questions to clarify. This might involve understanding the input format, edge cases, or the expected output.

Example: "Can I assume the input string will only contain ASCII characters, or should I also consider Unicode characters? Also, what should I return if the string is empty?"

Consider Edge Cases: Before starting to code, think about possible edge cases and ask the interviewer if they should be considered. This shows that you're thorough and thoughtful in your approach.

Example: "Should I consider edge cases like a string with all unique characters or all the same character? What if the input string contains special characters or numbers?"

23.3 Structuring Your Approach

Breaking Down the Problem

Organizing your approach to problem-solving is key to demonstrating your ability to tackle challenges methodically and efficiently. While thinking aloud is important, structuring your solution in a clear, step-by-step manner ensures that your process is easy to follow.

Divide the Problem into Sub-Problems: Start by breaking the problem into smaller, manageable chunks. Identify the key components and sub-problems that need to be solved before tackling the larger issue. This approach not only shows that you understand the problem but also allows you to focus on solving one piece at a time.

Example: For a problem involving searching for a pattern in a string, break it down into steps like parsing the string, matching the pattern, and handling edge cases where the pattern is not found.

Prioritize Steps: Once the problem is broken down, prioritize which components need to be addressed first. Consider what will have the most significant impact on solving the problem or what might be the most complex to address.

Example: "I'll start by setting up the basic structure of the solution and getting that to work before moving on to the more complex sections, like optimizing the runtime."

Choose an Appropriate Algorithm: Based on your breakdown, decide which algorithm or data structure is best suited to solve each sub-problem. Justify your choice to the interviewer by explaining why it's efficient for this problem.

Example: "For this problem, I'm thinking of using the sliding window technique because it allows us to efficiently find the longest substring without repeating characters in linear time."

Plan for Edge Cases: Before jumping into implementation, think about potential edge cases that might cause your solution to fail. Address these upfront by discussing how you'll handle unusual or extreme inputs. This demonstrates foresight and thoroughness in your approach.

Example: "I'll make sure to account for cases where the input is empty or where all elements are the same, as these can sometimes cause unintended behaviors in the algorithm."

Outline Your Plan Verbally: Before you start coding, explain your plan to the interviewer. This not only shows that you have a clear strategy but also allows the interviewer to provide feedback or suggestions.

Example: "Here's my plan: I'll initialize two pointers to define the sliding window. As I iterate through the string, I'll expand the window while checking for repeating characters. If a repetition is found, I'll move the left pointer to the right until the repetition is removed from the window."

Iterate as You Go: As you implement your solution, keep iterating on it as you test and validate your assumptions. After each step, review whether the current approach is working as expected or if adjustments are needed.

Example: "Now that I have the core logic in place, I'll test it with different inputs to make sure it handles them as expected. If something isn't working, I'll adjust the logic or add error handling to address it."

23.4 Writing Pseudocode

Writing pseudocode is a great way to outline your solution before diving into actual coding. It helps to organize your thoughts and can make the coding process smoother.

Keep it Simple: Pseudocode should be simple and focus on the logic rather than syntax. Use plain language and clear steps to describe what each part of your code will do.

Example: For the sliding window problem:

```
Initialize a set to keep track of characters in the current window
Initialize two pointers, both starting at the beginning of the string
Iterate through the string with the right pointer
  If the character is not in the set
    Add it to the set
    Update the maximum length
  If the character is in the set
    Move the left pointer until the character is removed from the window
```

Discuss Edge Cases: As you write your pseudocode, mention any edge cases you need to handle. This shows that you're thinking ahead and considering all possible scenarios.

Example: "I'll need to check if the string is empty at the start and handle it separately. Also, I'll handle cases where the entire string consists of unique characters."

Use It as a Guide for Coding: Once your pseudocode is ready, use it as a blueprint for writing the actual code. It should guide you through the coding process, ensuring you stay on track.

23.5 Writing Clean and Efficient Code

Best Practices for Code Clarity

Writing clear, readable code is just as important as finding the correct solution. It makes your thought process easier to follow and reduces the chance of making errors.

- **Use Meaningful Variable Names**: Choose variable names that clearly describe their purpose. Avoid single-letter names unless they're used in a well-known context (like 'i' in a loop).

Example: Instead of using a and b as variables, use leftPointer and rightPointer to describe their roles in a sliding window problem.

- **Break Down Complex Logic**: If your solution involves complex logic, break it down into smaller, manageable functions. This not only makes your code cleaner but also easier to debug.

  Example: If you're implementing a complex algorithm, create helper functions to handle distinct parts of the logic. For instance, if you're solving a graph traversal problem, separate the logic for initializing the graph from the traversal algorithm itself.

- **Comment Your Code Sparingly**: While you should aim to write self-explanatory code, brief comments can help clarify your logic, especially if you're using a less common approach.

  Example: "// Move the left pointer to ensure all characters in the window are unique."

Optimizing Code for Time and Space Complexity

Efficiency is key in coding interviews. While a brute-force solution might work, it's often not the most optimal, and interviewers expect you to consider the performance of your code.

- **Analyze Your Solution**: Before writing your final code, take a moment to analyze its time and space complexity. Explain your analysis to the interviewer to show that you're mindful of performance.

  Example: "The sliding window approach I'm using will have a time complexity of O(n), where n is the length of the string. The space complexity is O(k), where k is the size of the set that stores the characters in the window."

- **Consider Trade-offs**: Sometimes optimizing for time can increase space complexity, and vice versa. Discuss any trade-offs you're making and why you believe your approach is the best for this problem.

  Example: "Although this approach uses extra space to store the set of characters, it significantly reduces the time complexity compared to a brute-force solution that would be O(n^2)."

- **Refactor If Needed**: If you realize that your initial solution isn't optimal, don't hesitate to refactor it. Explain your thought process as you make improvements.

Example: "I noticed that this part of the code could be optimized by using a hashmap instead of a set, which allows us to track character indices more efficiently."

23.6 Testing Your Solution

Writing Test Cases

Before you consider your solution complete, it's crucial to test it thoroughly. Testing not only verifies that your code works but also shows the interviewer that you understand the importance of validation.

- **Start with Simple Test Cases**: Begin by testing your solution with simple cases that should be easy to handle. This will confirm that your basic logic is correct.

  Example: For the sliding window problem, test with a short string like "abcabcbb" where the expected output is 3.

- **Move to Edge Cases**: Next, test your solution against edge cases, such as empty strings, strings with all unique characters, or strings with all repeating characters.

  Example: Test with an empty string (""), a string with all unique characters ("abcdef"), and a string with all identical characters ("aaaaaa").

- **Consider Stress Testing**: If time allows, test your solution with large inputs to ensure it performs well under extreme conditions. This is especially important for algorithms where efficiency is key.

  Example: Test with a very long string of random characters to ensure that your solution still runs within acceptable limits.

Debugging Techniques

Even with the best preparation, bugs can creep into your code. Knowing how to debug effectively is crucial for solving problems during the interview.

- **Use Print Statements Wisely**: If you're stuck, strategically placed print statements can help you understand where your code is going wrong. Use them to check the values of variables at key points in your logic.

Example: Print the current state of the window and the values of your pointers during each iteration to see how they're moving and where the logic might fail.

- **Check for Off-by-One Errors**: These are common in coding, especially when working with loops and array indices. Review your loop boundaries carefully to ensure you're not missing any elements or going out of bounds.

  Example: If your loop runs from 0 to n-1, ensure that n is correctly defined as the length of the array or string and that you're not accidentally skipping the first or last element.

- **Rethink Your Approach if Necessary**: If you're unable to find the bug, it might be worth reconsidering your approach. Sometimes, a different perspective can reveal flaws in your logic that you hadn't noticed before.

  Example: If you're repeatedly running into the same issue, take a step back and think about the problem from a different angle. Discuss alternative approaches with the interviewer if you feel stuck.

23.7 Handling Difficult Situations

What to Do When You're Stuck

It's not uncommon to get stuck during an interview. What matters is how you handle it.

- **Take a Moment to Breathe**: If you're stuck, don't panic. Take a deep breath and give yourself a moment to clear your thoughts. A brief pause can help you refocus and approach the problem with fresh eyes. Example: If you hit a roadblock, say, "Let me take a moment to think about this," and use that time to mentally step back from the problem.
- **Break Down the Problem Again**: Go back to the problem statement and break it down again. Sometimes, reiterating the problem and the approach can help you identify where you went wrong. Example: "Let's revisit the problem. The goal is to find the longest substring without repeating characters. I'm currently trying to expand the window, but something seems off...".
- **Explain your stuck point:** Communicate your thoughts to the interviewer. Explain exactly where you are having trouble and what

you are considering doing next. For example, "I'm trying to optimize this part of the algorithm, but I'm unsure how to reduce the time complexity further. I'm considering whether a different data structure might help." This keeps the dialogue open and might prompt the interviewer to offer a hint or nudge you in the right direction.

- **Use Helper Functions** When faced with a complex problem, break it down into smaller parts by creating helper functions. This approach allows you to focus on smaller, more manageable tasks. For example, if the problem requires several steps, write helper functions for each step, like findMax(), sortList(), and mergeResults(). This makes the overall problem easier to solve and demonstrates a methodical approach to problem-solving
- **Ask for a Hint**: Don't hesitate to ask the interviewer for guidance if you're genuinely stuck. They can provide hints or ask questions that might help you rethink the problem. For example, "I'm stuck on how to efficiently handle duplicates in this array—could you provide some direction on whether to use a hash map or a different approach?" Asking for help shows that you're collaborative and willing to seek assistance when necessary.

Handling Feedback and Criticism

During the interview, the interviewer may offer feedback or critique your approach. It's important to handle this professionally and use it as an opportunity to improve.

- **Listen Carefully**: Pay close attention to any feedback or suggestions the interviewer provides. Even if it's critical, view it as constructive and a chance to learn. Example: If the interviewer points out that your solution could be more efficient, listen carefully to their reasoning and consider how you can incorporate their advice into your approach.
- **Respond Positively**: Thank the interviewer for their feedback and acknowledge any areas where you need to improve. Showing that you're open to learning and growth is a positive trait. Example: "Thank you for pointing that out. I see how the approach you suggested could improve the efficiency. Let me try to implement that now."
- **Incorporate Feedback Immediately**: If you receive feedback during the interview, try to adjust your approach or code accordingly. This shows that you're adaptable and capable of quick thinking. Example: If

the interviewer suggests a different data structure, try to incorporate it into your solution on the spot, explaining how it improves your code.

23.8 Effective Communication

Thinking Out Loud: Sharing Your Thought Process

Throughout the interview, it's crucial to communicate your thought process clearly. This not only helps the interviewer understand your approach but also provides insight into how you tackle problems.

- **Explain Every Step**: As you work through the problem, explain each decision you make. This includes why you're choosing a particular algorithm, how you're structuring your code, and what edge cases you're considering. Example: "I'm choosing a Hashmap here because it allows for constant time lookups, which is essential for keeping this operation efficient."
- **Talk Through Challenges**: If you encounter a challenge or a difficult part of the problem, talk it through with the interviewer. This can help you work through the issue and shows the interviewer how you approach problem-solving. Example: "I'm noticing that the current approach might not handle this edge case efficiently. I'm considering either adjusting the loop or adding a conditional check..."
- **Summarize Your Approach**: Once you've completed your solution, summarize your approach and explain how you arrived at it. This final explanation helps reinforce your understanding and allows the interviewer to see your complete thought process. Example: "To summarize, I used a sliding window approach to maintain a set of unique characters, moving the window as necessary to ensure no duplicates. This allowed us to find the longest substring in linear time."

23.9 Must-Do Things and Things to Avoid

Must-Do Things

► Stay Positive and Confident

Even when faced with challenging problems, your ability to remain calm and composed reflects well on your ability to handle stress and pressure. Smiling a bit and maintaining eye contact (in a virtual or in-person interview) can create a good impression, showing that you are approachable and confident. Your tone should convey enthusiasm for the role and the problem at hand. Confidence is key, but it should be balanced with humility—acknowledge the challenges without appearing overconfident.

► Collaborate with the Interviewer

The interview should be seen as a collaborative effort rather than a one-sided evaluation. Engage the interviewer by discussing your approach and reasoning openly. This demonstrates your teamwork skills and shows that you value feedback and input from others. For instance, as you outline your solution, invite the interviewer to ask questions or provide insights. This can lead to valuable discussions that enhance your solution and show your ability to work well in a team environment.

► Admit Knowledge Gaps

If you encounter a concept or detail you're unfamiliar with, don't try to bluff your way through. Admit your knowledge gaps openly and honestly. This is better than pretending to know something and getting caught out later. You can say something like, "I'm not very familiar with this specific algorithm, but I would approach it by first understanding its time complexity and then breaking down the steps to implement it." This shows that you are willing to learn and are aware of your limitations, which is a valuable trait in any employee.

Things to Avoid

► Avoid Immediate Solutions

Rushing into coding without fully understanding the problem is a common mistake. Before writing any code, take the time to think about the problem, identify potential pitfalls, and clarify any doubts. Start by carefully reading the problem statement, then rephrase it in your own words to ensure you've understood it correctly. This step can save you time in the long run by preventing errors and unnecessary rework.

► Don't Assume Details

"Assumptions are made and most assumptions are wrong"
– Albert Einstein

Never assume anything about the problem without verifying it first. For example, don't assume the input will always be sorted or that the data will fit into memory. Always ask questions to clarify these details. Assumptions can lead to mistakes that might be easily avoided with a simple question. For example, "Is the input guaranteed to be sorted, or do I need to handle that myself?" or "Should I expect the possibility of an empty input array?"

▶ **Limit the Use of Jargon**

While it's important to use technical language correctly, avoid overloading your explanations with jargon. The goal is to communicate clearly and effectively, ensuring that the interviewer understands your thought process. When you do use technical terms, be prepared to explain them in plain language if asked. For instance, instead of saying, "I'll use a DAG for this topological sort," you might say, "I'll use a Directed Acyclic Graph, which is a type of graph that helps in scheduling tasks in a specific order."

▶ **Don't Skip Over Your Thought Process**

Skipping steps in your explanation can leave the interviewer guessing about your reasoning. Make sure to articulate each part of your thought process, even if it seems straightforward. For example, if you're implementing a loop, explain why you chose a specific starting point or why the loop runs until a certain condition is met. This level of detail shows that you've thought through the problem thoroughly and aren't just coding by instinct.

▶ **Don't Be Defensive About Feedback**

Receiving feedback is an integral part of the interview process. It's important to listen carefully, avoid being defensive, and use the feedback to improve your solution. For instance, if the interviewer suggests a more efficient algorithm, thank them for the suggestion and discuss how you might implement it. This shows that you're coachable and open to learning, both of which are key qualities for any job.

23.10 Things to Do When You Code

Write Production-Level Code

Your code should be clean, efficient, and maintainable, just as it would be in a production environment. This means using meaningful variable names, adhering to consistent formatting, and writing modular code.

Each function should do one thing well and be easy to understand. For instance, rather than having a single long function that handles everything, break it down into smaller functions like getUserInput(), processData(), and displayResults(). This not only makes your code easier to debug but also demonstrates your ability to write scalable and maintainable software.

Check for Edge Cases

Always consider special or extreme cases that could break your solution. For example, if you're writing a function that sorts a list, think about what happens if the list is empty, contains only one element, or is already sorted. Testing for these edge cases ensures your code is robust and can handle a wide range of inputs. During the interview, explicitly mention these edge cases and how you plan to handle them. This shows that you're thorough and detail-oriented.

Validate Input

Ensuring that the input to your functions is valid is crucial. For example, if a function expects a list of numbers, what should it do if it receives a string or an empty list? Write your code to handle such scenarios gracefully, perhaps by throwing a meaningful exception or returning an error message. This practice prevents bugs and ensures your code is reliable and user-friendly.

Modularize Your Code

Breaking your code into smaller, reusable functions makes it easier to read, test, and maintain. Each function should perform a single task and do it well. For example, if you're writing a program that processes user data, separate the logic into functions like readData(), processData(), and writeData(). This modular approach makes your code more organized and easier to debug or extend.

Use Meaningful Variable and Method Names

Use clear, descriptive names for variables and methods. This not only makes your code easier to understand but also helps avoid confusion when you or others revisit the code later. For instance, instead of using names like a or b, use userInput or sortedList. Good naming conventions make your code self-explanatory and reduce the need for extensive comments.

Understand Time and Space Complexity

Being aware of the time and space complexity of your code is crucial for writing efficient algorithms. For instance, if you're using a nested loop, consider whether there's a way to reduce the time complexity from O(n^2) to O(n log n) or better. Discussing these considerations during the interview shows that you understand the importance of efficiency and can write code that scales well.

Dry-Run Your Code

Before running your code, mentally walk through it using sample inputs. This helps you catch logical errors and ensures your code behaves as expected. For example, if you're writing a sorting algorithm, go through the process step by step with a small list to ensure the logic is sound. Dry-running is an effective way to debug your code before you even hit the run button.

Code Clean-Up

After completing your solution, take the time to refactor and clean up your code. Remove any unnecessary comments or debug statements, and ensure the code is neatly formatted. This final step shows attention to detail and a commitment to writing high-quality code. Clean, well-organized code is easier to maintain and demonstrates professionalism.

PART 4

RESOURCES LIBRARY

Please scan the QR code to access the soft copy of the entire Resource Library.

Resources Library for DSA

📅 Month 1

♣ Pick a Language

a. Get an idea about programming - https://www.freecodecamp.org/news/what-is-programming-tutorial-for-beginners/
b. Pick a language and start learning - https://www.w3schools.com/
c. Setting up the basics

   i. Video Tutorials :

   Tutorial-1 : IDE installation - https://www.youtube.com/watch?v=DMWD7wfhgNY
   Tutorial 2 : C++ Setup - https://www.youtube.com/watch?v=FEeFG9OR-QU
   Tutorial 3 : Java Setup - https://www.youtube.com/watch?v=SQykK40fFds
   Tutorial 4 : Python Setup - https://www.youtube.com/watch?v=kRkkPIA-yEU&pp=ygUMUHl0aG9uIHNldHVw

♣ Learn Basic Syntax, Data Types, Variables, Operators

a. Basic Fundamentals For Each Language

   i. C++ Tutorial (w3schools) - https://www.w3schools.com/cpp/

   Video tutorial 1: C++ Tutorial for Beginners : https://www.youtube.com/watch?v=ZzaPdXTrSb8
   Video Tutorial 2 : C++ Fundamental Algorithms : https://www.youtube.com/watch?v=u67pZ_hCufA

   ii. Python - https://www.w3schools.com/python/default.asp

   Video tutorial : Learn Python - Full Course for Beginners : https://www.youtube.com/watch?v=rfscVS0vtbw

iii. Java - https://www.w3schools.com/java/default.asp

Video tutorial : Java Programming for Beginners [Course] : https://www.youtube.com/watch?v=A74TOX803D0

b. Cheat Sheets to remember everything

i. Python Cheat Sheet : https://leetcode.com/discuss/study-guide/2122306/Python-Cheat-Sheet-for-Leetcode
ii. C++ Cheat Sheet : https://github.com/jsjtzyy/LeetCode/blob/master/C%2B%2B cheat sheet for interview
iii. Java Cheat Sheet : https://github.com/jsjtzyy/LeetCode/blob/master/Java cheat sheet for interview

♣ **Conditional Statements, Loops, and Functions**

a. Courses for live examples of basics in action

i. Video tutorial : Full Course C++ : https://www.youtube.com/watch?v=vLnPwxZdW4Y
ii. Video tutorial : Full Course Python : https://www.youtube.com/watch?v=rfscVS0vtbw
iii. Video tutorial 1 : Full Course Java : https://www.youtube.com/watch?v=A74TOX803D0
iv. Video Tutorial 2 : Java : https://www.youtube.com/watch?v=pgBk8HC7jbU

b. Conditional Statements (https://www.geeksforgeeks.org/conditional-statements-in-programming/)

i. Java : https://www.w3schools.com/java/java_conditions.asp
ii. Python : https://www.w3schools.com/python/python_conditions.asp
iii. C++ : https://www.w3schools.com/cpp/cpp_conditions.asp

c. Loops (https://www.geeksforgeeks.org/loops-programming/)

i. C++

1. While Loops : https://www.w3schools.com/cpp/cpp_while_loop.asp
2. For Loops : https://www.w3schools.com/cpp/cpp_for_loop.asp

ii. Java
   1. While Loops : https://www.w3schools.com/java/java_while_loop.asp
   2. For Loops : https://www.w3schools.com/java/java_for_loop.asp

iii. Python
   1. While Loops : https://www.w3schools.com/python/python_while_loops.asp
   2. For Loops : https://www.w3schools.com/python/python_for_loops.asp

d. Functions (https://www.geeksforgeeks.org/functions-programming/)
   i. C++ : https://www.w3schools.com/cpp/cpp_functions.asp
   ii. Java : https://www.w3schools.com/java/java_methods.asp
   iii. Python : https://www.w3schools.com/python/python_functions.asp

♣ Understand Object-Oriented Programming (OOP) Concepts

Video Tutorial 1 : What is OOPS : https://www.youtube.com/watch?v=7GwptabrYyk

Video Tutorial 2 : Pillars of OOPS : https://www.youtube.com/watch?v=pTB0EiLXUC8

a. Java
   - Reading Material : https://www.geeksforgeeks.org/object-oriented-programming-oops-concept-in-java/
   - Head First Java Book : https://www.rcsdk12.org/cms/lib/NY01001156/Centricity/Domain/4951/Head_First_Java_Second_Edition.pdf

b. C++
   - Reading Material : https://www.geeksforgeeks.org/object-oriented-programming-in-cpp/

c. Python
   - Video tutorial - OOPS Python : https://www.youtube.com/watch?v=ZDa-Z5JzLYM&list=PL-osiE80TeTsqhIuOqKhwlXsIBIdSeYtc
   - Reading Material : OOPS Concept : https://www.geeksforgeeks.org/python-oops-concepts/

♣ Learn About Time & Space Complexity

a. Video tutorial – Basic understanding : https://www.youtube.com/watch?v=BgLTDT03QtU
b. Reading Material : Big O - Cheatsheet : https://www.freecodecamp.org/news/big-o-cheat-sheet-time-complexity-chart/

♣ Big O, Big Ω, Big Θ Notations

a. Video Tutorials –

   Tutorial 1 : Asymptotic Notations : https://www.youtube.com/watch?v=A03oI0znAoc
   Tutorial 2 : Big O, Omega, Theta notations: https://www.youtube.com/watch?v=0oDAlMwTrLo

b. Reading Material : https://www.prepbytes.com/blog/daa/difference-between-big-oh-big-omega-and-big-theta/

♣ Learn About Arrays, Strings, Hashmaps

► Arrays:

Reading Material : https://www.geeksforgeeks.org/array-data-structure-guide/

Problems to Try Out:

a. Basic to Advanced Array Questions with Techniques : https://leetcode.com/discuss/interview-question/operating-system/4417164/Basic-to-Advanced-Array-Questions-with-Techniques
b. Easy Questions List - Leetcode : https://leetcode.com/problemset/?topicSlugs=array&difficulty=EASY&page=1

► Strings:

Reading Material : https://www.geeksforgeeks.org/string-data-structure/

Problems to Try Out:

a. Types of String Problems : https://leetcode.com/discuss/general-discussion/1134565/approaching-almost-any-string-question
b. Easy Questions List - Leetcode : https://leetcode.com/problemset/?topicSlugs=string&page=1&difficulty=EASY

► Hashmaps:

1. Video Tutorial : About maps in Data Structure : https://study.com/academy/lesson/maps-in-data-structures-definition-methods.html
2. Reading Material : https://www.geeksforgeeks.org/hashing-data-structure/

Problems to Try Out:

a. Hashing Guide 1 Leetcode : https://leetcode.com/discuss/study-guide/4781120/Hashing-and-Prefix-Sum-%3A-Definitive-Guide
b. Easy Questions List - Leetcode : https://leetcode.com/problemset/?page=1&difficulty=EASY&topicSlugs=hash-table

Prerequisites Before Entering Month 2: LeetCode Step-by-Step Guide

1. Leetcode Guide : https://leetcode.com/discuss/career/450215/How-to-use-LeetCode-to-help-yourself-efficiently-and-effectively-(for-beginners)

Month 2

♣ Recursion

1. Video Tutorial : Understand Recursion : https://www.youtube.com/watch?v=IJDJ0kBx2LM
2. Recursion Guide + Problems - Leetcode Blog : https://leetcode.com/discuss/study-guide/1733447/become-master-in-recursion

Problems to Try Out:

a. Reverse Linked List : https://leetcode.com/problems/reverse-linked-list/
b. Merge Two Sorted Lists : https://leetcode.com/problems/merge-two-sorted-lists/
c. Palindrome Linked List : https://leetcode.com/problems/palindrome-linked-list/
d. Remove Linked List Elements : https://leetcode.com/problems/remove-linked-list-elements/
e. Reverse String : https://leetcode.com/problems/reverse-string/
f. Power of Two : https://leetcode.com/problems/power-of-two/
g. Fibonacci Number : https://leetcode.com/problems/fibonacci-number/
h. Power of Four : https://leetcode.com/problems/power-of-four/
i. Find the Winner of the Circular Game : https://leetcode.com/problems/find-the-winner-of-the-circular-game/
j. Power of Three : https://leetcode.com/problems/power-of-three/
k. Add Two Numbers : https://leetcode.com/problems/add-two-numbers/
l. Decode String : https://leetcode.com/problems/decode-string/
m. Swap Nodes in Pairs : https://leetcode.com/problems/swap-nodes-in-pairs/
n. Reorder List : https://leetcode.com/problems/reorder-list/
o. Pow(x, n) : https://leetcode.com/problems/powx-n/

♣ Backtracking

- **What to Focus On:**

a. Mastering the backtracking approach for solving problems.
b. Implementing solutions for classic problems like the N-Queen problem and Sudoku solver.

- **Resources:**

  Video Tutorial : Backtracking Algorithm : https://www.youtube.com/watch?v=Zq4upTEaQyM

- **Problems to Try Out:**

  a. Generate Parentheses : https://leetcode.com/problems/generate-parentheses/
  b. Permutations : https://leetcode.com/problems/permutations/
  c. Combination Sum : https://leetcode.com/problems/combination-sum/
  d. Letter Combinations of a Phone Number : https://leetcode.com/problems/letter-combinations-of-a-phone-number/
  e. Subsets : https://leetcode.com/problems/subsets/
  f. Combinations : https://leetcode.com/problems/combinations/
  g. All Paths From Source to Target : https://leetcode.com/problems/all-paths-from-source-to-target/
  h. Word Ladder II : https://leetcode.com/problems/word-ladder-ii/
  i. Letter Case Permutation : https://leetcode.com/problems/letter-case-permutation/
  j. Restore IP Addresses : https://leetcode.com/problems/restore-ip-addresses/
  k. N-Queens : https://leetcode.com/problems/n-queens/
  l. Sudoku Solver : https://leetcode.com/problems/sudoku-solver/
  m. Word Search II : https://leetcode.com/problems/word-search-ii/
  n. Expression Add Operators : https://leetcode.com/problems/expression-add-operators/
  o. Palindrome Partitioning II : https://leetcode.com/problems/palindrome-partitioning-ii/

♣ **Basic Data Structures**

- **What to Focus On:**

  a. Strengthening your understanding of basic data structures: Stack, Queue, LinkedList, Deque, and Priority Queue.
  b. Implementing these structures and solving related problems like reversal and cycle detection.

♣ Stack

- **What to Focus On:**
  a. Understanding stack operations and applications.
  b. Solving problems related to expression evaluation and function call management.
- **Resources:**
  Video Tutorial : Introduction to Stack : https://www.youtube.com/watch?v=I37kGX-nZEI
- **Problems to Try Out:**
  a. Trapping Rain Water : https://leetcode.com/problems/trapping-rain-water/
  b. Valid Parentheses : https://leetcode.com/problems/valid-parentheses/
  c. Largest Rectangle in Histogram : https://leetcode.com/problems/largest-rectangle-in-histogram/
  d. Palindrome Linked List : https://leetcode.com/problems/palindrome-linked-list/
  e. Decode String : https://leetcode.com/problems/decode-string/
  f. Min Stack : https://leetcode.com/problems/min-stack/
  g. Longest Valid Parentheses : https://leetcode.com/problems/longest-valid-parentheses/
  h. Binary Tree Inorder Traversal : https://leetcode.com/problems/binary-tree-inorder-traversal/
  i. Flatten Binary Tree to Linked List : https://leetcode.com/problems/flatten-binary-tree-to-linked-list/
  j. Daily Temperatures : https://leetcode.com/problems/daily-temperatures/
  k. Maximal Rectangle : https://leetcode.com/problems/maximal-rectangle/
  l. Reorder List : https://leetcode.com/problems/reorder-list/
  m. Next Greater Element II : https://leetcode.com/problems/next-greater-element-ii/
  n. Basic Calculator II : https://leetcode.com/problems/basic-calculator-ii/
  o. Remove Duplicate Letters : https://leetcode.com/problems/remove-duplicate-letters/

♣ Queue

- **What to Focus On:**

  a. Learning queue operations and their use in scheduling tasks and managing buffers.

- **Resources:**

  Video Tutorial : Introduction to Queue : https://www.youtube.com/watch?v=ypJwoz_SXTo

- **Problems to Try Out:**

  a. Merge k Sorted Lists : https://leetcode.com/problems/merge-k-sorted-lists/description/
  b. Sliding Window Maximum : https://leetcode.com/problems/sliding-window-maximum/description/
  c. Kth Largest Element in an Array : https://leetcode.com/problems/kth-largest-element-in-an-array/description/
  d. Top k Frequent Elements : https://leetcode.com/problems/top-k-frequent-elements/description/
  e. Find Median from Data Stream : https://leetcode.com/problems/find-median-from-data-stream/
  f. Task Scheduler : https://leetcode.com/problems/task-scheduler/
  g. Kth Smallest Element in a Sorted Matrix : https://leetcode.com/problems/kth-smallest-element-in-a-sorted-matrix/
  h. Sort Characters By Frequency : https://leetcode.com/problems/sort-characters-by-frequency/
  i. Ugly Number II : https://leetcode.com/problems/ugly-number-ii/
  j. The Skyline Problem : https://leetcode.com/problems/the-skyline-problem/
  k. Network Delay Time : https://leetcode.com/problems/network-delay-time/
  l. Flatten Nested List Iterator : https://leetcode.com/problems/flatten-nested-list-iterator/
  m. Implement Queue using Stacks : https://leetcode.com/problems/implement-queue-using-stacks/
  n. Find K Pairs with Smallest Sums : https://leetcode.com/problems/find-k-pairs-with-smallest-sums/

o. Maximum Sum Circular Subarray : https://leetcode.com/problems/maximum-sum-circular-subarray/
p. Shortest Subarray with Sum at Least K : https://leetcode.com/problems/shortest-subarray-with-sum-at-least-k/

♣ **Linked List**

- **What to Focus On:**
  a. Understanding linked list structures and operations like insertion, deletion, and traversal.
  b. Solving problems related to list reversal and cycle detection.
- **Resources:**

  Video Tutorial : Linked List explained : https://www.youtube.com/watch?v=N6dOwBde7-M
- **Problems to Try Out:**
  a. Add Two Numbers : https://leetcode.com/problems/add-two-numbers/
  b. LRU Cache : https://leetcode.com/problems/lru-cache/
  c. Reverse Linked List : https://leetcode.com/problems/reverse-linked-list/
  d. Merge k Sorted Lists : https://leetcode.com/problems/merge-k-sorted-lists/
  e. Merge Two Sorted Lists : https://leetcode.com/problems/merge-two-sorted-lists/
  f. Remove Nth Node From End of List : https://leetcode.com/problems/remove-nth-node-from-end-of-list/
  g. Intersection of Two Linked Lists : https://leetcode.com/problems/intersection-of-two-linked-lists/
  h. Palindrome Linked List : https://leetcode.com/problems/palindrome-linked-list/
  i. Copy List with Random Pointer : https://leetcode.com/problems/copy-list-with-random-pointer/
  j. Linked List Cycle : https://leetcode.com/problems/linked-list-cycle/
  k. Flatten Binary Tree to Linked List : https://leetcode.com/problems/flatten-binary-tree-to-linked-list/

l. Reverse Nodes in k-Group : https://leetcode.com/problems/reverse-nodes-in-k-group/
m. Linked List Cycle II : https://leetcode.com/problems/linked-list-cycle-ii/
n. Sort List : https://leetcode.com/problems/sort-list/
o. Swap Nodes in Pairs : https://leetcode.com/problems/swap-nodes-in-pairs/

♣ Reversal In Linked List

- **Resources:**

  Video Tutorial : Reversed Linked List: https://www.youtube.com/watch?v=G0_I-ZF0S38&t=31s

- **Problems to Try Out:**

a. Reverse Bits : https://leetcode.com/problems/reverse-bits/
b. Reverse String : https://leetcode.com/problems/reverse-string/
c. Reverse Linked List : https://leetcode.com/problems/reverse-linked-list/
d. Reverse String II : https://leetcode.com/problems/reverse-string-ii/
e. Reverse Only Letters : https://leetcode.com/problems/reverse-only-letters/
f. Reverse Prefix of Word : https://leetcode.com/problems/reverse-prefix-of-word/
g. Reverse Vowels of a String : https://leetcode.com/problems/reverse-vowels-of-a-string/
h. Reverse Words in a String III : https://leetcode.com/problems/reverse-words-in-a-string-iii/
i. Existence of a Substring in a String After Its Reverse : https://leetcode.com/problems/existence-of-a-substring-in-a-string-and-its-reverse/
j. A Number After a Double Reversal : https://leetcode.com/problems/a-number-after-a-double-reversal/
k. Make Two Arrays Equal by Reversing Subarrays : https://leetcode.com/problems/make-two-arrays-equal-by-reversing-subarrays/
l. Reverse Integer : https://leetcode.com/problems/reverse-integer/
m. Reverse Linked List II : https://leetcode.com/problems/reverse-linked-list-ii/

n. Evaluate Reverse Polish Notation : https://leetcode.com/problems/evaluate-reverse-polish-notation/
o. Reverse Words in a String : https://leetcode.com/problems/reverse-words-in-a-string/

♣ Cycle Detection in LinkedIn List

- Video Tutorial : Floyd's cycle detection algorithm : https://www.youtube.com/watch?v=PvrxZaH_eZ4
- Reading Material : Full Approach Guide - Leetcode : https://leetcode.com/discuss/interview-question/1409034/6-cycle-in-directed-graph
- **Problems to Try Out:**

a. Linked List Cycle Detection : https://www.codechef.com/practice/course/linked-lists/LINKLISTF/problems/PREP58
b. Linked List Cycle : https://leetcode.com/problems/linked-list-cycle/description/

♣ Deque

- Video Tutorial : Deque in Data Structure : https://www.youtube.com/watch?v=pqg0SOPRlJ4
- **Problems to Try Out:**

a. Strange Printer : https://leetcode.com/problems/strange-printer/?envType=daily-question&envId=2024-08-21
b. Design Circular Deque : https://leetcode.com/problems/design-circular-deque/

♣ Priority Queue

- Video Tutorial : Priority Queue Explained : https://www.youtube.com/watch?v=XDxLEUgVDMM
- **Problems to Try Out:**

a. Kth Largest Element in a Stream : https://leetcode.com/problems/kth-largest-element-in-a-stream/
b. Last Stone Weight : https://leetcode.com/problems/last-stone-weight/
c. Top K Frequent Elements : https://leetcode.com/problems/top-k-frequent-elements/
d. Merge k Sorted Lists : https://leetcode.com/problems/merge-k-sorted-lists/

e. Find K Closest Elements : https://leetcode.com/problems/find-k-closest-elements/
f. K Closest Points to Origin : https://leetcode.com/problems/k-closest-points-to-origin/
g. Minimum Cost to Connect Sticks : https://leetcode.com/problems/minimum-cost-to-connect-sticks/
h. Task Scheduler : https://leetcode.com/problems/task-scheduler/
i. Reorganize String : https://leetcode.com/problems/reorganize-string/
j. Distant Barcodes : https://leetcode.com/problems/distant-barcodes/
k. Maximum Frequency Stack : https://leetcode.com/problems/maximum-frequency-stack/
l. Minimum Number of Refueling Stops : https://leetcode.com/problems/minimum-number-of-refueling-stops/
m. Super Ugly Number : https://leetcode.com/problems/super-ugly-number/
n. Find Median from Data Stream : https://leetcode.com/problems/find-median-from-data-stream/
o. Swim in Rising Water : https://leetcode.com/problems/swim-in-rising-water/

♣ Kadane's Algorithm

- **Resources:**

  Video Tutorial : Kadane's Algorithm Tutorial : https://www.youtube.com/watch?v=YxuK6A3SvTs

- **Problems to Try Out:**

  a. Maximum Subarray Problem : https://leetcode.com/problems/maximum-subarray/
  b. Maximum Difference Of 0's And 1's In A Binary String : https://leetcode.com/problems/ones-and-zeroes/
  c. Maximum Sum Circular Subarray : https://leetcode.com/problems/maximum-sum-circular-subarray/
  d. Smallest Sum Contiguous Subarray : https://leetcode.com/problems/minimum-size-subarray-sum/
  e. Largest Sum Increasing Contiguous Subarray : https://leetcode.com/problems/maximum-ascending-subarray-sum/

♣ Difference Array

- **Resources:**

  Video Tutorial : Difference Array Explanation (YouTube) : https://www.youtube.com/watch?v=96RG7EBF8LI

- **Problems to Try Out:**

  a. Find the Distinct Difference Array : https://leetcode.com/problems/find-the-distinct-difference-array/
  b. Difference Between Element Sum and Digit Sum of an Array : https://leetcode.com/problems/difference-between-element-sum-and-digit-sum-of-an-array/
  c. Find the Difference : https://leetcode.com/problems/find-the-difference/
  d. Minimum Absolute Difference : https://leetcode.com/problems/minimum-absolute-difference/
  e. Odd String Difference : https://leetcode.com/problems/odd-string-difference/
  f. Highest Salaries Difference : https://leetcode.com/problems/highest-salaries-difference/
  g. Find the Difference of Two Arrays : https://leetcode.com/problems/find-the-difference-of-two-arrays/
  h. Minimum Absolute Difference in BST : https://leetcode.com/problems/minimum-absolute-difference-in-bst/
  i. Maximum Difference Between Increasing Elements : https://leetcode.com/problems/maximum-difference-between-increasing-elements/
  j. Divisible SQL Vs NoSQLn-Divisible Sums Difference : https://leetcode.com/problems/divisible-and-non-divisible-sums-difference/
  k. Permutation Difference Between Two Strings : https://leetcode.com/problems/permutation-difference-between-two-strings/

♣ Intervals

- **Resources:**

  Video Tutorial : Merge Overlapping Intervals : https://www.youtube.com/watch?v=IexN60k62jo

- **Problems to Try Out:**
    a. Merge Intervals : https://leetcode.com/problems/merge-intervals/
    b. Non-overlapping Intervals : https://leetcode.com/problems/non-overlapping-intervals/
    c. Remove Covered Intervals : https://leetcode.com/problems/remove-covered-intervals/
    d. Intervals Between Identical Elements : https://leetcode.com/problems/intervals-between-identical-elements/
    e. Partition Array Into Disjoint Intervals : https://leetcode.com/problems/partition-array-into-disjoint-intervals/
    f. Divide Intervals Into Minimum Number of Groups : https://leetcode.com/problems/divide-intervals-into-minimum-number-of-groups/
    g. Interval List Intersections : https://leetcode.com/problems/interval-list-intersections/
    h. Insert Interval : https://leetcode.com/problems/insert-interval/
    i. Remove Interval : https://leetcode.com/problems/remove-interval/
    j. Custom Interval : https://leetcode.com/problems/custom-interval/
    k. Find Right Interval : https://leetcode.com/problems/find-right-inter val/
    l. Find Interview Candidates : https://leetcode.com/problems/find-interview-candidates/
    m. Longest Well-Performing Interval : https://leetcode.com/problems/longest-well-performing-interval/
    n. Interleaving String : https://leetcode.com/problems/interleaving-string/
    o. Accepted Candidates From the Interviews : https://leetcode.com/problems/accepted-candidates-from-the-interviews/

Month 3

♣ Maths and Number Theory

- **Resources:**

  Reading Material : Number Theory - CodeChef Guide : https://www.codechef.com/learn/course/number-theory

- **Problems to Try Out:**

  a. Add Digits : https://leetcode.com/problems/add-digits/
  b. Three Divisors : https://leetcode.com/problems/three-divisors/
  c. Find Greatest Common Divisor of Array : https://leetcode.com/problems/find-greatest-common-divisor-of-array/
  d. Smallest Even Multiple : https://leetcode.com/problems/smallest-even-multiple/
  e. Number of Common Factors : https://leetcode.com/problems/number-of-common-factors/
  f. Count Primes : https://leetcode.com/problems/count-primes/
  g. Mirror Reflection : https://leetcode.com/problems/mirror-reflection/
  h. Simplified Fractions : https://leetcode.com/problems/simplified-fractions/
  i. The kth Factor of n : https://leetcode.com/problems/the-kth-factor-of-n/
  j. Number of Subarrays With GCD Equal to K : https://leetcode.com/problems/number-of-subarrays-with-gcd-equal-to-k/
  k. Largest Component Size by Common Factor : https://leetcode.com/problems/largest-component-size-by-common-factor/
  l. Graph Connectivity With Threshold : https://leetcode.com/problems/graph-connectivity-with-threshold/
  m. Count Ways to Make Array With Product : https://leetcode.com/problems/count-ways-to-make-array-with-product/
  n. Maximize Score After N Operations : https://leetcode.com/problems/maximize-score-after-n-operations/
  o. Number of Different Subsequences GCDs : https://leetcode.com/problems/number-of-different-subsequences-gcds/

♣ Binary Exponentiation

- **Resources:**

  Video Tutorial : Binary Exponentiation Tutorial : https://www.youtube.com/watch?v=9VEqjAZxmeA

- **Problems to Try Out:**

a. Codeforces Problem 630I - Parking Lot : https://codeforces.com/problemset/problem/630/I
b. LeetCode Problem - Count Good Numbers : https://leetcode.com/problems/count-good-numbers/
c. CodeChef Problem - RIFFLES : https://www.codechef.com/JAN221B/problems/RIFFLES
d. Codeforces Problem 222E - Decoding Genome : https://codeforces.com/contest/222/problem/E
e. Codeforces Problem 852B - Geometric Progression : https://codeforces.com/contest/852/problem/B
f. Codeforces Problem 1117D - Magic Carpet : https://codeforces.com/problemset/problem/1117/D
g. SPOJ Problem - LASTDIG : https://www.spoj.com/problems/LASTDIG/
h. SPOJ Problem - LOCKER : https://www.spoj.com/problems/LOCKER/
i. UVa Live Problem 3722 - Power of Cryptography : https://vjudge.net/problem/UVALive-3722
j. SPOJ Problem - ZSUM : https://www.spoj.com/problems/ZSUM/
k. Codeforces Problem 498E - Cinema : https://codeforces.com/contest/498/problem/E

♣ **GCD (Greatest Common Divisor)**

- **Resources:**

Video Tutorial : GCD Explanation (YouTube) : https://www.youtube.com/watch?v=yHwneN6zJmU&t=91s

- **Problems:**

a. GCD and LCM Problem : https://leetcode.com/problems/greatest-common-divisor-of-strings/description/
b. Find Greatest Common Divisor of Array : https://leetcode.com/problems/find-greatest-common-divisor-of-array/
c. GCD Sort of an Array : https://leetcode.com/problems/gcd-sort-of-an-array/
d. Count Primes : https://leetcode.com/problems/count-primes/
e. Greatest Common Divisor of Strings : https://leetcode.com/problems/greatest-common-divisor-of-strings/

f. X of a Kind in a Deck of Cards : https://leetcode.com/problems/x-of-a-kind-in-a-deck-of-cards/
g. Largest Component Size by Common Factor : https://leetcode.com/problems/largest-component-size-by-common-factor/
h. Number of Different Subsequences GCDs : https://leetcode.com/problems/number-of-different-subsequences-gcds/
i. Count the Number of Ideal Arrays : https://leetcode.com/problems/count-the-number-of-ideal-arrays/
j. Minimum Deletions to Make Array Divisible : https://leetcode.com/problems/minimum-deletions-to-make-array-divisible/
k. Number of Subarrays With GCD Equal to K : https://leetcode.com/problems/number-of-subarrays-with-gcd-equal-to-k/

♣ Integer Factorization

- **Resources:**

  Video Tutorial: Integer Factorization Techniques (YouTube) : https://www.youtube.com/watch?v=LT7XhVdeRyg

- **Problems to Try Out:**

  a. Largest Component Size by Common Factor : https://leetcode.com/problems/largest-component-size-by-common-factor/description/
  b. Distinct Prime Factors of Product of Array : https://leetcode.com/problems/distinct-prime-factors-of-product-of-array/description/
  c. Minimum Factorization : https://leetcode.com/problems/minimum-factorization/description/
  d. Greatest Common Divisor Traversal : https://leetcode.com/problems/greatest-common-divisor-traversal/description/
  e. Count Primes : https://leetcode.com/problems/count-primes/
  f. Ugly Number : https://leetcode.com/problems/ugly-number/
  g. Ugly Number II : https://leetcode.com/problems/ugly-number-ii/
  h. Ugly Number III : https://leetcode.com/problems/ugly-number-iii/
  i. Largest Component Size by Common Factor : https://leetcode.com/problems/largest-component-size-by-common-factor/
  j. Number of Distinct Prime Factors of Product of Array : https://leetcode.com/problems/distinct-prime-factors-of-product-of-array/
  k. Smallest Value After Replacing With Sum of Prime Factors : https://leetcode.com/problems/smallest-value-after-replacing-with-sum-of-prime-factors/

l. Find Kth Factor of N : https://leetcode.com/problems/the-kth-factor-of-n/
m. Count the Number of Ideal Arrays : https://leetcode.com/problems/count-the-number-of-ideal-arrays/

♣ **Primality Tests (Linear Sieve, Sieve of Eratosthenes)**

- **Resources:**

  Video Tutorials –

  Tutorial-1 : Sieve of Eratosthenes - Khan Academy : https://www.youtube.com/watch?v=klcIklsWzrY

- **Problems to Try Out:**

  a. Count Primes : https://leetcode.com/problems/count-primes/
  b. Prime Palindrome : https://leetcode.com/problems/prime-palindrome/
  c. Find the Kth Prime : https://leetcode.com/problems/the-kth-factor-of-n/
  d. Super Ugly Number : https://leetcode.com/problems/super-ugly-number/
  e. Prime Subtraction Operation : https://leetcode.com/problems/prime-subtraction-operation/
  f. Largest Component Size by Common Factor : https://leetcode.com/problems/largest-component-size-by-common-factor/
  g. Find Greatest Common Divisor of Array : https://leetcode.com/problems/find-greatest-common-divisor-of-array/
  h. Replace Non-Coprime Numbers in Array : https://leetcode.com/problems/replace-non-coprime-numbers-in-array/
  i. Number of Good Ways to Split a String : https://leetcode.com/problems/number-of-good-ways-to-split-a-string/
  j. Sum of Beauty of All Substrings : https://leetcode.com/problems/sum-of-beauty-of-all-substrings/

♣ **Sum of Divisors / Number of Divisors**

- **Resources:**

  Video Tutorial : Divisors - Sum and Count : https://www.youtube.com/watch?v=5ltOfUUb-7U

- **Problems to Try Out:**
  a. Count of Smaller Numbers After Self : https://leetcode.com/problems/count-of-smaller-numbers-after-self/
  b. Count Primes : https://leetcode.com/problems/count-primes/
  c. The Kth Factor of N : https://leetcode.com/problems/the-kth-factor-of-n/
  d. Number of Good Ways to Split a String : https://leetcode.com/problems/number-of-good-ways-to-split-a-string/
  e. Find Greatest Common Divisor of Array : https://leetcode.com/problems/find-greatest-common-divisor-of-array/
  f. Three Divisors : https://leetcode.com/problems/three-divisors/
  g. Maximum Sum of an Hourglass : https://leetcode.com/problems/maximum-sum-of-an-hourglass/
  h. Largest Component Size by Common Factor : https://leetcode.com/problems/largest-component-size-by-common-factor/
  i. Sum of Beauty of All Substrings : https://leetcode.com/problems/sum-of-beauty-of-all-substrings/
  j. Replace Non-Coprime Numbers in Array : https://leetcode.com/problems/replace-non-coprime-numbers-in-array/

♣ Permutations and Combinations (Star and Bars, The Inclusion-Exclusion Principle)

- **Resources:**

  Video Tutorials –

  Tutorial – 1 : Print all Permutation : https://www.youtube.com/watch?v=YK78FU5Ffjw
  Tutorial – 2 : Stars and Bars Explained : https://www.youtube.com/watch?v=epY_8lcKxCU

- **Problems to Try Out:**
  a. Permutations : https://leetcode.com/problems/permutations/
  b. Combinations : https://leetcode.com/problems/combinations/
  c. Letter Combinations of a Phone Number : https://leetcode.com/problems/letter-combinations-of-a-phone-number/
  d. Subsets : https://leetcode.com/problems/subsets/
  e. Combination Sum : https://leetcode.com/problems/combination-sum/

f. Permutations II : https://leetcode.com/problems/permutations-ii/
g. Combination Sum II : https://leetcode.com/problems/combination-sum-ii/
h. Subsets II : https://leetcode.com/problems/subsets-ii/
i. Generate Parentheses : https://leetcode.com/problems/generate-parentheses/
j. Factor Combinations : https://leetcode.com/problems/factor-combinations/
k. Count Vowels Permutation : https://leetcode.com/problems/count-vowels-permutation/
l. Count Numbers with Unique Digits : https://leetcode.com/problems/count-numbers-with-unique-digits/
m. Unique Paths III : https://leetcode.com/problems/unique-paths-iii/
n. Beautiful Arrangement : https://leetcode.com/problems/beautiful-arrangement/
o. Reconstruct Itinerary : https://leetcode.com/problems/reconstruct-itinerary/

♣ **Pigeonhole Principle**

- **Resources:**

  Video Tutorials -

  Tutorial 1 : About the principle : https://www.youtube.com/watch?v=B2A2pGrDG8I

  Tutorial 2 : Pigeonhole Principle explained with example : https://www.youtube.com/watch?v=ROnetLvbl6M

- **Problems to Try Out:**

a. Majority Element : https://leetcode.com/problems/majority-element/
b. Find the Duplicate Number : https://leetcode.com/problems/find-the-duplicate-number/
c. Missing Number : https://leetcode.com/problems/missing-number/
d. Contains Duplicate : https://leetcode.com/problems/contains-duplicate/
e. Kth Largest Element in an Array : https://leetcode.com/problems/kth-largest-element-in-an-array/

f. Minimum Window Substring : https://leetcode.com/problems/minimum-window-substring/
g. Longest Substring Without Repeating Characters : https://leetcode.com/problems/longest-substring-without-repeating-characters/
h. Subarray Sum Equals K : https://leetcode.com/problems/subarray-sum-equals-k/description/
i. Longest Consecutive Sequence : https://leetcode.com/problems/longest-consecutive-sequence/

♣ Bit Manipulation

- **Resources:**

  Video Tutorial : Bit Manipulation Basics : https://www.youtube.com/watch?v=NLKQEOgBAnw

  Reading Material : All Types of Patterns for Bits Manipulations and How to use it (Blog) : https://leetcode.com/discuss/interview-question/3695233/all-types-of-patterns-for-bits-manipulations-and-how-to-use-it

- **Problems to Try Out:**

  a. Add Binary : https://leetcode.com/problems/add-binary/
  b. Single Number : https://leetcode.com/problems/single-number/
  c. Number of 1 Bits : https://leetcode.com/problems/number-of-1-bits/
  d. Power of Two : https://leetcode.com/problems/power-of-two/
  e. Palindrome Permutation : https://leetcode.com/problems/palindrome-permutation/
  f. Find the Duplicate Number : https://leetcode.com/problems/find-the-duplicate-number/
  g. Maximum Product of Word Lengths : https://leetcode.com/problems/maximum-product-of-word-lengths/
  h. Hamming Distance : https://leetcode.com/problems/hamming-distance/
  i. Stickers to Spell Word : https://leetcode.com/problems/stickers-to-spell-word/
  j. K-th Symbol in Grammar : https://leetcode.com/problems/k-th-symbol-in-grammar/

k. Transform to Chessboard : https://leetcode.com/problems/transform-to-chessboard/
l. Chalkboard XOR Game : https://leetcode.com/problems/chalkboard-xor-game/
m. Shortest Path to Get All Keys : https://leetcode.com/problems/shortest-path-to-get-all-keys/
n. Triples with Bitwise AND Equal To Zero : https://leetcode.com/problems/triples-with-bitwise-and-equal-to-zero/
o. Can I Win : https://leetcode.com/problems/can-i-win/

♣ **Search Algorithms**

♣ Linear Search

- **Resources:**

  Video Tutorial : Linear Search Explained : https://www.youtube.com/watch?v=Hr5cP7LOUkU

  Reading Material : Linear Search Explained (Leetcode) : https://leetcode.com/discuss/study-guide/1837620/getting-idea-about-searching-or-familiar-with-linear-search-and-binary-search

- **Problems to Try Out:**

  a. Find Numbers with Even Number of Digits : https://leetcode.com/problems/find-numbers-with-even-number-of-digits/
  b. Find Pivot Index : https://leetcode.com/problems/find-pivot-index/
  c. Check If N and Its Double Exist : https://leetcode.com/problems/check-if-n-and-its-double-exist/
  d. Maximum Population Year : https://leetcode.com/problems/maximum-population-year/
  e. Lucky Numbers in a Matrix : https://leetcode.com/problems/lucky-numbers-in-a-matrix/
  f. Find the Difference : https://leetcode.com/problems/find-the-difference/
  g. Find All Numbers Disappeared in an Array : https://leetcode.com/problems/find-all-numbers-disappeared-in-an-array/
  h. Find Common Characters : https://leetcode.com/problems/find-common-characters/
  i. Find Smallest Letter Greater Than Target : https://leetcode.com/problems/find-smallest-letter-greater-than-target/

a. Find the Town Judge : https://leetcode.com/problems/find-the-town-judge/
b. Search a 2D Matrix II : https://leetcode.com/problems/search-a-2d-matrix-ii/
c. Find Peak Element : https://leetcode.com/problems/find-peak-element/
d. Search in Rotated Sorted Array : https://leetcode.com/problems/search-in-rotated-sorted-array/
e. First Missing Positive : https://leetcode.com/problems/first-missing-positive/
f. Minimum Size Subarray Sum : https://leetcode.com/problems/minimum-size-subarray-sum/

♣ Binary Search

- **Resources :**

Video Tutorials

Tutorial 1 : Binary Search Tutorial : https://www.youtube.com/watch?v=eVuPCG5eIr4&t=10s

Tutorial 2 : Linear vs Binary Search : https://www.youtube.com/watch?v=sSYQ1H9-Vks&t=110s

Reading Material : Binary Search Guide - Leetcode

- **Problems to Try Out:**

a. Merge Two Binary Trees : https://leetcode.com/problems/merge-two-binary-trees/
b. Cousins in Binary Tree : https://leetcode.com/problems/cousins-in-binary-tree/
c. Evaluate Boolean Binary Tree : https://leetcode.com/problems/evaluate-boolean-binary-tree/
d. Maximum Odd Binary Number : https://leetcode.com/problems/maximum-odd-binary-number/
e. Maximum Depth of Binary Tree : https://leetcode.com/problems/maximum-depth-of-binary-tree/
f. Minimum Depth of Binary Tree : https://leetcode.com/problems/minimum-depth-of-binary-tree/

g. Binary Number With Alternating Bits : https://leetcode.com/problems/binary-number-with-alternating-bits/
h. Binary Prefix Divisible by 5 : https://leetcode.com/problems/binary-prefix-divisible-by-5/
i. Average of Levels in Binary Tree : https://leetcode.com/problems/average-of-levels-in-binary-tree/
j. Special Positions in a Binary Matrix : https://leetcode.com/problems/special-positions-in-a-binary-matrix/
k. Second Minimum Node in a Binary Tree : https://leetcode.com/problems/second-minimum-node-in-a-binary-tree/
l. Sum of Root To Leaf Binary Numbers : https://leetcode.com/problems/sum-of-root-to-leaf-binary-numbers/
m. Minimum Changes To Make Alternating Binary String : https://leetcode.com/problems/minimum-changes-to-make-alternating-binary-string/
n. Prime Number of Set Bits in Binary Representation : https://leetcode.com/problems/prime-number-of-set-bits-in-binary-representation/
o. Convert Binary Number in a Linked List to Integer : https://leetcode.com/problems/convert-binary-number-in-a-linked-list-to-integer/
p. Find the Longest Balanced Substring of a Binary String : https://leetcode.com/problems/find-the-longest-balanced-substring-of-a-binary-string/

♣ Ternary Search

- **Resources:**

  Video Tutorials : Ternary Search : https://www.youtube.com/watch?v=lCrzxiwXjDk

  Reading Material : Ternary Search Guide : https://cp-algorithms.com/num_methods/ternary_search.html

- **Problems To Try:**

a. Find the Peak Element : https://leetcode.com/problems/find-peak-element/
b. Search in Rotated Sorted Array : https://leetcode.com/problems/search-in-rotated-sorted-array/
c. Find Minimum in Rotated Sorted Array : https://leetcode.com/problems/find-minimum-in-rotated-sorted-array/

d. Maximum Number in Mountain Array : https://leetcode.com/problems/peak-index-in-a-mountain-array/
e. Kth Smallest Element in a Sorted Matrix : https://leetcode.com/problems/kth-smallest-element-in-a-sorted-matrix/
f. Find Minimum in Rotated Sorted Array II : https://leetcode.com/problems/find-minimum-in-rotated-sorted-array-ii/
g. Search a 2D Matrix : https://leetcode.com/problems/search-a-2d-matrix/
h. Find the Smallest Divisor Given a Threshold : https://leetcode.com/problems/find-the-smallest-divisor-given-a-threshold/
i. Maximum Average Subarray I : https://leetcode.com/problems/maximum-average-subarray-i/
j. Search in Rotated Sorted Array II : https://leetcode.com/problems/search-in-rotated-sorted-array-ii/
k. Minimize Max Distance to Gas Station : https://leetcode.com/problems/minimize-max-distance-to-gas-station/description/
l. Find Peak Element in 2D Array : https://leetcode.com/problems/find-a-peak-element-ii/
m. Guess Number Higher or Lower II : https://leetcode.com/problems/guess-number-higher-or-lower-ii/
n. Kth Smallest Prime Fraction : https://leetcode.com/problems/k-th-smallest-prime-fraction/description/

Month 4

♣ **Sort Algorithms**

♣ Bubble Sort

- **Resources:**

  Video Tutorial : Bubble Sort Tutorial : https://www.youtube.com/watch?v=Jdtq5uKz-w4

- **Problems to Try Out:**

  a. Sort Colors : https://leetcode.com/problems/sort-colors/
  b. Sort Array By Parity : https://leetcode.com/problems/sort-array-by-parity/
  c. Sort Array By Parity II : https://leetcode.com/problems/sort-array-by-parity-ii/
  d. Sort Integers By The Number of 1 Bits : https://leetcode.com/problems/sort-integers-by-the-number-of-1-bits/
  e. Sort Characters By Frequency : https://leetcode.com/problems/sort-characters-by-frequency/
  f. Relative Sort Array : https://leetcode.com/problems/relative-sort-array/
  g. Minimum Number of Arrows to Burst Balloons : https://leetcode.com/problems/minimum-number-of-arrows-to-burst-balloons/
  h. Wiggle Sort II : https://leetcode.com/problems/wiggle-sort-ii/
  i. Sort Array By Increasing Frequency : https://leetcode.com/problems/sort-array-by-increasing-frequency/
  j. Sort the Matrix Diagonally : https://leetcode.com/problems/sort-the-matrix-diagonally/
  k. Max Chunks To Make Sorted : https://leetcode.com/problems/max-chunks-to-make-sorted/
  l. Sort An Array : https://leetcode.com/problems/sort-an-array/
  m. Custom Sort String : https://leetcode.com/problems/custom-sort-string/
  n. Maximum Product of Two Elements in an Array : https://leetcode.com/problems/maximum-product-of-two-elements-in-an-array/
  o. Sort Integers By Power Value : https://leetcode.com/problems/sort-integers-by-the-power-value/

♣ Insertion Sort

- **Resources:**

  Video Tutorial : Insertion sort : https://www.youtube.com/watch?v=8mJ-OhcfpYg

  Reading Material : Insertion sort reading material : https://www.w3schools.com/dsa/dsa_algo_insertionsort.php

- **Problems to Try Out:**

  a. Insertion Sort List : https://leetcode.com/problems/insertion-sort-list/
  b. Sort Colors : https://leetcode.com/problems/sort-colors/
  c. Wiggle Sort II : https://leetcode.com/problems/wiggle-sort-ii/
  d. Pancake Sorting : https://leetcode.com/problems/pancake-sorting/
  e. Sort Array By Parity : https://leetcode.com/problems/sort-array-by-parity/
  f. Sort Array By Parity II : https://leetcode.com/problems/sort-array-by-parity-ii/
  g. Sort the Matrix Diagonally : https://leetcode.com/problems/sort-the-matrix-diagonally/
  h. Sort Transformed Array : https://leetcode.com/problems/sort-transformed-array/
  i. Sort Integers By Power Value : https://leetcode.com/problems/sort-integers-by-the-power-value/
  j. Max Chunks To Make Sorted : https://leetcode.com/problems/max-chunks-to-make-sorted/
  k. Max Chunks To Make Sorted II : https://leetcode.com/problems/max-chunks-to-make-sorted-ii/
  l. Longest Word in Dictionary : https://leetcode.com/problems/longest-word-in-dictionary/
  m. Largest Number : https://leetcode.com/problems/largest-number/
  n. Custom Sort String : https://leetcode.com/problems/custom-sort-string/
  o. Sort the Matrix Diagonally : https://leetcode.com/problems/sort-the-matrix-diagonally/

♣ Merge Sort

- **Resources:**

  Video Tutorials –

  Tutorial 1 : Merge sort : https://www.youtube.com/watch?v=3j0SWDX4AtU

  Tutorial 2 : Merge Sort Tutorial : https://www.youtube.com/watch?v=ogjf7ORKfd8

  Reading Material : Merge sort algorithm : https://www.geeksforgeeks.org/merge-sort/

- **Problems to Try Out:**

  a. Merge Intervals : https://leetcode.com/problems/merge-intervals/
  b. Sort List : https://leetcode.com/problems/sort-list/
  c. Merge Sorted Array : https://leetcode.com/problems/merge-sorted-array/
  d. Interval List Intersections : https://leetcode.com/problems/interval-list-intersections/
  e. Merge Two Sorted Lists : https://leetcode.com/problems/merge-two-sorted-lists/
  f. Kth Smallest Element in a Sorted Matrix : https://leetcode.com/problems/kth-smallest-element-in-a-sorted-matrix/
  g. Intersection of Two Arrays II : https://leetcode.com/problems/intersection-of-two-arrays-ii/
  h. Count of Smaller Numbers After Self : https://leetcode.com/problems/count-of-smaller-numbers-after-self/
  i. Smallest Range II : https://leetcode.com/problems/smallest-range-ii/
  j. Sort Transformed Array : https://leetcode.com/problems/sort-transformed-array/
  k. Reverse Pairs : https://leetcode.com/problems/reverse-pairs/
  l. Max Chunks To Make Sorted II : https://leetcode.com/problems/max-chunks-to-make-sorted-ii/
  m. Interval List Intersections : https://leetcode.com/problems/interval-list-intersections/

n. Largest Number : https://leetcode.com/problems/largest-number/
o. Minimum Number of Arrows to Burst Balloons : https://leetcode.com/problems/minimum-number-of-arrows-to-burst-balloons/

♣ Selection Sort

- **Resources:**

  Video Tutorial : Selection Sort Tutorial : https://www.youtube.com/watch?v=WYVKZ4Mla5c

  Reading Material : Selection sort in data structure : https://www.w3schools.in/data-structures/sorting-techniques/selection-sort-algorithm

- **Problems to Try Out:**

  a. Kth Largest Element in an Array : https://leetcode.com/problems/kth-largest-element-in-an-array/
  b. Kth Smallest Element in a Sorted Matrix : https://leetcode.com/problems/kth-smallest-element-in-a-sorted-matrix/
  c. Select Sort an Array : https://leetcode.com/problems/sort-an-array/
  d. Max Chunks To Make Sorted : https://leetcode.com/problems/max-chunks-to-make-sorted/
  e. Kth Smallest Element in a Sorted Matrix : https://leetcode.com/problems/kth-smallest-element-in-a-sorted-matrix/
  f. Find Median from Data Stream : https://leetcode.com/problems/find-median-from-data-stream/
  g. Top K Frequent Elements : https://leetcode.com/problems/top-k-frequent-elements/
  h. Find Median from Data Stream : https://leetcode.com/problems/find-median-from-data-stream/

♣ Quick Sort

- **Resources:**

  Video Tutorial : Quick Sort Tutorial : https://www.youtube.com/watch?v=Vtckgz38QHs

- **Problems to Try Out:**

  a. Kth Largest Element in an Array : https://leetcode.com/problems/kth-largest-element-in-an-array/

b. 3Sum : https://leetcode.com/problems/3sum/
c. 4Sum : https://leetcode.com/problems/4sum/
d. Merge Intervals : https://leetcode.com/problems/merge-intervals/
e. Sort Colors : https://leetcode.com/problems/sort-colors/
f. Group Anagrams : https://leetcode.com/problems/group-anagrams/
g. Kth Smallest Element in a Sorted Matrix : https://leetcode.com/problems/kth-smallest-element-in-a-sorted-matrix/
h. Top K Frequent Elements : https://leetcode.com/problems/top-k-frequent-elements/
i. Find Median from Data Stream : https://leetcode.com/problems/find-median-from-data-stream/
j. Task Scheduler : https://leetcode.com/problems/task-scheduler/
k. Largest Number : https://leetcode.com/problems/largest-number/
l. Sort List : https://leetcode.com/problems/sort-list/
m. Queue Reconstruction by Height : https://leetcode.com/problems/queue-reconstruction-by-height/
n. Max Chunks To Make Sorted II : https://leetcode.com/problems/max-chunks-to-make-sorted-ii/
o. Wiggle Sort II : https://leetcode.com/problems/wiggle-sort-ii/

♣ HeapSort

- **Resources:**

  Video Tutorials –

  Tutorial 1 : Heapsort : https://www.youtube.com/watch?v=2DmK_H7IdTo

  Tutorial 2 : Heap sort visualization : https://www.youtube.com/watch?v=mgUiY8CVDhU

  Reading Material : Understanding Heapsort : https://www.baeldung.com/cs/understanding-heapsort

- **Problems to Try Out:**

  a. Queue Reconstruction by Height : https://leetcode.com/discuss/study-guide/1212004/Binary-Trees-study-guide
  b. Find Median from Data Stream : https://leetcode.com/problems/find-median-from-data-stream/

c. Top K Frequent Elements : https://leetcode.com/problems/top-k-frequent-elements/
d. Task Scheduler : https://leetcode.com/problems/task-scheduler/
e. Find Median from Data Stream : https://leetcode.com/problems/find-median-from-data-stream/

♣ **Trees**

♣ Binary Trees

- **Resources:**

  Video Tutorial -

  Tutorial 1 : Binary Trees Basics : https://www.youtube.com/watch?v=H5JubkIy_p8

  Tutorial 2 : Binary tree Code explanation : https://www.youtube.com/watch?v=Gt2yBZAhsGM

  Reading Material : Binary Trees Guide - LeetCode Blog : https://leetcode.com/discuss/study-guide/1212004/Binary-Trees-study-guide

- **Problems to Try Out:**

Refer to problems on leach code study guide page (https://leetcode.com/discuss/study-guide/1212004/Binary-Trees-study-guide). Pick a few from each sections on the page. Minimum try to solve -

a. Binary Tree Inorder Traversal,
b. Same Tree,
c. Symmetric Tree,
d. Maximum Depth of Binary Tree,
e. Invert Binary Tree,
f. Binary Tree Level Order Traversal,
g. Binary Tree Paths,
h. Construct Binary Tree from Preorder and Inorder Traversal,
i. Kth Smallest Element in a BST,
j. Binary Tree Right Side View,
k. Binary Tree Maximum Path Sum,
l. Flatten Binary Tree to Linked List,
m. Lowest Common Ancestor of a Binary Tree,
n. Path Sum III,
o. Pseudo-Palindromic Paths in a Binary Tree

♣ Tree Traversals

- **Resources:**
  Video Tutorial : Binary Tree Traversal Concept : https://www.youtube.com/watch?v=9RHO6jU--GU
- **Problems to Try Out:**
  a. Binary Tree Inorder Traversal : https://leetcode.com/problems/binary-tree-inorder-traversal/
  b. Binary Tree Postorder Traversal : https://leetcode.com/problems/binary-tree-postorder-traversal/
  c. Binary Tree Preorder Traversal : https://leetcode.com/problems/binary-tree-preorder-traversal/
  d. N-ary Tree Preorder Traversal : https://leetcode.com/problems/n-ary-tree-preorder-traversal/
  e. N-ary Tree Postorder Traversal : https://leetcode.com/problems/n-ary-tree-postorder-traversal/
  f. Construct Binary Tree from Preorder and Inorder Traversal : https://leetcode.com/problems/construct-binary-tree-from-preorder-and-inorder-traversal/
  g. Binary Tree Level Order Traversal : https://leetcode.com/problems/binary-tree-level-order-traversal/
  h. Binary Tree Zigzag Level Order Traversal : https://leetcode.com/problems/binary-tree-zigzag-level-order-traversal/
  i. Construct Binary Tree from Inorder and Postorder Traversal : https://leetcode.com/problems/construct-binary-tree-from-inorder-and-postorder-traversal/
  j. Construct Binary Search Tree from Preorder Traversal : https://leetcode.com/problems/construct-binary-search-tree-from-preorder-traversal/
  k. Binary Tree Level Order Traversal II : https://leetcode.com/problems/binary-tree-level-order-traversal-ii/
  l. Construct Binary Tree from Preorder and Postorder Traversal : https://leetcode.com/problems/construct-binary-tree-from-preorder-and-postorder-traversal/
  m. N-ary Tree Level Order Traversal : https://leetcode.com/problems/n-ary-tree-level-order-traversal/

n. Flip Binary Tree to Match Preorder Traversal : https://leetcode.com/problems/flip-binary-tree-to-match-preorder-traversal/
o. Vertical Order Traversal of a Binary Tree : https://leetcode.com/problems/vertical-order-traversal-of-a-binary-tree/
p. Recover a Tree from Preorder Traversal : https://leetcode.com/problems/recover-a-tree-from-preorder-traversal/

♣ Binary Search Trees (BST)

- **Resources:**

  Tutorial 1 : Binary Search Tree Concept : https://www.youtube.com/watch?v=mtvbVLK5xDQ

  Tutorial 2 : Code example using C++ : https://www.youtube.com/watch?v=sf_9w653xdE

- **Problems to Try Out:**

  a. Unique Binary Search Trees II : https://leetcode.com/problems/unique-binary-search-trees-ii
  b. Validate Binary Search Tree : https://leetcode.com/problems/validate-binary-search-tree/
  c. Convert Sorted Array to Binary Search Tree : https://leetcode.com/problems/convert-sorted-array-to-binary-search-tree/
  d. Binary Search Tree Iterator : https://leetcode.com/problems/binary-search-tree-iterator/
  e. Kth Smallest Element in a BST : https://leetcode.com/problems/kth-smallest-element-in-a-bst/
  f. Lowest Common Ancestor of a Binary Search Tree : https://leetcode.com/problems/lowest-common-ancestor-of-a-binary-search-tree/
  g. Closest Binary Search Tree Value : https://leetcode.com/problems/closest-binary-search-tree-value/
  h. Delete Node in a BST : https://leetcode.com/problems/delete-node-in-a-bst/
  i. Minimum Absolute Difference in BST : https://leetcode.com/problems/minimum-absolute-difference-in-bst/
  j. Convert BST to Greater Tree : https://leetcode.com/problems/convert-bst-to-greater-tree/
  k. Trim a Binary Search Tree : https://leetcode.com/problems/trim-a-binary-search-tree/

l. Search in a Binary Search Tree : https://leetcode.com/problems/search-in-a-binary-search-tree/
m. Construct Binary Search Tree from Preorder Traversal : https://leetcode.com/problems/construct-binary-search-tree-from-preorder-traversal/
n. All Elements in Two Binary Search Trees : https://leetcode.com/problems/all-elements-in-two-binary-search-trees/
o. Balance a Binary Search Tree : https://leetcode.com/problems/balance-a-binary-search-tree/

♣ **Sliding Window**

- **Resources:**

  Video Tutorial : Sliding window tutorial : https://www.youtube.com/watch?v=MK-NZ4hN7rs

- **Problems to Try Out:**

  a. Longest Substring Without Repeating Characters : https://leetcode.com/problems/longest-substring-without-repeating-characters/
  b. Minimum Window Substring : https://leetcode.com/problems/minimum-window-substring/
  c. Sliding Window Maximum : https://leetcode.com/problems/sliding-window-maximum/
  d. Find All Anagrams in a String : https://leetcode.com/problems/find-all-anagrams-in-a-string/
  e. Minimum Size Subarray Sum : https://leetcode.com/problems/minimum-size-subarray-sum/
  f. Permutation in String : https://leetcode.com/problems/permutation-in-string/
  g. Max Consecutive Ones III : https://leetcode.com/problems/max-consecutive-ones-iii/
  h. Longest Repeating Character Replacement : https://leetcode.com/problems/longest-repeating-character-replacement/
  i. Longest Substring with At Least K Repeating Characters : https://leetcode.com/problems/longest-substring-with-at-least-k-repeating-characters/
  j. Maximum Length of Repeated Subarray : https://leetcode.com/problems/maximum-length-of-repeated-subarray/

k. Subarray Product Less Than K : https://leetcode.com/problems/subarray-product-less-than-k/
l. Subarrays with K Different Integers : https://leetcode.com/problems/subarrays-with-k-different-integers/
m. Shortest Subarray with Sum at Least K : https://leetcode.com/problems/shortest-subarray-with-sum-at-least-k/
n. Maximum Points You Can Obtain from Cards : https://leetcode.com/problems/maximum-points-you-can-obtain-from-cards/
o. Contains Duplicate III : https://leetcode.com/problems/contains-duplicate-iii/
p. Contains Duplicate II : https://leetcode.com/problems/contains-duplicate-ii/

♣ Divide and Conquer

- **Resources:**

  Video Tutorial : Divide and Conquer Algorithm : https://www.youtube.com/watch?v=ib4BHvr5-Ao

- **Problems to Try Out:**

  a. Maximum Subarray : https://leetcode.com/problems/maximum-subarray/
  b. Median of Two Sorted Arrays : https://leetcode.com/problems/median-of-two-sorted-arrays/
  c. Merge k Sorted Lists : https://leetcode.com/problems/merge-k-sorted-lists/
  d. Kth Largest Element in an Array : https://leetcode.com/problems/kth-largest-element-in-an-array/
  e. Majority Element : https://leetcode.com/problems/majority-element/
  f. Construct Binary Tree from Preorder and Inorder Traversal : https://leetcode.com/problems/construct-binary-tree-from-preorder-and-inorder-traversal/
  g. Top K Frequent Elements : https://leetcode.com/problems/top-k-frequent-elements/
  h. Search a 2D Matrix II : https://leetcode.com/problems/search-a-2d-matrix-ii/
  i. Sort List : https://leetcode.com/problems/sort-list/
  j. Convert Sorted Array to Binary Search Tree : https://leetcode.com/problems/convert-sorted-array-to-binary-search-tree/

k. Count of Smaller Numbers After Self : https://leetcode.com/problems/count-of-smaller-numbers-after-self/
l. K Closest Points to Origin : https://leetcode.com/problems/k-closest-points-to-origin/
m. Convert Sorted List to Binary Search Tree : https://leetcode.com/problems/convert-sorted-list-to-binary-search-tree/
n. Construct Binary Tree from Inorder and Postorder Traversal : https://leetcode.com/problems/construct-binary-tree-from-inorder-and-postorder-traversal/
o. The Skyline Problem : https://leetcode.com/problems/the-skyline-problem/

♣ Two Pointers

- **Resources:**

  Video Tutorial –

  Tutorial 1 : Two Pointers Explained : https://www.youtube.com/watch?v=On03HWe2tZM

  Tutorial 2 : comprehensive guide : https://algodaily.com/lessons/using-the-two-pointer-technique

  Reading Material : When to use : https://www.geeksforgeeks.org/when-should-i-use-two-pointer-approach/

- **Problems to Try Out:**

  a. Trapping Rain Water : https://leetcode.com/problems/trapping-rain-water/
  b. 3Sum : https://leetcode.com/problems/3sum/
  c. Container With Most Water : https://leetcode.com/problems/container-with-most-water/
  d. Find the Duplicate Number : https://leetcode.com/problems/find-the-duplicate-number/
  e. Next Permutation : https://leetcode.com/problems/next-permutation/
  f. Remove Nth Node From End of List : https://leetcode.com/problems/remove-nth-node-from-end-of-list/
  g. Move Zeroes : https://leetcode.com/problems/move-zeroes/
  h. Intersection of Two Linked Lists : https://leetcode.com/problems/intersection-of-two-linked-lists/

i. Palindrome Linked List : https://leetcode.com/problems/palindrome-linked-list/
j. Rotate Array : https://leetcode.com/problems/rotate-array/
k. Linked List Cycle : https://leetcode.com/problems/linked-list-cycle/
l. Partition Labels : https://leetcode.com/problems/partition-labels/
m. Find Median from Data Stream : https://leetcode.com/problems/find-median-from-data-stream/
n. Linked List Cycle II : https://leetcode.com/problems/linked-list-cycle-ii/

Month 5

♣ Greedy Algorithms

1. Video Tutorial: Video tutorials on greedy algorithms: https://www.youtube.com/watch?v=DIX2p7vb9co&list=PLgUwDviBIf0rF1w2Koyh78zafB0cz7tea

2. Book : Dynamic-Programming (Kamal Rawat) : https://www.flipkart.com/dynamic-programming-coding-interviews-bottom-up-approach-problem-solving/p/itmeqewxyebhu7xw

- **Problems to Try Out:**
  a. Container With Most Water : https://leetcode.com/problems/container-with-most-water/
  b. Jump Game : https://leetcode.com/problems/jump-game/
  c. Jump Game II : https://leetcode.com/problems/jump-game-ii/
  d. Best Time to Buy and Sell Stock II : https://leetcode.com/problems/best-time-to-buy-and-sell-stock-ii/
  e. Partition Labels : https://leetcode.com/problems/partition-labels/
  f. Task Scheduler : https://leetcode.com/problems/task-scheduler/
  g. Shortest Unsorted Continuous Subarray : https://leetcode.com/problems/shortest-unsorted-continuous-subarray/
  h. Queue Reconstruction by Height : https://leetcode.com/problems/queue-reconstruction-by-height/
  i. Gas Station : https://leetcode.com/problems/gas-station/
  j. Remove K Digits : https://leetcode.com/problems/remove-k-digits/
  k. Wildcard Matching : https://leetcode.com/problems/wildcard-matching/
  l. Split Array Largest Sum : https://leetcode.com/problems/split-array-largest-sum/
  m. Candy : https://leetcode.com/problems/candy/
  n. Minimum Number of Refueling Stops : https://leetcode.com/problems/minimum-number-of-refueling-stops/
  o. Smallest Range Covering Elements from K Lists : https://leetcode.com/problems/smallest-range-covering-elements-from-k-lists/

♣ Graphs

- Video Tutorial –

  Tutorial 1 : Video tutorials on Graphs : https://www.youtube.com/watch?v=bvWVs0tJUOY

  Tutorial 2 : https://www.youtube.com/watch?v=-VgHk7UMPP4

- **Problems to Try Out:**
  a. Course Schedule : https://leetcode.com/problems/course-schedule/
  b. Course Schedule II : https://leetcode.com/problems/course-schedule-ii/
  c. Minimum Height Trees : https://leetcode.com/problems/minimum-height-trees/
  d. Evaluate Division : https://leetcode.com/problems/evaluate-division/
  e. Clone Graph : https://leetcode.com/problems/clone-graph/
  f. Number of Provinces : https://leetcode.com/problems/number-of-provinces/
  g. Cheapest Flights Within K Stops : https://leetcode.com/problems/cheapest-flights-within-k-stops/
  h. Is Graph Bipartite? : https://leetcode.com/problems/is-graph-bipartite/
  i. All Paths From Source to Target : https://leetcode.com/problems/all-paths-from-source-to-target/
  j. Critical Connections in a Network : https://leetcode.com/problems/critical-connections-in-a-network/
  k. Reconstruct Itinerary : https://leetcode.com/problems/reconstruct-itinerary/
  l. Most Stones Removed with Same Row or Column : https://leetcode.com/problems/most-stones-removed-with-same-row-or-column/
  m. Find Eventual Safe States : https://leetcode.com/problems/find-eventual-safe-states/
  n. Reorder Routes to Make All Paths Lead to the City Zero : https://leetcode.com/problems/reorder-routes-to-make-all-paths-lead-to-the-city-zero/
  o. Find the City With the Smallest Number of Neighbors at a Threshold Distance : https://leetcode.com/problems/find-the-city-with-the-smallest-number-of-neighbors-at-a-threshold-distance/

♣ **Search Algorithms in Graphs**

♣ Breadth First Search (BFS)

- Video tutorial on BFS. : https://www.youtube.com/watch?v=xlVX7dXLS64

- **Problems to Try Out:**

  a. Course Schedule : https://leetcode.com/problems/course-schedule
  b. Cheapest Flights Within K Stops : https://leetcode.com/problems/cheapest-flights-within-k-stops
  c. Reconstruct Itinerary : https://leetcode.com/problems/reconstruct-itinerary
  d. Network Delay Time : https://leetcode.com/problems/network-delay-time
  e. All Paths From Source to Target : https://leetcode.com/problems/all-paths-from-source-to-target
  f. Find the Town Judge : https://leetcode.com/problems/find-the-town-judge
  g. Keys and Rooms : https://leetcode.com/problems/keys-and-rooms
  h. Number of Operations to Make Network Connected : https://leetcode.com/problems/number-of-operations-to-make-network-connected
  i. Find Eventual Safe States : https://leetcode.com/problems/find-eventual-safe-states
  j. Shortest Path Visiting All Nodes : https://leetcode.com/problems/shortest-path-visiting-all-nodes
  k. Reorder Routes to Make All Paths Lead to the City Zero : https://leetcode.com/problems/reorder-routes-to-make-all-paths-lead-to-the-city-zero
  l. Minimum Number of Vertices to Reach All Nodes : https://leetcode.com/problems/minimum-number-of-vertices-to-reach-all-nodes
  m. Shortest Path with Alternating Colors : https://leetcode.com/problems/shortest-path-with-alternating-colors
  n. Find If Path Exists in Graph : https://leetcode.com/problems/find-if-path-exists-in-graph
  o. Parallel Courses II : https://leetcode.com/problems/parallel-courses-ii

♣ Depth First Search (DFS)

- Video tutorial on DFS algorithm : https://www.youtube.com/watch?v=7fujbpJ0LB4
- **Problems to Try Out:**

  a. Number of Islands : https://leetcode.com/problems/number-of-islands

b. Validate Binary Search Tree : https://leetcode.com/problems/validate-binary-search-tree
c. Lowest Common Ancestor of a Binary Tree : https://leetcode.com/problems/lowest-common-ancestor-of-a-binary-tree
d. Course Schedule : https://leetcode.com/problems/course-schedule
e. Binary Tree Maximum Path Sum : https://leetcode.com/problems/binary-tree-maximum-path-sum
f. Path Sum III : https://leetcode.com/problems/path-sum-iii
g. Diameter of Binary Tree : https://leetcode.com/problems/diameter-of-binary-tree
h. Flatten Binary Tree to Linked List : https://leetcode.com/problems/flatten-binary-tree-to-linked-list
i. Course Schedule II : https://leetcode.com/problems/course-schedule-ii
j. Serialize and Deserialize Binary Tree : https://leetcode.com/problems/serialize-and-deserialize-binary-tree
k. House Robber III : https://leetcode.com/problems/house-robber-iii
l. Binary Tree Right Side View : https://leetcode.com/problems/binary-tree-right-side-view
m. Binary Tree Level Order Traversal : https://leetcode.com/problems/binary-tree-level-order-traversal
n. Kth Smallest Element in a BST : https://leetcode.com/problems/kth-smallest-element-in-a-bst
o. All Nodes Distance K in Binary Tree : https://leetcode.com/problems/all-nodes-distance-k-in-binary-tree

♣ **Shortest Path Algorithms**

♣ Dijkstra's Algorithm

- Video tutorial on Dijkstra's algorithm. : https://www.youtube.com/watch?v=pVfj6mxhdMw
- **Problems to Try Out:**

  a. Cheapest Flights Within K Stops : https://leetcode.com/problems/cheapest-flights-within-k-stops
  b. Network Delay Time : https://leetcode.com/problems/network-delay-time

c. Path with Maximum Probability : https://leetcode.com/problems/path-with-maximum-probability
d. Minimum Cost to Make at Least One Valid Path in a Grid : https://leetcode.com/problems/minimum-cost-to-make-at-least-one-valid-path-in-a-grid
e. Find the City With the Smallest Number of Neighbors at a Threshold Distance : https://leetcode.com/problems/find-the-city-with-the-smallest-number-of-neighbors-at-a-threshold-distance
f. The Maze II : https://leetcode.com/problems/the-maze-ii
g. The Maze III : https://leetcode.com/problems/the-maze-iii
h. Path with Minimum Effort : https://leetcode.com/problems/path-with-minimum-effort
i. Reachable Nodes in Subdivided Graph : https://leetcode.com/problems/reachable-nodes-in-subdivided-graph
j. Number of Restricted Paths From First to Last Node : https://leetcode.com/problems/number-of-restricted-paths-from-first-to-last-node

♣ Bellman-Ford Algorithm

- Video tutorial on Bellman-Ford algorithm. : https://www.youtube.com/watch?v=obWXjtg0L64
- **Problems to Try Out:**

a. Network Delay Time : https://leetcode.com/problems/network-delay-time
b. Min Cost to Connect All Points : https://leetcode.com/problems/min-cost-to-connect-all-points
c. Is Graph Bipartite? : https://leetcode.com/problems/is-graph-bipartite
d. Cheapest Flights Within K Stops : https://leetcode.com/problems/cheapest-flights-within-k-stops
e. Network Delay Time : https://leetcode.com/problems/network-delay-time
f. Find the City With the Smallest Number of Neighbors at a Threshold Distance : https://leetcode.com/problems/find-the-city-with-the-smallest-number-of-neighbors-at-a-threshold-distance
g. Shortest Path with Alternating Colors : https://leetcode.com/problems/shortest-path-with-alternating-colors

h. All Pairs Shortest Path : https://leetcode.com/problems/find-the-city-with-the-smallest-number-of-neighbors-at-a-threshold-distance
i. Path with Maximum Probability : https://leetcode.com/problems/path-with-maximum-probability

♣ Floyd-Warshall Algorithm

- Video Tutorial On Floyd-Warshall algorithm : https://www.youtube.com/watch?v=4NQ3HnhyNfQ
- **Problems to Try Out:**

a. Cheapest Flights Within K Stops : https://leetcode.com/problems/cheapest-flights-within-k-stops?envType=problem-list-v2&envId=9idenloe
b. Network Delay Time : https://leetcode.com/problems/network-delay-time?envType=problem-list-v2&envId=9idenloe
c. Number of Ways to Arrive at Destination : https://leetcode.com/problems/number-of-ways-to-arrive-at-destination?envType=problem-list-v2&envId=9idenloe
d. Evaluate Division : https://leetcode.com/problems/evaluate-division?envType=problem-list-v2&envId=9idenloe
e. Find the City With the Smallest Number of Neighbors at a Threshold Distance : https://leetcode.com/problems/find-the-city-with-the-smallest-number-of-neighbors-at-a-threshold-distance?envType=problem-list-v2&envId=9idenloe
f. Course Schedule IV : https://leetcode.com/problems/course-schedule-iv?envType=problem-list-v2&envId=9idenloe

♣ Minimum Spanning Tree Algorithms

♣ Prim's Algorithm

- Video tutorial on Prim's algorithm : https://www.youtube.com/watch?v=jsmMtJpPnhU
- **Problems to Try Out:**

a. Minimum Cost to Connect All Points : https://leetcode.com/problems/min-cost-to-connect-all-points/
b. Minimum Cost to Make at Least One Valid Path in a Grid : https://leetcode.com/problems/minimum-cost-to-make-at-least-one-valid-path-in-a-grid/

c. Minimum Number of Vertices to Reach All Nodes : https://leetcode.com/problems/minimum-number-of-vertices-to-reach-all-nodes/
d. Shortest Path with Alternating Colors : https://leetcode.com/problems/shortest-path-with-alternating-colors/
e. Minimum Path Sum : https://leetcode.com/problems/minimum-path-sum/description/
f. Path with Maximum Minimum Value : https://leetcode.com/problems/path-with-maximum-minimum-value/
g. Minimum Effort Path : https://leetcode.com/problems/path-with-minimum-effort/
h. Shortest Path in a Grid with Obstacles Elimination : https://leetcode.com/problems/shortest-path-in-a-grid-with-obstacles-elimination/
i. Network Delay Time : https://leetcode.com/problems/network-delay-time/
j. Shortest Path Visiting All Nodes : https://leetcode.com/problems/shortest-path-visiting-all-nodes/
k. Prim's Minimum Spanning Tree (MST) Algorithm : https://cp-algorithms.com/graph/mst_prim.html
l. Shortest Path with Alternating Colors : https://leetcode.com/problems/shortest-path-with-alternating-colors/
m. Find the City With the Smallest Number of Neighbors at a Threshold Distance : https://leetcode.com/problems/find-the-city-with-the-smallest-number-of-neighbors-at-a-threshold-distance/
n. Minimum Cost to Reach Destination in Time : https://leetcode.com/problems/minimum-cost-to-reach-destination-in-time/

♣ Kruskal's Algorithm

- Video tutorial on Kruskal algorithm : https://www.youtube.com/watch?v=JZBQLXgSGfs
- **Problems to Try Out:**

a. Connecting Cities With Minimum Cost : https://leetcode.com/problems/connecting-cities-with-minimum-cost/
b. Optimize Water Distribution in a Village : https://leetcode.com/problems/optimize-water-distribution-in-a-village/
c. Minimum Cost to Repair Edges : https://leetcode.com/discuss/interview-question/357310

d. Number of Operations to Make Network Connected : https://leetcode.com/problems/number-of-operations-to-make-network-connected/
e. Union-Find to Detect Cycle in a Graph : https://leetcode.com/problems/course-schedule/solutions/149177/detecting-cycles-in-undirected-graph-union-find/
f. Critical Connections in a Network : https://leetcode.com/problems/critical-connections-in-a-network/
g. Find if Path Exists in Graph : https://leetcode.com/problems/find-if-path-exists-in-graph/
h. Island Connections : https://leetcode.com/problems/number-of-islands/
i. Most Stones Removed with Same Row or Column : https://leetcode.com/problems/most-stones-removed-with-same-row-or-column/
j. Graph Valid Tree : https://leetcode.com/problems/graph-valid-tree/
k. Accounts Merge : https://leetcode.com/problems/accounts-merge/
l. Redundant Connection : https://leetcode.com/problems/redundant-connection/
m. Earliest Moment When Everyone Become Friends : https://leetcode.com/problems/the-earliest-moment-when-everyone-become-friends/
n. Remove Max Number of Edges to Keep Graph Fully Traversable : https://leetcode.com/problems/remove-max-number-of-edges-to-keep-graph-fully-traversable/

♣ Topological Sort

- Video tutorial on topological sort : https://www.youtube.com/watch?v=eL-KzMXSXXI
- **Problems to Try Out:**

a. Course Schedule : https://leetcode.com/problems/course-schedule
b. Course Schedule II : https://leetcode.com/problems/course-schedule-ii
c. Minimum Height Trees : https://leetcode.com/problems/minimum-height-trees

d. Longest Increasing Path in a Matrix : https://leetcode.com/problems/longest-increasing-path-in-a-matrix
e. Find Eventual Safe States : https://leetcode.com/problems/find-eventual-safe-states
f. Course Schedule IV : https://leetcode.com/problems/course-schedule-iv
g. Number of Ways to Arrive at Destination : https://leetcode.com/problems/number-of-ways-to-arrive-at-destination
h. Rank Transform of a Matrix : https://leetcode.com/problems/rank-transform-of-a-matrix
i. Sort Items by Groups Respecting Dependencies : https://leetcode.com/problems/sort-items-by-groups-respecting-dependencies
j. Loud and Rich : https://leetcode.com/problems/loud-and-rich
k. Number of Restricted Paths From First to Last Node : https://leetcode.com/problems/number-of-restricted-paths-from-first-to-last-node
l. Largest Color Value in a Directed Graph : https://leetcode.com/problems/largest-color-value-in-a-directed-graph
m. Strange Printer II : https://leetcode.com/problems/strange-printer-ii
n. Find All Possible Recipes From Given Supplies : https://leetcode.com/problems/find-all-possible-recipes-from-given-supplies
o. Parallel Courses III : https://leetcode.com/problems/parallel-courses-iii

♣ Cycle Detection

- Video tutorial on cycle detection. : https://www.youtube.com/watch?v=MFOAbpfrJ8g
- **Problems to Try Out:**

a. Detect Cycle in an Undirected Graph Using BFS : https://takeuforward.org/data-structure/detect-cycle-in-an-undirected-graph-using-bfs/
b. Detect Cycle in an Undirected Graph Using DFS : https://takeuforward.org/data-structure/detect-cycle-in-an-undirected-graph-using-dfs/
c. Detect a Cycle in Directed Graph - Topological Sort (Kahn's Algorithm) : https://takeuforward.org/data-structure/detect-a-cycle-in-directed-graph-topological-sort-kahns-algorithm-g-23/

♣ Lowest Common Ancestor (LCA)

- Video tutorial on LCA. : https://www.youtube.com/watch?v=sD1IoalFomA
- **Problems to Try Out:**
  a. Lowest Common Ancestor of a Binary Tree : https://leetcode.com/problems/lowest-common-ancestor-of-a-binary-tree/
  b. Lowest Common Ancestor of Deepest Leaves : https://leetcode.com/problems/lowest-common-ancestor-of-deepest-leaves/
  c. Lowest Common Ancestor of a Binary Tree III : https://leetcode.com/problems/lowest-common-ancestor-of-a-binary-tree-iii/

♣ **Dynamic Programming (DP)**

Video Tutorial –

Tutorial 1 : Mastering Dynamic Programming :https://www.youtube.com/watch?v=Hdr64lKQ3e4

Tutorial 2 : What Is Dynamic Programming : https://www.youtube.com/watch?v=yfTlyYTnfKM

♣ Memoization

Video Tutorial : Algorithms: Memoization and Dynamic Programming : https://www.youtube.com/watch?v=P8Xa2BitN3I

- **Problems to Try Out:**
  a. Climbing Stairs : https://leetcode.com/problems/climbing-stairs
  b. Word Break : https://leetcode.com/problems/word-break
  c. Longest Increasing Path in a Matrix : https://leetcode.com/problems/longest-increasing-path-in-a-matrix
  d. Partition to K Equal Sum Subsets : https://leetcode.com/problems/partition-to-k-equal-sum-subsets
  e. Word Break II : https://leetcode.com/problems/word-break-ii
  f. Different Ways to Add Parentheses : https://leetcode.com/problems/different-ways-to-add-parentheses
  g. Fibonacci Number : https://leetcode.com/problems/fibonacci-number
  h. All Possible Full Binary Trees : https://leetcode.com/problems/all-possible-full-binary-trees
  i. Can I Win : https://leetcode.com/problems/can-i-win

j. Remove Boxes : https://leetcode.com/problems/remove-boxes
k. N-th Tribonacci Number : https://leetcode.com/problems/n-th-tribonacci-number
l. Shopping Offers : https://leetcode.com/problems/shopping-offers
m. Sort Integers by The Power Value : https://leetcode.com/problems/sort-integers-by-the-power-value
n. Integer Replacement : https://leetcode.com/problems/integer-replacement
o. Minimum Number of Days to Eat N Oranges : https://leetcode.com/problems/minimum-number-of-days-to-eat-n-oranges

♣ Tabulation

Video tutorial on tabulation : https://www.youtube.com/watch?v=WNkqbqyvR_0&pp=ygUNVGFidWxhdGlvbiBEUA%3D%3D

- **Problems to Try Out:**

a. Longest Increasing Subsequence : https://leetcode.com/problems/longest-increasing-subsequence/
b. Largest Divisible Subset : https://leetcode.com/problems/largest-divisible-subset/
c. Russian Doll Envelopes : https://leetcode.com/problems/russian-doll-envelopes/
d. Maximum Length of Pair Chain : https://leetcode.com/problems/maximum-length-of-pair-chain/
e. Number of Longest Increasing Subsequence : https://leetcode.com/problems/number-of-longest-increasing-subsequence/
f. Delete and Earn : https://leetcode.com/problems/delete-and-earn/
g. Longest String Chain : https://leetcode.com/problems/longest-string-chain/
h. Partition Equal Subset Sum : https://leetcode.com/problems/partition-equal-subset-sum/
i. Last Stone Weight II : https://leetcode.com/problems/last-stone-weight-ii/
j. Partition to K Equal Sum Subsets : https://leetcode.com/problems/partition-to-k-equal-sum-subsets/
k. Longest Common Subsequence : https://leetcode.com/problems/longest-common-subsequence/

l. Edit Distance : https://leetcode.com/problems/edit-distance/
m. Distinct Subsequences : https://leetcode.com/problems/distinct-subsequences/
n. Minimum ASCII Delete Sum for Two Strings : https://leetcode.com/problems/minimum-ascii-delete-sum-for-two-strings/
o. Palindrome Partitioning II : https://leetcode.com/problems/palindrome-partitioning-ii/

♣ Dynamic Programming (DP) Problem List Topic Wise

1. Linear Dp : https://leetcode.com/list/50vlu3z5
2. String and Dp : https://leetcode.com/list/50v8wybv
3. Dp with Tree and Graph : https://leetcode.com/list/50v8rtm7
4. Knapsack based Dp : https://leetcode.com/list/50vif4uc
5. Dp with bits manipulation : https://leetcode.com/list/50vt8ied
6. Dp on math problems : https://leetcode.com/list/50w545lj
7. Classical dp problems : https://leetcode.com/list/50wroh7h
8. Grid based dp : https://leetcode.com/list/50izszui
9. Multidimensional Dp : https://leetcode.com/list/50wob6ze
10. Digit problems with dp : https://leetcode.com/list/50vtbd3v
11. Interval problems with dp : https://leetcode.com/list/50vtr1g3

Month 6

♣ KMP (Knuth-Morris-Pratt) Algorithm

- Video Tutorial : KMP algorithm for pattern matching : https://www.youtube.com/watch?v=V5-7GzOfADQ&t=4s
- **Problems to Try Out:**
  a. Implement strStr() : https://leetcode.com/problems/implement-strstr/
  b. Repeated Substring Pattern : https://leetcode.com/problems/repeated-substring-pattern/
  c. Longest Substring Without Repeating Characters : https://leetcode.com/problems/longest-substring-without-repeating-characters/
  d. Longest Palindromic Substring : https://leetcode.com/problems/longest-palindromic-substring/
  e. Find the Index of the First Occurrence in a String : https://leetcode.com/problems/find-the-index-of-the-first-occurrence-in-a-string/description/
  f. Find All Anagrams in a String : https://leetcode.com/problems/find-all-anagrams-in-a-string/
  g. Minimum Window Substring : https://leetcode.com/problems/minimum-window-substring/
  h. Substring with Concatenation of All Words : https://leetcode.com/problems/substring-with-concatenation-of-all-words/
  i. Zigzag Conversion : https://leetcode.com/problems/zigzag-conversion/
  j. Longest Common Prefix : https://leetcode.com/problems/longest-common-prefix/
  k. Distinct Subsequences : https://leetcode.com/problems/distinct-subsequences/
  l. Edit Distance : https://leetcode.com/problems/edit-distance/
  m. Wildcard Matching : https://leetcode.com/problems/wildcard-matching/
  n. Longest Repeating Substring : https://leetcode.com/problems/longest-duplicate-substring/
  o. Word Search : https://leetcode.com/problems/word-search/

♣ String Hashing

- Video tutorial on string hashing. : https://www.youtube.com/watch?v=KEs5UyBJ39g
- **Problems to Try Out:**

  a. Repeated DNA Sequences : https://leetcode.com/problems/repeated-dna-sequences
  b. Longest Duplicate Substring : https://leetcode.com/problems/longest-duplicate-substring
  c. Distinct Echo Substrings : https://leetcode.com/problems/distinct-echo-substrings
  d. Longest Repeating Substring : https://leetcode.com/problems/longest-repeating-substring
  e. Find Substring With Given Hash Value : https://leetcode.com/problems/find-substring-with-given-hash-value
  f. Check If a String Contains All Binary Codes of Size K : https://leetcode.com/problems/check-if-a-string-contains-all-binary-codes-of-size-k
  g. Maximum Length of Repeated Subarray : https://leetcode.com/problems/maximum-length-of-repeated-subarray
  h. Longest Happy Prefix : https://leetcode.com/problems/longest-happy-prefix
  i. Number of Distinct Substrings in a String : https://leetcode.com/problems/number-of-distinct-substrings-in-a-string
  j. Longest Chunked Palindrome Decomposition : https://leetcode.com/problems/longest-chunked-palindrome-decomposition
  k. Number of Distinct Islands : https://leetcode.com/problems/number-of-distinct-islands
  l. Number of Distinct Islands II : https://leetcode.com/problems/number-of-distinct-islands-ii
  m. Shortest Palindrome : https://leetcode.com/problems/shortest-palindrome
  n. Encode and Decode TinyURL : https://leetcode.com/problems/encode-and-decode-tinyurl
  o. Subtree of Another Tree : https://leetcode.com/problems/subtree-of-another-tree

♣ Z Function

- Video tutorial on Z-function computation : https://www.youtube.com/watch?v=6mzNnEGimPA

- **Problems to Try Out:**
  a. Longest Duplicate Substring : https://leetcode.com/problems/longest-duplicate-substring
  b. Shortest Palindrome : https://leetcode.com/problems/shortest-palindrome
  c. Longest Happy Prefix : https://leetcode.com/problems/longest-happy-prefix
  d. Find All Anagrams in a String : https://leetcode.com/problems/find-all-anagrams-in-a-string
  e. Substring with Concatenation of All Words : https://leetcode.com/problems/substring-with-concatenation-of-all-words
  f. Minimum Window Substring : https://leetcode.com/problems/minimum-window-substring
  g. Longest Palindromic Substring : https://leetcode.com/problems/longest-palindromic-substring
  h. Palindrome Partitioning II : https://leetcode.com/problems/palindrome-partitioning-ii
  i. Longest Repeating Character Replacement : https://leetcode.com/problems/longest-repeating-character-replacement
  j. Wildcard Matching : https://leetcode.com/problems/wildcard-matching
  k. Regular Expression Matching : https://leetcode.com/problems/regular-expression-matching
  l. Longest Common Prefix : https://leetcode.com/problems/longest-common-prefix
  m. Edit Distance : https://leetcode.com/problems/edit-distance
  n. Interleaving String : https://leetcode.com/problems/interleaving-string

♣ Disjoint Set Union (DSU)

- Video tutorial on Disjoint Set : https://www.youtube.com/watch?v=ID00PMy0-vE
- **Problems to Try Out:**
  a. Longest Consecutive Sequence : https://leetcode.com/problems/longest-consecutive-sequence?envType=problem-list-v2&envId=5lhmb4mj
  b. Graph Valid Tree : https://leetcode.com/problems/graph-valid-tree?envType=problem-list-v2&envId=5lhmb4mj

c. Satisfiability of Equality Equations : https://leetcode.com/problems/satisfiability-of-equality-equations?envType=problem-list-v2&envId=5lhmb4mj
d. Checking Existence of Edge Length Limited Paths : https://leetcode.com/problems/checking-existence-of-edge-length-limited-paths?envType=problem-list-v2&envId=5lhmb4mj
e. SmallestStringwithSwaps:https://leetcode.com/problems/smallest-string-with-swaps?envType=problem-list-v2&envId=5lhmb4mj
f. Lexicographically Smallest Equivalent String : https://leetcode.com/problems/lexicographically-smallest-equivalent-string?envType=problem-list-v2&envId=5lhmb4mj
g. Number of Provinces : https://leetcode.com/problems/number-of-provinces?envType=problem-list-v2&envId=5lhmb4mj
h. Number of Operations to Make Network Connected : https://leetcode.com/problems/number-of-operations-to-make-network-connected?envType=problem-list-v2&envId=5lhmb4mj
i. Remove Max Number of Edges to Keep Graph Fully Traversable : https://leetcode.com/problems/remove-max-number-of-edges-to-keep-graph-fully-traversable?envType=problem-list-v2&envId=5lhmb4mj
j. Synonymous Sentences : https://leetcode.com/problems/synonymous-sentences?envType=problem-list-v2&envId=5lhmb4mj
k. Number of Islands II : https://leetcode.com/problems/number-of-islands-ii?envType=problem-list-v2&envId=5lhmb4mj
l. The Earliest Moment When Everyone Become Friends : https://leetcode.com/problems/the-earliest-moment-when-everyone-become-friends?envType=problem-list-v2&envId=5lhmb4mj
m. Minimize Malware Spread : https://leetcode.com/problems/minimize-malware-spread?envType=problem-list-v2&envId=5lhmb4mj
n. MinimizeMalwareSpreadII:https://leetcode.com/problems/minimize-malware-spread-ii?envType=problem-list-v2&envId=5lhmb4mj
o. NumberofDistinctIslandsII:https://leetcode.com/problems/number-of-distinct-islands-ii?envType=problem-list-v2&envId=5lhmb4mj

♣ Tries

- Video tutorial on Tries : https://www.youtube.com/watch?v=3CbFFVHQrk4
- **Problems to Try Out:**

a. Word Break : https://leetcode.com/problems/word-break

b. Implement Trie (Prefix Tree) : https://leetcode.com/problems/implement-trie-prefix-tree
c. Word Search II : https://leetcode.com/problems/word-search-ii
d. Word Break II : https://leetcode.com/problems/word-break-ii
e. Top K Frequent Words : https://leetcode.com/problems/top-k-frequent-words
f. Design Add and Search Words Data Structure : https://leetcode.com/problems/design-add-and-search-words-data-structure
g. Maximum XOR of Two Numbers in an Array : https://leetcode.com/problems/maximum-xor-of-two-numbers-in-an-array
h. Number of Matching Subsequences : https://leetcode.com/problems/number-of-matching-subsequences
i. Palindrome Pairs : https://leetcode.com/problems/palindrome-pairs
j. Search Suggestions System : https://leetcode.com/problems/search-suggestions-system
k. Concatenated Words : https://leetcode.com/problems/concatenated-words
l. Stream of Characters : https://leetcode.com/problems/stream-of-characters
m. Replace Words : https://leetcode.com/problems/replace-words
n. Longest Word in Dictionary : https://leetcode.com/problems/longest-word-in-dictionary
o. Map Sum Pairs : https://leetcode.com/problems/map-sum-pairs

♣ Binary Indexed Tree (BIT) / Fenwick Tree

- Video tutorial on BIT/Fenwick tree : https://www.youtube.com/watch?v=uZx-eqyu0Cg
- **Problems to Try Out:**

a. The Skyline Problem : https://leetcode.com/problems/the-skyline-problem/
b. Count of Smaller Numbers After Self : https://leetcode.com/problems/count-of-smaller-numbers-after-self/
c. Count of Range Sum : https://leetcode.com/problems/count-of-range-sum/
d. Reverse Pairs : https://leetcode.com/problems/reverse-pairs/
e. Create Sorted Array through Instructions : https://leetcode.com/problems/create-sorted-array-through-instructions/

f. The Skyline Problem : https://leetcode.com/problems/the-skyline-problem
g. Range Sum Query - Mutable : https://leetcode.com/problems/range-sum-query-mutable
h. Range Sum Query 2D - Mutable : https://leetcode.com/problems/range-sum-query-2d-mutable
i. Count of Smaller Numbers After Self : https://leetcode.com/problems/count-of-smaller-numbers-after-self
j. Count of Range Sum : https://leetcode.com/problems/count-of-range-sum
k. Queue Reconstruction by Height : https://leetcode.com/problems/queue-reconstruction-by-height
l. Reverse Pairs : https://leetcode.com/problems/reverse-pairs
m. Count Subarrays with More Ones than Zeros : https://leetcode.com/problems/count-subarrays-with-more-ones-than-zeros
n. Number of Longest Increasing Subsequence : https://leetcode.com/problems/number-of-longest-increasing-subsequence
o. K Empty Slots : https://leetcode.com/problems/k-empty-slots

♣ Segment Tree

- Video tutorial on Segment Tree : https://www.youtube.com/watch?v=Oq2E2yGadnU
- **Problems to Try Out:**

a. Count of Smaller Numbers After Self : https://leetcode.com/problems/count-of-smaller-numbers-after-self
b. The Skyline Problem : https://leetcode.com/problems/the-skyline-problem
c. Number of Longest Increasing Subsequence : https://leetcode.com/problems/number-of-longest-increasing-subsequence
d. Range Sum Query - Mutable : https://leetcode.com/problems/range-sum-query-mutable
e. Reverse Pairs : https://leetcode.com/problems/reverse-pairs
f. My Calendar I : https://leetcode.com/problems/my-calendar-i
g. Count of Range Sum : https://leetcode.com/problems/count-of-range-sum
h. My Calendar II : https://leetcode.com/problems/my-calendar-ii
i. Range Module : https://leetcode.com/problems/range-module
j. Rectangle Area II : https://leetcode.com/problems/rectangle-area-ii

k. My Calendar III : https://leetcode.com/problems/my-calendar-iii
l. Create Sorted Array through Instructions : https://leetcode.com/problems/create-sorted-array-through-instructions
m. Online Majority Element In Subarray : https://leetcode.com/problems/online-majority-element-in-subarray
n. Falling Squares : https://leetcode.com/problems/falling-squares
o. Minimum Possible Integer After at Most K Adjacent Swaps On Digits : https://leetcode.com/problems/minimum-possible-integer-after-at-most-k-adjacent-swaps-on-digits

Resources Library for System Design

▶ System Design Key Concepts

1. Scalability : https://blog.algomaster.io/p/scalability
2. Reliability and Availability : https://www.atlassian.com/incident-management/kpis/reliability-vs-availability
3. CAP Theorem : https://www.splunk.com/en_us/blog/learn/cap-theorem.html
4. Database Transactions : https://redis.io/glossary/acid-transactions/
5. Consistent Hashing : https://highscalability.com/consistent-hashing-algorithm/
6. Rate Limiting : https://www.cloudflare.com/learning/bots/what-is-rate-limiting/
7. API Design : https://swagger.io/resources/articles/best-practices-in-api-design/
8. Fault Tolerance : https://www.cockroachlabs.com/blog/what-is-fault-tolerance/
9. Consensus Algorithms : https://w3.cs.jmu.edu/kirkpams/OpenCSF/Books/csf/html/DistConsensus.html
10. Gossip Protocol : https://highscalability.com/gossip-protocol-explained/
11. Service Discovery : https://blog.algomaster.io/p/0204da93-f0e9-49b9-a88a-cb20b9931575
12. Disaster Recovery : https://cloud.google.com/learn/what-is-disaster-recovery
13. Distributed Tracing : https://www.dynatrace.com/news/blog/what-is-distributed-tracing/

► System Design Building Blocks

1. Databases and its Types : https://www.confluent.io/learn/database/
2. Content Delivery Network (CDN) : https://www.ibm.com/topics/content-delivery-networks
3. Domain Name System (DNS) : https://www.cloudflare.com/learning/dns/what-is-dns/
4. Caching : https://auth0.com/blog/what-is-caching-and-how-it-works/
5. Distributed Caching : https://redis.io/glossary/distributed-caching/
6. Load Balancing : https://aws.amazon.com/what-is/load-balancing
7. SQL Vs NoSQL : https://www.mongodb.com/resources/basics/databases/nosql-explained/nosql-vs-sql
8. Database Indexes : https://www.progress.com/tutorials/odbc/using-indexes
9. Consistency Patterns : https://systemdesign.one/consistency-patterns/
10. HeartBeats : https://blog.algomaster.io/p/heartbeats-in-distributed-systems
11. Circuit Breaker : https://martinfowler.com/bliki/CircuitBreaker.html
12. Idempotency : https://www.cockroachlabs.com/blog/idempotency-in-finance/
13. Database Scaling : https://www.mongodb.com/resources/basics/scaling
14. Data Replication : https://redis.com/blog/what-is-data-replication/
15. Data Redundancy : https://www.talend.com/uk/resources/what-is-data-redundancy/
16. Database Architectures : https://www.mongodb.com/developer/products/mongodb/active-active-application-architectures/
17. Failover : https://www.cloudflare.com/learning/performance/what-is-server-failover/
18. Proxy Server : https://www.fortinet.com/resources/cyberglossary/proxy-server
19. Message Queues : https://www.ibm.com/topics/message-queues
20. Checksums : https://linuxsecurity.com/features/what-are-checksums-why-should-you-be-using-them
21. WebSockets : https://websocket.org/guides/road-to-websockets/
22. Bloom Filters : https://www.enjoyalgorithms.com/blog/bloom-filter

23. API Gateway : https://www.nginx.com/learn/api-gateway/
24. Microservices Guidelines : https://newsletter.systemdesign.one/p/netflix-microservices
25. Distributed Locking : https://martin.kleppmann.com/2016/02/08/how-to-do-distributed-locking.html
26. oAuth2.0 and OpenID Connect: https://developer.okta.com/docs/concepts/oauth-openid/
27. oAuth vs JWT : https://frontegg.com/blog/oauth-vs-jwt

► System Design Tradeoffs

1. System Design Tradeoffs : https://www.geeksforgeeks.org/tradeoffs-in-system-design/
2. Vertical vs Horizontal Scaling : https://www.cockroachlabs.com/blog/vertical-scaling-vs-horizontal-scaling/
3. Stateful vs Stateless Design : https://redis.io/glossary/stateful-vs-stateless-architectures/
4. Selecting a cache strategy : https://docs.oracle.com/cd/E16459_01/coh.350/e14510/readthrough.htm
5. Pull vs Push Architecture : https://www.geeksforgeeks.org/pull-vs-push-api-architecture-system-design/
6. Long-polling vs WebSockets : https://www.pubnub.com/blog/evaluating-long-polling-vs-websockets/
7. Latency vs Throughput : https://aws.amazon.com/compare/the-difference-between-throughput-and-latency/
8. Batch vs Real Time Stream : https://www.confluent.io/en-gb/learn/batch-vs-real-time-data-processing/

► System Design Architectural Patterns

1. Microservices Architecture Pattern : https://learn.microsoft.com/en-us/azure/architecture/guide/architecture-styles/microservices
2. Serverless Architecture : https://www.datadoghq.com/knowledge-center/serverless-architecture/
3. Event-Driven Architecture : https://www.confluent.io/learn/event-driven-architecture/
4. Peer-to-Peer (P2P) Architecture : https://community.fs.com/article/client-server-vs-peer-to-peer-networks.html/

▶ Additional Topics For System Design

Additional topics essential for in-depth learning

1. InterviewBit - Low-Level Design Interview Questions by Anshuman Singh, Abhimanyu Saxena : https://www.interviewbit.com/low-level-design-interview-questions/
2. freeCodeCamp-DesignPatternsAllDevelopersNeedtoKnowbyQuincy Larson : https://www.freecodecamp.org/news/the-basic-design-patterns-all-developers-need-to-know/
3. Content Delivery Network (CDN) : https://www.cloudflare.com/learning/cdn/what-is-a-cdn/
4. System Design BluePrint : https://medium.com/bytebytego-system-design-alliance/system-design-blueprint-the-ultimate-guide-e27b914bf8f1
5. Uptime calculation for SLA : https://uptime.is/
6. CAP Theorem : https://www.bmc.com/blogs/cap-theorem/
7. Event-Driven Architecture: Request/Reply Processing : https://www.developertoarchitect.com/lessons/lesson1.html
8. How Kafka Differs From Standard Messaging : https://www.developertoarchitect.com/lessons/lesson2.html
9. Disk IO Part 1 : https://medium.com/databasss/on-disk-io-part-1-flavours-of-io-8e1ace1de017
10. Disk IO Part 2 : https://medium.com/databasss/on-disk-io-part-2-more-flavours-of-io-c945db3edb13
11. Disk IO Part 3 : https://medium.com/databasss/on-disk-io-part-3-lsm-trees-8b2da218496f
12. The Log: What every software engineer should know about real-time data's unifying abstraction : https://lnkd.in/gQ7WsE8k
13. SQL Vs NoSQL Database by Sc Gupta : https://www.ml4devs.com/articles/datastore-choices-sql-vs-nosql-database/
14. Consistent Hashing : https://www.baeldung.com/cs/consistent-hashing
15. Microservices Guidelines : https://newsletter.systemdesign.one/p/netflix-microservices
16. Connection Pooling : https://www.cockroachlabs.com/blog/what-is-connection-pooling/
17. Strong vs Eventual Consistency : https://hackernoon.com/eventual-vs-strong-consistency-in-distributed-databases-282fdad37cf7

18. Consistency Patterns : https://systemdesign.one/consistency-patterns/
19. REST vs RPC : https://aws.amazon.com/compare/the-difference-between-rpc-and-rest/
20. HeartBeat : https://martinfowler.com/articles/patterns-of-distributed-systems/heartbeat.html
21. Ambassador Pattern : https://learn.microsoft.com/en-us/azure/architecture/patterns/ambassador
22. Database Scaling : https://thenewstack.io/techniques-for-scaling-applications-with-a-database/
23. Database Sharding : https://www.mongodb.com/features/database-sharding-explained
24. Domain Name System (DNS) : https://www.cloudflare.com/learning/dns/what-is-dns/
25. Bloom Filters : https://www.enjoyalgorithms.com/blog/bloom-filter
26. API Gateway : https://www.nginx.com/learn/api-gateway/
27. Distributed Locking : https://martin.kleppmann.com/2016/02/08/how-to-do-distributed-locking.html
28. Data Replication : https://redis.com/blog/what-is-data-replication/
29. Data Redundancy : https://www.egnyte.com/guides/governance/data-redundancy

► Real World Use Cases

1. How browsers work : https://developer.mozilla.org/en-US/docs/Web/Performance/How_browsers_work
2. Keeping Netflix reliable using Load Shedding : https://netflixtechblog.com/keeping-netflix-reliable-using-prioritized-load-shedding-6cc827b02f94
3. Netflix Fault Tolerance in a high volume distributed system : https://lnkd.in/gGFensR4
4. Building In-Video Search : https://netflixtechblog.com/building-in-video-search-936766f0017c
5. How Uber predicts Arrival Times : https://www.uber.com/en-IN/blog/deepeta-how-uber-predicts-arrival-times/
6. How LedgerStore stores trillion indexes at Uber : https://www.uber.com/en-IN/blog/how-ledgerstore-supports-trillions-of-indexes/?uclick_id=bb28014d-a32a-45a5-b67d-0e87d1bed96c

7. How Uber Serves 40 Million reads per second : https://www.uber.com/en-IN/blog/how-uber-serves-over-40-million-reads-per-second-using-an-integrated-cache/
8. Distributed Tracing at Uber : https://www.uber.com/en-IN/blog/distributed-tracing/
9. Capturing a Billion Emojis at Hotstar : https://blog.hotstar.com/capturing-a-billion-emojis-62114cc0b440
10. How Pinterest Built a Real Time User Action Counting System for Ads : https://lnkd.in/gSRg368z
11. How Pinterest runs Kafka at scale : https://lnkd.in/gb5skEtU
12. How Airbnb avoids double payments in a Distributed Payments System : https://medium.com/airbnb-engineering/avoiding-double-payments-in-a-distributed-payments-system-2981f6b070bb
13. Airbnb Delayed Job Queuing System : https://medium.com/airbnb-engineering/dynein-building-a-distributed-delayed-job-queueing-system-93ab10f05f99
14. Unified Payment Data Reads at Airbnb : https://medium.com/airbnb-engineering/unified-payments-data-read-at-airbnb-e613e7af1a39
15. One million online users in a single discord server : https://discord.com/blog/maxjourney-pushing-discords-limits-with-a-million-plus-online-users-in-a-single-server
16. How Discord stores billions of messages : https://discord.com/blog/how-discord-stores-billions-of-messages
17. How Discord stores trillions of messages : https://discord.com/blog/how-discord-stores-trillions-of-messages
18. Building Faster Indexing at DoorDash : https://doordash.engineering/2021/07/14/open-source-search-indexing/
19. Building and Operating S3 the biggest storage system : https://www.allthingsdistributed.com/2023/07/building-and-operating-a-pretty-big-storage-system.html
20. How Canva scaled Media uploads from Zero to 50 Million per Day : https://www.canva.dev/blog/engineering/from-zero-to-50-million-uploads-per-day-scaling-media-at-canva/
21. Stripe's payments APIs - The first 10 years : https://stripe.com/blog/payment-api-design
22. Real time messaging at Slack : https://slack.engineering/real-time-messaging/

Books Worth Reading

1. Head First Design Patterns by Eric Freeman, Ph.D. : https://amzn.eu/d/enZHQ5f
2. Head First Object-Oriented Analysis & Design by Brett McLaughlin : https://amzn.eu/d/6rMyQyO
3. Clean Code by Robert C. Martin (Uncle Bob) : https://github.com/martinmurciego/good-books/blob/master/Clean Code_ A Handbook of Agile Software Craftsmanship - Robert C. Martin.pdf
4. Clean Architecture by Robert Martin : https://amzn.eu/d/aghQlf3
5. Refactoring: Improving the Design of Existing Code by Martin Fowler : https://refactoring.com/
6. Patterns of Enterprise Application Architecture by Martin Fowler : https://amzn.eu/d/eHQY71A
7. Design Patterns: Elements of Reusable Object-Oriented Software : https://github.com/GunterMueller/Books-3/blob/master/Design Patterns Elements of Reusable Object-Oriented Software.pdf
8. Domain-Driven Design: Tackling Complexity in the Heart of Software by Eric Evans: https://www.amazon.co.uk/Domain-Driven-Design-Tackling-Complexity-Software/dp/0321125215

Top Tech Blogs for Latest Trends

1. Netflix TechBlog : https://netflixtechblog.com/
2. Google Developers Blog : https://developers.googleblog.com/en/
3. Engineering at Meta (Articles) : https://engineering.fb.com/category/web/
4. Meta Developers blog : https://developers.facebook.com/blog/
5. Data Management Guide : https://martinfowler.com/data/
6. Refactoring.Guru - Design Patterns : https://refactoring.guru/design-patterns
7. Alexander Shvets - SourceMaking Design Patterns : https://sourcemaking.com/design_patterns
8. GeeksforGeeks - Software Design Patterns by Sandeep Jain : https://www.geeksforgeeks.org/software-design-patterns/
9. AWS Blogs - https://aws.amazon.com/blogs
10. LinkedIn Engineering Blog - https://linkedin.com/blog/engineering